Cases in Microeconomics

Jose A. Gomez-Ibañez
Joseph P. Kalt

with the Case Program, the Kennedy School of Government

PRENTICE HALL
Englewood Cliffs, New Jersey 07632

Library of Congress Cataloging-in-Publication Data

Gómez-Ibáñez, José A.
    Cases in microeconomics / Jose A. Gomez-Ibañez, Joseph P. Kalt,
and Kennedy School of Government.
        p.   cm.
    ISBN 0-13-118886-0
    1. Microeconomics--Case studies.   2. United States--Economic
policy--1981- --Case studies.   I. Kalt, Joseph p.   II. John F.
Kennedy School of Government.   III. Title.
    HB172.G62 1990
    338.5--dc20
                                                89-38951
                                                   CIP

Editorial/production supervision: Merrill Peterson
Interior design: Joan Stone
Manufacturing buyer: Peter Havens

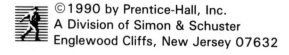 ©1990 by Prentice-Hall, Inc.
A Division of Simon & Schuster
Englewood Cliffs, New Jersey 07632

Printed in the United States of America

10 9 8 7 6 5 4 3 2 1

ISBN 0-13-118886-0

Prentice-Hall International (UK) Limited, *London*
Prentice-Hall of Australia Pty. Limited, *Sydney*
Prentice-Hall Canada Inc., *Toronto*
Prentice-Hall Hispanoamericana, S.A., *Mexico*
Prentice-Hall of India Private Limited, *New Delhi*
Prentice-Hall of Japan, Inc., *Tokyo*
Simon & Schuster Asia Pte. Ltd., *Singapore*
Editora Prentice-Hall do Brasil, Ltda., *Rio de Janeiro*

Contents

_____ *chapter 3* _____

Social Justice in Economic Policy, 107

_____ *chapter 4* _____

Public Sector Investment and Pricing,   174

Preface

The cases in this book were developed and first taught at the John F. Kennedy School of Government, Harvard University's graduate school for professional training in public management, policy, and politics. Kennedy School students have always, as a major part of their training, been expected to understand the principles of microeconomics. Behind that requirement lies the belief that Kennedy School graduates—like anyone who enters the public arena—will often be called upon to apply the principles of microeconomics to practical problems: to decide whether or how government should regulate a market, to anticipate whether there will be price increases or declines in key industries, to set user fees for public services, or to evaluate the worth of public programs and investments.

Despite the school's traditional emphasis on microeconomics, however, we found, in our own teaching, that students frequently failed to recognize the economic principles inherent in the public policy problems they faced. Ordinary textbook-and-lecture methods were not producing the problem-solving habits of mind the school sought. These microeconomic cases are tools we developed as a means of helping our students to recognize the workings of economics in the world around them—and, in turn, to develop the skills and intuition needed to apply microeconomics concepts creatively to the complex real-world problems they will face as graduates and as citizens. We hope and believe the cases can do the same for you.

WHAT IS A CASE?

Since the term "case" is used in so many different ways, it may be useful to clarify at the outset what *we* mean by cases. Each of the cases presented in this book describes a real situation in which a specific decision must be made by a public or private official or manager. The cases summarize the various pressures and considerations that the official or manager must weigh in making the decision, as well as the often incomplete or contradictory information available at the time. Should the secretary of transportation require that all new cars produced in the United States be equipped with airbags or automatic seat belts instead of manual seat belts, for example, or should the Arizona state legislature fund organ transplants as part of its program to pay for the health expenses of the indigent? Should the California Public Utilities Commission allow regulated public utilities to drop their electricity prices for some industrial customers to meet competition from certain unregulated electricity suppliers? Should the Urban League support a proposal to lower the minimum wage for teenagers?

Your instructor may choose to use these cases in two ways. The first way is as background reading or illustrations for the instructor's lecture. In the lecture, for example, the instructor might explain how the case illustrates typical dilemmas that public and private managers face and the principles of economics that can be used to help them reach a reasonable strategy or decision. The second way is to challenge the students themselves to grapple with the decision maker's dilemma, formulate a strategy and a recommendation, and come to class prepared to explain and defend their recommendations. In this second approach, which is often termed "case method teaching," the instructor does not lecture but instead moderates a classroom discussion among the students in which the students compare their different approaches and, learning from each other, together reach a richer understanding of the dilemmas and principles involved in the decision.

Cases require more preparation and work on the part of the student than the usual reading assignments, particularly if they are used as the basis for a case method discussion rather than for a lecture. For a student to get the most out of a case and for the discussion (or even a lecture) to be fruitful, the student must immerse himself or herself in the case, attempting to formulate his or her own position and strategy before class, and must participate actively in the class discussion. Most students find this process both intellectually interesting and frustrating, especially because the most stimulating cases are ones in which reasonable people might—and, invariably, do—disagree about the appropriate course of action, either because conflicting principles or considerations are involved or because the evidence is inconclusive. To justify and mitigate these extra burdens, we offer here a rationale for the case method and some pointers on how to prepare a case and participate in case discussions.

WHY USE CASES?

Why is it worth the effort for you to struggle before class to understand the case to the point where you can formulate and defend your own course of action? Wouldn't it be simpler and more efficient if the instructor just told you what the ''answer'' to the case was, since the instructor has more experience and has carefully considered the case already? The fundamental principles behind the case method are that the best-learned lessons are the ones you teach yourself, through your own struggles, and that many of the most useful kinds of understanding and judgment cannot be told but must be learned through practical experience. When instructors assign problem sets or papers in a course, they are motivated by a similar concern: In working through the problem set on your own or in writing the paper you reach a deeper understanding of the concepts and ideas than you would if you only read the text or listened passively to lectures. Case method teaching extends this principle to make preparing for class and the class session itself an active learning experience for you. By using complex, real-world problems as the focus, it challenges you to learn skills that will be appropriate to the practical problems you will face as a public official, private manager, or responsible citizen.

One of the principal purposes of the cases is to develop a more practical and lasting understanding of the principles of microeconomics by forcing you to work through these economic principles and concepts in real-world problems. Take, for example, the concept of marginal cost, which is so central to economic analysis. From a lecture or a microeconomics textbook, you probably already understand that marginal cost is the increase in total cost caused by producing one more unit of output. Given the total cost schedule or function in a problem set, you can easily identify the marginal cost at various levels of output. But imagine now that you are put in the position of a real manager of a private firm or of a public regulatory authority, as you will be in the cases that follow, who must decide both how to set the price of a product or service and whether it will be profitable at that price. You will quickly discover that identifying the relevant marginal cost is much more difficult in the real world than it is in an introductory textbook. Which costs are likely to be fixed and which are likely to vary with output? How should one allocate overhead costs among the different products the firm produces? How should one value firm or agency resources (ranging from machinery to the time and attention of senior managers) that have a variety of alternative uses? How should one consider intangibles such as the goodwill of customers or clients or the reputation of the firm or agency? What is the relevant cost when the firm or agency faces an uncertain future and must choose between a variety of strategies that have different implications for its vulnerability to future competition and environmental challenges? By working through these practical problems for yourself, you will reach a much deeper understanding of the concept of marginal cost and acquire the confidence that you can apply it to situations far more complex and realistic than those presented in simplified textbook examples or problem sets.

Another purpose of these cases is to develop an appreciation of how and when economics can be relevant to the complex and tangible problems of the real world. Too often economics texts use the same idealized examples to illustrate economic concepts: national defense or a lighthouse to illustrate the concept of a public good; agricultural price supports to illustrate the effects of subsidies; rent control to illustrate the effects of price controls. Students often get the sense that these examples are contrived, selected because they are among the few real-world issues that clearly illustrate the economic concept. Even then, they are sometimes presented in a simplified form that glosses over important political, institutional, or ethical dimensions of the problem. Isn't the persistence of agricultural price supports or rent control, despite economists' oft-repeated concerns about their effects, proof that economic considerations are often of secondary importance in the real world? If economic considerations present only one of many perspectives that might be relevant to a problem, what role should economic analysis play in formulating a course of action? Does economics have anything to contribute in a situation where political pressures and administrative constraints narrow the options considerably, for example, or where basic considerations about human rights and social justice are obviously critical?

The cases presented here are selected, of course, because economics offers some insight into the problems they raise, but the administrative, political, ethical, and other noneconomic considerations are not glossed over. You will quickly recognize what you suspected already: Economic concepts do not provide the sole or complete guide for action in, say, deciding whether the state should fund kidney or liver transplants for the poor in Arizona, or even whether the U.S. government should provide Harley-Davidson with temporary protection from Japanese motorcycle imports. A good professional economist develops, over many years of working with real-world problems, intuition and judgment about when to apply economics and how to integrate economic considerations with other perspectives. By working through a series of cases in which the noneconomic considerations are presented fairly, you will begin to develop that judgment for yourself.

Finally, working through these cases will also foster the tolerance for ambiguity, the willingness to learn from others, and the ability to formulate a persuasive and balanced argument that are hallmarks of a good manager and a good citizen. In each case there may be some courses of action that are more easily or persuasively defended than others, but, because the cases are drawn from the real world, there is seldom one "correct" answer. In preparing the case you will be forced to sift through contradictory and incomplete evidence and weigh considerations which suggest conflicting courses of action. In discussion, moreover, your classmates will almost surely raise persuasive evidence, perspectives, or arguments that had not occurred to you and that may conflict with your initial recommendation. In the real world, as in the cases, managers and citizens must often make decisions involving conflicting considerations and ambiguous evidence. By working with cases, therefore, you will practice the skills of weighing and balancing these conflicting considerations and evidence, learning from others, and finally developing a persuasive yet balanced argument of your own for a course of action.

The cases presented here were developed because there were few existing cases suitable for a general applied microeconomics course. Business schools pioneered in teaching by the case method, and there are numerous business administration casebooks, the best known of which are produced by the Harvard Business School. But although two Harvard Business School cases are reproduced in this book (*Avon Corporation* and *The West Side Highway Proposal*) most business administration cases are designed to teach more specialized concepts in, for example, finance, production management, or human resources, concepts less appropriate for a general microeconomics course. Business administration cases also, understandably, present decisions from the perspective of the private corporation and thus do not often capture the wider public concerns or issues that motivate many graduate and undergraduate students to study economics. Schools of public administration and public policy have also long used case method teaching, and the John F. Kennedy School of Government's Case Program is the leading producer of teaching cases in public management. Until recently, however, most of the cases developed and used in schools of public administration were designed for courses in political leadership, management, or administration rather than quantitative methods or economics. This casebook represents one of the Kennedy School's efforts to expand the use of cases across the curriculum.

PREPARING THE CASE

How much you will get out of a case discussion depends greatly on how much effort you put into preparing it before class. Most students unaccustomed to cases are initially overwhelmed by the prospect of preparing one. That task can be imposing since a variety of factors, some economic and some not, come into play and the facts are sometimes confusing or unclear. Fear not, however. Preparing a case involves slightly different skills than you may be accustomed to using in a typical classroom reading or homework assignment, but with a little application and practice you'll find it manageable.

Reading the Case. Perhaps the most common mistake is to think that you can prepare by reading the case through once and then thinking about it. Most cases require at least two readings, often more, to help you formulate an understanding of the problem and a well-reasoned course of action. In your first reading, try to familiarize yourself with the basic situation. Your instructor may furnish discussion questions to help focus your attention on particular aspects of the case, and you should read these discussion questions before you read the case. Whether or not you are given discussion questions, however, you should develop a basic checklist of questions to keep in mind during this first reading, such as

- Who is the decision maker in this case and what specific decision does he or she have to make?
- What are the objectives of the decision maker?
- Who are the other important actors in the case and what are their objectives?
- What are the key issues in dispute in the case? How do they bear on the discussion?
- What is the environment in which the decision maker operates, and what specific constraints or opportunities does that environment establish? For example, what is the product or service produced, what is the relevant market, who are the competitors or regulators? Does the decision maker face constraints of money, time, institutional authority, or other resources?
- What are the possible courses of action for the decision maker?
- What are the likely consequences of each course of action? What assumptions or arguments about the nature of the problem or the environment does one have to believe to make each course of action seem reasonable or likely to be successful? How plausible are those assumptions or arguments? How might other actors react?

After the first reading, attempt to formulate one or, better still, several plausible courses of action and then reread the case, searching for evidence that supports or undercuts the various courses of action you are considering. Keep on reformulating your understanding of the problem and rereading the case to test that understanding until you feel comfortable with your position.

Above all, try to immerse yourself in the case when reading and thinking about it. Try to imagine yourself as the decision maker and take his or her problem to heart. What should you, the decision maker, do? What do you need to know to decide? What will be the consequences if you are wrong?

Using Evidence and Numbers. One of the most difficult problems in preparing a case is sorting through the mass of information and evidence. Usually the case provides considerable background information on the firm, agency, or market involved, which is of varying relevance to the decision at hand. Often the case describes a dispute between several actors, each championing a different course of action and advancing evidence to support the claims. Important skills in preparing a case, as in real life, are deciding what information is important and evaluating apparently conflicting evidence.

One of the basic reasons for reading a case at least twice is to help you avoid being overwhelmed and paralyzed by all the available information. It is difficult to identify and evaluate the key evidence on a first reading. After you have familiarized yourself with the basic facts of the case and formulated a few hypotheses about the nature of the problem and the most plausible courses of action, ask yourself what evidence is needed to support (or oppose) those courses of action. Reread the case looking for that evidence. If you decide that a key issue in the decision is whether the market is competitive, for example, reread the case with an eye for evidence that there are structural barriers to competition or that the firms are able to maintain prices above their costs.

You should be slightly skeptical about the information presented or the interpretation placed on it by various actors in the case. Does the evidence an actor cites really support his or her argument persuasively, for example, or are there alternative interpretations that one could draw from that data? Obviously you won't have the time to question every bit of evidence presented in a case. If the evidence appears critical to the debate or decision, however, ask yourself what it really implies and whether it is as compelling as it seems.

It is often helpful to use numbers and make calculations to test and develop your arguments. Numbers can help you decide whether a particular problem is important or unimportant. If economies of scale may be a barrier to competition, for example, how large are fixed costs relative to variable costs? Simple calculations may also help resolve key issues in the case. If a critical question is the profitability of a product, for example, you may want to make a few calculations of likely costs, revenues, or profits.

As in real life, you may be faced with many numbers but be unable to find exactly the ones you think you need. As with other forms of evidence, you can avoid getting lost in the numbers by formulating your hypotheses first before you begin a detailed search through the tables or turn on your calculator. If you can't find the particular numbers you think you require, don't be afraid to make approximations from the numbers you have. If you aren't given the marginal cost of a product or service, for example, maybe you can find or calculate a close proxy. Be mindful of the limitations of your approximations, of course, such as whether they are likely to overestimate or underestimate the true figures.

It is especially easy to get confused when making calculations. A few simple rules will help you avoid being diverted and overwhelmed by a mass of numbers that you create.*

- Always ask why you are calculating a number before you begin.
- If a calculation is complex, break it down into components and write them down as you go.
- Keep track of the units of measurement you are using at each step (for example 5 cents per kilowatt hour × 1,000 kilowatt hours per month = 5,000 cents per month).
- After each calculation, and before proceeding, ask yourself what the result means and whether it is surprising.

---

*These suggestions are based on a longer list in "How to Avoid Getting Lost in the Numbers," Harvard Business School note no. 9-682-010.

- If you are surprised, check your calculation for errors or try calculating the number from other sources.

Informal Discussion Groups. After preparing by yourself, if possible arrange to meet with a group of your fellow students to talk about the case before class. An informal discussion will give you a chance to test your ideas on others and to reflect on their different perspectives on the issues.

PARTICIPATING IN CLASS DISCUSSION

The purpose of the case discussion is to develop and test the ideas of the class so that together students reach a richer and deeper understanding of the issues raised by the case. In contrast to a lecture class, the instructor's role is not to present the evidence, arguments, and answer but rather to moderate the students' discussion and create an environment in which the contributions of individual students build upon one another to illuminate the problem more fully. The instructor usually poses the initial question to start the class discussion and calls upon individual students to contribute. At points during the class, the instructor may summarize the debate, highlighting and synthesizing the issues involved, and then ask the class to address another aspect of the problem. Many instructors like to use the last few minutes of the class to review the principal issues raised by the class or to pose a few follow-up questions for students to think about after class.

The quality of the class discussion depends ultimately, however, on the quality of the students' preparation and participation in class. You should think of your class as a team of colleagues that has been asked to work together to solve a challenging problem.

One of the hallmarks of a good team member is a willingness to push his or her ideas and to give a brief explanation of the reasoning behind them. The class will move forward only if students are prepared to share their insights and perspectives on the case, and the best ideas are of little use if you are not prepared to support them carefully and persuasively.

Equally important, you should be prepared to listen to your classmates and keep an open mind. Your classmates will almost surely raise ideas and arguments you have not thought of, and you should be prepared to change your mind and incorporate their ideas when you find them persuasive. An important part of listening is choosing the right moment to add your contribution to the class discussion, trying to ensure that your comments build upon the comments of your classmates. If you want to raise a completely different issue than the one the class is discussing, it may be helpful to wait until the class has fleshed out the issue on the table, or to explain the link between that issue and the issue you think should be considered next.

A corollary is that you should not be afraid to be challenged or to be wrong. Sometimes students leave a case discussion discouraged because many issues and arguments were raised that they had not considered before class. Remember that these cases would not be worth discussing if they were so simple and straightforward that you could understand them completely on your own, without the help of your classmates. Often the class gains the greatest insights when you are brave enough to crawl out on a limb and make an argument that, on close inspection, has some unanticipated flaws. The classroom should be a place where you can test your own ideas and learn from each other.

Finally, enjoy yourself. There is enormous satisfaction in struggling with a complex problem and, through your efforts and the help of your friends, coming to a better understanding of it. We hope these cases will help you do both.

ACKNOWLEDGMENTS

This book represents a group effort. Although our names appear as authors, it is the product of both our work and the work of the dedicated writers, editors, and staff of the Kennedy School Case Program. Without them, neither this volume nor the new kind of microeconomics course we envisioned would exist.

When we agreed, in 1986, to take over the applied microeconomics course at the John F. Kennedy School of Government, we did so only on the condition that the school make a commitment to developing at least half a dozen new cases for the course, which had previously been taught by lecture. Under the tireless leadership of the Case Program director at that time, Professor Dorothy Robyn—herself a keen economics thinker with a special interest in market regulation—the school's casewriters took up our challenge eagerly. Working together with us—often completing the final versions of cases but minutes before they were due to be distributed in class—Professor Robyn and the casewriters became an integral part of the teaching team in a course whose success surpassed our highest initial hopes. Instead of the six cases originally planned, almost twenty were ultimately written. Some of the best appear in this book.

We began this project with no intention of producing a book. But the success of these cases in the classroom, along with their innovative nature, encouraged Howard Husock, Dorothy Robyn's successor as Case Program director, to seek a publisher. Without his vision and encouragement, this book would never have happened. He prodded us to write teaching notes and devoted casewriters and editorial staff to polishing them and gaining publications permission where necessary.

As Howard and Dorothy would be the first to remind us, the backbone of this effort was the work of the individual casewriters. They are David Kennedy, Pamela Varley, Vlad Jenkins, Nancy Kates, Linda Kincaid, Carl Danner, and Dorothy Robyn herself. The cases were edited by Esther Scott and prepared for publication by Jane Licciardello and Karen Johnson.

The authors would also like to thank their students, teaching assistants, and faculty colleagues, who helped test and improve these cases. Our students in the intermediate applied microeconomics course at the

Kennedy School have unwittingly served as our guinea pigs and have taught us a great deal in the process; to them we extend our gratitude and, where appropriate, our apologies. Our teaching assistants offered valuable insights along the way. Professors William C. Apgar, H. James Brown, and John R. Meyer, all of the Kennedy School, used many of these cases in an introductory graduate economics course and have made useful suggestions. Professor Marc Roberts, also of the Kennedy School, originally encouraged and tutored us in the teaching of economics by the case method. Professor Helen Ladd of Duke University has also used several of these cases in both undergraduate and graduate economics courses and has offered helpful comments as well.

Finally, as good economists we know that someone has to pay the bills. This work could not have been done without the commitment of financial resources made by the Kennedy School faculty case committee and Kennedy School Dean Graham Allison.

Tony Gomez-Ibañez
Joe Kalt
Cambridge, MA

chapter 1

Market Operations: Supply, Demand, and Welfare

The bulk of the cases in this volume concern issues of public policy. Accordingly, the cases of this first section are aimed at illustrating some of the basic tools of analysis needed to be able to engage in "applied welfare economics," the analysis of the costs and benefits, and the winners and losers, of economic and policy decisions. These conceptual tools include opportunity cost (the highest valued alternative use of resources); marginalism in decision making (the principle that the net benefits of an economic decision are maximized when incremental benefits are pushed to the point where they equal incremental costs); efficiency in resource allocation (allocating resources to their highest valued uses); consumer and producer gains from trade and production; equilibrium balancing of supply and demand; and "other things equal" methods of reasoning.

California Water Pricing introduces the cases of this volume. Although it is short, it is replete with instances of, and opportunities for, economic ways of reasoning. In particular, the case addresses the question of whether marketplace transactions will tend to ration scarce resources to their highest valued uses. The case also raises the question of whether it is appropriate to allow value to depend, as economics assumes, on the revealed preferences of individuals, no matter how frivolous such preferences may seem. At present, urban water users in California are revealing, through their willingness to pay for water, considerably higher-valued uses for water than the uses to which farmers are putting their water allocations. Farmers in California have been receiving water priced far below the charges that urban users bear. The potential for gains from trade between low-valued agricultural water uses and higher-valued nonagricultural urban uses is obvious but has been blocked by institutional and legal barriers in the California water rights system.

The core of *California Water Pricing* is aimed at dissection of the consequences of forcing or allowing the trading of water in California. Particular emphasis is placed on the incidence of higher water prices *within* the farm sector. This entails examination of the supply-and-demand determinants of the burden of higher water prices as a function of different crops' water usage, substitution capabilities, and demand conditions. The case also illustrates how relatively uncomplicated factual evidence, interpreted through economic reasoning, can be brought to bear on real-world problems.

California Water Pricing illustrates the concept of efficiency in resource *distribution.* The case of *Avon Corporation* introduces issues surrounding *technical* efficiency, that is, minimizing resource input costs for any given level of production of a good. *Avon Corporation* also serves to describe the theory of the profit-maximizing firm and concretely illustrates the role of total, average, and marginal costs in production decisions. While the case does not emphasize public policy matters, it does lay the groundwork for derivation of industry supply curves, which is essential for analyses of, for example, market power and monopoly, public utility regulation, and producers' sources of profits.

Revving Up for Relief: Harley-Davidson at the ITC serves as an integrative case. In 1982, the famous U.S. manufacturer of high-powered motorcycles successfully petitioned the U.S. International Trade Commission (ITC) for import protection. The decision of the ITC focused on the question of the dominant cause of a decline in Harley-Davidson's fortunes. Answering this question requires that the various possible causes of Harley-Davidson's problems—imports, changes in consumer desires, poor management, a weak economy—be isolated. This requires that the influence of "other things" be analytically held "equal" while investigating with economic reasoning the causal influence of a particular individual factor. For example, if everything else had been as it was but Harley-Davidson had utilized better management techniques, would the company be in its current troubles? It turns out that the timing of Harley-Davidson's troubles is strongly correlated with both the appearance of Japanese competition and economy-wide recession. Which of these is the dominant cause of Harley-Davidson's difficulties?

Part B of the Harley-Davidson case examines the remedy for harm from import competition that the company sought before the ITC, a remedy that consisted of very stiff tariffs on imported motorcycles. Such tariffs would alter the U.S. motorcycle market by making imports more expensive and raising the returns to producing motorcycles in the United States. Who would this help and who would it harm? Harley-Davidson stockholders and workers, motorcycle consumers, retail motorcycle dealers, the recipients of tariff revenues, and foreign producers all have stakes in the answer to this question. The case indicates that a tariff is a kind of tax, and the location (or "incidence") of the burdens and benefits of a tax of this type turns on such factors as the responsiveness of consumer demand to price increases, the responsiveness of the supplies of motorcycles and retailing services to changes in prices, and the mobility of workers across industries.

Of course, the case of Harley-Davidson implicitly raises the issue of whether the proposed remedy for the company's problems would constitute sound economic policy for the nation as a whole. The criterion that economics brings to this debate is that of efficiency—maximizing the value yielded to consumers by the nation's resources. Is this value higher if we prop up a domestic motorcycle industry, or would we be better off in the aggregate if that industry's resources were allowed to move into other sectors of the economy to produce other things consumers want? In a situation such as the Harley-Davidson case, where there are likely to be both winners and losers from either decision, application of the standard of economic efficiency amounts to an assessment of whether the winners' gains outweigh the losers' losses. The need for this kind of assessment, however, also points up some of the limitations of economics, for economics has little to say about whether the distribution of benefits and burdens across winners and losers is equitable and fair. Such judgments fall under the purview of social ethics and political philosophy, rather than economics. The cases of the third section of this volume focus on this distinction more completely.

California Water Pricing

Like energy in the East, water has proved to be a limiting natural resource in the western states. The appropriate allocation of this scarce commodity is perhaps nowhere more important than in California, a semi-arid state with a gigantic agricultural sector and a burgeoning population. And yet, the state's historical approach to water has established a pattern of consumption far removed from what many people consider ideal.

The evolution of California water law is a story in several chapters. Early settlers adopted the approach prevalent in the eastern states which gave water rights to the owner of land adjacent to a river or stream. That system of "riparian" rights (from the Latin word for bank) sufficed while settlement was sparse, but proved unsuitable as demand grew for nonriparian land. California gold miners were the first to systematically appropriate water for use at off-stream sites. Over time, miners fashioned a sophisticated system of water rights based on the principle of "first in time, first in right," with codes specifying the maximum size of claims, limits on the number of claims per miner, and conditions for forfeiture. Reflecting the special demands of an arid climate, the doctrine of "prior appropriation" served to establish ownership rights that were generally well-defined, enforced, and transferable.

Despite its sophistication, the prior appropriation system began to unravel in the late 1800s. Faced with frontier disputes, eastern-trained judges often enforced riparian precedent, and the resulting mix of riparian and prior appropriation doctrine led to a confusion that stifled the establishment of private property in water. The miners' system was gradually

This case was written by Assistant Professor Dorothy Robyn for use at the John F. Kennedy School of Government, Harvard University. It draws heavily on Philip A. Guentert, "Agricultural Water Pricing in California" (Policy Analysis Exercise, Kennedy School of Government, 1983), and on an earlier case by Professor Helen Ladd. Certain institutional and administrative facts have been altered. (0987)

replaced by a system of state control of water, which restricted water sale and transfer in significant ways.

The decline of private water rights also removed a key incentive for conservation. In an effort to reduce waste, a 1928 California constitutional amendment limited water rights to an amount "reasonably required for beneficial use." Conservation was not treated as a beneficial use, however, and so the amendment perversely reinforced farmers' "use it or lose it" mentality toward water. For more than 50 years, the "beneficial use" doctrine—combined with state control of water allocation—punished conservation and discouraged the voluntary transfer of existing allotments to parties who could make better use of the water.

The water system that developed within this legal framework is physically and institutionally complex. California has 1,251 major dams and the two biggest irrigation projects on earth (the gargantuan Central Valley Project, operated by the federal government since 1902, diverts one-third of the Colorado River's flow, primarily to southern California farms and ranches; the State Water Project, begun in 1959, serves chiefly Los Angeles and Kern County). These engineering feats satisfy only 60 percent of California's enormous thirst for water. The rest comes from under the ground.

Most of the state's water, 85 percent of which goes for irrigation, is delivered by some 2,500 local water agencies. These delivery agencies, or retailers, are supplied by wholesalers who purchase water from federal, state, and local sources at markedly different rates. Federal water goes for the heavily subsidized rate of roughly $10 per acre-foot (volume of water covering an acre to a depth of one foot). Water from state reservoirs costs wholesalers from $30–$60 per acre-foot. Underground supplies cost approximately $100 per acre-foot. Retailers, in turn, are charged a "rolled-in" (i.e., weighted) average of wholesale acquisition costs.

At the retail level, there is no single price for water. Although retailers' revenues cover their costs (water districts are barred from making a profit), in many areas, especially those dominated by farmers, agricultural users pay less than residential users. A recent study done for a major Los Angeles petrochemical firm put the average water price for agriculture at $10 per acre-foot, compared to an average residential water price of approximately $100 per acre-foot. This pricing structure results in such anomalies as the current, and profitable, practice of irrigating hay in Death Valley. According to a 1978 study by the Rand Corporation, the gross inefficien-

cies created by charging farmers less than the true cost of water result in a $5 billion loss to society.

Recent years have seen a growing interest in alternatives to the current system. A 1982 statewide referendum, defeated with heavy opposition from farm interests (see Exhibit 1), would have encouraged marginal cost pricing by local water districts. That same year, the California Water Code was amended to allow for the temporary sale of "conserved" water without loss of water rights (an earlier bill had defined conservation as a beneficial use). More recently, debate has focused on additional means to expand the ability of those holding water rights—individuals as well as water districts—to buy, sell, and transport surplus water with no danger of losing future rights (see Exhibit 2). While the eventual movement to some kind of market-oriented system of water allocation seems likely, strong political and institutional obstacles remain.

MARGINAL COST PRICING

The nature and degree of potential opposition begin to emerge from some simple tables showing the differential effects a system of marginal cost pricing for water might have: There are 13 major water basins in California (see Exhibit 3), and most of the variation in average water prices occurs between basins (see Exhibit 4). Price increases from a marginal cost scheme would differ substantially by region, both because agricultural water prices are closer to the true marginal cost in some regions and because the true marginal cost is lower in some regions. (Costs within basins are assumed to be uniform.) Since certain re-

EXHIBIT 1

"No" Vote on Water Referendum

Westside San Joaquin	80%
San Joaquin Basin	80
Mountain Valley	79
North San Joaquin	78
Sacramento Valley	77
High desert	75
Imperial Valley	74
Central coast	70
Delta	69
North coast	67
South coast	63
North bay	67
South bay	53

Source: Compiled from county tabulations in the *Los Angeles Times,* November 4, 1982, p. 19, column I.

Push to Lift Curbs on Water Sales

By Ann Cony
Bee Staff Writer

Legislative attempts to create an open market for the buying and selling of state water have brought together some unlikely bedfellows.

The irony is not lost on Ron Khachigian, senior vice president of Blackwell Land Co. Inc., which operates one of the largest corporate farms in California.

"I'm sitting at a witness table with the Environmental Defense Fund, and here I am a real conservative farmer, and we're both espousing the marketing of water," Khachigian said.

For different reasons, Blackwell and the Environmental Defense Fund are supporting a bill that would require state water agencies to make their canals and aqueducts available to third parties that have concluded water sales.

Sponsored by Assemblyman Richard Katz, D-Sepulveda, the bill (AB 2746) was approved by the Assembly in May. It's one of two water-marketing bills that will be awaiting Senate action when lawmakers return from a recess on Monday.

Those bills and a third one signed recently by the governor are designed to remove institutional, logistical and financial roadblocks to water trading. None is monumental in and of itself.

However, "they're all adding to a policy and a body of law that allows [water marketing] to happen," said Clyde MacDonald of the Assembly Office of Research. "They're like bricks in a building: They're all important."

The Legislature has been working on fundamental changes in water policy for the last seven years or so, pushing water marketing as one means of using a scarce resource more efficiently, MacDonald said.

Four years ago a law was passed to allow farmers and others to sell surplus state water without abandoning their rights to use their water allocations in the future.

But there still are potential barriers to water trading, proponents say.

Katz has said that farmers who support water trading fear that big water districts will block sales by denying access to their canals. His bill would guarantee water traders access to transportation systems as long as space is available and they're willing to pay a fair fee.

The measure has been opposed by some water bureaucracies but supported by a broad coalition that includes environmentalists, the California Farm Bureau and financially strapped irrigation districts where farmers are having trouble paying their water bills.

For farmers, water trading offers flexibility and a new weapon in their survival arsenal. In a free water market, a farmer can sell some or all of his water rights, for any length of time, without selling the land to which the water rights were originally attached.

Environmental groups support water marketing as one way of encouraging water conservation, and hope it will lessen the need for building expensive or environmentally disruptive additions to the state's water delivery system.

Katz' bill will be before the Senate Appropriations Committee on Monday, along with a water-marketing bill by Assembly Democrats Jim Costa of Fresno and Phil Isenberg of Sacramento.

The Costa-Isenberg bill (AB 3722) is designed to help overcome bureaucratic inertia. It directs the state Department of Water Resources to "facilitate" the voluntary transfer or exchange of water and serve as an information clearinghouse, maintaining lists of would-be buyers and sellers.

A third bill, sponsored by Assemblyman David Kelley, R-Hemet, was approved by the Legislature last month and has been signed into law by the governor. It removes a seven-year limit on the term of contracts for the transfer of water. Removal of the time limit eliminates an economic roadblock to water transfers that would require construction of canals, pipelines, pumps or other expensive structures. The Farm Bureau and other proponents say the seven-year limit on contracts would have made some of those deals impossible to finance.

Observers say that the Katz and Costa-Isenberg bills have a good chance of joining the Kelley bill in becoming law but that none of the measures will trigger immediate wheeling and dealing in water.

Numerous farms are reportedly anxious to sell water, but "until we have a situation where there's not enough water, we're not going to have very many buyers," said MacDonald.

That is expected to change, however, with the next drought.

Eventually, "I think we will use water marketing," MacDonald said. "I think there's no question about it."

EXHIBIT 2

Source: Reprinted with permission from *The Sacramento Bee,* August 10, 1986, pp. D1-2.

EXHIBIT 3
California's Water Basins

gions tend to produce certain crops, the shift to a marginal cost pricing scheme would affect some crops more than others (see Exhibit 5).

Water is also much more important for some California crops than others. The "factor share" of water—the percentage of total costs accounted for by water—ranges from 1.0 percent for celery to 35.8 percent for grain hay (see Exhibit 6). Moreover, the additional value created by marginal applications of water differs markedly across crops. For example, the marginal application of an acre-foot of water produces $62.00 worth of lemons on average across the

EXHIBIT 4

Water Price Increases from Marginal Cost Pricing by Water Basin ($ per Acre-Foot)

Basin	Current Average Price	Marginal Cost	Change
North coast	20	50	30
Sacramento Valley	30	40	10
North bay	20	80	60
Delta	20	50	30
South bay	20	20	0
North San Joaquin	10	70	60
Mountain valley	20	50	30
San Joaquin	20	90	70
Central coast	10	100	90
Westside San Joaquin	20	100	80
South coast	30	90	60
High desert	40	80	40
Imperial Valley	10	90	80

Source: Derived from Philip Guentert, *Agricultural Water Pricing in California,* Policy Analysis Exercise, Kennedy School of Government, Harvard University, 1983.

EXHIBIT 5

Average Price Increase for Water by Crop
($ per Acre-Foot)

Lettuce	80
Carrots	70
Celery	70
Grapes	70
Oranges	70
Barley	60
Cotton	60
Melons	60
Sorghum	60
Peaches	50
Pears	50
Onions	50
Wheat	50
Alfalfa hay	40
Almonds	40
Apricots	40
Field corn	40
Grain hay	40
Lima beans	40
Prunes	40
Sugar beets	40
Tomatoes	40
Irrigated pasture	30
Rice	30
Walnuts	30

Source: Derived from Philip Guentert, *Agricultural Water Pricing in California,* Policy Analysis Exercise, Kennedy School of Government, Harvard University, 1983.

EXHIBIT 6

Average Factor Share of Water by Crop
(% Costs)

Grain hay	35.8
Irrigated pasture	34.7
Alfalfa hay	25.9
Field corn	21.7
Barley	20.2
Rice	19.7
Wheat	17.8
Sorghum	14.2
Oranges	14.2
Sugar beets	13.6
Onions	12.5
Cotton	11.3
Almonds	6.8
Melons	6.7
Carrots	6.5
Walnuts	6.3
Grapes	5.9
Tomatoes	5.3
Lettuce	4.7
Prunes	4.3
Lima beans	4.0
Apricots	3.5
Pears	3.0
Peaches	2.3
Celery	1.0

Source: Derived from Philip Guentert, *Agricultural Water Pricing in California,* Policy Analysis Exercise, Kennedy School of Government, Harvard University, 1983.

state, but only $8.83 worth of lima beans (see Exhibit 7).

In addition, farmers in different regions use different amounts of water to produce a given crop. The coefficient of variation—which represents the degree of inter-region variation in the ratio of water to non-water inputs—is much greater for onions and pears, for example, than for rice and lima beans (see Exhibit 8).

Farmers of a given crop also incur different costs of production, largely because some land is more fertile than other. No consistent data are available with which to estimate the precise size of the cost variations, but it is clear that some farmers operate on marginal land while others farm land that returns large profits to owners.

Finally, crops differ with respect to their place in the domestic and international market, which has implications for a marginal cost pricing scheme. For example, California farmers produce 99.9 percent of the U.S. almond crop, which represents 20.7 percent of the total world production. About 60.7 percent of California's almonds are exported outside the state.

In contrast, California only produces 2.9 percent of the nation's wheat, but 78.1 percent of it is exported (see Exhibit 9).

URBAN WATER ACQUISITION STRATEGIES

The various metropolitan water districts of California (MWDs), water wholesalers that represent primarily urban and often rapidly growing regions of the state, are eager to secure rights to additional supplies of water. At present, these districts negotiate with water authorities in agricultural areas for medium and long-term supply contracts. When the MWDs can induce farm regions to forego the use of water, it becomes available for purchase under the provisions of the California Water Code, as amended in 1982:

§1011. Reduction of water use due to conservation efforts

(a) When any person entitled to the use of water under an appropriative right fails to use

EXHIBIT 7

Mean Marginal Value Products
($ per Acre-Foot)

Lemons	62.00
Cotton	55.98
Melons	53.53
Carrots	53.27
Onions	51.50
Oranges	46.86
Sweet corn	40.00
Grapes	39.61
Wheat	37.74
Barley	37.17
Alfalfa hay	36.37
Sugar beets	32.78
Tomatoes	32.75
Walnuts	32.45
Almonds	32.26
Grain hay	31.37
Sorghum	32.78
Prunes/plums	28.49
Irrigated pasture	20.93
Celery	20.77
Asparagus	17.40
Field corn	17.27
Rice	16.89
Lettuce	16.84
Peaches	10.59
Artichokes	10.00
Apricots	9.41
Broccoli	10.00
Lima beans	8.83

Source: Derived from Philip Guentert, *Agricultural Water Pricing in California,* Policy Analysis Exercise, Kennedy School of Government, Harvard University, 1983.

EXHIBIT 8

Coefficient of Variation of Input Ratios[1]

Onions	.829
Pears	.532
Grain hay	.475
Sorghum	.445
Prunes	.419
Lettuce	.403
Carrots	.395
Almonds	.393
Peaches	.302
Tomatoes	.266
Field corn	.265
Wheat	.250
Grapes	.244
Irrigated pasture	.242
Apricots	.235
Walnuts	.230
Cotton	.219
Alfalfa hay	.181
Celery	.195
Oranges	.187
Barley	.163
Sugar beets	.138
Melons	.123
Rice	.119
Lima beans	.005

[1]Defined as the standard deviation of the set of ratios divided by their mean.

Source: Derived from Philip Guentert, *Agricultural Water Pricing in California,* Policy Analysis Exercise, Kennedy School of Government, Harvard University, 1983.

all or any part of the water because of water conservation efforts, any cessation or reduction in the use of such appropriated water shall be deemed equivalent to a reasonable beneficial use of water to the extent of such cessation or reduction in use. No forfeiture of the appropriative right to the water conserved shall occur upon the lapse of the forfeiture period applicable to water appropriated pursuant to the Water Commission Act or this code or the forfeiture period applicable to water appropriated prior to December 19, 1914. . . .

For purposes of this section, the term "water conservation" shall mean the use of less water to accomplish the same purpose or purposes of use allowed under the existing appropriate right. Where water appropriated for irrigation purposes is not used by reason of land fallowing or crop rotation, the reduced usage shall be deemed water conservation for purposes of this section.

(b) Water, or the right to the use of water, the use of which has ceased or been reduced as the result of water conservation efforts as described in subdivision (a), may be sold, leased, exchanged, or otherwise transferred pursuant to any provision of law relating to the transfer of water or water rights, including, but not limited to, provisions of law governing any change in point of diversion, place of use, and purpose of use due to the transfer.

Needless to say, when negotiating with agricultural water districts, the MWDs find farmers reluctant to part with water acquired at prices so favorable to agriculture. Accordingly, the metropolitan water districts are considering asking for statewide legislation that would require all water authorities, urban and agricultural, to price their water at no less than each district's marginal cost.

EXHIBIT 9

California Crops in the World Marketplace

	CA Prod. (Tons)	CA % of US Prod.	CA % World Prod.	US Imports (Tons)	US Exports (Tons)	% CA Prod. Exported
Almonds	159,000	99.9	20.7	688		60.7
Walnuts	195,000	99.4	27.1	145	49,887	30.8
Artichokes	174,000	98.0	19.5		9,795	18.7
Broccoli	180,000	94.9				10.8
Grapes	3,924,000	90.4	N.B.[1]	27,240[2]	192,130	18.1[3]
Tomatoes	7,270,600	85.5	14.0	368,720[4]	167,840	2.1[5]
Plums[6]	273,000	79.2	10.2	3,229	206,500	≈25
Lemons	844,000	75.5	27.4	12	198,913	31.4
Lettuce	1,912,500	73.2	23.6			5.1
Celery	530,600	66.2				7.2
Peaches	914,500	64.7	19.1		99,312	≈10
Melons	306,500	63.8	5.7			
Carrots	520,800	54.0	7.6			5.2
Asparagus	53,500	50.3				16.3
Lima beans	46,300	48.2				
Pears	300,400	39.3	5.4	8,159	35,667	6.9
Onions	545,100	34.7	2.8	34,800	87,900	29.1
Sugar beets	8,476,000	29.0	N.B.[7]	3,867,000	203,000	
Rice	1,504,400	23.6	0.4	1,102	2,287,949	79.0
Cotton[8]	465,700	23.3	1.8	29,970	827,750	87.5
Oranges	2,062,500	20.2	5.8	30,980	529,743	25.8
Barley	1,450,100	15.8	0.9	337,998	545,472	
Apples	230,000	6.1	0.8	42,953	120,978	
Hay[9]	7,642,000	5.8				4.1[10]
Wheat	1,866,800	2.9	0.5	43,130	25,179,022	78.1
Sorghum[11]	417,300	2.0			6,663,916	
Corn	775,200	0.5	0.2	49,117	27,397,696[12]	

[1] 24,943,687 acres worldwide; 524,420 acres in California.

[2] Raisins and fresh equivalent.

[3] Fresh only (no wine).

[4] All products.

[5] Processing tomatoes only (no fresh).

[6] Including prunes.

[7] 11,506,910 tons sugar, cane and beet. Imports in tons cane and beet sugar. Exports in tons centrifugal sugar only.

[8] Lint only (not seed).

[9] Of total CA production, 6,608,000 is alfalfa.

[10] Alfalfa only.

[11] Grain only.

[12] Corn and cornmeal.

Source: Derived from Philip Guentert, *Agricultural Water Pricing in California,* Policy Analysis Exercise, Kennedy School of Government, Harvard University, 1983.

ASSIGNMENT FOR CLASS DISCUSSION

Come to class prepared to discuss the following questions:

1. Which crops and which regions of California would be most affected, and how would they be affected, by a shift to a system of

water allocation in which farmers are required to pay prices set at marginal cost for their water?

2.   A move to marginal cost pricing would most likely cause a shift of water usage away from agriculture and toward urban areas. Do you believe such a shift would be appropriate? By what criteria would you address such a question?

3.   Consider the problems of implementing a new pricing system for California's water. What if, instead of having to pay marginal cost prices, farmers were simply permitted to sell the water they are currently using on an open market? What impact would this have on water prices, water usage by farmers and others, and California's output of agricultural crops?

Avon Corporation
Price Formulation for an Electric Adjustable Speed Drive

Avon Corporation manufactured a wide line of electrical products which were sold as stationary power equipment for use in industrial plants and also as components to be built into end products by original equipment manufacturers. The company sold to end users and to OEMs, both through the company's direct salesforce and through distributors. Avon salesmen generally handled large OEM accounts, and distributors covered small and medium-sized OEMs and end users. The prices charged by Avon Corporation to direct accounts and to distributor accounts were the same.

Early in 1956, Avon engineers had completed work on the development of a new type of electric adjustable speed drive. This machine consisted of an AC motor coupled to a device by means of which the speed output of the motor could be increased or decreased.

The new type of electric adjustable speed drive would have wide use as a source of power for conveyor belts in mines, warehouses, and factories. The new product could also serve as a source of adjustable speed power in machine tools, materials handling equipment, draw presses, printing presses, power shovels, and other types of heavy equipment, both stationary and mobile. Avon executives believed that over the long run the new product could easily

account for a substantial portion of Avon's sales and profits, even though they expected that other companies would introduce closely similar units. The new design, they thought, was probably not patentable.

With the completion of the design engineering on this machine, Avon executives began to make long-range plans for the production and marketing of this product. Engineering personnel were assigned to the task of developing information on what it would cost to make the new product and on the capital investment which would be required to make and sell it. Sales Department personnel were requested to survey the markets for various types of adjustable speed drives, and to estimate sales volume for the new product. In particular, members of the Sales Department were asked to recommend a price schedule for the Avon adjustable speed drive.

TYPES OF ADJUSTABLE SPEED DRIVES

As of 1956 there were three types of adjustable speed drives, the mechanical adjustable speed (MAS) drive, the electric adjustable speed (EAS) drive, and the adjustable voltage DC (AVDC) drive. While all three products performed similar functions each was based on different design principles and for each there were certain applications for which it was particularly suited. The three products sold at different price levels. MAS drive prices were the lowest of the three and AVDC drive prices the highest. Each of the three had its advantages and limitations, and these are noted in the discussion which follows.

Mechanical Adjustable Speed Drives. For this type of drive, speed adjustment was achieved mechanically through a system of variable pitch pulleys and V-belts. Speed had to be adjusted by means of a handwheel mounted on the unit, and control settings could only be changed when the unit was in operation.

The primary advantage which this product had was low price. The OEM price on a 5 H.P. unit, for example, was $750 as compared to $1,470 for an EAS drive and $1,685 for an AVDC drive of the same horsepower rating.

As for limitations of the mechanical adjustable speed drive, a major one was that remote control could be achieved only by means of complicated and expensive systems using chain drives or geared motors. In addition, V-belts, pulleys, and bearings required frequent replacement in these units. Finally, a mechanical adjustable speed drive was more than twice the size of an electric adjustable speed drive and was bulky to install at the work location.

Electric Adjustable Speed Drives. Among the major advantages of this equipment were smooth acceleration, simplicity, compactness, and ease of installation. The motor could be started without a load, and then the load could be accelerated smoothly to the desired speed by means of remote controls. It was possible to obtain a zero to full speed range which was substantially stepless for intermittent operation.

As for its undesirable features, EAS drives were generally regarded as somewhat inefficient because they used a great amount of power at low speeds. In addition, this equipment heated up under conditions of sustained low-speed operation. Overheating and unsatisfactory operation also resulted where frequent jogging, inching, or reversing were required. In some instances, vibration problems had been encountered with electric adjustable speed drives because of the way in which these machines were constructed.

The new Avon product was an electric adjustable speed drive, the design of which was based on somewhat different principles than EAS drives which were then available. As compared with existing EAS drives, the new Avon product had certain advantages. It required less maintenance and was easier to

maintain. It was somewhat more efficient since it required less power input relative to output than existing EAS equipment. Finally, power output could be somewhat more closely controlled and kept within a narrower range.

Adjustable Voltage DC Drives. In applications requiring great precision, adjustable voltage DC drives were used. An AVDC drive consisted of an AC motor which drove a DC generator which in turn provided power for a DC motor. The speed of the drive shaft of the DC motor could be precisely adjusted through a remote control system by controlling the power going into the DC generator and the DC motor.

AVDC drives were used, for example, to power the rolls in a steel rolling mill. In making steel sheet the speeds of all rolls in the line had to be closely coordinated to avoid having the sheet either buckle or stretch.

More efficient than electric adjustable speed drives, the AVDC drive did not have the disadvantage of high power losses and overheating at low speed operation. In addition, the AVDC drive could be installed so that only the DC motor was at the work location. This component by itself was much smaller than an EAS drive unit. Even with its improvements over existing EAS drives, the new Avon unit still fell short of AVDC drives in performance.

Avon Corporation was one of several manufacturers of AVDC drives. The company's sales of this product in 1955 had amounted to $1.2 million.

REASONS FOR ADDING AN ELECTRIC ADJUSTABLE SPEED DRIVE TO THE AVON LINE

The Avon management had originally authorized research and development work on a new type EAS drive because they believed attractive profits were available. In addition they recognized a need to include a product of this type in the line. Avon salesmen and distributors had reported, not infrequently, that they had lost sales of AVDC drives when the prospective customer had been persuaded to purchase an EAS drive. The competition from EAS drives, it was believed, would be even greater if manufacturers of this equipment had wider distribution than they had. Recognizing that the EAS drive was not completely efficient, salesmen nevertheless believed it to be an effective and worthwhile product for many applications. They sometimes exhibited reluctance to attempt to sell an AVDC drive when EAS equipment was quite adequate for the application. Thus one salesman reported as follows:

> While the efficiencies of our drives are equal to or better than the efficiency of electric adjustable speed drives at the normal operating speed (two-thirds of full speed), we still cannot show it to be economically sound on single motored conveyors to purchase our equipment over the EAS drive because it would take something in the order of 10 to 15 years' worth of savings in power to make up the difference in price.

Another salesman made the following comment in a call report:

> While we never did admit to [Customer X] that we did not have as good a proposition from an overall engineering aspect as they could obtain from [Competitor A] using an EAS drive, we did feel deep in our hearts that we do not have any equipment developed which could truly match up to the EAS drive for this particular type of drive. Certainly we could match this performance if we were given the-sky-as-the-limit for price, and providing we were allowed to furnish as much equipment as necessary to do the job. Nevertheless, we must be realistic and admit that if simplicity is combined with relatively low price it is a good buy for the customer. We are proud of these factors when they are in our favor.

MANUFACTURING COST ANALYSIS

Because of the way it was designed, Avon's new drive could be manufactured at lower costs than existing EAS drives of equivalent capacity. In calculating what it would actually cost to make the new product, Avon engineers had worked from drawings of a 5 H.P. model. This size was known to be a very popular one in the case of existing EAS drives.

Engineering analysis indicated that if the rate of production (of all sizes) was over 200 units per week, the 5 H.P. units could be made for a unit cost of $599 exclusive of selling and administrative overhead. (Selling and administrative overhead was regarded as fixed, and in calculating costs Avon accountants estimated this overhead at 10% of net sales.)

Unit costs, it was further estimated, would increase by 20% if the rate of production was 100 units a week instead of 200 or more and by 40% if the rate

of production was 50 units a week. If production was as low as 30 units a week, unit costs of production would be 50% greater (or $900 for the 5 H.P. model).

ESTIMATES OF REQUIRED INVESTMENT

Engineering estimates indicated that to produce at the rate of 200–400 units per week would require an additional investment in plant of $2,500,000 and an investment in equipment of $1,500,000.[1] An additional investment of $460,000 in inventory would be needed if 400 units a week were produced. At lower levels of production correspondingly lower investments in inventory would be needed. Inventory investment was calculated on the assumption that a ten times inventory turnover could be achieved.

Finally, it would be necessary to include in the total investment figure an amount to cover receivables. On the basis of previous experience this amount could be roughly calculated at 8% of sales. The investment in receivables, however, would be partially offset by Avon's accounts payable, an amount that was estimated at 4% of sales.

If the rate of production was 100–150 units a week the investment in plant and in equipment would be $2,000,000 and $1,000,000 respectively. To manufacture between 25 and 50 units a week Avon would need to construct a plant which would cost $1,650,000 and which would be equipped with machinery costing $800,000.

When asked how long it would take to build plant capacity for the new electric adjustable speed drive and to get into production, executives in the Engineering Department stated that more than a year would be required. Because engineering personnel were already overburdened and because the work on the new product was quite extensive, it was believed that production could not be started before January 1958.

MARKET ANALYSIS

By means of field surveys and through the use of published information, market research personnel in the Sales Department estimated that the 1956 market for adjustable speed drives of all types amounted to $53.8 million. Mechanical drives accounted for $30.7

---

[1]Avon Corporation, it may be noted, depreciated capital investment in buildings at 2-1/2% a year and equipment investment at 10% a year. In this case the depreciation would be charged directly to the cost of manufacture of the new product.

million of this amount; electric drives for $9.1 million; and adjustable voltage DC drives for $14.0 million. Five medium-sized companies, it was learned, manufactured electric drives. Three of these companies and four others made and supplied mechanical drives. At least fifteen concerns, including Avon Corporation, manufactured adjustable voltage DC drives.

Again through the use of published information and by working closely with Avon field sales offices, market research personnel prepared estimates of unit sales of each of the three types of drives by size. It was found that unit sales of the lower horsepower ratings were greatest. Thus in the case of the EAS drive, about 13% of unit sales were represented by 1 H.P. units and only 1.6% of sales were accounted for by 100 H.P. units.

Price schedules for each of the three types of adjustable speed drives were also obtained. These prices are shown in Exhibits 1a and 1b.

ESTIMATES OF MARKET POTENTIAL FOR THE NEW AVON DRIVE

Members of the Sales Department recognized that the share of the $53.8 million market for adjustable speed drives which could be claimed by the new type

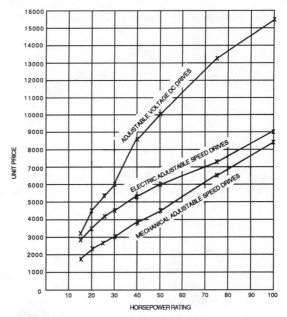

EXHIBIT 1b
OEM Prices for Three Types of Adjustable Speed Drives
15–100 Horsepower

EXHIBIT 1a
OEM Prices for Three Types of Adjustable Speed Drives
1–15 Horsepower

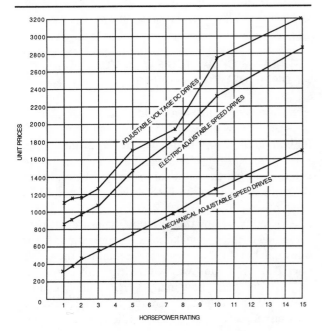

EAS drive depended greatly on the prices charged for it. This product could be sold at the same prices at which existing EAS drives were then sold, or at higher prices. On the other hand, it was quite conceivable, in view of the production costs which were estimated for the new product, that the prices for the new Avon drive could be lowered to the prices of the mechanical adjustable speed drive, $750 in the case of the 5 H.P. model.

Because there was a possibility that the Avon drive could be priced at this low level, a detailed analysis was then made of the various applications for adjustable speed drives to determine in which of these applications the existing equipment could be replaced by a new EAS drive selling at the MAS drive price level. This analysis indicated that even though the new EAS drive was priced at the MAS drive price level, there were still many applications in which other types of drives had strong functional advantages. These advantages would probably overcome any price disadvantages that might exist.

It was estimated, however, that potentially the new type drive sold at MAS drive prices could account for approximately half, or $27 million, of the 1956 market for adjustable speed drives of all types. About $15.5 million of this amount would come from the existing market for MAS drives and $2.4 million from the market for AVDC drives. The $27 million figure included the $9.1 million of volume which could be obtained by replacing all existing EAS drives.

On the other hand, if Avon priced the new drive at the price level which obtained for EAS drives, it was possible that a $2.5 million market existed for it as of 1956.

AVON'S MARKET SHARE

In calculating how much of the potential market for the new product Avon could obtain, Sales Department personnel assumed that it would take the company five years to achieve its full market share. This assumption was especially valid, they believed, because other companies were already well entrenched in the adjustable speed drive market.

Avon personnel, therefore, began to think in terms of the 1963 market. Hence, it was necessary first to judge the size of the 1963 market before estimating Avon's sales potential.

By computing and projecting the growth rate of industries which purchased adjustable speed drives, either for in-plant use or as components, it was estimated that the demand of these customers in 1963 for drives of all types would be 147% of their demand in 1956. Hence the 1963 adjustable speed drive market would be about $79 million as compared to $53.8 million in 1956. Similarly the share of the 1963 market which could be accounted for by a new design EAS drive, selling at MAS drive prices, would be $40 million as compared to $27 million in 1956.

With a new product at substantially reduced prices, it was conceivable, Avon sales executives believed, that the company could claim 50% of this $40 million market. In the electrical industry, there were several examples where the innovating company had, through aggressive market development, retained half the market even though many other producers had come in. These examples, furthermore, had involved some relatively small and medium-sized companies.

If on the other hand the Avon drive was sold at the same price level as existing EAS drives, the company, it was estimated, probably could develop a sales volume of about $3.4 million by 1963. The particular advantages of the Avon drive and the aggressive sales effort of the Avon salesforce could be counted on as factors in achieving this sales goal. Futhermore, it was anticipated that with the growth of user industries, a $3.4 million sales volume would be in addition to the total volume which would otherwise exist for EAS drives and would not be taken from present suppliers.

In making these estimates of Avon's market share at two price levels, Sales Department personnel had made certain assumptions regarding factors which would condition competitive reactions to the introduction of the new drive. First, it was assumed that manufacturers of existing EAS drives could, in a year's time, redesign their products to incorporate some of the design features in the new Avon drive, features that affected both performance and manufacturing cost. To duplicate the new unit completely, however, competitors would need to allow a minimum of 1 1/2–2 years for product design and production engineering. No specialized machinery was needed to make the new drive, and it was possible for existing manufacturers of all types of adjustable speed drives to manufacture the new unit in their plants.

In appraising the possibility that competitors might elect initially to reduce prices on existing units, the following information was relevant. It was estimated that the gross margin was about 20% on MAS drives. Other expenses such as sales and administrative overhead probably averaged 12% and profit before taxes, 8%. While MAS drive manufacturers also made and sold other electrical products, MAS drive sales in each instance contributed significantly to total sales. Two, out of seven, manufacturers together accounted for more than 50% of the total output of MAS drives.

Avon engineers estimated that on EAS drives, gross margin was about 50%, other expenses 12%, and profit before taxes, 38%. In the case of each of the five companies making EAS drives, this product was its major product. One of the five concerns accounted for 50% of the total output of EAS drives.

ESTIMATES OF AVON'S SALES VOLUME AT DIFFERENT PRICE LEVELS

The foregoing calculations indicated that Avon's sales of the new drive in 1963 could fall between $20 million and $3.4 million depending primarily on price. With this range estimated, it was useful next to determine what the sales volume would be at different price levels between EAS drive prices and MAS drive prices.

In approaching this question, Sales Department personnel decided to make sales volume estimates for one model in the line, first, rather than for the whole line. The 5 H.P. unit was selected for this purpose.

To determine how many 5 H.P. units would be sold if Avon's total sales of the new electric drive were either $20 million or $3.5 million, Avon person-

EXHIBIT 2

Estimates of Avon's Annual Sales of the New Electric Adjustable Speed Drives by Size Rating at Two Price Levels, 1963

H.P. Rating	OEM Price per Unit		Avon Sales in Units		Avon Sales in Dollars (000 Omitted)	
	MAS Drives	EAS Drives	At MASD Prices	At EASD Prices	At MASD Prices	At EASD Prices
1	$ 317	$ 855	2,500	190	$ 792,500	$ 162,450
1.5	372	910	2,350	185	874,200	168,350
2	445	970	2,350	185	1,045,750	179,450
3	560	1,070	2,250	175	1,260,000	187,250
5	750	1,470	2,200	170	1,650,000	249,900
7.5	985	1,815	2,100	170	2,068,500	308,550
10	1,275	2,310	1,550	155	1,976,250	358,050
15	1,720	2,840	1,100	110	1,892,000	312,400
20	2,280	3,610	800	75	1,824,000	270,750
25	2,655	4,100	680	70	1,805,400	287,000
30	3,020	4,525	470	55	1,419,400	248,875
40	3,850	5,360	330	40	1,270,500	214,400
50	4,575	5,975	270	30	1,235,250	179,250
75	6,500	7,355	70	25	455,000	183,875
100	8,525	8,970	30	15	255,750	134,550
			19,050	1,650	$19,824,500	$3,445,100

nel applied the information they had developed as to unit sales of adjustable speed drives by sizes. Their calculations are shown in Exhibit 2.

This breakdown indicated that Avon's sales of the 5 H.P. model selling at $1,470 would be 170 units. At $750, however, 2,200 units could be sold, it was estimated.

As a next step, members of the Sales Department attempted to estimate how much the sales volume of the 5 H.P. drive would decline as the price of this unit was increased above $750. They believed that, as price increased, volume would decline, not in direct proportion, but exponentially. That is, an increase in price from $750 to $850, for example,

EXHIBIT 3

Estimated Unit Sales of the Avon 5 H.P. EAS Drive at Different Price Levels

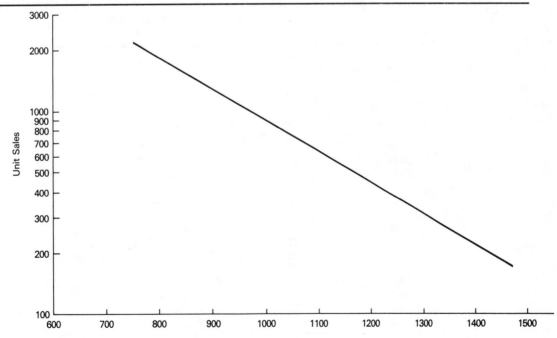

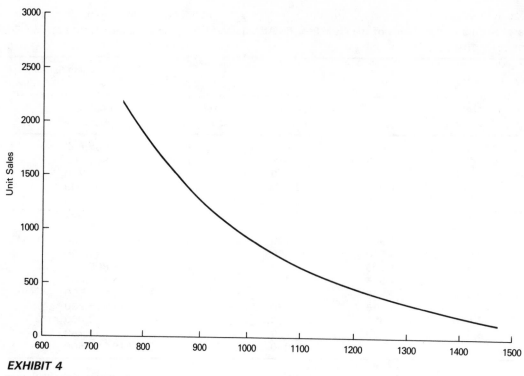

EXHIBIT 4

Estimated Unit Sales of the Avon 5 H.P. EAS Drive at Different Price Levels

EXHIBIT 5

Avon Corporation

Estimated Unit Sales of the Avon 5 H.P. EAS Drive at Different Price Levels

Price	Unit Sales	Price	Unit Sales
$ 750	2,200	$1,120	590
760	2,130	1,140	550
780	1,980	1,160	510
800	1,845	1,180	480
820	1,720	1,200	445
840	1,600	1,220	415
860	1,490	1,240	385
880	1,390	1,260	360
900	1,290	1,280	335
920	1,200	1,300	310
940	1,120	1,320	290
960	1,045	1,340	270
980	975	1,360	250
1,000	905	1,380	235
1,020	845	1,400	220
1,040	785	1,420	205
1,060	730	1,440	190
1,080	680	1,460	175
1,100	635	1,480	170

would reduce unit volume by a greater amount than an increase from $1,370 to $1,470. Therefore, the volume-price calculations shown in Exhibit 2 for 5 H.P. equipment were plotted on semilog paper and the two points connected by a straight line (see Exhibit 3). Points on this line were read off and plotted on conventional graph paper (see Exhibit 4). In addition a table was prepared from these charts which indicated the number of 5 H.P. units which would be sold at various prices ranging between $750 and $1,470 (see Exhibit 5).

Members of the Sales Department wondered what pricing recommendations they should make to Avon's management on the basis of the various estimates they had made as to market size at different price levels and Avon's market share. They recognized that they had had to make a number of assumptions in arriving at these estimates. Nevertheless, they believed that their calculations were as good as could be developed in the light of many unknown market factors.

ASSIGNMENT FOR CLASS DISCUSSION

Come to class prepared to explain what price Avon should set for its new product. (*Note:* for simplicity's sake, assume that the manufacturing cost figures in the case include depreciation and an adequate return on the investment, accounts receivables, and inventory.)

Revving Up for Relief: Harley-Davidson at the ITC (A)

Only the Harley when ridden down a straight highway makes a rider smile. Nothing else feels or sounds quite like it, and when you ride a Harley, nothing needs explaining. It's all said. You feel good, just looking at it.

Cycle World, May 1980

On September 1, 1982, Harley-Davidson, the sole U.S.-headquartered motorcycle manufacturer, petitioned the federal government for temporary relief from high levels of Japanese heavyweight motorcycles and motorcycle components. Harley claimed that the Japanese had exported a great many more heavyweight motorcycles to the U.S. than market demand warranted and, to reduce unprecedented inventories, were selling models at prices so low that Harley could not compete. Harley sought a "temporary respite from imports to regain its competitiveness and attain a strong market position over the long-term."

The body to whom Harley made its petition was the U.S. International Trade Commission. Created in 1916 as the U.S. Tariff Commission, the ITC is an independent, quasi-judicial entity charged with investigating possible injury from imports to U.S. producers and workers. The six commissioners—appointed by the president for non-renewable nine-year terms—also make policy recommendations to the president concerning specific remedies (e.g., tariffs, quotas, and orderly marketing agreements), if warranted.

Even before the evidence from Harley-Davidson and its Japanese competitors was in, the decision facing the ITC looked to be a tough one. In the fall of 1982, gloomy forecasts of a deepening U.S. recession had combined with a postwar-high 10.4% unemployment rate to intensify already-widespread protectionist sentiment. American antagonism toward imports was mounting steadily, and proposed remedies were directed especially toward Japan and its skyrocketing trade surplus. At the same time, the Reagan administration, less than two years old, had voiced strong support for free trade, and Reagan had already overruled one ITC recommendation to extend existing trade protection.

This case was written by Assistant Professor Dorothy Robyn with assistance from Don Lippincott for use at the John F. Kennedy School of Government, Harvard University. (0987)

Harley-Davidson and the U.S. Motorcycle Market.[1] Established in Milwaukee in 1903 by William Harley and the three Davidson brothers, Harley-Davidson had become all but "synonymous with the word motorcycle" after half a century of operations. In 1955, for example, Harley had 60–70% of the (largely heavyweight) American market, with sales of roughly $20 million. Britain's BSA, Triumph, and Norton companies and the Italian Moto-Guzzi served the rest of that market, which—with motorcycle ownership constant at around 500,000—was largely stagnant between 1950 and 1960.

In 1959, two Japanese producers—Honda and Yamaha—entered the U.S. market. Honda, which with sales of $55 million was already the world's largest motorcycle manufacturer, established a U.S. subsidiary (other foreign producers relied on distributors) and began offering very small, lightweight motorcycles. Technically superior to anything comparable produced in the U.S., these cycles sold for under $250 retail, compared to $1,000 to $1,500 for the bigger American and British machines. A marketing effort backed by heavy expenditures on advertising ("You meet the nicest people on a Honda") sought to counter the unsavory image of "bikers."

Honda's strategy (subsequently adopted by other Japanese producers), combined with demographic changes that increased the number of 14 to 24 year olds by half between 1960 and 1970, produced a radical change in the size and shape of the U.S. motorcycle market. Sales rose from 40,000–50,000 units in 1960 to well over a million in 1974, by which time more than 2.4% of all Americans owned motorcycles. Lightweight models—a negligible part of the market in 1960—dominated it by 1966; while they lost ground to middleweight models in the late 1960s and early 1970s, Japanese manufacturers were by then producing motorcycles of that size as well. In short, by 1974, Japanese producers were dominating a market shared by U.S. and European companies only 15 years earlier.

Because the overall U.S. market for motorcycles grew so dramatically, Harley prospered throughout most of this decade and a half of change. By 1970, its market share had dropped below 5%, but Harley was marking its seventh consecutive year of revenue growth, and sales exceeded $50 million. In 1973, Honda, Suzuki, and Kawasaki entered the over-750cc market segment, and in 1974, Kawasaki—then the leading Japanese producer of heavyweight motorcycles—opened a plant in Lincoln, Nebraska designed to produce up to 100,000 bikes per year. While Harley's share of the heavyweight market plummeted from 99.6% in 1972 to 44% in 1975, the company's fraction of the total U.S. market for motorcycles grew continuously during that time.

In 1978, faced with mounting Japanese inventories and price cuts, Harley petitioned the ITC for relief from Japanese motorcycles of all sizes, alleging that imports were being sold, or were likely to be sold, at less than fair value, in violation of the Antidumping Act of 1921. The ITC determined unanimously that while such dumping may indeed have occurred, Harley had not been injured—as evidenced by the fact that the company had been consistently profitable from 1972–77 and that the demand for heavyweights was growing.

By late 1982, Harley's condition had deteriorated. Three years earlier, Honda of America had begun domestic production in Marysville, Ohio. With a work force of some 450, the Ohio plant was turning out 50,000 motorcycles annually, including Honda's top-of-the-line models. Kawasaki was by then employing roughly 350 workers in its Nebraska plant to produce 1000cc heavyweights. Harley's sales had slipped from just over 50,000 in 1979 to just over 30,000 in 1982, and its share of the large cycle market had dropped from 21% to 14% in the same three-year period. Once again, Harley turned to the ITC.

Harley filed its 1982 complaint under Section 201 of the 1974 Trade Act, which—unlike those sections of the law under which the overwhelming majority of relief petitions before the ITC are filed—does not require proof of an unfair foreign trade practice (e.g., pricing below cost, or "dumping") or government subsidy to be affirmed. Section 201 is known as the "escape clause" since it allows countries—under special circumstances—to impose temporary import relief which would normally not be permissible for signatories to the General Agreement on Tariffs and Trade (GATT), an international framework of rules designed to promote free trade. Congress intended this clause to provide "additional time to permit a seriously injured domestic industry to become competitive under relief measures, and, at the same time, to create incentives for the industry to adjust, if possible, to competitive conditions in the absence of long-term restrictions." However, to receive tariff or quota relief under 201, not only must an industry demonstrate serious injury (or the threat of such injury) from increasing imports competing directly with its products, but no other cause (such as the general economic climate, poor management,

---

[1]This section draws heavily on the following: Harvard Business School, *Note on the Motorcycle Industry-1975*, (#578–210); and *Harley Davidson/Marketing Strategies for Motorcycles-1977*, (#9-584-032).

etc.) can be considered a more important cause of injury:

> The Commission shall . . . make an investigation to determine whether an article is being imported into the United States in such increased quantities as to be a substantial cause of serious injury, or the threat thereof, to the domestic industry producing an article like or directly competitive with the imported article.

THE DEBATE OVER INJURY

Harley-Davidson

When the ITC convened a hearing on November 30, 1982, Harley opened its case by attempting to show that it was the only U.S. producer of heavyweight motorcycles. This definitional point was important because by excluding production and sales figures of Kawasaki USA and Honda of America, Harley could make a stronger case for injury to the domestic industry.

Although the ITC had ruled in 1978 that Kawasaki USA was a domestic producer, Harley argued that the U.S. operations of Kawasaki and Honda "are not true motorcycle manufacturing facilities because [they] are limited to the assembly of motorcycle components, which are largely of Japanese origin, and the manufacture of minor components." Moreover, since the domestic content of the final products was less than 50%, Harley maintained, they should be considered foreign imports.

A second definitional argument was that the term "heavyweight" should include 750cc engines and motorcycles (industry sources generally limited the term to engines and motorcycles with displacement greater than 750cc). Harley spokesmen maintained that the 750cc models—manufactured exclusively by Japanese producers—were "like and directly competitive with" Harley's (larger) models, consistent with the language of Section 201. Harley-Davidson Chairman Vaughn L. Beals cited a recent trade press study that included new owners of a particular Harley 1000cc model; 43% of those questioned said they had also considered a 750cc model (see Exhibit 1).

Moving from definitional to substantive arguments, Harley addressed the criteria for 201 relief:

1. Dramatic Increases in Imports Have Occurred. Citing new motorcycle registration data (a proxy for retail sales), Harley claimed that U.S. sales of Japanese heavyweight machines had gone from 143,052 in 1977 to 200,353 in 1981—a 40% increase (see Exhibit 2). Taking into account projected 1982 sales, the Japanese would be able to claim 84% of the

---

EXHIBIT 1

Engine Size of Other Motorcycles Considered

	Total Buyers	BMW R100 Buyers	Harley-Davidson XLH/XLS 1000 Buyers	Honda GL 1100 Buyers	Kawasaki KZ 550 Buyers	Suzuki GS 550 Buyers	Suzuki GS 1100 Buyers	Yamaha XJ 750 Buyers
Less than 400cc	3%	5%	3%	5%	2%	3%	1%	3%
400–499cc	5	—	1	1	9	18	—	1
500–599cc	23	3	4	2	59	54	2	10
600–699cc	16	2	17	2	22	45	1	15
700–799cc	30	12	43	7	38	21	12	69
800–899cc	5	10	4	6	3	2	44	16
900–999cc	15	17	16	72	18	8	83	30
1,000–1,199cc	45	80	54	30	18	3	9	6
1,200cc or more	11	22	12	30	1	3	9	6
Total	*	*	*	*	*	*	*	*
Average engine size	865cc	1,045cc	925cc	1,100cc	690cc	640cc	1,040cc	835cc

Base: Buyers who considered other makes.

*Totals exceed 100% due to multiple responses.

Question 9c: Please indicate below in order of preference the other makes and models you considered. Also, indicate whether or not you went to a dealer to look at the motorcycle. (If you considered more than three, list the three most seriously considered.)

Source: Ziff-Davis Publishing Co. survey (1982), presented as testimony before the US International Trade Commission, Investigation No. TA-201-47.

EXHIBIT 2

U.S. Sales of Heavyweight Motorcycles: Total, Harley-Davidson, Japanese, and Total Imports 1977–1982
(Sales in Units; Market Share in Percent)

	Total		Harley-Davidson		Japanese		Total Imports	
	Sales	Market Share	Sales	Market Share	Sales	Market Share	Sales	Market Share
1977	200,174	100.0	41,972	21.0	143,052	71.5	158,202	79.0
1978	209,789	100.0	44,469	21.2	152,993	72.9	165,320	78.8
1979	253,824	100.0	51,760	20.4	190,000	74.9	202,064	79.6
1980	238,892	100.0	40,567	17.0	192,643	80.6	198,325	83.0
1981	246,712	100.0	41,321	16.7	200,353	81.2	205,391	83.3
1982[1]	220,000E	100.0	31,500E	14.3E	185,640E	84.4E	188,500E	85.7E
1982 Jan.–Sept.	193,557	100.0	28,648	14.8	162,311	83.9	164,909	85.2

E = Estimated

[1]Estimated by Harley-Davidson based on 9 months data and seasonal adjustment factors.

Source: R. L. Polk registration data, presented in testimony before the US International Trade Commission, Investigation No. TA-201-47.

U.S. heavyweight market, up from 71.5% in 1977. Looking just at 790+cc motorcycles imported fully assembled from Japan, Department of Commerce data indicated that between 1977 and 1982 U.S. inventories had increased by more than 152,000 units (see Exhibit 3).

2. Imports Have Caused Serious Injury. Although the total U.S. heavyweight motorcycle market increased by 23% between 1977 and 1981, Harley spokesmen argued, Harley-Davidson's sales showed a net decline of 2%. Sales in 1982 were projected to reach only 31,500 units, a 25% drop from their 1977 level, and a 39% drop from their peak sales level in 1979. This loss of sales and market share was responsible for tremendous declines in production and capacity utilization, profits, and employment—the very definition of economic injury under Section 201.[2]

As evidence of idling facilities, Harley cited "dramatic" production declines from 1980 to 1982, and a steep drop in its capacity utilization—from 85% in 1980 to 51% in 1982. To demonstrate unprofitability, Harley provided (proprietary) tables showing operating losses in the millions for 1981 and 1982 as well as concomitant cutbacks in capital investment, engineering, and R & D. A banker from Harley's chief lender, Citicorp, testified that the motorcycle manufacturer had been a successful corpora-

[2]Among the symptoms of economic injury to domestic producers that the ITC is required by law to consider are: (a) significant idling of productive facilities; (b) inability to operate at a reasonable profit; and (c) significant unemployment or underemployment.

tion for over 80 years with unparalleled, "almost fanatical customer support." He maintained that no one could have predicted the unprecedented importation of Japanese motorcycles into the U.S. "far in excess of demand" and the "drastic price reductions" of the Japanese firms that were threatening the company's lifeblood. Although Harley management appeared to be doing everything it could to stay afloat, he warned, the company's "very survival [was] threatened":

> As a result of its disproportionate loss of sales, [Harley] is in an overadvanced situation. In other words, we are extending credit to Harley-Davidson in excess of the amounts available under the formula terms of the loan agreement. . . . Under the circumstances, a lender is entitled to declare the borrower in default under the loan agreement. Our continuing support of Harley-Davidson, therefore, is extraordinary.

With respect to unemployment, which Harley termed the "most devastating effect" of the increased imports, grim statistics indicated that roughly 36% of its work force—or 1,159 employees—had lost their jobs during the preceding nine-month period (see Exhibit 4). Other evidence included temporary plant closings and reduction of management salaries and benefits during the past year.

3. Imports Have Been a "Substantial Cause" of Injury. As prima facie evidence that imports had been a "substantial cause" of its injury, Harley un-

EXHIBIT 3

Estimated Changes in U.S. Inventories of Heavyweight Japanese Motorcycles (790cc and Over), Based on U.S. Imports for Consumption and U.S. Registrations (Units)

	U.S. Registrations of Japanese Motorcycles (790 + cc)[1]	Imports for Consumption from Japan[2]	Estimated Inventory Increase[3]
1977	30,378	38,615	8,237
1978	45,048	68,768	23,720
1979	62,383	88,379	25,996
1980	84,924	123,237	38,313
1981	71,479	116,011	44,532
1982 (Jan.–Sept.)	81,169	92,732	11,563
Total inventory increase, 1977–September 1982			152,361

[1]Total registrations of Japanese heavyweight motorcycles, less estimated registrations of U.S.-assembled motorcycles and registrations of motorcycles with engine displacements between 700cc and 790cc.
[2]TSUSA number 692.5075.
[3]Calculated as imports less registrations.
Source: R. L. Polk registration data. U.S. Department of Commerce (IM146), presented in testimony before the U.S. International Trade Commission, Investigation No. TA-201-47.

derscored the simultaneity of the decline in its own market share with the rise in the Japanese percentage. By way of explanation, Harley's chief economic consultant, Stanley Nehmer, pointed to the pattern of price suppression by Japanese producers.

Although demand was exceptionally strong in 1979, Japanese producers kept their prices low enough to increase their market share. In 1980, however, when confronted with a drop in the level of demand from the previous year, Japanese producers cut import prices and instituted aggressive dealer and consumer incentive programs, so that they increased both their share of U.S. sales and their sales volume. Conversely, Harley-Davidson suffered a 22 percent

EXHIBIT 4

Total Number of Employees Engaged in United States (Harley-Davidson) Production and Sale of Heavyweight Motorcycles
(700 + cc) (1977–1982)[1]

Year	Hourly	Salaried	Total
1977	1903	1097	3000
1978	2054	1189	3243
1979	2204	1262	3476
1980	2148	1321	3469
1981	2167	1153	3320
1982[2]	1216	945	2161

[1]Year end total.
[2]July.
Source: Harley-Davidson.

loss of volume, and a sharp drop in market share that year. These trends have continued in 1981 and 1982, and the Japanese have steadily gained market share and volume.

As further evidence of price-cutting, Nehmer cited Commerce Department data showing that between 1977 and 1982, the "average unit value" of imports from Japan of motorcycles of 790cc and above had declined both in current dollars and in real (1977) dollars (see Exhibit 5):

The Japanese price cutting strategy appears to have become especially aggressive during 1982 [when] for the first time since 1979-80, overall market demand has declined. . . . [I]n spite of the downturn in the market, imports . . . are literally flooding the market.

The impact of these price cuts on Harley's market share had been dramatic, Nehmer concluded (see Exhibit 6).

This impact had been seriously aggravated, moreover, by the introduction of Japanese models that virtually copied elements of Harley styling, its traditional area of distinction. Harley Chairman Vaughn Beals cited several trade publication articles including one describing a conversation with a Japanese designer in the industry:

One Japanese stylist told me, "We are very conscious of beauty. We know what looks right to the Japanese, but in areas of Western design,

EXHIBIT 5

Heavyweight Motorcycles from Japan: Quantity, Value, and Average Unit Value of U.S. Imports for Consumption of Motorcycles with Engine Displacement of 790cc and Over, 1977–1981 and First Nine Months of 1981 and 1982

	Quantity (Units)	Value [1] (Current Dollars)	Average Unit Value (Current Dollars)	Average Unit Value[2] (1977 Dollars)
1977	38,615	64,300,850	1,665	1,665
1978	68,768	133,740,290	1,945	1,804
1979	88,379	185,180,121	2,095	1,749
1980	123,237	241,080,179	1,956	1,439
1981	116,011	235,865,402	2,033	1,369
1981 (Jan.–Sept.)	81,491	168,053,244	2,062	1,389
1982 (Jan.–Sept.)	92,732	168,620,970	1,818	1,184

[1]Customs value basis.

[2]Deflated using U.S. Producer Price Index, indexed based on 1977 = 100.

Source: U.S. Department of Commerce (IM146), Bureau of Labor Statistics, Producer Price Index, presented in testimony before the U.S. International Trade Commission, Investigation No. TA-201-47.

EXHIBIT 6

Indices of Harley-Davidson's Market Share and the Average Unit F.O.B. Value of Imports from Japan of 790+cc Motorcycles, 1977–1982 *(1977 = 100)*

[1]Deflated to 1977 dollars using the *Producer Price Index.*

[2]1982 figures annualized based on 9 months' seasonally adjusted data.

Source: R. L. Polk registration data and the Bureau of Labor Statistics, Producer Price Index, presented in testimony before the U.S. International Trade Commission, Investigation No. TA-201-47.

such as motorcycles, we are not so sure of ourselves. So we tend to copy what others are doing successfully such as Harley-Davidson. We hire European stylists because we assume they know better than we do what Westerners like.''

As part of this strategy of duplication, Beals claimed, the Japanese had introduced the ''dresser'' or long-distance touring bike, and the ''V''-configuration engine—the ''heart'' of the Harley motorcycle, the thing that ''automatically conveys [its] masculine image . . . its sleek look.'' Harley consultant Stanley Nehmer addressed the economic implications of this strategy.

These models were first introduced by the Japanese in 1980, and accounted for only a small share of total 1980 sales [see Exhibit 7]. With the introduction of a series of new Japanese V-configuration and ''dresser'' models in 1981 and 1982, however, these ''Harley-type'' motorcycles have obtained a substantial and growing share of the total heavyweight market, almost totally at Harley-Davidson's expense.

4. Imports Have Been the Most Important Cause of Injury. Finally, Harley advocates argued that high interest rates, unemployment, and other macroeconomic factors had been a much less important source of injury than Japanese imports. Had Harley maintained its 1979 market share (20.4%) during 1980-82, Nehmer calculated, it would have sold an additional 41,892 motorcycles. Of this falloff

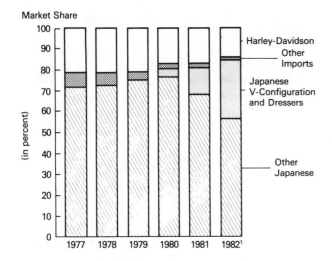

Market Share

EXHIBIT 7

Relative U.S. Market Shares Held by Various Heavyweight Motorcycles, 1977–1982

[1]1982 Estimate based on 9 months' data and seasonal adjustment factors.

Source: R. L. Polk registration data, presented in testimony before the U.S. International Trade Commission, Investigation No. TA-201-47.

in sales relative to 1979 levels, 27.1% (or 11,337 units) was attributable to declining overall demand, and 72.9% to increased import sales (see Exhibit 8).

Harley stressed that it was pursuing an aggressive recovery plan, including quality control, an advanced inventory system, and plans to develop a new "family" of lower-end heavyweights. In the first year of this program, Harley boasted, it had doubled the number of defect-free shipments and lowered its break-even point from 53,000 to 35,000 cycles sold per year. However, without immediate import relief, Harley's chairman cautioned, the "prospects for completing these vital programs, quite frankly, are bleak."

Japanese Producers

Unanimously contesting the validity of the Harley petition were U.S. subsidiaries of the "Big Four" Japanese cycle producers: Honda, Kawasaki, Suzuki, and Yamaha. The Japanese companies challenged Harley's definition of terms as well as its substantive claims regarding injury.

On the question of who qualified as a domestic

EXHIBIT 8

Importance of Increasing Imports Relative to Declining Demand as an Explanation for the Decline in Harley-Davidson's Sales of Heavyweight (700+cc) Motorcycles Since 1979

	1979	1980	1981	1982[1]	Cumulative 1980–1982 Lost Sales
Total heavyweight motorcycle sales in the United States	253,824	238,892	246,712	220,000E	—
Sales of Harley-Davidson Motorcycles in the United States	51,760	40,567	41,321	31,500E	—
Projected sales of Harley-Davidson motorcycles at 1979 market share[2]	—	48,734	50,329	44,880E	—
Total decline in Harley-Davidson motorcycles sales from 1979 levels	—	11,193	10,439	20,260E	41,892
Net decline in Harley-Davidson's sales due to increased import sales	—	8,167	9,008	13,380E	30,555
Net decline in Harley-Davidson's sales due to declining demand	—	3,026	1,431	6,880E	11,337
Share of decline in Harley-Davidson's sales due to increased import sales (percent)	—	73.0	86.3	66.0E	72.9
Share of declining Harley-Davidson sales due to declining demand (percent)	—	27.0	13.7	34.0E	27.1

E = Estimated.

[1]Estimated on the basis of January-September 1982 data and seasonal adjustment factors presented in the Polk Report.

[2]Projection made based on Harley-Davidson 1979 market share of 20.4 percent. Harley-Davidson's market shares in 1977 and 1978 were 21.0 and 21.2 percent, respectively.

Source: Testimony before the U.S. International Trade Commission, Investigation No. TA-201-47.

producer, the Japanese manufacturers disputed Harley's less-than-50%-local-content rule as legally irrelevant and underscored the sizable capital investment by Honda of America and Kawasaki USA, who together employed more than 800 American workers.

The "Big Four" also sought to redefine which of their products should be included in the injury claim. First, they argued that 750cc cycles were not "like or directly competitive with" Harley products—limited to 1000cc and 1340cc cycles—as required by Section 201. Price was the major explanation, they maintained: 1982 dealer costs for the lowest priced 1000cc bike were $500 greater than for the most expensive 750cc cycle, and dealer markups only accentuated the disparity.

> Such a pricing pattern indicates that producers have positioned their models to appeal to the broadest range of consumers, while minimizing the competitive overlap between engine categories. It appears, therefore, that any competition between producers would take place within each engine size category but not to any significant degree between categories.

The Japanese producers also cited a consultant's survey of motorcycle owners which found a very low incidence of cross-pricing between Harleys and bikes in the 700–899cc range.

Second, Japanese producers maintained that their importation of power train components was in no way injurious to the U.S., since no domestic industry for such components existed, nor would one exist in the absence of imports. Moreover, the importation of power train components reflected current practice by domestic producers throughout the motor vehicle industry.

As to the question of injury, the Japanese producers made two fundamental arguments. Japanese-brand cycles weren't competitive with Harleys; even within the same (large) engine size category, the two markets were distinct. Consistent with that, Harley's financial troubles were not caused by Japanese competition; rather, they stemmed from the 1981-82 recession and associated unemployment.

Absence of Competition. Looking just at the 1000cc and larger bikes, Japanese producers compared "dealer net prices" for Japanese and Harley brands across four models: dressed tourers, standard tourers, cruisers, and sportsters. Harleys were consistently more expensive—on average, by $1600, $1800, $1500, and $400 for the four models respectively. Harleys and Japanese models were in "distinctly separate market segments," they concluded.

As additional evidence of non-competitiveness, Japanese producers cited performance characteristics compiled by *Cycle Guide* for selected Harley and Japanese-brand cruisers and dressed tourers. In both instances, the Japanese bikes recorded superior characteristics in seven important categories, including top speed, fuel consumption, braking, and price (see Exhibit 9). In the dressed tourers, the superior Honda GL1100A listed for $6600 versus $7900 for the Harley FLH classic. In the cruisers, the Kawasaki Z1100 Spectre listed for $4300 versus $7300 for the Harley FXRS. The Japanese concluded that, given the superior technical performance and significantly lower costs to the consumer, "There would appear to be no reason for a rational purchaser to select a Har-

EXHIBIT 9

Comparative Performance Characteristics of Selected Harley-Davidson and Japanese Brand Motorcycles, 1982 Models

| | Dressed Tourers | | Cruisers | |
	Honda GL1100A	H-D FLH Classic	Kawasaki Z1100 Spectre	H-D FXRS
Engine displacement (cc)	1,085	1,339	1,090	1,339
Quarter-mile time (seconds)	13	15	12	14
Speed end of quarter-mile (mph)	99	82	110	93
Top speed (mph)	139	101	142	109
Weight (lbs.)	724	752	553	594
Fuel consumption (mpg)	40–50	32–42	36–44	40–47
Stopping distance from 60 mph (in feet)	145	180	132	124
Suggested list price	$6,600	$7,900	$4,300	$7,300

Source: Cycle Guide, November, 1982, p. 4, as presented in testimony before the U.S. International Trade Commission, Investigation No. TA-201-47.

EXHIBIT 10

Proportion of Variation (R^2) in Harley-Davidson Sales Explained by Blue-Collar Employment

Period	Number of Data Points	R^2	T Statistic[1]	D-W Statistic
$Q_1 77 - Q_2 82$	22	0.54	4.93	1.6
$Q_1 78 - Q_2 82$	18	0.59	4.80	1.7
$Q_1 79 - Q_2 82$	14	0.73	5.65	2.3
$Q_1 80 - Q_2 82$	10	0.63	3.70	2.5
$Q_1 81 - Q_2 82$	6	0.69	3.01	3.2

[1]The T Statistic in each case indicates a confidence level of 95% or better that the regression is valid.

Source: ICF Inc. (December 13, 1982), presented as post-hearing submission to the U.S. International Trade Commission, Investigation No. TA-201-47.

ley . . . [and that] head-to-head competition [w]ould have eliminated Harley from the market long ago."

Finally, Japanese producers pointed to a consultant's survey which revealed that only 55 of 262 (21%) Harley owners polled said they had priced a Japanese alternative, and only 80 of 794 (10.1%) Japanese cycle owners had priced Harleys. This was true despite the fact that a large number of dealers sold both Harleys and Japanese bikes, and shoppers had only to walk across the floor. Thus, the Japanese

concluded, Harley owners were indeed "a breed apart."

Harley-Davidson's Sales Performance. Economic conditions, not Japanese competition, were the primary cause of Harley's injuries, the "Big Four" maintained: Heavyweight motorcycles are a "big-ticket luxury consumer product," and their purchase is therefore highly sensitive to changes in the general economy. Using quarterly employment data,

EXHIBIT 11

Proportion of Variation (R^2) in Harley-Davidson Sales Explained by Sales of Japanese Motorcycles

Period	Number of Data Points	Sales of Japanese-Brand Motorcycles Specified as Independent Variables					
		700cc and Larger		900cc and Larger		1000cc and Larger	
		R	R^2	R	R^2	R	R^2
$Q_1 77 - Q_2 82$	22	0.14	0.02	−0.13	0.02	0.26	0.07
$Q_1 78 - Q_2 82$	18	0.13	0.02	−0.21	0.04	0.29	0.08
$Q_1 79 - Q_2 82$	14	0.30	0.09	−0.19	0.04	0.47	0.22
$Q_1 80 - Q_2 82$	10	0.44	0.20	0.37	0.14	0.54	0.30
$Q_1 81 - Q_2 82$	6	0.45	0.20	0.49	0.24	0.44	0.19

Period	Number of Data Points	Sales of Japanese-Brand Motorcycles Specified as Independent Variables					
		700cc and Larger		900cc and Larger		1000cc and Larger	
		R	R^2	R	R^2	R	R^2
1st half 77–1st half 82	11	0.06	0.00	−0.24	0.06	0.19	0.03
1st half 78–1st half 82	9	0.03	0.00	−0.35	0.12	0.20	0.04
1st half 79–1st half 82	7	0.21	0.04	−0.39	0.16	0.41	0.17
1st half 80–1st half 82	5	0.56	0.32	0.46	0.21	0.60	0.36

Source: ICF Inc. (December 13, 1982), presented as a post-hearing submission to the U.S. International Trade Commission, Investigation No. TA-201-47.

the Japanese producers' chief economic consultant, John Reilly of ICF, Inc., found that 73% of the variation in Harley sales between 1979 and 1982 was explained by the level of blue collar employment (see Exhibit 10). (Use of semi-annual employment data produced an even higher proportion of variation explained.) By comparison, the level of sales of Japanese-brand motorcycles explained less of the variation in Harley sales (see Exhibit 11).

Revving Up for Relief: Harley-Davidson at the ITC (B)

THE DEBATE OVER IMPORT RELIEF

Harley's Proposal

To allow for recovery from the injury imports had caused, Harley requested a five-year increase in the existing 4.4% tariff on imported 700cc and larger heavyweight motorcycles and power train components: 48% for the first three years, 40% in the fourth year, and 30% in the fifth year. The American manufacturer sought to restore the approximate price differential between Japanese and Harley heavyweights that existed in 1979. Using statistics on "average unit value" of 790cc and larger imports, Harley computed that the real value of imports had dropped by $883 between 1979 and 1982; stated differently, a tariff rate of 48% was necessary to restore import values to their 1979 level (see Exhibit 1). (Harley lacked data on 700cc-790cc cycles, but maintained that a comparable price decline had occurred in that segment of the market.)

The effect of the proposed tariff on sales of existing Japanese models would be delayed due to the "massive" size of current inventories, Harley recognized. But the tariff would immediately limit the ability of Japanese producers to introduce low-priced new models aimed at the upscale niche, with direct benefits to Harley-Davidson: increased sales, a reduction in costly rebate and dealer support programs, and a renewal of creditors' confidence.

In addition to improving its own bottom line, Harley argued, the proposed import relief should provide other benefits to the U.S. economy as well. Most important, Harley could re-employ workers it had been forced to lay off—1,159 of them during the first seven months of 1982. Harley's U.S. secondary suppliers would also benefit from the company's increased production. And although U.S. consumers would face higher retail prices for motorcycles in the short run, the proposed import relief should encourage competition, and hence lower prices, in the long run. The benefits of current low import prices were less than it would seem, moreover, Harley explained, because they were based chiefly on excessive inventories:

> Whereas Harley-Davidson's experience suggests that sales can be maintained adequately with six months worth of dealer inventories, available information suggests that the Japanese have approximately one and a half to two years of inventories on hand. This implies that the importers and dealers of Japanese motorcycles have at least one year of *excess* inventories, the annual carrying costs of which may be as high as $400-$500 per unit. These carrying costs represent a deadweight loss to the economy.

Japanese Producers' Response

In a post-hearing brief, Japanese cycle producers challenged Harley's case for a steep import tariff. The challenge was twofold. First, the proposed remedy wasn't justified: Harley's analysis of the tariff (48%) necessary to restore Japanese cycle prices to their 1979 level was flawed. Second, even if such a steep tariff were necessary to restore 1979 prices, the adverse economic impact it would have—on consumers, dealers, and workers—was unacceptably large.

Flawed Analysis. Harley's analysis of Japanese motorcycle prices—which was based on the declining value of imported cycles between 1979 and 1982 (see Exhibit 1) was flawed in three respects, Japanese producers argued. First, "import values" (i.e., f.o.b. values) of Japanese cycles understated the

EXHIBIT 1

Calculation of the Average Increase in the Tariff Rate Needed to Restore the Prices of Imported Heavyweight Motorcycles to Their 1979 Level[1]

Actual average unit value of imports in 1979	$2,124
Projected average unit value of imports in 1982 (2,124 × 1.28[2])	$2,719
Actual average unit value of imports for the first nine months of 1982	$1,836
Difference between projected and actual value	$883
Percentage point increase in tariff rate needed to bring the actual unit value to the projected unit value	48

[1]Based on the average unit value of imports of 790cc and above heavyweight motorcycles.

[2]Percentage increase in the U.S. PPI between 1979 and January–September, 1982.

Source: Testimony before the U.S. International Trade Commission, Investigation No. TA-201-47.

price dealers paid, which is "what should be of concern to Harley-Davidson." Second, import-value data excluded 750cc motorcycles, which accounted for more than half of all sales of Japanese 700cc and larger cycles. Third, import data by definition ignored domestic content—in particular that of Honda's most expensive motorcycles, which had been produced in the U.S. since 1981—and hence distorted the trend in the real value of Japanese-brand heavyweights.

The "Big Four" producers offered, as an alternative, data drawn from their consultant's survey of Japanese manufacturers. Figures for 1977-82 on the volume of cycles shipped annually to dealers and the price to dealers of the average cycle in each shipment, expressed both in current dollars and in constant 1967 dollars (see Exhibit 2), provided the basis for a series of calculations designed to dispute Harley's findings.

First, using 1967 dollars as the measuring rod, the Japanese producers calculated the decline in Japanese-brand cycle prices between 1979 and 1982—that is, the amount necessary to restore prices to their 1979 level, Harley's stated goal. This amount—$46, or $141 in 1982 dollars[1]—was far less than Harley's comparable figure of $883.

The Japanese brief then calculated the tariff rate necessary to increase the average price of an imported 1982 Japanese motorcycle, as specified by Harley ($1,836), by $141. The result: 7.7% (see Exhibit 3). To pass that same amount on to dealers, the Japanese concluded using their own data on dealer costs, would result in a 4.7% price increase to dealers (see Exhibit 3).

Finally, the Japanese brief repeated those same calculations using a base period of 1977-1979, on the grounds that the 1979 base year chosen by Harley

was the year in which real prices of Japanese motorcycles to dealers reached their peak. Those calculations indicated that to restore 1982 prices to their 1977-79 level would require a tariff rate of 4.5% and a price increase to dealers of 2.7% (see Exhibit 4).

Economic Impact. Putting aside their statistical refutation of Harley's proposed tariff, the Japanese producers turned to an assessment of its economic impact. They looked in turn at "potential impacts" on motorcycle dealers (and indirectly, consumers), accessories producers, and workers throughout the industry.

(a) Dealers. If the $883 figure computed by Harley (see Exhibit 1) were applied to 700cc and larger Japanese-brand motorcycles, it would increase their average retail price by 23.3%, the brief asserted (see Exhibit 5). The Japanese producers' analysis assumed a 25% dealer markup on cost. The analysis also assumed that the tariff would apply to all Japanese motorcycles, whether imported or not.

Taking that estimated percentage price increase, the brief calculated the likely decline in sales of motorcycles subject to the tariff (see Exhibit 6). Assuming a demand for motorcycles that is moderately elastic (E = −1.0) with respect to price (on the rationale that cycles are non-essential and that their price represents a significant share of the average purchaser's annual income), sales would decline by 45,293 units, from a base of 194,389. (The base figure—derived from Exhibit 2—equalled the average number of Japanese cycles shipped annually from 1977–81.) Assuming an even more elastic demand (E = −1.5), sales would fall by nearly 68,000 units. At an average dealer markup of $757 (25% of $3,026), this sales drop would reduce dealers' total net revenues by $34.2 to $51.4 million.

Of course, two effects could serve to offset those losses, the Japanese producers' analysis recognized: possible increases in sales of 650cc and smaller

[1](1) $1,035–$989 = $46. (2) ($46) (306.1/100) = $141.

EXHIBIT 2

Average Prices of Shipments of Japanese Brand 750cc and Larger Motorcycles to Dealers, 1977–1982, and January–September 1982 (in Current Dollars and in Constant 1967 Dollars)

Period	Units Shipped	Total Value ($ 000)	Average Unit Price	PPI Industrial Products	Average Unit Price[1] ($1967)
1977	164,537	314,720	1,913	195.1	981
1978	168,691	364,033	2,158	209.4	1,031
1979	185,050	453,054	2,448	236.5	1,035
1980	217,346	580,345	2,670	274.8	972
1981	223,909	635,172	2,837	304.1	933
1982 (9 months)	150,338	454,937	3,026	306.1	989

[1](Average unit price ÷ PPI) × 100 = unit value ($1967).

Source: ICF analysis based upon questionnaire responses by Honda, Kawasaki, Suzuki, and Yamaha. The shipments and shipment values reported in the Honda of America Manufacturing producer questionnaire were for transfers of motorcycles to American Honda, which sells the motorcycles to dealers. The data reflect American Honda's actual shipments to dealers and shipment values of motorcycles produced domestically by Honda American Manufacturing, as reported to ICF by American Honda. Presented to U.S. International Trade Commission, Investigation No. TA-201-47.

EXHIBIT 3

Tariff Rate and Price Effects Based upon the Harley-Davidson Method Applied to a Correct Calculation of the Change in the Real Price of Japanese-Brand 750cc and Larger Motorcycles between 1979 and January–September 1982 (in 1982 Dollars)

Average unit value of 1982 imports from Japan[1]	$1,836
Price increase required to restore 1979 real unit value	$141
Tariff rate [($141 ÷ $1,836)(100)]	7.7
Average 1982 price to dealers	$3,026
Average price increase to pass tariff cost on to dealers[2]	$141
Percent price increase to dealers	4.7

[1]The calculations in Exhibit 3 are based upon an average import value of $1,836 for 1982 as specified by Harley-Davidson. Based upon questionnaire responses, the USITC reported average 1982 import unit value of $2,123.

[2]The importer and the dealer would incur an inventory carrying cost on the amount represented by the tariff. For the purpose of simplification, such costs, which would amount to about eight dollars per unit, have been omitted from the analysis.

Source: ICF, Inc. Presented to U.S. International Trade Commission, Investigation No. TA-201-47.

EXHIBIT 4

Tariff Rate and Price Effects Based upon a 1977–1979 Base Period (in 1982 Dollars)

Average unit value of 1982 imports from Japan	$1,836
Price increase required to restore 1977–1979 real unit value	$83[1]
Tariff rate [($83 ÷ $1,836) (100)]	4.5
Average 1982 price to dealers	$3,026
Average price increase to pass tariff cost on to dealers	$83
Percent price increase to dealer	2.7

[1]Japanese producers obtained the $83 figure as follows:
1. For 1977–79, the average price of Japanese-brand motorcycles sold to dealers was $1,016 in 1967 dollars (derived from Exhibit 2).
2. Restoration of the 1982 average import price to the 1977–79 level would require a price increase of $27 in 1967 dollars ($1016–$989 = $27).
3. In 1982 dollars, that represents $83 [($27)(306.1 ÷ 100) = $83].

Source: ICF, Inc. Presented to U.S. International Trade Commission, Investigation No. TA-201-47.

EXHIBIT 5

Average Retail Price Increase for 700cc and Larger Japanese-Brand Motorcycles
Implied by Harley-Davidson's Tariff Recommendations

Average 1982 retail price[1]	$3,783
Average price increase to pass tariff cost on to consumers	$883
Percent retail price increase	23.3

[1]Based upon a dealer markup of 25 percent on cost, which is equal to the difference between listed dealer net prices for Japanese-brand machines and suggested retail prices.

Source: ICF, Inc. Presented to U.S. International Trade Commission, Investigation No. TA-201-47.

Japanese motorcycles and of Harley-Davidson motorcycles. Recognizing that "the vast majority of 700cc and larger motorcycle buyers are experienced riders who are either trading up from smaller machines or replacing heavyweight machines," the Japanese assumed that only 20% of those who would decline to buy 750cc and 850cc motorcycles would instead purchase a 650cc cycle. Offset sales of 650cc cycles would thus range from 4,710 to 7,065 units, depending on the elasticity of demand (throughout their brief, Japanese producers assumed that their customers' elasticity ranged from −1.0 to −1.5). At an average dealer profit of $500 per cycle,[2] such sales would offset the decline in dealer revenues by $2.4 million–$3.6 million.

With respect to offset purchases of Harleys, the Japanese producers accepted, for the sake of argument, their opponent's view that "there is a significant cross-elasticity of demand relative to price between Harley products and 700cc and larger Japanese-brand machines."

. . . it will be assumed, to reflect Harley's point of view, that a tariff rate increase of 48 percent would be required [to restore Japanese brand prices to their 1979 level], and that the result of

[2]That figure represented a 25% dealer markup on $2,000, the estimated average net cost for 550cc-650cc motorcycles.

the tariff would be to increase Harley's sales to 42,500 units per year. (Harley claims that it needs to sell 40–45,000 units per year to make a satisfactory long-run profit.) Further reflecting Harley's point of view, sales of 42,500 units would reflect a sales gain of 6,200 units from a base sales level of 36,300 units. The base sales figure was derived by applying Harley's 15.2 percent market share [in 1982] of 700cc and larger motorcycles to a normal year's total sales of 239,000 units.

The Japanese producers calculated that with this sales gain of 6,200 cycles, Harley dealers' net revenue (profit) would rise by $1,443—or $8.9 million. (The $1,443 figure represented 30% of Harley's net price to dealers during the first nine months of 1982 and was based on the difference between Harley's listed dealer prices and suggested retail prices for 1982.) The corresponding loss to Japanese-brand dealers, given an average profit of $757 per cycle, would be $4.7 million. Thus, tariff-induced sales of Harley cycles would offset the total decline in dealer revenues by $4.2 million ($8.9 million less $4.7 million). Taking both offsetting effects of the proposed tariff into account, then, the loss to dealers would range from $27.6 million to $43.6 million, the Japanese brief concluded (see Exhibit 7).

(b) Accessories producers. A sharp decline in

EXHIBIT 6

Decline in Sales of Japanese-Brand 700cc and Larger Motorcycles Associated with a
23.3 Percent Retail Price Increase

	Elasticity of −1.0	*Elasticity of* −1.5
Base sales	194,389	194,389
Sales decline	45,293[1]	67,940[2]
Sales after price increase	149,096	126,449

[1][(23.3 ÷ 100)(−1.0)(194,389)] = −45,293.

[2][(23.3 ÷ 100)(−1.5)(194,389)] = −67,940.

Source: ICF, Inc. Presented to U.S. International Trade Commission, Investigation No. TA-201-47.

EXHIBIT 7

Effect of Proposed Tariff on Total Dealer Net Revenues (Million Dollars)

	Low	High
Revenues lost due to decline in Japanese-brand 700cc and larger motorycles	$ 34.2	$ 51.4
Revenues gained from sales of 650cc and smaller motorcycles	2.4	3.6
Revenues gained from increased Harley sales	4.2	4.2
Net revenue decline	$ 27.6	$ 43.6

Source: ICF, Inc. Presented to U.S. International Trade Commission, Investigation No. TA-201-47.

new motorcycle sales, argued Japanese producers, would stem the demand for related products, such as helmets, gloves, boots, mirrors, wind screens, and baggage carriers. "Assuming conservatively" that accessory purchases average $150 per new cycle sold, the loss of revenues to producers would amount to $6.1 million if elasticity of demand is low, $9.1 million if elasticity is high (see Exhibit 8).

(c) Workers. Workers throughout the motorcycle industry would be hurt by the proposed tariff, Japanese producers cautioned. For dealers, whose overhead costs are largely fixed, the losses indicated in Exhibit 7 would lead to the layoff of from 1,910 to 3,028 workers, assuming an average annual wage rate of $14,400 (equal to the rate of non-supervisory employees in U.S. auto dealerships). For accessories producers, the lost revenue would translate into 359 to 535 layoffs, given an annual wage ($17,000) equal to that for all blue-collar manufacturing employees in the U.S. Honda and Kawasaki would also be forced to lay off U.S. workers—between 211 and 317 of them, assuming that (1) sales of U.S.-produced Japanese cycles drop at the same rate as sales of all Japanese cycles, and (2) the decline in hours worked in U.S. plants is proportional to the decline in sales of U.S.-produced Japanese cycles. (The brief also noted that "Honda and Kawasaki [might] find continued domestic production to be uneconomical, thus

putting all employment in the domestic production of [heavyweight] motorcycles in jeopardy.") In total, Japanese producers concluded, the proposed tariff would jeopardize 2,500–3,900 non-Harley jobs.

To determine employment effects on Harley, Japanese producers reasoned as follows: Harley produced at a rate of 32,000 units per year during 1982 with a labor force of 2,161 employees. An increase in annual production to 42,500 units (roughly the amount Harley claimed it would have to sell to make a satisfactory long-run profit) would raise output one-third. Assuming a proportional increase in employment, Harley would need roughly an additional 700 workers; but taking into account economies of scale, a reasonable estimate is that the proposed tariff would produce 500 new Harley jobs.

The Japanese producers acknowledged that were Harley to go out of business, all of the roughly 2,600 jobs involved might be lost. But they noted that Harley had been profitable in the late 1960s and early 1970s at a sales level of 15,000–35,000 cycles, and that a hard-core market of that size could sustain a reorganized and trimmed down company. In sum, even assuming all 2,600 Harley jobs were at stake, the proposed tariff would only preserve 100 domestic jobs overall. And under other assumptions, 3,400 U.S. jobs could be lost (see Exhibit 9). "The remedy proposed by Harley," the Japanese brief concluded,

EXHIBIT 8

Revenue Lost by Motorcycle Accessories Producers Due to Decline in Motorcycle Sales

	Low	High
Decline in Japanese-brand sales (thousand units)[1]	46.8	67.0
Increase in Harley sales (thousand units)	6.2	6.2
Net sales decline (thousand units)	40.6	60.8
Revenue lost by accessories producers at $150 per unit (million dollars)	$ 6.1	$ 9.1

[1]Sales lost due to demand decline for 700cc and larger motorcycles + sales lost to Harley − increase in 650cc and smaller motorcycles = decline in Japanese-brand sales.

Source: ICF, Inc. Presented to U.S. International Trade Commission, Investigation No. TA-201-47.

EXHIBIT 9

Potential Net Employment Effects of the Tariff Rate Increase Recommended by Harley-Davidson

	Low	High
Assuming all Harley jobs at stake		
Other U.S. jobs lost[1]	2,500	3,900
Harley-Davidson jobs preserved[2]	(2,600)	(2,600)
Net jobs lost (preserved)	(100)	1,300
Assuming 500 Harley jobs at stake		
Other U.S. jobs lost[1]	2,500	3,900
Harley-Davidson jobs preserved[2]	(500)	(500)
Net jobs lost (preserved)	2,000	3,400

[1]Includes provision for gains in revenues and employment by Harley dealers.
[2]Direct employment at Harley-Davidson.
Source: ICF, Inc. Presented to U.S. International Trade Commission, Investigation No. TA-201-47.

"is, therefore, far more likely to do serious damage during a period of desperately high unemployment than it is to produce even a temporary benefit."

Intangibles. While the ITC members were charged with assessing the narrow economic criteria contained in Section 201, it would be hard for them to ignore the larger economic implications of their decision. Other U.S. industries lobbying hard against foreign imports—steel and machine-tools among them—waited and watched, as did those wary of an all-out trade war. The commissioners would also not be likely to ignore the special symbolism of Harley-Davidson: a peculiarly American product—loud, daring, and ruggedly individualistic—and the last true survivor of a once-prosperous U.S. industry.

ASSIGNMENT FOR CLASS DISCUSSION

Assume you are a member of the International Trade Commission facing the question of trade protection for Harley-Davidson. Come to class prepared to issue a decision. In forming your decision, you will want to consider the following:

1. According to the ITC's criteria, has Harley-Davidson been sufficiently harmed by imports of motorcycles to justify restrictions on such imports? On what information in the case does your answer depend?

2. In addition to the rise of import competition, are there other possible causes of Harley-Davidson's economic condition? Has Harley-Davidson adequately isolated the impact of import competition and demonstrated that it is the dominant cause of the company's problems?

3. If tariff relief is granted to Harley-Davidson, what will be the impact on the well-being of motorcycle consumers, motorcycle dealers, Harley-Davidson's stockholders and employees, parts companies from whom Harley-Davidson purchases supplies, and Japanese producers? Can you describe the effects of a tariff graphically?

chapter 2

Market Failure
and Its Remedies

The previous three cases illustrated how markets can be used to help encourage producers and consumers to use scarce resources more efficiently. Markets do not always encourage efficiency, however, and the five cases in this section of the casebook explore various ways in which markets may fail to do so and the possible mechanisms by which the public sector may intervene in private markets to correct these failures.

One important cause of market failure is a lack of competition among firms. Economists often distinguish between two extremes: perfect competition and monopoly. In a perfectly competitive industry, each firm is so small that its output decisions do not appreciably affect total industry supply and, as a result, each firm takes the market price as given. The monopolist, by contrast, recognizes that it faces a downward-sloping demand curve: The more it produces, the lower the market price will be. Both firms follow the profit-maximizing rule of increasing output to the point where marginal cost equals marginal revenue. But for the firm in the perfectly competitive industry marginal revenue is the market price, since its output decisions do not affect price, while for the monopolist the marginal revenue is less than the market price, since it recognizes that additional output will reduce market price. As a result, the monopolist will produce less output and sell it at a higher price than would a perfectly competitive industry facing the same costs.

In practice, one rarely finds industries that are either perfectly competitive or perfect monopolies. Economists evaluating the level of competition usually think in terms of the degree of ''market power'' that individual firms in that industry enjoy; that is, the degree to which a firm's output decisions can affect market price. In some cases it is possible to measure the degree of market power empirically by observing the extent to which an individual firm's output decisions affect market price or whether a firm can charge a higher price for comparable output than its competitors. In other cases one must infer the degree of market power from various structural characteristics of the industry that might inhibit competition, most notably barriers to the entry of new firms. Barriers to entry may be technological (such as economies of scale so large that a single firm is the least-cost supplier to the entire market), created by a government action (such as an exclusive franchise or a patent), or created by firm behavior (such as tied sales).

The first three cases in this section deal with the problem of assessing the level of competition in an industry and alternative government remedies to maintain competition or regulate uncompetitive industries. In *Cable Wars,* cities and the cable TV industry are engaged in a dispute over whether cable TV is a natural monopoly whose prices should be regulated or just one segment of a highly competitive entertainment and information industry. *The Northwest/Republic Airline Merger* explores a potential government policy to maintain competition: review of mergers between companies. In this case, the U.S. government must decide whether the merger of two airlines is in the public interest or not. *Competitive Bypass of Pacific Gas and Electric* deals with the electric utility industry, which has traditionally been considered a natural monopoly and, as a result, is subject to government regulation of rates. The electric utility argues that it is now facing increasing competition from alternative energy sources and the State of California must decide whether it should approve the utility's request to allow it to lower its rates for selected customers who have alternative energy sources.

Other important causes of market failure include externalities, public goods, and asymmetric information. Externalities occur when the actions of a producer or consumer impose costs or benefits on others through a mechanism other than market prices; the common example of an externality is pollution from a plant which imposes costs on surrounding neighbors. Public goods are a special class of goods or services: It is impossible to exclude people from enjoying the benefits of these and thus the private market will not supply them. The national defense or a public health effort to eradicate an infectious mosquito are public goods, since it is difficult to exclude citizens from benefiting from these goods if they are not willing to pay for them. Finally, consumers may not be able to make wise decisions if they are poorly informed about important characteristics of the good or service they are considering purchasing. It is impossible, and unnecessary, for consumers and producers to be perfectly informed about all the characteristics of a good or service; but the market will work reasonably well if both have a similar, though imperfect, level of information. But if one party, usually the consumer, has significantly less information than the other, then the amount produced and consumed may not be efficient.

The last two cases in this section involve problems of externalities and information. *Controlling Acid Rain* deals with a classic externality:

The sulfur emissions from midwestern utilities are deposited on the Northeast. But Congress must decide how serious the damage from the sulfur emissions is, how much sulfur emissions should be controlled, and who should pay for the cleanup. In *Rescission of the Passive Restraints Standard,* the U.S. government must decide whether to require that new cars be equipped with airbags or automatic seat belts. Is the decision of most motorists not to use their seat belts or not to buy cars with airbags sensible or does it reflect a market failure that justifies government intervention?

Cable Wars

INTRODUCTION

The average American household spends between six and seven hours a day watching television, according to the A. C. Nielsen Company. While over-the-air broadcasters command the largest share of this audience, cable television has made substantial inroads, especially since 1972 (see Exhibit 1). By 1982, 36 percent of all households subscribed to cable (56 percent of those with access to the service) and the Washington Center for Public Policy Research was estimating that 50 to 60 percent would subscribe by the end of the decade.

But the boom of the late seventies and early eighties brought cable operators a new and messy problem. As cable systems spread from small rural areas to larger urban markets, their owners found themselves embroiled in tense battles with municipal regulators. They charged that city officials shame-

lessly abused their regulatory authority, demanding huge concessions just for the privilege of doing business. Municipal leaders countered that—despite the best efforts of local regulators—cable operators exploited their monopoly status and delivered inadequate service.

By 1982, the cable industry and, albeit reluctantly, the cities—each for their own reasons—wanted Congress to clarify the regulatory authority of municipalities. There was, however, no consensus within Congress on the question. At the urging of several members of the House of Representatives, the National Cable Television Association (NCTA) and the National League of Cities (NLC) began to work together on compromise legislation. Debate over this legislation raged for two years, both in private negotiations and in formal congressional hearings.[1]

BACKGROUND

Until the late seventies, cable television operators worried far less about municipal regulation than about federal regulatory control. The Federal Com-

EXHIBIT 1
Growth of Cable Television from 1952 to 1980

Year	Growth of Cable Operating Systems	Total Subscribers
1952	70	14,000
1960	640	650,000
1965	1,325	1,275,000
1970	2,490	4,500,000
1975	3,506	9,800,000
1980	4,225	15,500,000

Source: Reprinted with permission from *Cable and Station Coverage Atlas 1980–81.* (Washington, DC: Television Digest, Inc., 1986.)

[1] In the course of creating a new federal policy for cable television, a number of broad regulatory issues were discussed, including the cross-ownership of print media, TV stations, and cable stations; First Amendment questions; the access of independent commercial programmers to cable channels; and the predicted collision of cable technology and telephone technology in the future. For purposes of this case study, we have concentrated on local regulatory concerns: rate and service regulation, franchise renewals, and franchise fees.

This case was written by Pamela Varley under the direction of Professor José A. Gomez-Ibañez for use at the John F. Kennedy School of Government, Harvard University. (1187)
Copyright © 1986 by the President and Fellows of Harvard College

munications Commission (FCC) all but froze the development of cable television from 1966 to 1972 in an effort to protect small local broadcast stations. But changing perceptions of the television business, combined with pressure from the cable industry, led the commission to gradually loosen these restraints during the seventies. In 1980, the FCC virtually halted its regulation of cable TV.

At the same time, the cable industry was benefiting from technological advances. In the mid seventies, cable companies began to offer subscribers satellite-transmitted specialty channels (e.g., Home Box Office, Playboy Channel, Entertainment and Sports Programming Network). These "pay channels" proved extremely popular. By 1984, more than 40 video programs were distributed to cable via satellite and 66 percent of all cable subscribers received at least one of them. In addition, some cable operators were able to provide a host of new services, including videotext, at-home shopping, home-banking, security services and electronic games.

The combination of federal deregulation and rapidly improving technology created a heady atmosphere of expansion and the expectation of high profitability for the industry. Cable operators enthusiastically set out to wire the nation's largest cities, anticipating that their residential density would make them extremely lucrative markets.

Savvy municipal leaders, for their part, were determined to prevent cable operators from making high profits in their cities without giving something in return.[2] For one thing, they wanted cable firms to pay a percentage of their revenues to the city to offset local regulatory costs and to pay for the privilege of stringing wire along public streets. Such revenues were limited, however, because FCC regulations capped "franchise fees" at three percent of a company's gross revenues.[3]

City leaders also wanted some service concessions. Typically, they wanted universal cable service—that is, service available in all neighborhoods of the city, not simply the denser, higher income areas where cable operators would realize the greatest returns. And they wanted the service available at af-

fordable rates. They wanted some channels devoted to local public access, educational, and government programming with training provided so that the lay public might use them. Sometimes they wanted programming tailored to the particular population of the city and its needs—for instance, foreign language programs to serve large concentrations of immigrants. They often wanted at least the capacity for a large number of channels, institutional networks, and such interactive services as home security and electronic banking, even if these services were not to be used immediately: With cable technology advancing at high speed, they did not want their communities stuck with systems which would be obsolete as soon as they were constructed.

In the "gold rush" for big-city franchises, cable operators submitted extremely ambitious proposals. Almost immediately, however, they began to realize that the cable market was not as bullish as they'd anticipated. In fact, many cable corporations—instead of finding a gold mine in big urban markets—found themselves using profits from their good old reliable 12-channel "cash cows" in the boondocks to cross-subsidize their fancy new "whistles and bells" systems in the cities.

Part of the problem was a rapid escalation of construction costs—particularly in urban areas. According to the *National Journal,* the average cost per subscriber of constructing a cable system rose from $120 in 1975 to $900 in 1984. What's more, cable firms found that fewer urban households than expected were subscribing to cable service. In Dallas, where Warner-Amex had built a fancy high-capacity system, only a scant 25 percent of households had signed up by 1984—far below the 50 percent penetration considered necessary for a comfortable rate of return. In addition, the cable industry had vastly overestimated the popularity of some of its new service offerings. Early in 1984, California telecommunications consultant John Mansell told the *National Journal* that virtually none of the 50 24-hour burglar and fire alarm services offered through cable systems was turning a profit. One of Warner's biggest and most expensive disappointments was QUBE, an interactive channel which offered such services as electronic shopping. "Technologically [QUBE] works," one industry representative told the *National Journal.* "But we couldn't figure out anything to sell on it that people would buy."

Finally, cable operators were uneasy about the growing development of new video technologies, including video cassette and disc players and an array of services able to deliver cable-like video programming. The most threatening in many cities was Satel-

---

[2]To construct a cable system, a company had to secure a "franchise" giving it permission to string cable above or beneath public streets. Typically, the city invited competitive bids and awarded an exclusive 15-year franchise to the firm with the most attractive proposal. These franchises usually required the cable company to provide particular facilities and services, submit to rate regulation for "basic" service, and pay the city a franchise fee.

[3]If the city could demonstrate to the FCC's satisfaction that its costs for regulating cable television exceeded three percent, it would be allowed to levy up to five percent.

lite Master Antenna Television or "private cable," a multichannel service installed in individual apartment and condominium complexes—often a cable operator's wealthiest customers.

The net result was that cable firms failed to fulfill a number of their franchise promises, scaled back their systems in a host of larger cities including Dallas, Pittsburgh, and Los Angeles, and delayed installing systems in Chicago, Detroit, Cleveland, Washington D.C., Baltimore, Philadelphia, and New York City.

GROWING HOSTILITY

In the process, relations between cities and cable operators deteriorated markedly. Indignant municipal leaders, who often had spent months or even years hammering out their franchise agreements, charged operators with acting in monstrous bad faith. For one thing, some city officials doubted the cable industry's claim of fiscal hard times. Despite its setbacks, "this is an industry that, according to the FCC, had an enviable net income of $40 million in 1981, and achieved over $3.5 billion in operating revenues—up 60 percent over the previous year, with total assets up 78 percent over the previous year," New York City Mayor Edward Koch told a House subcommittee in 1983. Cable television might not be the golden goose the industry once expected, but city officials believed the operators should still live up to their contractual agreements.

"[I]t reminds me very much of hiring a company to pick up trash," remarked Denver City Councillor Cathy Reynolds at a later hearing. "I don't want the gentleman with whom I have a contract to provide dump trucks for our asphalt plant to say, 'Well, the economy has gone bad. I can't provide you trucks this year.'"

"I just have a question for the Councilwoman," shot back Stephen Effros, director of the Community Antenna Television Association (CATA), a trade organization for small cable firms. "Have you required them to teach trash collection? Have you required them to give free trash containers? Have you required them to provide portions of their truck for other people to use at all times with no fee?"

Cable operators admitted that they were not meeting their franchise obligations but argued that cities were making outrageous demands. William J. Bresnan, chairman and chief executive officer of Group W Cable, rattled off a few of the industry's favorite horror stories at a 1983 House subcommittee hearing:

> In Sacramento, California the winning bidder had to promise to plant 20,000 trees. The city even specified the kinds of trees. In Newton, Massachusetts the winning cable franchise winner had to promise to build the city a new library. In Miami, the cable TV company must pay $200,000 a year for a police department anti-drug abuse campaign.

The entire national telecommunications system, he concluded, was being "held for ransom" by local government.

Speaking to the oft-cited trees-in-Sacramento story, Paul Zeltner, mayor of Lakewood, California, countered:

> The trees were proposed by an overly ambitious cable operator. The trees were never proposed or required by the franchising authority. Most cities establish franchising "minimums" and allow cable operators to provide extras, as long as the extras are financially viable. If the cable industry has promised too much, it is because of the lack of self-restraint by a few members of the cable industry.

Municipal leaders had a few stories of their own. Zeltner complained that following "a two-year process of intensive community participation," the city of Lakewood had finalized a franchise agreement with a cable operator, only to have him return a few months later and argue that "significant changes in circumstances" were forcing him to eliminate "more than 80 percent" of the local programming and community service commitments that had won his firm the franchise in the first place.

In Raleigh, North Carolina, even after 15 years of service, the cable company had still failed to wire low income, primarily black areas of the city and was criticized, more generally, for poor quality service, according to *Access* magazine. Of the 8,000 respondents to a questionnaire mailed to 40,000 Raleigh households, nearly all reported dissatisfaction with the company.

THE NEED FOR CONGRESSIONAL ACTION

The combatants on both sides dug in their heels. The cable operators fought city regulators in the courts and the cities stood their ground. But by 1982, new developments had substantially raised the stakes for both sides.

Some 60 percent of the franchises were due to expire between 1983 and 1987, according to CATA Director Effros, and cable operators feared that cities might deny their requests for franchise renewals, forcing them to take a loss on a substantial capital investment. More commonly, an operator might be forced to choose between the untenable option of losing the franchise and the expensive option of substantially changing or upgrading the system.

At the same time, city officials worried that decisions of the courts, the FCC, and state public utilities commissions were gradually eroding their regulatory authority. Already the courts had prohibited cities from regulating rates charged for pay channels and the FCC had limited municipal franchise fees to three percent of gross revenues. Even more unnerving, a 1982 Supreme Court decision held that cities were not immune to antitrust obligations, throwing into question their right to award exclusive cable franchises. With cable operators filing a steady stream of cases in the courts, the cities feared that, absent a clear statement from Congress, cable television would be de facto deregulated.

Thus, both the NLC and the NCTA had reasons for wanting Congress to clarify cities' regulatory authority, and both sides were willing to negotiate for a compromise. As the two groups sat down at the bargaining table, however, they were poles apart on the substantive issues. The cities wanted Congress to codify their current regulatory power and remove the FCC's three percent cap on franchise fees. The cable operators, on the other hand—who initially argued for complete deregulation of the industry—wanted strict limits on municipal regulatory power at the very least, including virtually automatic franchise renewals, rate deregulation, and exemption from franchise agreements if "circumstances" changed "significantly" after the contract was signed.

ISSUES ON THE TABLE

Service Requirements and Franchise Fees

Dallas Mayor Jack Evans told a Senate subcommittee in 1983:

The franchising process . . . is a model of the free enterprise system working feverishly. In this instance, local governments, acting as the customer, describe and define the qualities and

specifics they seek in the product, the cable television system. The private cable companies then compete for the franchise. . . . Through this procedure, the marketplace ensures the best possible cable television system which can be sustained by the jurisdiction.

The cable industry, however, argued that the cities' service requirements were not only cumbersome and expensive, but unwanted by consumers. "Of the time available for access programming . . . only 3.7 percent actually gets used," said NCTA President Thomas Wheeler. The same was true for high channel capacity and fancy interactive systems. "The cities tell us we have to build the 50- to 100-channel systems, but the cable consumers do not buy 50 to 100 channels," Wheeler said. "All of our studies show that the cable consumers buy four to six channels."

One NCTA-commissioned study prepared by Ernst and Whinney, a leading accounting firm, analyzed the "cost of regulation" for an anonymous 35-channel system in one of the top 50 television markets and concluded that $5.60 per subscriber per month—or 22 percent of the average subscriber's bill—paid for services or facilities required by regulation.[4] The biggest of these regulatory expenses were the system's interactive capability, local programming facilities and services, free services to government and educational facilities, 24-hour repair service, and payment of the franchise fee.

Franchise fees were a classic case of backhanded taxation, argued industry representatives. In addition to property taxes, the nation's 5800 cable operators paid $194.6 million in franchise fees in 1984, or 2.4 percent of the industry's $8 billion in revenues, according to NCTA President Wheeler. In some cases, he added, a small percentage of gross revenues might represent a large chunk of the operator's net income.

Municipal leaders, however, argued that it was important for the public—through its elected leaders—to guide the development of an industry with

[4]The methodology of this study was harshly criticized in a paper prepared by Hyman Goldin of the Massachusetts Cable Commission and Yale Brauenstein, professor at Brandeis University. They charged the analysts with failing to document their claims or demonstrate that the system was representative, failing to differentiate properly between regulatory requirements and normal business practices, and incorrectly measuring capital and service costs. (For example, the study allocated to "regulation" the cost of digging tunnels to lay a second cable for interactive service even though these tunnels had already been excavated to lay the original cable.)

the potential to be a powerful information and communication tool. According to Frank Greif, cable communications director for Seattle, Washington:

> Eventually, the economic viability of urban areas may well be determined by the quality of . . . their communications infrastructure. It is therefore imperative that cities play a leading role in determining how this new infrastructure is developed, just as cities have planned the development of other infrastructure components such as bridges, streets, sewage and water facilities and transit systems.

Similarly, public access proponents defended such services—even if underused in the short run—because over the long run, they would increase information sources at the local level and provide more democratic access to television. According to Samuel Simon, director of the Telecommunications Research and Action Center:

> After many years of frustration on the part of public access advocates, we are seeing now the emergence of this new medium. . . . It is my view that within three to five years, given the proper environment, cable access television is going to blossom [but] like any new phenomenon, it needs intensive nurturing and help to make it to maturity.

Rate Regulation

The cable industry also objected to the regulation of "basic" cable rates[5] for several reasons. For one, such regulation was unnecessary, industry representatives argued, because cable television operated in a competitive market. According to NCTA President Wheeler, rates in 855 communities which had voluntarily deregulated rates were "virtually identical" to rates in regulated communities. A 1984 study of a few small communities conducted by Thomas Hazlett, an economist at the University of California at Davis, also found little overall difference between rates in regulated and unregulated communities. In the unregulated communities, rates ran 18 percent higher for basic service, but 10 percent lower for a "complete" package including basic and premium services (see Exhibit 2).

In addition, cable operators contended, the regulation of basic rates hampered their ability to price and package their services according to the dictates of the marketplace. According to Denver telecommunications consultant Paul Bortz:

> A tremendous challenge is posed in marketing an increasingly complex mix of pay television services such as movies and sports and a wide

[5]Cities had already been restricted by the courts from regulating rates charged for pay channels, but were still allowed to regulate basic rates. The services included in the basic package varied from city to city, however.

EXHIBIT 2

Unregulated Monthly Cable Rates in San Diego County vs. National Averages from Hazlett Study

Community	Basic	HBO	The Movie Channel	Bravo	Playboy	Total Package
Carlsbad	$10.95	$ 9.95	$11.95	$ 5.95	$ 7.95	$46.75
North County	9.75	9.95	11.95	5.95	7.95	45.55
Fallbrook	11.95	7.00	9.00	N/A	7.00	N/A
Lake San Marcos	10.95	9.75	11.95	5.95	6.95	45.55
Del Mar	8.90	8.75	9.95	4.95	6.95	39.50
Shadowridge	9.95	9.95	9.95	5.95	7.95	43.75
Average (unregulated)	10.41	9.23	10.79	5.75	7.63	43.81[1]
Deflated Average (1982 dollars)	10.01	8.88	10.38	5.53	7.34	42.13
National Average (1982)	8.47	9.58	9.67	9.66	9.36	46.74

[1]Includes Fallbrook over four services listed.

Source: Reprinted with permission from Thomas W. Hazlett, "Competitive vs. Franchise Monopoly in Cable Television," *Contemporary Policy Issues,* IV (Long Beach, CA: Western Economic Association International, Spring 1986), 80–97.

array of services ranging from 24-hour news to cultural programming. The difficulty of packaging services in a way that will appeal to consumers and develop adequate revenues to cover the costly investments being made by cable companies should not be underestimated.

Finally, cable operators objected to the cities' use of rate regulation as a "club" with which to enforce franchise agreements. "All too often this authority is used as a lever to pry from the cable operator concessions or commitments wholly unrelated to the question of setting reasonable rates," said NCTA President Wheeler.

Municipal leaders, on the other hand, defended rate regulation as a hedge against the market power of cable companies and a necessity if cable television was to remain available to the broadest possible cross-section of the public. According to John Gunther, director of the U.S. Conference of Mayors, while cable companies tended to keep basic rates low to win a franchise and attract customers, "as the system begins to mature beyond the beginning phases, cities have been experiencing a rapid increase in the pace of basic service rate increases."

The state of Connecticut's Department of Public Utility Control, in a statement to the House subcommittee, wrote:

Although [the cable industry argues] that the marketplace would place a limit on cable rates, we have no evidence to suggest that cable service is sufficiently elastic to provide a meaningful check on cable rates. Although there must be some limit to what most people would be willing to pay for cable services, we have apparently not reached it yet in this state. For example, in 1981, New Milford Cablevision, serving 4600 subscribers in a four-town franchise, was granted the increase it required to raise basic rates from $9.50 to $11.50 per month. Yet the number of subscribers continued to grow, as did the company's revenues.

Some economists also disputed the claim that comparable rates in regulated and unregulated communities signalled the presence of a competitive market. For example, Robert Entman, a professor of public policy at Duke University, noted that studies comparing rates in regulated and unregulated communities typically had neglected an important consideration: service quality. In his own 1982 study,[6] using channels-per-dollar as a proxy for quality, Entman found that across 61 systems, a range of one to five channels was provided per subscriber dollar. Newer systems in the sample were most likely to provide more channels per dollar, he discovered, but secondarily, rate regulated communities offered more per dollar (see Exhibit 3). The density of homes in the community, the level of penetration, and the require-

[6]Entman cautioned that his sample—though representative—was not truly random, and thus his conclusions were "only suggestive."

EXHIBIT 3
Effects of Rate Regulation and Other Variables upon Cable Services from Entman Study

Explanatory Variable	Dependent Variable: Channels per Dollar			
	B	Beta	Standard Error of B	F
Age of system	−.553	−.531	.014	16.047
Rate regulation[1]	.564	.342	.194	8.486
Homes per mile of wire	−.705	−.172	.001	2.292
Penetration	.536	.122	.563	0.907
Franchise fee	−.011	−.013	—	0.009
(Constant)	2.176			

$R^2 = .285$
Standard error = .728.
F = 5.58; Significance (df: 4,56) = .134.

[1]Rate regulation is a "dummy" variable coded 1 if the city has full rate regulatory authority over the system that serves it, zero otherwise. The zero category included systems serving more than one town in which some jurisdictions regulate and others do not, and systems where rate increases are regulated only if they exceed the Consumer Price Index or some fraction thereof. Essentially identical results were obtained using other coding schemes.

Source: US House of Representatives, Committee on Energy and Commerce, Hearing 98–73, June 22, 1983.

ment of a franchise payment appeared to have little effect, he added.

Municipal leaders also defended the use of rate regulation to enforce cable franchises, arguing that it was virtually the only tool available to cities, short of such drastic alternatives as revoking a franchise or going to court. Entman wrote:

> [C]onsumers rarely know franchise provisions. They will be unaware of broken promises. Subscribers will not drop cable for failure to cover city council meetings if they do not know coverage is a possibility. Consumers already hooked up will not disconnect in solidarity with neighboring townsfolk who are not wired on schedule. Officials can use rate regulation power to enforce franchise provisions that are not subject to market pressure.

Furthermore, city officials argued, there was no record of cities abusing their authority to regulate rates. In fact, in nearly all cases, rate requests were ultimately approved in full.

Franchise Renewals

The cable industry was perhaps most outraged by the power of cities to put a cable operator out of business (or threaten to) by refusing to renew his or her franchise. Trygve Myhren, chairman and chief economic officer of the American Television and Communication Corporation, called the refranchising process "one of the most disturbing examples of a low-productivity exercise available in today's economy."

The issue was of particular concern in smaller towns with older 12-channel systems (see Exhibit 4). "The small community mayor . . . sees *Newsweek* magazine and it says 108 channels is state of the art," said the CATA's Effros. But, he added, smaller cable operators simply could not afford to deliver that kind of service to their communities.

EXHIBIT 4

Channel Capacity for Cable Television Systems in 1980

Number of Systems	Channel Capacity
163	Less than 12
2493	12
884	13–20
910	21–30
678	More than 30

Source: Federal Communications Commission.

The franchise renewal process was also ripe for political abuse, cable operators argued. Bresnan, of Group W Cable, told the story of Marquette, Michigan, where he said the operator had been denied his renewal so that the city could award the franchise to a local firm in which several city officials held a financial interest: "After the city's action, the new franchisees obtained the existing cable system at a distressed sale price. Now that system is up for sale only months after it was taken away from the original cable operator, with a tidy profit expected for those who won out in the political arena."

NCTA President Wheeler added that in Spencer, Iowa, when a cable operator refused to sell his recently upgraded 35-channel system to a local group, "the city council revised its cable ordinance to require 54 channels as the price of refranchising." In Amberly, Ohio, after the city lost a suit against a cable operator for raising rates on pay channels, city officials "announced that they will have the last say on the matter when the operator's franchise comes up for renewal," he said.

The precarious nature of the franchise renewal process had all kinds of financial ramifications for companies, as well, according to ATC's Myhren. He said that while the typical cable franchise extends 15 years, most operators do not pay off their initial investment and begin to make a profit for the first eight to ten years. In addition, some costly components of the system, including amplifiers and converters, wear out after eight or ten years. The operator must then decide whether to invest millions of dollars in replacing this equipment, said Myhren. But with franchise renewal in question, the operator—or the operator's bank—may decide not to reinvest.

> Obviously the person who loses here is the consumer, because the refranchising process today makes it logical and reasonable for a responsible cable operator to let his cable system, signal quality, and customer service run down sharply in the last five to seven years of the franchise.

Municipal leaders, on the other hand, argued that an "automatic" franchise renewal would be akin to granting an operator a monopoly in perpetuity. It is the "temporary nature of cable franchises," Rep. Robert Matsui (D-CA) told a House subcommittee in 1983, that "preserves some essence of the competitive marketplace," creating an incentive for improved service as the renewal date approaches. Sue Miller Buske, director of the National Federation of Local Cable Programmers, related the plight of Santa Cruz County, California, an area where "the only significant access that residents have to television services is through the cable system" and where the cable operator enjoyed a penetration rate of more than 90 percent:

> Santa Cruz city and county have provided an exceptionally lucrative franchise area for the cable company and no significant improvements or changes have been made to the cable system over the last 15 years. Service responsiveness is poor, signal quality is not very good, and the cable company has not consistently met the guidelines set forth in the franchise. New services, including community access services, have not been provided to cable subscribers. If [the cable industry gets its way] it would make it difficult for Santa Cruz County to renegotiate an acceptable franchise with the existing cable company, or to obtain, in some other manner, appropriate cable television services to meet the needs of residents of this community.

City officials added that nearly 100 percent of franchises that have expired so far have been renewed. "Failure to renew is extraordinary because the incumbent operator has strong competitive advantages over outside bidders," said Matsui.

CABLE TELEVISION: IS IT A MONOPOLY?

During the course of various House and Senate subcommittee hearings, both the city regulators and cable operators invoked the well-being of consumers in defending their positions about regulation of cable TV. Underlying these arguments were questions about whether or not cable television was a natural monopoly. Two issues—the presence of economies of scale, and the competitive potential of alternative technologies—were critical to the debate.

Economies of Scale

In a study commissioned by the City of Monroe, Georgia, analysts Alan Pearce, Roger Peterson, and Mary Fredrickson claimed that large economies of scale—considered characteristic of any natural monopoly—were present in the cable television business:

> [A] cable operator must invest in headend equipment, satellite dishes, towers, antenna, and cable distribution facilities before providing service to a single customer. Although some additional investment, in drops and converters, will be required to provide service to additional customers, this investment is relatively minor compared to the initial investment in facilities required for all customers. Because this large initial investment is invariant with respect to the number of customers served, the average unit (per customer) cost will decline in inverse proportion to the total number of customers served. Under these conditions of economies of scale, construction of duplicate fixed facilities will be wasteful and economically inefficient.

Indeed, one "rule of thumb" in the cable industry is that at least a 50 percent penetration of households is necessary for a comfortable return on investment to a cable operator. Thus, argued the analysts, "If the maximum subscriber penetration that could be expected would be 60 percent in an average market, it would be likely that only one operator would survive under competitive market conditions." They noted that a study conducted by the Rand Corporation in 1974 also found large economies of scale in the cable business (see Exhibit 5).

But in the early eighties, other economists began to challenge this view. A 1983 study of larger, modern cable systems prepared by Bruce Owen and Peter Greenhalgh of Economists, Inc., showed only "modest" economies of scale. The Owen and Greenhalgh study simulated competition between two companies based on cost predictions listed in the franchise applications of 160 cable companies (both winners and losers) in 35 cities between 1979 and 1982.[7] They were all high-capacity systems with interactive capability and separate institutional networks. The average system was serving a community of 61,156 households and would eventually offer 73 channels. The analysts concluded that "in head to head competition between two cable systems down the same streets, there is about a 14 percent penalty in unit costs per subscriber" (see Exhibits 6 and 7). Another analysis conducted by Columbia Business School Professor Eli Noam, based on actual 1981 cost data for 4200 cable systems, concluded that overall, for every 10 percent increase in a cable system's scale, there was a corresponding one percent decrease in unit cost to the operator.

Other evidence on scale economies came from communities that had awarded more than one cable

---

[7]The authors themselves acknowledged certain problems with using these cost figures as a base. For one thing, they are "not actual operating data, but rather promises made in the context of franchise competitions . . . [and] biases . . . may arise from 'gamesmanship' in the . . . bidding process."

EXHIBIT 5

Summary of 1974 Rand Corporation Study

The Rand Corporation[1] developed a financial model which illustrates the economies of cable television built in different environments. Three cable systems in three communities are used here to demonstrate that costs per subscriber will increase substantially if cable television systems are permitted to compete for the same blocks of households.

- System A, serving a town of 25,000 people, with poor to fair off-the-air reception.
- System B, serving a medium-sized city of 150,000 people, with good off-the-air reception.
- System C, serving a city of 750,000 people, with excellent off-the-air reception.

Item	System A	System B	System C
Population in franchise area	25,000	150,000	750,000
Households in franchise area	8,000	48,000	240,000
In the 100 largest television markets?	no	yes	yes

	Total Capital Investment ($)		
Item	System A	System B	System C
Fixed facilities	$ 85,000	$ 364,000	$ 2,199,000
Cable distribution plant	497,000	3,818,000	15,648,000
Subscriber equipment:			
30 percent penetration	33,000	361,000	5,310,000
50 percent penetration	51,000	559,000	8,670,000
100 percent penetration	84,000	923,000	16,495,000
Pre-operating expenses capitalized:	40,000	100,000	200,000
Total capital investment:			
30 percent penetration	655,000	4,643,000	23,357,000
50 percent penetration	673,000	4,841,000	26,717,000
100 percent penetration	706,000	5,205,000	34,542,000
Capital investment per subscriber:			
30 percent penetration	273	322	324
50 percent penetration	168	202	223
100 percent penetration	88	108	144

[1]See Walter S. Baer, *Cable Television: A Handbook for Decision Making* (The Rand Corporation, 1974), pg. 40–55.

Source: Booz Allen Applied Research, Inc.

EXHIBIT 6

Predicted Cost per Subscriber per Month from Owen and Greenhalgh Study (Translog Equation)

	Subscribers		Channels in Use	
	Average Cost	Marginal Cost	Average Cost	Marginal Cost
Average system (30,481 subs.)	$39.33	$30.01	70¢	27¢
Large system (90,000 subs.)	$34.17	$19.08	61¢	37.2¢

Source: US House of Representatives, Committee on Energy and Commerce, Hearing 98–73, May 25, 1983.

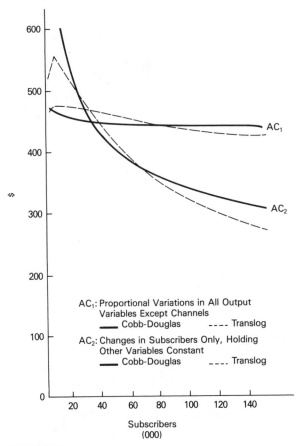

EXHIBIT 7
Annual Costs per Subscriber from Owen and Greenhalgh Study

Note: Cobb-Douglas and translog embody different assumptions about how costs vary with outputs.
Source: US House of Representatives, Committee on Energy and Commerce, Hearing 98–73, May 25, 1983.

company a franchise. Examples of mature multiple franchises were rare among the 5800 communities with cable service, but according to the ATC's Myhren, "It is important to keep in mind that government regulation is in many cases the most important factor contributing to the appearance of a monopoly. The franchise process is an enormous entry barrier that has limited the ability of would-be competitors to provide service."

In any event, the number of multiple franchise awards appeared to be rising. A study conducted by California-based Paul Kagan Associates in the early 1980s showed that 69 multiple franchises had been awarded since 1978, compared with 24 such awards before 1978. In Allentown, Pennsylvania—a town with poor over-the-air broadcast reception—two

companies had coexisted since the early seventies and virtually everyone in town subscribed to one service or the other. Both companies offered free installation and below-average rates of $7 to $8 for basic service and $9 to $10 for premium service. According to the Monroe study, however, both companies were pulling in lower than average returns, and the analysts speculated that "personal animosity" between the two operators might have fueled and sustained the competitive situation.

The Monroe study examined the other 23 communities which had awarded multiple franchises prior to 1978. The analysts found that "thirteen have resolved competition by consolidation, merger, or buy out (see Exhibit 8). Six now have side-by-side competition rather than overbuilding.[8] One municipality was never wired by the second franchisee and is seeking new bids." Like Allentown, the other three communities had genuine competition between franchises, but according to the study:

> The same destructive competition that has led to consolidations in thirteen other municipalities has occurred in the four continuing overbuilds. Circumstances exist, however, which have prevented the failure or withdrawal of either company in these cases. In each case the competitors have continued operation despite the lower returns on investment they receive because of price-cutting and duplication of fixed costs (organizational expense, headend equipment). Personal animosity, as evidenced by price wars, defamatory advertising, and protracted litigation in some cases, appears to have affected the decision to overbuild and continue operation.

As for the more recent round of multiple franchise awards, the study stated, "[B]ecause of the length of time that it takes to build a cable system and begin to operate it as a functioning business, it is far too early to collect data and draw conclusions from this data," but the analysts predicted that "the trend toward consolidation will continue and that the same consequences stemming from overbuilding will result."

In fact, critics of multiple franchising con-

[8]In cable TV jargon, an "overbuilt" area is one in which households have access to more than one cable firm. By contrast, some cities are served by more than one cable company, but the companies exist "side by side" and do not compete for the same households.

EXHIBIT 8

Explanation of 13 Multiple Franchise Consolidations

City/State	Companies Franchised	Start up/Award Dates	Resolution
Aberdeen, SD	2	1970	One company survived.
Austin, TX	2	1962–63	Cass Cable sold to Capital Cable after one year and construction of 300 miles.
Burlington, WA	2	1952	One company survived.
Charlotte, NC	2	1967	ATC bought out independents in 1972.
Corning, NY	2	1954	One company survived.
Danville, NY	2	1956	One company survived.
Longview, WA	3	1965	Two systems built. One bought out the other in less than one year.
Owensboro, KY	2	1967	One company survived.
Pensacola, FL	2	1970	One company survived.
Salisbury, MD	2	1960	Both sold to General TV in 1962.
Tallahassee, FL	3	1962, late 60s	All three sold to Clearwater Cable TV in 1967.
Warrensburg, MO	2	1966	One company survived after acquisition by Warner.
Williamsport, PA	5	1950s–1960s	One company survived. Acquired by Times-Mirror.

Source: Booz Allen Applied Research, Inc., ''Analysis of Overlapping Franchises, Overbuilding and Dividing Urban Markets in the CATV Industry,'' (Atlanta, Georgia), October 9, 1979.

tended that consumers were generally hurt by the competition. Entman pointed to the case of Paramus, New Jersey (7700 households), where two companies, simultaneously granted franchise rights, quickly embarked on a wiring race in hopes of being the first to offer service. While cable facilities were in place over 95 percent of the city in just 20 months, the operators cut corners, created traffic snarls, and damaged public and private property in their haste. The New Jersey Office of Cable TV estimated that the competition resulted in $1.6 million in waste and duplicated facilities. In the end, one company sold out to the other. Entman concluded:

> It is conceivable that if both companies had survived over the long haul, the competition would have helped enhance their responsiveness to consumers. But since one of the companies gave up and sold out to the other, consumers— who had to bear the costs of competition— probably wound up losers.

The Nature of Cable Service and Marketplace Competitors

At a hearing of the House Committee on Energy and Commerce, John Dingell (D-MI) stated:

> In 1934, the total number of homes wired for telephone was not significantly different from that percentage of the population which has cable today. For many people of that time, tele-

phones were as much a luxury as cable appears to be now. . . . [T]he situation that now faces the nation is that there is a cornucopia potentially available, but the dangers are great. Among them is the danger of changing our society from one which is integrated by the telecommunications system into one which is divided by it—with a patchwork of different classes, groups, and regions with different systems and different degrees of access to the information age.

He called on Congress to encourage new technological advances ''while preserving the basic values of universality and affordability.''

But according to CATA President Peter Athanas, too much of the public discussion about cable television ''has focused on our potential as opposed to our reality, on our capability as opposed to what people really want from us today.'' To cable operators, cable television was primarily the business of selling video programming to consumers. It was an entertainment service, not a necessity. And its long-run prospects were far from clear. Some cable operators speculated that cable television might go the way of the trolley car—a relic, abandoned in the wake of a new technology.

Even in the video market alone, argued Entman, ''the very versatility of cable makes it difficult to settle on what cable 'services' are and how much competition they face.''

For some, cable may mean the availability of 24-hour news and sports. These are currently available nowhere but cable. . . . It is also uniquely able to provide such programming as covering city council meetings. . . . For others, [cable] might mean stock market quotes, weather, and clearer broadcast TV reception, which can all be obtained without cable in most places.

In addition, marketplace competition varied markedly from community to community, and in a number of locations—typically those with poor over-the-air reception—cable television firms enjoyed penetration rates of 80 to 100 percent.

But NCTA President Wheeler argued that even where a single, popular cable system was in place, "So what?"

We may be the only broadband wire running down the street, but we must compete like mad to convince consumers to receive their video services from over the wire instead of by microwave, scrambled broadcast signals or discs and cassettes.

CBS' Senior Vice President James Parker submitted a 1982 rundown of cable television's video competitors (excerpted below) to a Senate subcommittee (see Exhibits 9 to 13):

- **Conventional TV:** "[T]he total number of operational broadcast stations has increased by 28 percent since 1970. As a result, 97 percent of all television households now receive four or more over the air television signals and almost two thirds of all households receive seven or more signals."
- **Subscription TV:** (Scrambled, over-the-air signals; not a new technology, but newly deregulated.) The number of subscription TV services had been increasing since the FCC deregulated it in 1978. An article in a 1982 issue of *Broadcasting* predicted there would be 4 million STV subscribers by 1985.
- **Multipoint distribution service:** (Signals transmitted over microwave frequencies.) As of 1982, these signals were single-channel systems, but it was possible that FCC action would make multichannel service available in the future. At the time, most MDS subscriptions were in hotels and apartment buildings, and the industry's growth had been slow, but "the number of new MDS stations per year has increased recently as a result of a 95 percent drop in the cost of necessary reception equipment (from $1500 to $100)," wrote CBS. A 1982 issue of *Media Science Newsletter* predicted that MDS would reach 3.2 million homes in 1990. A 1982 issue of *Broadcasting* speculated that if permitted, multichannel MDS systems might attract as many as 6 to 12 million viewers by 1990.
- **Low power TV:** Another recent FCC deregulation decision had opened up the possibility of expanding the number of these short range broadcast signals. It was hard to predict how successful these channels might be, but according to CBS, "applications have been filed for eight or more LPTV channels . . . in 94 percent of the top 50 markets and in half of the top 50 markets, authorizations have been sought for 18 or more LPTV channels."
- **Video cassette recorders/Video disc players:** "Since 1975 when VCRs were first introduced, an estimated 3 million units have been sold and industry experts predict that by 1990, sales will reach 15.3 million," wrote CBS. As of 1982, an estimated 300,000 VDPs had been sold, with predictions of sales of 4.8 million by 1990.
- **Satellite master antenna TV or "private cable":** (The closest substitute for cable's video services, offering improved broadcast reception and satellite-fed multiple channel service to apartments, hotels and other multi-unit buildings.) This business was serving between 100,000 and 250,000 in 1982, and "the industry is targeting 11 million U.S. homes located in apartment buildings with five or more units."
- **Direct satellite broadcasting:** (These orbiting satellites would transmit multichannel service to satelite dishes on individual rooftops.) Not yet available in 1982; no actual projections hazarded about the impact, but several projects were in the works.

"Although the new media are so recently arrived that they still have comparatively small dollar shares of the business," they might grow rapidly, Parker said. "From a technological point of view, there is now—as there was not a few years ago—substantial demand and supply side elasticity in video media markets."

But because most of these technologies were very new, city leaders argued, it was hard to predict how the video marketplace would actually shake out. For instance, VCRs might be spreading like wildfire, but were they competitive with cable television? Ent-

EXHIBIT 9

Status of Video Outlets in 1982

	Cable					
	Percentage of Homes Passed	*Average Number of Channels*	*MDS Channels*	*Total UHF and VHF Channels*	*Video Cassette Recorders*	*Radio Stations*
1. New York	40	31	3	14	392,800	39/78
2. Los Angeles	24	24	5	18	253,548	32/73
3. Chicago	5	34	2	12	181,676	39/67
4. Philadelphia	29	28	6	11	146,239	30/44
5. San Francisco	64	27	3	12	119,786	28/52
6. Boston	23	25	3	9	115,294	21/50
7. Detroit	5	31	3	8	101,818	23/38
8. Washington, D.C.	9	27	1	9	89,840	20/40
9. Cleveland	30	27	3	6	85,348	21/32
10. Dallas-Forth Worth	2	38	2	9	83,351	20/39
11. Pittsburgh	49	15	1	8	74,867	22/37
12. Houston	25	26	2	5	78,360	26/35
13. Minneapolis-St. Paul	5	29	1	6	66,881	27/35
14. St. Louis	4	22	1	6	62,888	21/37
15. Seattle-Tacoma	41	23	3	7	66,382	26/47
16. Atlanta	12	35	1	6	66,382	23/32
17. Miami	28	35	2	9	67,879	17/37
18. Tampa-St. Petersburg	44	21	2	8	57,398	13/33
19. Baltimore	14	30	1	6	52,906	22/28
20. Denver	2	27	1	5	53,405	22/32
21. Indianapolis	19	23	2	7	48,913	20/24
22. Sacramento	23	21	2	6	49,911	18/24
23. San Diego	79	32	2	4	42,424	19/34
24. Portland	2	18	3	5	48,414	24/33
25. Kansas City	37	29	1	6	42,424	16/31
26. Hartford	69	33	2	7	47,915	12/28
27. Cincinnati	17	43	1	7	42,923	19/27
28. Milwaukee	9	25	1	7	41,426	19/25
29. Buffalo	53	28	1	5	37,433	16/18
30. Nashville	10	32	1	5	39,929	17/24
31. Phoenix	10	32	5	8	44,920	20/33
32. Columbus	52	21	2	4	35,437	15/19
33. Providence	15	32	1	5	33,440	13/19
34. Memphis	19	36	1	5	34,938	20/23
35. Charlotte	19	16	1	7	36,934	13/16
36. New Orleans	23	32	2	5	35,936	23/25
37. Greenville, S.C.	30	22	1	8	33,939	11/17
38. Grand Rapids	42	19	2	5	34,439	17/18
39. Oklahoma City	29	34	1	7	32,442	17/24
40. Orlando	43	23	1	5	36,435	12/24
41. Raleigh	24	24	2	5	33,440	11/20
42. Louisville	5	21	1	6	31,943	16/22
43. Charleston, W. Va.	34	14	0	6	31,943	10/13
44. Birmingham	29	26	1	5	29,447	20/23
45. Salt Lake City	13	25	6	6	31,444	19/24
46. Harrisburg	64	17	1	7	27,451	8/17
47. Norfolk	41	30	1	6	29,947	13/31
48. Wilkes-Barre	54	20	0	4	28,449	6/22
49. Albany	59	27	1	4	27,950	12/22
50. Dayton	62	29	1	5	28,948	12/19
64. Des Moines	44	32	1	4	21,961	14/14
75. Springfield	49	27	1	6	19,465	9/10
100. Waco	62	12	1	3	12,977	8/8
125. Eugene	59	12	0	2	9,982	13/15
150. Odessa	60	12	1	4	7,487	9/14

Source: US House of Representatives, Committee on Energy and Commerce, Hearing 98-26, February 16–17, 1983.

EXHIBIT 10

Availability and Use of Electronic Mass Media: 1970–90

	[In millions]					
	1970	*1975*	*1980*	*1982*	*1986*	*1990*
Number of TV households	59	70	78	83	90	97
Basic cable:						
Homes with access	9	20	35	45	75	82
Subscribers	5	11	19	28	41	58
Pay cable:						
Homes with access		4	26	42[1]	70[1]	76[1]
Subscriptions		0.5	9	23	46	65
STV and MDS:						
Homes with access		3	22	35	49	59
Subscribers		NA	1	3	6	8
Low power TV:						
Homes with access				NA	0.4	10
Subscribers				NA	.36	0.8
Direct broadcast satellite:						
Homes with access					72	97
Subscribers					2	11
Videocassette recorders:						
Homes with access		70	78	83	90	97
Owners		.3	2	5	13	15
Videodisc players:						
Homes with access			78	83	90	97
Owners			.02	0.3	3	7
Videogames:						
Homes with access		70	78	83	90	97
Owners		NA	11	15	22	29

[1]In 1982, 93 percent of the television households passed by basic cable had access to at least one pay cable service. Assuming that the basic-to-pay ratio remains constant through 1990 (a conservative estimate given the anticipated expansion in channel capacities, see supra pay cable will be available to 70 million households in 1986 and to 76 million households in 1990.

NA = Not available.

Source: Donaldson, Lufkin & Jenrette, ''Industry Viewpoint: Cable '82'' at7, 9, 35 (October 1982); Paul Kagan Assocs., Inc., ''Cable TV Databook'' 36, 51 (1982); *Media Science Newsletter,* June 1–15, 1982, at 2; Doyle Dane Bernbach, Inc., ''The Media Scene: What Will It Look LIke?'' 11 (1982); Television Digest, Inc., ''Television Factbook,'' Services Vol., at 79–a, 83–a (1981–82 ed.); Titsch Publishing, Inc., ''Cablefile'' 93 (1982); Paul Kagan Assocs., Inc., ''MDS Databook'' 13 (October 1982).

Table prepared by Alan Pearce, PhD., January 18, 1983.

EXHIBIT 11

Television Stations on Air: 1970–83

Year (Jan. 1)	Total VHF	Total UHF	Total Commercial	Total Educational	Grand Total
1983[1]	633	472	812	293	1,105
1980	625	386	734	277	1,011
1978	617	365	716	266	982
1976	608	352	701	259	960
1974	605	333	697	241	938
1972	598	308	693	213	906
1970	581	281	677	185	862

[1]As of Dec. 13, 1982.

Sources: Television Digest, Inc., ''Television Factbook,'' Services Vol., at 75–a (1982–82); *TV Digest Weekly,* December 20, 1982, at 1.

Number of Units
(Millions)

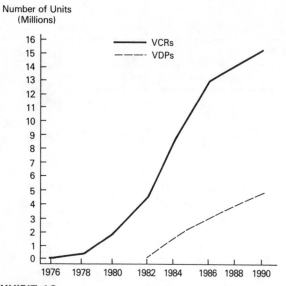

EXHIBIT 12

Cumulative Sales of VCRs and VDPs: 1976–90

Sources: Doyle Dane Bernbach, Inc., *The Media Scene: What Will It Look Like?* 9 (1982); Television Digest, Inc., *Television Factbook*, Services Vol., at 79-a (1981–82 ed.).

man, for example, suspected not: "More likely, those with the taste and budget for cassette recorders would subscribe to cable, then tape shows to be viewed at their convenience. Videocassette is more a complement to cable than a substitute."

Telecommunications consultant Paul Bortz predicted that in the long run, multichannel services—private cable and perhaps eventually direct broadcast satellites—would compete with cable television, but that single channel services like subscription television and multipoint distribution services, while currently performing well in some locations, would ultimately survive in only "a handful of markets."

Cable operators argued that, while the video future was admittedly unclear, cable television firms were certain to be at a competitive disadvantage if they and they alone were subject to municipal regulation. "Cable and only cable pays franchise fees to municipal governments," Group W's Bresnan protested. "Cable and only cable provides free telecommunications services to local governments. Cable and only cable provides and maintains access facilities and equipment for local programming." NCTA President Wheeler added:

No one can predict who the winners will be and who the losers will be. . . . A good bet is that

EXHIBIT 13

Authorized and Proposed DBS Systems: Number of Channels and Service Start Dates

Company	Number of Proposed Channels (Fully Implemented Systems)	Proposed Service Start Date
Permittees:		
CBS Inc.	3	late 1980's
Direct Broadcast Satellite Corp	6	mid-1985
Graphic Scanning Corp	2	1986
RCA American Communications, Inc.	6	1986[2]
Satellite Television Corp	3	1986[2]
U.S. Satellite Broadcasting Co., Inc. (Hubbard)	3	mid-1980's
Video Satellite Systems, Inc.	2[1]	1986
Western Union Telegraph Co.	4[1]	1985
Applicants:		
Advance Inc.	7	1984[3]
National Christian Network	4	NA
Oak Satellite Corp	12[1]	1988[3]
Satellite Development Trust	3	1986[3]
Satellite Syndicated Systems	6	1986[3]

[1]During their interim phases of operation, the Video Satellite, Western Union, and Oak Satellite Corp. systems will offer 1, 2, and 6 channels, respectively.

[2]ETZ: Eastern Time Zone.

[3]Dates provided by applicants (assumed issuance of construction permits in 1982).

NA = Not available.

Sources: Broadcasting, Nov. 8, 1982, at 40; Communications Daily, Aug. 3, 1982, at 2; DBS applications on file at the FCC, Gen. Docket No. 80–603; DBS News, Aug. 1982, at 3, 8, 9.

the winners will be those that adapt the best to meet the challenges of the competitive marketplace. To be able to respond to consumer needs and competitive challenges, the winners will need flexibility. The losers will be those who either fail to respond or those who cannot respond because the regulatory burdens they must carry are too great.

But the current reality, contended Entman, was that "cable service can fall far short of delivering the optimal level of consumer choice and satisfaction while still being profitable." New York City Mayor Edward Koch also argued that talk of cable television's competitors was largely speculative:

> Right now, there is no effective competition to cable television. Alternative service providers such as satellite and microwave systems carry only limited entertainment programming and serve only a limited audience. If cable systems were left to marketplace forces alone, the poor might never receive any cable service—just as they do not now receive the services of the alternatives to cable.

ASSIGNMENT FOR CLASS DISCUSSION

Read the case and come to class prepared to recommend whether Congress should restrict cities' powers to regulate cable TV rates and service. In preparing your argument, please consider:

1. What are the different aspects of cable TV franchises' behavior that municipalities regulate?
2. Which elements of municipal regulation might be justified by natural monopoly? What are possible rationales for other elements?
3. How plausible is the natural monopoly rationale for regulation? What evidence do you have in the case to support your position?
4. Supposing there is a monopoly, what are the possible remedies? What are the advantages and disadvantages of each remedy?

The Northwest/Republic Airline Merger

INTRODUCTION

On January 28, 1986, NWA, Inc., the parent company of Northwest Airlines, and Republic Airlines, Inc., both based in Minneapolis, Minnesota, filed an application with the U.S. Department of Transportation (DOT) for permission to merge. Northwest's business was primarily in international and long- and medium-haul domestic air travel. It had a fleet of large airplanes suited for those markets, and 4.1% of the domestic air travel market in 1985. Republic flew primarily in short- and medium-haul domestic markets, with a fleet of smaller aircraft, and 4.0% of the domestic market in 1985. Northwest ranked eighth among the U.S.'s top twenty domestic carriers; Republic ninth (see Exhibit 1). The two airlines argued to the DOT that their combined fleets and route systems would complement each other and that the merged carrier would thus be a more efficient and effective competitor, both internationally and domestically.

There were also potential domestic anticompet-

This case was written by David M. Kennedy under the direction of Professors José Gomez-Ibañez and Joseph Kalt for use at the John F. Kennedy School of Government, Harvard University. (1087)
Copyright © 1986 by the President and Fellows of Harvard College

EXHIBIT 1

Percent of Domestic Revenue Passenger Miles by Carrier Rank
1978–1984 (Even Years) and 1985

Carrier Rank	1978		1980		1982		1984		1985		1985[1]		1985[2]	
	Carrier	%	Carrier	%	Carrier	%	Carrier	%	Carrier	%	Carrier	%	Carrier	%
1	UA	21.6	UA	18.9	UA	18.3	UA	18.4	UA	14.9	UA	14.9	CO/NY/EA	16.8
2	AA	13.8	AA	12.1	AA	13.5	AA	13.9	AA	14.8	AA	14.8	UA	14.9
Top 2		35.4		31.0		31.8		32.3		29.7		29.7		31.7
3	DL	12.3	DL	12.1	EA	11.3	EA	10.9	EA	11.2	EA	11.2	AA	14.8
Top 3		47.7		43.1		43.1		43.2		40.9		40.9		46.5
4	EA	11.4	EA	11.7	DL	10.9	DL	10.4	DL	10.3	DL	10.3	DL	10.3
Top 4		59.1		54.8		54.0		53.6		51.2		51.2		56.8
5	TW	9.7	TW	9.2	TW	7.4	TW	6.1	TW	6.1	NW/RC	8.1	NW/RC	8.1
Top 5		68.8		64.0		61.4		59.7		57.3		59.3		64.9
6	WA	5.2	PA	4.4	RC	4.4	NW	4.0	PE/FL/RU	5.3	TW	6.1	TW/OZ	7.3
7	CO	4.6	NW	4.2	NW	4.1	CO	3.8	CO	5.1	PE/FL/RU	5.3	PE/FL/RU	5.3
8	BN	3.9	WA	3.9	WA	3.9	WA	3.6	NW	4.1	CO	5.1	WA	3.6
9	NA	3.7	BN	3.7	CO	3.9	RC	3.5	RC	4.0	WA	3.6	AL	3.6
10	NW	2.7	CO	3.6	PA	3.4	AL	3.4	WA	3.6	AL	3.6	PI/EM	3.1
Top 10		88.9		83.8		81.1		78.0		79.4		83.0		87.8
11	AL	2.2	RC	3.5	AL	2.9	PE	2.7	AL	3.6	PI/EM	3.1	WN/MC	2.4
12	RW	1.4	AL	2.7	PI	1.9	PI	2.6	PI/EM	3.1	WN/MC	2.4	PA	1.9
13	FL	1.3	FL	1.5	FL	1.7	PA	2.5	WN/MC	2.4	PA	1.9	PS	1.3
14	PA	1.1	PI	1.2	WN	1.4	FL	2.1	PA	1.9	PS	1.3	WO	1.2
15	NC	0.9	TI	1.1	PS	1.3	WN	1.9	PS	1.3	WO	1.2	AS	0.9
Top 15		95.8		93.8		90.3		89.8		91.7		92.9		95.5
16	TI	0.9	WO	1.0	BN	1.1	PS	1.3	WO	1.2	OZ	1.1	HP	0.8
17	PI	0.8	WN	1.0	CL	1.1	WO	1.2	OZ	1.1	AS	0.9	BN	0.8
18	OZ	0.8	PS	1.0	OZ	1.0	OZ	1.1	AS	0.9	HP	0.8	OC	0.7
19	SO	0.7	OZ	0.8	TI	1.0	BN	0.8	HP	0.8	BN	0.8	ML	0.4
20	—	—	OC	0.5	WO	0.9	AS	0.8	BN	0.8	OC	0.7	HA	0.3
Top 20		99.0		98.1		95.4		95.0		96.5		97.2		98.5

[1]With NW/RC combined.

[2]With NW/RC, CO/NY/EA, and TW/OZ combined.

Airline Codes:

UA = United	AA = American	DL = Delta	EA = Eastern	TW = TWA	WA = Western
CO = Continental	BN = Braniff	NA = National	NW = Northwest	AL = USAir	RW = Hughes Air West
FL = Frontier	PA = Pan American	NC = North Central	TI = Texas Int'l	PI = Piedmont	OZ = Ozark
SO = Southern	WN = Southwest	PS = PSA	OC = Air Cal	CL = Capitol	AS = Alaska
PE = People Express	HP = America West	MC = Muse/Transtar	EM = Empire	RU = Britt	HA = Hawaiian
ML = Midway	WO = World	RC = Republic			

Source: U.S. Department of Transportation.

itive aspects of the proposed merger: A concerned Alfred Kahn, a Cornell economist who as chairman of the Civil Aeronautics Board (CAB) had successfully championed the deregulation of the airline industry in the late 1970s, testified before Congress in February of 1986 that "the union of Northwest and Republic will join together two carriers that are the only or almost the only competitors on a number of routes, that are direct competitors . . . over some 205 routes, that control 80 percent of the gates at the Minneapolis-St. Paul airport. . . ." Kahn urged strongly that the proposed merger be subjected to close scrutiny under the antitrust laws.

The DOT, under its congressional mandate, was responsible for carrying out that examination, and for vetoing the merger if it appeared likely to lessen competition substantially or to create a monopoly. (The Department of Justice's [DOJ] antitrust division, sometimes together with the Federal Trade Commission [FTC], had enforcement authority for all industries, except those such as air transportation, communications, railroads, and banking, which are subject to specialized federal economic regulation. The DOT had only exercised merger authority over airlines since 1985, when the CAB was dissolved.) It requested written testimony on the matter from its own Office of Public Counsel (OPC), a part of the DOT's general counsel charged with representing the public interest in certain departmental proceedings, and from the DOJ's antitrust division. That testimony, backed up by an oral hearing in April, 1986, went to a departmental administrative law judge (ALJ) for disposition. That decision was open to review by Secretary of Transportation Elizabeth Dole.

The administration performing the review of the merger was widely recognized to be unusually, perhaps overly, friendly to such consolidations; Kahn, in urging close review of the Northwest/Republic combination, noted particularly that the DOT "has yet to encounter a merger with which it was willing to interfere." The DOJ eventually recommended the merger's rejection, but it did so with some regret. "The one concern I have with the position we took was the fact that it might send out a signal that somehow we're hostile to consolidations in the airline industry, and we're not," said Charles F. Rule, Deputy Assistant Attorney General in the antitrust division. "Almost any other merger involving these airlines we would have applauded. . . ." The DOT recommended that the ALJ approve the merger. The ALJ would have to decide between them.

DEREGULATION

Two arms of the same administration could disagree so thoroughly about the same case in part because the airline industry was, in 1986, in considerable flux. For forty years, from 1938 to 1978, the federal Civil Aeronautics Board (CAB) had regulated domestic airlines, controlling which firms could enter the industry, whether existing firms could merge, which routes they could serve, and what prices they could charge. By the mid-1970s a consensus had emerged among economists that the CAB's regulatory practices had resulted in a highly inefficient industry.[1]

Carriers generally supported regulation, but Congress passed the Airline Deregulation Act (ADA) in 1978, deregulating most aspects of the industry and providing for the CAB's dissolution on New Year's Eve, 1984 (the board continued to fulfill certain functions, like antitrust oversight, from 1978–1984 when such authority passed to the DOT upon the CAB's "sunset").

The transition to deregulation was not easy; some major carriers like Braniff were unable to adapt and went bankrupt. Extraneous events impinged as well: The recession of 1981–1982, combined with high oil prices and the PATCO air traffic controllers strike, were extremely painful for carriers. The deregulators' hopes were largely fulfilled, however. Prices, in general, fell. A new breed of low-cost carriers, like New York Air and People Express, entered the market (Continental emerged from its bankruptcy, union broken, as one of these). Carriers' efficiencies, measured by such things as the percentage of seats filled per flight, rose.

There was also a wave of mergers and acquisitions. Traditionally, the competitive implications of mergers had been considered primarily in terms of two key measures of market concentration among existing firms. High market concentration factors—the percentage of sales in a given market made by the several larger firms in that market—were considered to increase the likelihood of anticompetitive collusion among those firms.[2] Large market shares—the proportion of a given commodity sold by a single firm in a given market—were likewise suspect because firms with such shares were considered less likely to lower their prices or improve their service in response to competition. This rationale was sometimes applied quite strictly; the Supreme Court in 1966 forbade a merger which would have joined firms with a combined 4.49% of the beer market, when the top eight firms had 59% of the market. The Justice Department, according to its official 1984 *Merger Guidelines,* routinely assessed both indicia

---

[1]The CAB protected established carriers—most significantly, the ten major trunk airlines and nine smaller local service carriers—from upstart competitors; between 1950 and 1974 the board received seventy-nine applications from firms wishing to enter the domestic industry, and granted none. It restricted the ability of the established carriers to operate as they saw fit; between 1969 and 1974 fewer than four percent of carriers' applications to serve new

routes were approved. And, it seemed clear, it distorted the market for passenger service by simultaneously setting fares and forbidding carriers to engage in price competition. The result was high prices: in 1975, the regulated, Boston-Washington fare was $41.67, against a fare of $26.21 in the San Diego-San Francisco corridor, roughly equivalent but unregulated by the CAB. Unable to attract additional passengers by cutting these fares, carriers competed instead by overscheduling—running frequent, often half-empty flights—or offering other service inducements like gourmet meals.

[2]Economists usually examine a four- or eight-firm concentration ratio: that is, the percentage of the market captured by the largest four or eight firms.

through the Herfindahl-Hirschman Index (HHI), a value calculated by summing the squares of the market shares of all the firms in a given market.[3] HHIs below 1000 were considered unconcentrated; between 1000 and 1800 moderately concentrated, and above 1800 highly concentrated. The *Guidelines* noted that while many factors affecting competition in a market entered into the department's decision to approve or challenge mergers, it generally would not challenge mergers in unconcentrated markets; was unlikely to challenge mergers in moderately concentrated markets which would result in a post-merger HHI increase of less than 100; and was likely to challenge mergers in concentrated markets which would result in a post-merger HHI increase of more than fifty. More broadly, the *Guidelines* indicated that if the department believed that a merger would result in "a small but significant and nontransitory" price increase in the market at issue, the merger was likely to be challenged. The *Guidelines* codified such an increase, for most purposes, as five percent for at least a year; this was generally called "the five percent test."

The courts, and agencies like the DOJ's antitrust division, recognized, however, that if it were very easy for firms to begin competing in particular markets—if "barriers to entry" were low—even high market share and concentration levels might not be too significant, since new firms would enter such markets if established firms were pricing exploitatively. The CAB's, and later the DOT's, approach to considering post-deregulation airline consolidations drew heavily on an economic analysis of the airline industry which had been developed during the period leading up to deregulation, and which saw market shares and concentrations in the industry as having little bearing on competition. In essence, this analysis held that airline markets—construed as national, regional, or as individual "city pairs"—are by their nature extremely competitive. Air routes are easily entered: if a potential competitor already has airplanes, they can easily be moved around to take advantage of ripe markets, and if not they can readily be purchased or leased. Routes can also be readily abandoned, since there are none of the large fixed costs associated with, say, the steel industry; what fixed costs do exist are associated mainly with airports and are borne by government. These two factors together, so the analysis went, all but eliminate barriers to entry and make air travel markets highly

"contestable" so that a carrier charging high prices on a particular route should very shortly be faced with lower-priced competition. Some economists argued that airline markets were so "perfectly contestable" that actual competition on any given route was not necessary to keep fares down to competitive levels: entry and exit from routes were so easy and quick that the mere threat of another carrier's entry was sufficient to drive fares down.

The CAB and the DOT thus had such confidence in the essential competitiveness of the industry that they regularly approved even mergers combining carriers flying the same routes which resulted in firms with sizable market shares on those routes. For instance, beginning in 1978, Texas International Airline attempted to acquire National Airlines, against National's wishes. The merged firms would have had a 51% market share in the busy Houston-New Orleans corridor; the top four firms in the corridor would have had a concentration factor of 91%. Under traditional antitrust principles the merger would have been very highly suspect. A federal administrative law judge rejected the merger on that basis, but the CAB overturned the decision, arguing that in the airline industry barriers to entry were so low, and potential competition so effective, that concentration and market shares had little relevance: if the merged carriers began monopolistic pricing other carriers would immediately enter the market. Ease of entry was demonstrated, even as the government considered the issue: by mid-1979, Southwest Airlines had begun service and captured 24% of the Houston-New Orleans market (in any event, National avoided the merger and joined instead with Pan American). The CAB and DOT continued to follow this line of thought in considering other airline mergers, generally preventing consolidation only when special factors, such as restricted access to airports or international agreements limiting the number of carriers on particular routes, might interfere with unfettered competition.

HUBBING IN MINNEAPOLIS

While most airline analysts continued to believe in the contestability of markets, the industry evolved in ways not foreseen by the deregulators. One significant new characteristic of the deregulated industry was the "hub-and-spoke" route system, which potentially had significant implications for the contestability of airline routes.

Under CAB regulation, carriers generally had operated numerous discrete, relatively unintegrated

---

[3]Thus, an industry with only four equally large firms would have an HHI of $4 \times (25^2) = 2500$, while an industry with ten equally large firms would have an HHI of $10 \times (10^2) = 1000$.

nonstop routes: owing to the vagaries of the board's route assignment practices, a passenger travelling from Miami to Madison, Wisconsin might well fly one carrier Miami-Minneapolis, only to be forced to change to another carrier for the Minneapolis-Madison leg. Under deregulation, airlines' marketing strategies emphasized retaining passengers for the whole of such trips. Since many city pairs generated too little traffic to justify non-stop service, carriers evolved hub-and-spoke systems: a carrier would establish a major operation, or hub, in, say, Minneapolis—as had both Northwest and Republic—and fly passengers from all over the country into the hub and then out again.

The systems were generally seen to benefit both passengers and carriers. Carriers argued that they could serve more markets efficiently, and offer more frequent service, by consolidating passengers going to and from local markets at the hub, and using large, fully loaded airplanes for long-haul markets. Passengers, they said, got more frequent and cheaper service, with the reduced likelihood of missed connections and lost baggage that came from remaining with one carrier for the entire trip. Although most carriers had one or two hubs each before deregulation, CAB route awards didn't usually facilitate their development. In the new industry, though, hub-and-spoke systems were increasingly important and strategic elements: some thirty-three new hubs had been formed nationwide since deregulation, and their development was accelerating.

Northwest and Republic operated hubs at the same airport in Minneapolis/St. Paul, from which they served and competed for a large number of small cities in the region, such as Bismarck and Fargo, North Dakota and Grand Rapids, Michigan, as well as larger cities like New York and St. Louis. Were the merger to be approved, the new carrier would have on the order of 71% of the flights and 78% of the enplanements at the airport. It was this aspect of the merger that chiefly disturbed the DOJ, and over this issue, and several surrounding it, that the two departments joined battle.

THE DOJ'S ANALYSIS

The DOJ submitted testimony to the DOT on March 27, 1986, arguing that the merger of the two carriers would lead to significantly increased concentration in twenty-six city pair markets served nonstop by both carriers out of Minneapolis/St. Paul (see Exhibit 2). It argued further that the ability of the merged carrier to dominate and exploit many of those markets was

not likely to be countered by the entry, or threat of entry, of another carrier because such a carrier would need to have a hub on one end-point of those routes—as the merged carrier would—and no other carrier was likely to establish a hub in Minneapolis/St. Paul.

The argument began with an attempt to pin down exactly what sort of market was at issue. DOJ's position was that nonstop airline service was sufficiently different from "single-plane" (one or more stops on the same plane en route to a destination), on-line connecting (change of planes, but same airline), and interline (change of airlines en route) service as to constitute a distinct product category. There was little question that passengers, all else being equal, preferred nonstop service, which was typically both quicker and involved less chance of missed connections and lost baggage. Federal surveys of airline traffic didn't distinguish between nonstop and single-plane service; the DOJ adduced in support of its position such data as that, for instance, there were twelve nonstop and single-plane flights a day out of Minneapolis/St. Paul to Atlanta, compared to eighteen connecting flights, but the nonstop/single-plane flights cornered 96.4% of the traffic (see Exhibit 3).

The question, under the *Merger Guidelines'* five-percent test, was whether nonstop was sufficiently different that a merged Northwest and Republic could impose a 5% price increase for a year that consumers would pay rather than switching to another kind of service. DOJ economist Gloria J. Hurdle, who performed the bulk of Justice's analysis, thought that it was. Taking a published 1974 estimate of the value of a typical traveler's time—$22/hour, when inflated to 1985 dollars—Hurdle reasoned that a nonstop carrier could therefore charge up to that much more for a nonstop flight that saved at least an hour (leaving aside the less quantifiable value of avoiding lost bags and missed connections). Given that on most routes out of Minneapolis one-stop and connecting alternatives to nonstops did in fact involve at least a one-hour differential, the five-percent test implied that for fares under $440 (.05 × 440 = 22) a five-percent fare increase would not be sufficient to drive passengers off nonstop flights. Most of the relevant fares were well under that amount; Hurdle noted that at least the lowest class of fares charged on all flights out of Minneapolis/St. Paul was typically not more than $200.

DOJ's stance on this point meant that, in its analysis of the implications of the proposed merger, only other carriers' nonstop flights would be considered competitive with the merged carrier's flights. If the merged carrier flew nonstop from Minneapolis/

EXHIBIT 2

26 City-Pair Markets Currently Served by Both Northwest and Republic at Minneapolis/
St. Paul
Shares and HHIs

(1)	(2) Combined NW-RC Market Share	(3) Change in HHI	(4) Post-merger HHI
1. Atlanta (ATL)	49	1,179	3,705
2. Bismarck (BIS)	100	4,992	10,000
3. Boston (BOS)	100	4,511	10,000
4. Chicago (ORD) (MDW)	60	1,671	3,974
5. Dallas (Ft. Worth) (DFW)	52	1,113	5,010
6. Denver (DEN)	39	710	2,803
7. Detroit (DTW)	100	5,000	10,000
8. Fargo (FAR)	100	4,763	10,000
9. Grand Forks (GKF)	100	4,943	10,000
10. Grand Rapids (GRR)	100	4,858	10,000
11. Kansas City (MCI)	100	4,986	10,000
12. Los Angeles (LAX)	100	4,258	10,000
13. Madison, WI (MSN)	100	4,972	10,000
14. Milwaukee (MKE)	100	4,993	10,000
15. New York (JFK) + (LGA)	81	1,830	6,837
16. Omaha (OMA)	100	4,793	10,000
17. Orlando (MCO)	100	4,891	10,000
18. Philadelphia (PHL)	100	4,759	10,000
19. Phoenix (PHX)	100	4,928	10,000
20. Portland (PDX)	100	4,997	10,000
21. Rochester (RST)	87	3,472	7,685
22. San Diego (SAN)	100	4,669	10,000
23. San Francisco (SFO)	100	4,712	10,000
24. Seattle (SEA)	100	3,819	10,000
25. St. Louis (STL)	53	1,379	4,758
26. Washington, D.C. (DCA)	100	3,097	10,000

Source: U.S. Department of Justice.

St. Paul to Miami, for instance, and another carrier flew the same route but with a stopover in Pittsburgh, the DOJ's argument ruled out the second carrier as a competitive force even if the second carrier's price was attractive. It was to become an extremely contentious point, but one the DOJ would hold to. "One thing that I think we have going for us [in the antitrust division] is the fact that we do a lot of merger analysis in a lot of different areas, and that sort of experience, over a long period of time, gives our economists a certain advantage because of an ability to build up human capital and bring their experience from other industries," said the antitrust division's Rule. "[The analysts here think that nonstop service is in a different market,] and it rings true from my experience, especially for businesspeople."

The DOJ's analysis thus went on to focus on nonstop flights to and from the twenty-six cities. Hurdle's argument centered on an examination of "feed" or "beyond passengers"—those passengers flying a spoke route into a hub in order to make a connection to elsewhere. Feed could be the decisive element in a carrier's decision whether to serve a particular spoke route: it might not make sense for a carrier to serve the Fargo-Minneapolis/St. Paul route if it could attract only local passengers flying that leg, whereas if it could attract additional fliers from Fargo wishing to go on to New York, serving the route might be sensible. With good feed, a carrier could serve a spoke even if it didn't profit on the spoke itself, as long as the additional revenue from the feed passengers continuing on was high enough. Hubs appealed to the industry precisely because of their ability to generate feed. "To be able to offer jet service to a small city," said Hurdle, "what you want to do is pick up passengers in that city, take them to your hub, and then transport the ones who aren't stopping in, say, Minneapolis on to New York or

EXHIBIT 3

Select City Pairs to or from Minneapolis
Comparison of Scheduled Service to Actual Traffic

(1)	(2) Scheduled Daily Service	(3) % Scheduled Service	(4) % Traffic
MSP-Atlanta			
Nonstop and Single Plane	12	40.0	96.4
Connecting	18	60.0	3.6
Total	30	100.0	100.0
MSP-Billings			
Nonstop and Single Plane	3	27.3	94.3
Connecting	8	72.7	5.7
Total	11	100.0	100.0
MSP-Boston			
Nonstop and Single Plane	10	27.8	87.6
Connecting	26	72.2	12.4
Total	36	100.0	100.0
MSP-Bozeman			
Nonstop and Single Plane	1	16.7	20.0
Connecting	5	83.3	80.0
Total	6	100.0	100.0
MSP-Cincinnati			
Nonstop and Single Plane	3	17.6	74.7
Connecting	14	82.4	25.3
Total	17	100.0	100.0
MSP-Cleveland			
Nonstop and Single Plane	10	34.5	76.7
Connecting	19	65.5	23.3
Total	29	100.0	100.0
MSP-Columbus			
Nonstop and Single Plane	2	10.0	77.3
Connecting	18	90.0	22.7
Total	20	100.0	100.0
MSP-Dallas/Fort Worth			
Nonstop and Single Plane	11	35.5	86.3
Connecting	20	64.5	13.7
Total	31	100.0	100.0
MSP-Denver			
Nonstop and Single Plane	18	72.0	99.2
Connecting	7	28.0	0.8
Total	25	100.0	100.0
MSP-Detroit			
Nonstop and Single Plane	34	70.8	89.5
Connecting	14	29.2	10.5
Total	48	100.0	100.0
MSP-Grand Rapids			
Nonstop and Single Plane	6	37.5	91.8
Connecting	10	62.5	8.2
Total	16	100.0	100.0
MSP-Indianapolis			
Nonstop and Single Plane	3	20.0	85.7
Connecting	12	80.0	14.3
Total	15	100.0	100.0

EXHIBIT 3
(continued)

(1)	(2) Scheduled Daily Service	(3) % Scheduled Service	(4) % Traffic
MSP-Kansas City			
Nonstop and Single Plane	8	32.0	90.1
Connecting	17	68.0	9.9
Total	25	100.0	100.0
MSP-Las Vegas			
Nonstop and Single Plane	3	14.3	53.8
Connecting	18	85.7	46.2
Total	21	100.0	100.0
MSP-Los Angeles			
Nonstop and Single Plane	9	20.5	84.7
Connecting	35	79.5	15.3
Total	44	100.0	100.0
MSP-Madison			
Nonstop and Single Plane	6	60.0	100.0
Connecting	4	40.0	0.0
Total	10	100.0	100.0
MSP-Memphis			
Nonstop and Single Plane	10	71.4	91.8
Connecting	4	28.6	8.2
Total	14	100.0	100.0
MSP-Miami			
Nonstop and Single Plane	5	14.7	53.7
Connecting	29	85.3	46.3
Total	34	100.0	100.0
MSP-Milwaukee			
Nonstop and Single Plane	10	66.7	99.6
Connecting	5	33.3	0.4
Total	15	100.0	100.0
MSP-New York			
Nonstop and Single Plane	24	38.7	97.3
Connecting	38	61.3	2.7
Total	62	100.0	100.0
MSP-Orange County			
Nonstop and Single Plane	2	13.3	55.6
Connecting	13	86.7	44.4
Total	15	100.0	100.0
MSP-Orlando			
Nonstop and Single Plane	10	24.4	71.9
Connecting	31	75.6	28.1
Total	41	100.0	100.0
MSP-Philadelphia			
Nonstop and Single Plane	8	25.0	91.0
Connecting	24	75.0	9.0
Total	32	100.0	100.0
MSP-Phoenix			
Nonstop and Single Plane	11	34.4	80.5
Connecting	21	65.6	19.5
Total	32	100.0	100.0

EXHIBIT 3
(continued)

(1)	(2) Scheduled Daily Service	(3) % Scheduled Service	(4) % Traffic
MSP-Portland			
Nonstop and Single Plane	6	30.0	73.4
Connecting	14	70.0	26.6
Total	20	100.0	100.0
MSP-Salt Lake City			
Nonstop and Single Plane	5	27.8	81.7
Connecting	13	72.2	18.3
Total	18	100.0	100.0
MSP-San Diego			
Nonstop and Single Plane	5	20.0	74.6
Connecting	20	80.0	25.4
Total	25	100.0	100.0
MSP-San Francisco			
Nonstop and Single Plane	5	13.2	85.4
Connecting	33	86.8	14.6
Total	38	100.0	100.0
MSP-Seattle			
Nonstop and Single Plane	10	45.5	91.8
Connecting	12	54.5	8.2
Total	22	100.0	100.0
MSP-Spokane			
Nonstop and Single Plane	5	50.0	74.3
Connecting	5	50.0	25.7
Total	10	100.0	100.0
MSP-St. Louis			
Nonstop and Single Plane	16	61.5	99.1
Connecting	10	38.5	0.9
Total	26	100.0	100.0
MSP-Tampa			
Nonstop and Single Plane	5	13.9	72.7
Connecting	31	86.1	27.3
Total	36	100.0	100.0
MSP-Washington, D.C.			
Nonstop and Single Plane	14	21.5	83.6
Connecting	51	78.5	16.4
Total	65	100.0	100.0

Source: U.S. Department of Justice.

Florida or wherever. The more points you can offer service to from the hub, the more passengers you're going to have on that local flight." Likewise, Hurdle argued, a carrier serving one or several of the twenty-six Minneapolis/St. Paul city pairs at issue, but without significant "beyond" flights to attract more passengers and generate additional revenue, would likely operate at a higher cost per passenger than a hub carrier, and thus be uncompetitive with the merged carrier.

Hurdle therefore used feed as a proxy for the likelihood that a competitive carrier would enter one of the twenty-six city pairs: more accurately, she used a proxy for feed as a proxy for that likelihood. Using a methodology developed specifically for the proposed merger, another DOJ analyst computed "potential entrant feed ratios" for carriers likely to enter the city pairs by first summing the enplanements of each such carrier at each end of the city pair. The analyst then took the largest such sum for each city pair and divided it by the summed enplanements for that city pair of the incumbent carrier with the lowest such number. "This ratio," wrote Hurdle, "shows the feed of the carrier not serving the route relative to that of the incumbent carrier with the lowest feed. A feed ratio that is one or larger indicates that the potential entrant has at least as much feed as the lowest-feed incumbent."[4]

The results seemed, to Hurdle, to establish several things (see Exhibit 4). First, in all of the city pairs except one, St. Louis, the least advantaged incumbent had a hub at one endpoint, and on twenty-three of the twenty-six all the carriers—Republic, Northwest, the least advantaged incumbent, and all other airlines serving the city pair—had a hub at at least one endpoint. "This suggests," wrote Hurdle, "that only hub carriers find it profitable to serve those routes." Second, in twenty-one of the city pairs, the best potential entrant's feed ratio was less than one, and in fourteen city pairs the entrant's feed ratio was less than 0.5. "I consider this," wrote Hurdle, "a substantial disadvantage" likely to prevent such carriers from entering those twenty-one routes.

Hurdle also noted that beside eliminating actual competitors on the twenty-six routes, the proposed merger would eliminate the two airlines as potential competitors with each other on twenty-one additional Minneapolis/St. Paul city pairs which one but not both of the airlines served. Feed ratios for these cities seemed illuminating as well:

For sixteen of those twenty-one city pairs . . . the feed ratio is greater than one, and in all cases the ratio is over 0.7, which suggests that there is a carrier with comparable feed currently contesting the route. Moreover, in all cases, that contestor is Northwest on Republic's routes, and in all but one case, that contestor is Republic on Northwest's routes. Furthermore, in fourteen of those cities where Northwest is a contestor with a feed ratio greater than 0.7, the carrier with the second highest feed ratio has a feed ratio less than 0.5. This means that if Northwest is eliminated as a contestor, there will be no other contestor with comparable feed on those routes. Similarly, in four cities served by Northwest where Republic is a contestor with a feed ratio greater than 0.7, the next best contestor has a feed ratio less than 0.5. Thus, there are eighteen additional city pairs where fares are likely to increase or service deteriorate following this transaction.

(See Exhibits 5 and 6.)

Thus, the DOJ argued, in order to prevent the merged carrier from pricing monopolistically, a competitor would have to build a hub in Minneapolis/St. Paul. How big a hub would it have to be? "I'm not an airline executive, so I don't have all the information about Minneapolis to tell me what cities you need to serve," said Hurdle.

[4]"For example," The DOJ's submission said, "the Atlanta-Minneapolis/St. Paul city pair is served by Northwest, Republic, Delta and Eastern. Northwest and Republic hub at Minneapolis/St. Paul. Delta and Eastern hub at Atlanta. The table below shows the enplanements by carrier at Atlanta and Minneapolis/St. Paul. This table also calculates the combined enplanements at both airports.

Incumbent Carriers	Enplanements at Atlanta	Enplanements at Minneapolis	Combined Enplanements at ATL and MSP
Delta	10,720,371	109,492	10,829,863
Eastern	8,505,242	76,438	8,581,680
Northwest	84,604	3,125,323	3,209,927
Republic	400,213	2,422,546	2,822,759
Large Non-Incumbents			
American	173,271	200,819	374,090
United	121,020	220,717	341,737
Piedmont	224,079	11,885	235,964

Republic is the incumbent carrier with the lowest combined enplanements. American is the potential entrant with the largest combined enplanements not currently serving the market. United is the second best entrant carrier. To calculate the feed ratio, one takes the ratio of the combined enplanements of the most advantaged entrant to the incumbent carrier with the lowest combined enplanements. In this case, it is American's combined enplanements of 374,090 to Republic's combined enplanements of 2,822,759 or 0.13. The most advantaged potential entrant feed ratio is therefore 0.13. Therefore, while American is the most advantaged carrier not currently serving the market, it nevertheless is at an extreme feed disadvantage relative to Republic."

EXHIBIT 4

Cities Served by Republic and Northwest from Minneapolis/St. Paul
Analysis of Potential Entry

(1) Minneapolis/ St. Paul To From	*(2)* Least Advantaged Incumbent	*(3)* First Best Entrant	*(4)* Feed Ratio	*(5)* Second Best Entrant	*(6)* Feed Ratio	*(7)* Other Non-stop Carriers
Atlanta, GA	RC	AA	0.13	UA	0.12	NW, DL, EA
Bismarck, ND	RC	UA	0.09	AA	0.08	NW
Boston, MA	RC	EA	0.72	DL	0.62	NW
Chicago, IL	ML	TW	0.71	CO	0.64	DL, UA, NW, AA, RC
Dallas, TX	RC	DL	1.64	WN	1.10	NW, AA
Denver, CO	RC	AA	0.21	DL	0.17	FL, NW, CO, UA
Detroit, MI	NW	AA	0.20	DL	0.17	RC, PA*a
Fargo, ND	RC	UA	0.10	AA	0.08	NW
Grand Forks, ND	RC	UA	0.09	AA	0.08	NW
Grand Rapids, MI	RC	UA	0.13	AA	0.11	NW
Kansas City, MO	EA	TW	0.54	AA	0.44	RC, NW
Los Angeles, CA	RC	UA	1.05	WA	0.93	NW
Madison, WI	RC	UA	0.10	AA	0.08	NW
Milwaukee, WI	RC	UA	0.12	AA	0.09	NW
New York, NY	RC	EA	2.06	TW	1.36	NW, PE, PA*a,b
Omaha, NE	RC	UA	0.18	AA	0.14	NW
Orlando, FL	RC	EA	0.48	DL	0.38	NW
Philadelphia, PA	RC	AL	0.52	EA	0.42	NW
Phoenix, AZ	RC	HP	0.69	WN	0.29	NW
Portland, OR	RC	UA	0.35	WA	0.13	NW, NW*, CHc,d
Rochester, MN	RC	UA	0.09	AA	0.08	NW, NW*, CHc,d
St. Louis, MO	EA	AA	2.05	UA	1.77	NW, RC, TW, OZ
San Diego, CA	RC	PS	0.36	UA	0.29	NW
San Francisco, CA	RC	UA	1.43	PS	0.62	NW
Seattle, WA	RC	UA	0.59	AS	0.33	NW
Washington, DC	RC	EA	0.70	AL	0.38	NW

Notes:
a The Pan Am listing (PA*) is actually a Republic flight. PA is not counted as an incumbent.
b TWA begins nonstop service on this city pair April 1, 1986.
c This city pair is served by Mesata Aviation (NW*). For this table, NW* was assumed to be part of Northwest.
d Bemidji Airlines (CH) was not used in calculating feed ratios.
Source: U.S. Department of Justice.

I would assume that you would need to serve New York, and I assume you would need to serve Washington, and that you would probably need to serve some Florida point, but beyond that I don't know what other cities you would have to serve to start out with. So what I did was look at what the executives of the two carriers had already done, and I saw which cities they served in common, and I said, well, those must be important cities to serve.

Those routes were, of course, the same twenty-six city pairs that had been the subject of analysis all along. Hurdle's assumption that a hub serving those cities would be viable was, she thought, perhaps overoptimistic: "in fact," she wrote, "both Republic and Northwest operate much larger hubs [at Minne-apolis now], so that entry on a hub basis at this small size may not be profitable."

The DOJ's analysis indicated that construction of a hub of that size was probably not possible within a reasonable time (DOJ used two years as its limit). Hurdle, arguing that "it is unlikely a carrier would build a hub and schedule frequencies such that its competitor has more frequencies than it has on every route," assumed that a viable competitor would offer at least the same number of flights on every route as the smaller of Northwest or Republic then did. That added up to seventy-nine flights. At eight daily departures per gate—a reasonable number, Hurdle thought, based on data from other hubs—the entrant would need ten gates, and something more than twenty airplanes. The gate space was potentially available at the Minneapolis/St. Paul airport, al-

EXHIBIT 5

Cities Served by Republic but Not Northwest from Minneapolis/St. Paul
Analysis of Potential Entry

(1) Minneapolis/ St. Paul To From	(2) Least Advantaged Incumbent	(3) First Best Entrant	(4) Feed Ratio	(5) Second Best Entrant	(6) Feed Ratio	(7) Other Nonstop Carriers
Appleton, WI	RC	NW	1.28	UA	0.09	—
Bemidji, MN	RC	NW	1.28	UA	0.09	CH[a]
Cincinnati, OH	RC	NW	1.23	DL	0.42	—
Columbus, OH	RC	NW	1.25	PE	0.15	—
Des Moines, IA	ZV	NW	510.25	UA	70.25	RC, ZK[b]
Eau Claire, WI	RC	NW	1.27	UA	0.09	—
Green Bay, WI	RC	NW	1.22	UA	0.09	—
Indianapolis, IN	RC	NW	1.22	AL	0.20	—
La Crosse, WI	RC	NW	1.27	UA	0.09	—
Las Vegas, NV	RC	NW	1.16	UA	0.30	—
Memphis, TN	RC	NW	0.74	DL	0.23	—
Minot, ND	RC	NW	1.27	UA	0.09	—
Orange Cty, CA	RC	NW	1.21	OC	0.20	—
Salt Lake, UT	WA	NW	1.36	UA	0.22	RC
Wausau, WI	RC	NW	1.26	UA	0.09	IU[c]

Notes:
[a]Bemidji Airlines (CH) was not used in calculating feed ratios.
[b]Great Lakes Aviation (ZK) was not used in calculating feed ratios.
[c]Midstate Airlines (IU) was not used in calculating feed ratios.
Source: U.S. Department of Justice.

though it would need to be leased from other airlines (almost certainly from the merged carrier) or, most likely, constructed (see Exhibit 7). Hurdle's examination of other carriers' hub formation made her think, however, that it was unlikely an applicant would go within two years from scratch to the 7,110 quarterly departures her hypothetical hub represented. "The only cases where that has occurred are when People Express constructed its hub at Newark and when Republic constructed its two hubs at Memphis and Detroit," she wrote.

In none of those cases was another carrier operating at that hub. All other examples of carriers that established hubs took longer than two years. This suggests both that carriers have not chosen to construct hubs where another carrier has already built a hub and also that in most cases the hub-building process takes longer than two years.

The DOJ therefore recommended that the merger be blocked on the grounds that the transac-

EXHIBIT 6

Cities Served by Northwest but Not Republic from Minneapolis/St. Paul
Analysis of Potential Entry

(1) Minneapolis/ St. Paul To From	(2) Least Advantaged Incumbent	(3) First Best Entrant	(4) Feed Ratio	(5) Second Best Entrant	(6) Feed Ratio	(7) Other Nonstop Carriers
Billings, MT	NW	RC	0.74	UA	0.08	—
Bozeman, MT	NW	RC	0.77	UA	0.07	—
Cleveland, OH	TW	RC	14.25	RC	6.63	TW
Miami, FL	NW	EA	1.28	UA	0.80	—
Spokane, WA	NW	RC	0.72	UA	0.11	—
Tampa, FL	NW	RC	0.71	EA	0.28	—

Source: U.S. Department of Justice.

EXHIBIT 7

Number of Gates by Airline at Minneapolis-St. Paul International Airport

Prime Tenant	Number of Gates	Subleases/Handles
Main Terminal		
Red concourse		
Northwest	12	
Ozark	4	Delta, Continental
Blue concourse		
Eastern	2	
Western	2	Midstate, TWA, People Express
American	2	
United	2	Piedmont
Republic	2	Frontier
USAir	1	
Midway	1	
Green concourse		
Republic	17	
Gold concourse		
Northwest	18	Mesaba
Hubert H. Humphrey terminal		
Joint use	3	
Regional terminal		
Joint use	4	
	70	

Source: Northwest Airlines.

tion would lessen competition in a number of city pair markets, and would likely lead to increased fares or reduced service. It reiterated the position, following the same rationale, in oral arguments presented at the April hearing.

DOT'S REJOINDER

The DOT's Office of the Public Counsel responded to the ALJ in a May 27, 1986 brief. The OPC followed Northwest's and Republic's briefs arguing that combining the two carriers' fleets of airplanes would be good for air travelers. "By melding these complementary strengths, this acquisition could ultimately lead to enhanced competition and more service in the increasingly competitive environment that exists in the U.S. domestic airline industry," the OPC wrote. It disagreed with the DOJ's analysis of the proposed merger in nearly every important detail.

DOT began by taking issue with the DOJ's contention that the relevant market was in nonstop service. "Common sense and the overwhelming evidence in the record conclusively demonstrate that in fact single-plane, rather than nonstop, and on-line connecting services are reasonably substitutable for nonstop service in most of the geographic markets in

this case," it wrote in the May brief. Some who worked on the OPC brief were blunter about the DOJ's position. "I think that's silly," said John Coleman, an ex-CAB staffer who moved on to the DOT's Office of Essential Air Services and helped prepare OPC's position on the merger. "That notion didn't pass our laugh test. What's affected is simply transportation between point A and point B; it's a seat."

Once the department had stopped laughing, it adduced four reasons for considering scheduled air transportation, rather than simply nonstop service, to be the relevant market. One was that, as the DOJ and virtually everybody else concerned with the industry recognized, carriers seemed to be moving away from offering predominantly nonstop service to hub-and-spoke systems based on single-plane or connecting service. "The underlying premise of this efficient way of operating is that connecting service is a viable alternative for nonstop service," OPC wrote, and quoted an expert witness for the merger applicants who had testified at the May hearing that "in an industry as competitive as this one, it is inconceivable that nearly every carrier could be as unresponsive to consumer demand as DOJ assumes." Another was that substantial numbers of fliers use connecting service even on routes where nonstop service is available; the OPC noted the Dallas-Ft. Worth/Minneapolis city pair, where on-line connecting service accounts for 18.6% of the local traffic despite nine daily nonstop and two more single-plane flights, and the Orlando/Minneapolis city pair, where 23.3% of the traffic is on-line connecting. The third was indications that yields—defined as average fares per passenger—on nonstop flights tended to decline when low-cost connecting service was or became available as competition (see Exhibit 8). The OPC cited the Dallas-Minneapolis city pair example in support of the point:

> During the year ended June 1985, three carriers with major hub complexes at either Dallas (American) or Minneapolis (Northwest and Republic) provided frequent nonstop service in the market. Overall average yields for all carriers in this market have dropped steadily since the first quarter of 1984 when Midway began carrying low-yield connecting traffic. Yields for each of the nonstop carriers, on the other hand, did not start declining until the third quarter of 1984 when low-yield connecting traffic appeared for Continental. At that point, yields of the three nonstop carriers also dropped sharply and steadily through the second quarter of 1985. While it is not clear whether improved connecting services, lower fares, or some combination of these two factors has been the competitive spur for this decline in yield, it is clear from this evidence that nonstop and connecting service compete for the same traffic and thus must be considered to be in the same product market.

The OPC also endorsed Northwest's and Republic's submissions that nonstop fares fell towards, or even matched, cheaper connecting fares when connecting service was introduced to a city pair market (see Exhibit 9). This was taken as evidence that both were in the same market, even though a nonstop fare at the same price as a connecting fare could be heavily restricted (conditional on advance purchase, cancellation penalties, or layover demands, or simply not available on many seats).

Finally, the OPC argued that "differences in fares, in and of themselves, do not delineate separate product markets" and that in any case Hurdle had not established anything by her use of the $22/hour calculation. First, OPC said, the $22/hour figure was old and suspect; second, even if she were correct in her contention that passengers would pay more for nonstop flights, she would have to demonstrate further that the premium was not legitimately related to a real difference in service quality (that is, cheap suits and expensive suits are still in the same market). This, said OPC, she had not done.

Having established, to its own satisfaction at any rate, that scheduled air transportation of whatever sort was the relevant market, OPC went on to argue that there was no need for a competitor to establish a hub in Minneapolis/St. Paul because the merged carrier's hub, and the feed associated with it, would confer on it no special advantage. It did so chiefly by looking at several other hubs that were then as, or nearly as, concentrated as Minneapolis/St. Paul would be were the merger approved. Concentration as such—that is, on particular city pairs—was beginning once again to be regarded by industry analysts with some suspicion, since several initial statistical studies of the deregulated industry had raised some questions about the validity of the perfect contestability theory, which had held that potential competition would keep fares down to competitive levels on even the most heavily concentrated routes. "I know of at least five" studies, former CAB chairman Kahn had said in his February congressional testimony, "every one of which concluded that contestability or potential competition has not in fact been as effective as the actual presence of competition." One of the most recent and comprehensive had indicated that new entry by a jet carrier into a previously monopolized route would bring fares down an average of 20%; when two carriers of roughly equal size served the same route steadily—that is, without new entry—fares were kept down 6% relative to monopoly markets.[5] Most of these studies were of the early years of deregulation, however, and said little specific about concentration in the relatively new hubs as opposed to particular routes. The DOT made do instead with what it could get. "[We don't have] the kind of data base that you'd like," said Coleman. "We haven't been able to prove things in the statistical sense, through regression analysis for example, but we did find the analogies."

The analogies came from twenty-four U.S. hubs, notably Pittsburgh, Salt Lake City, and Charlotte, where USAir, Western, and Piedmont respectively had the three most concentrated hubs in the country (USAir had 80% of the enplanements and 78% of the seats offered in Pittsburgh, making it very similar to a post-merger Minneapolis/St. Paul). DOT analyzed load factors—average percentage of seats filled on a carrier's flights—and yields for the hubs. Higher load factors or yields at the three hubs would have indicated that the carriers were taking ad-

[5] Elizabeth S. Bailey, David R. Graham, and Daniel P. Kaplan, *Deregulating the Airlines* (Cambridge, Mass.: MIT Press, 1985).

EXHIBIT 8

Trends in Yield (¢) Nonstop Minneapolis Markets (Large Aircraft Markets)

Miles	Between Minneapolis and	Service[1]	1983 1st Qtr.	1983 2nd Qtr.	1983 3rd Qtr.	1983 4th Qtr.	1984 1st Qtr.	1984 2nd Qtr.	1984 3rd Qtr.	1984 4th Qtr.	1985 1st Qtr.	1985 2nd Qtr.
76	Rochester, Minn.	RC,NW	42.9	43.5	37.7	35.3	41.6	35.4	36.1	36.1	36.9	35.0
85	Eau Claire	RC	47.8	60.6	65.3	59.5	69.5	71.2	68.5	65.0	67.5	65.7
113	Brainard	RC,NW	48.2	48.9	48.3	50.7	48.3	55.0	53.7	48.3	39.1	42.9
120	La Crosse	RC	47.3	47.3	46.5	46.7	50.5	50.1	50.6	53.3	47.1	48.0
144	Duluth	RC	42.8	43.1	42.0	44.8	44.9	44.3	44.3	44.4	44.5	43.7
172	Hibbing	RC,NW	37.0	33.0	30.8	31.3	34.1	33.6	34.6	32.6	33.9	36.6
182	Wausau	RC	27.2	27.4	30.9	31.0	35.6	36.5	37.6	37.6	41.1	35.6
197	Sioux Falls	RC,NW	31.8	34.4	33.4	37.6	27.7	28.0	34.9	38.8	34.9	35.0
199	Bemidji	RC,NW	32.7	31.9	31.3	30.6	31.9	32.3	33.0	32.0	24.2	27.1
223	Fargo	RC,NW,XX	30.7	28.9	24.4	24.1	24.9	25.7	26.7	26.6	26.9	26.4
228	Madison	RC,NW	34.3	37.5	36.7	35.6	35.7	35.5	39.4	42.3	33.7	32.4
232	Des Moines	RC	40.1	39.4	36.8	38.3	37.4	37.5	36.0	33.6	33.9	26.1
232	Appleton	RC	35.6	37.6	37.8	37.9	38.7	38.4	37.0	37.0	36.9	36.4
252	Green Bay	RC	28.8	30.5	30.2	31.0	34.1	32.3	33.5	31.6	37.1	28.8
257	Aberdeen	RC	29.8	31.9	32.7	34.1	33.8	33.0	32.6	33.1	29.7	30.7
282	Omaha	RC,NW	19.4	25.1	27.0	26.7	31.1	31.8	31.0	23.5	29.6	26.5
284	Grand Forks	RC,NW	23.8	23.2	21.4	21.5	22.0	22.7	23.4	35.2	22.9	23.0
297	Milwaukee	RC,NW,XX	29.9	30.1	27.8	25.6	32.4	33.7	32.8	15.9	31.0(ML)	28.0
344	Chicago	DL,ML,NW,RC,UA	19.5	22.1	21.7	24.7	20.9	18.0	16.6	21.9	18.4	21.2
386	Bismarck	RC,NW	21.2	21.0	20.2	19.9	21.0	21.7	22.5	26.1	22.1	20.7
404	Kansas City	RC,NW,XX	17.9	21.5	24.7	24.7	24.5	23.7	26.4	26.3	22.3	14.3
448	St. Louis	RC,OZ,NW,TW,XX	22.0	22.4	22.6	23.8	24.6	24.1	26.7	19.9	22.6(AA)	18.7
449	Minot	RC	21.6	21.5	20.2	20.4	20.8	20.9	20.3	21.7	19.8	17.7
503	Indianapolis	RC,XX	22.8	22.2	24.5	24.6	25.9	25.1	21.4	22.2	18.7	16.9
534	Detroit	NW,RC,XX	21.0	19.9	15.2(ML)	15.8	18.2	18.9	20.0	25.0(ML)	20.8	17.5(PE)
596	Cincinnati	RC,(DL),XX	22.2	22.0	23.1	23.6	25.4	23.9	23.4	22.4	19.7	17.9(DL,PE)
624	Cleveland	NW,(AA,UA),XX	19.9	20.4	18.8	20.5	21.9	22.5	22.0	18.6	20.7	17.8(PE)
627	Columbus, Ohio	RC,XX	20.0	19.0	17.0	20.9	24.6	23.3	21.3	18.6	14.3	13.4(PE)
693	Denver	RC,NW,CO,FL,UA	15.6	17.9	18.0	16.2(CO)	13.7	13.2	12.9	11.3(FL)	11.6	13.0
699	Memphis	RC,XX	20.8	19.5	19.4	19.1	20.3	18.9	19.8	19.4	17.8	13.0(DL)
726	Pittsburgh	AL,(RC),XX	22.6	20.0	18.7	18.3	20.2	19.8	19.8	20.2	16.3	11.0(PE)
748	Billings	NW,XX	15.0	20.1	20.2	20.7	19.5	20.0(UA)	20.8	18.6(FL)	17.9	13.4
859	Dallas	RC,NW,AA,(DL),XX	12.8	14.6	15.9	17.4	17.2(ML)	16.6	15.3(CO)	14.5	14.4	13.2
906	Atlanta	RC,NW,DL,EA,XX	15.3	16.9	17.3	16.8	17.9	17.0	15.8(UA)	15.5	16.3	14.9(AA,DL)

EXHIBIT 8
(continued)

			1983				1984				1985	
Miles	Between Minneapolis and	Service¹	1st Qtr.	2nd Qtr.	3rd Qtr.	4th Qtr.	1st Qtr.	2nd Qtr.	3rd Qtr.	4th Qtr.	1st Qtr.	2nd Qtr.
919	Washington	RC,NW,XX	12.9	13.8	14.2	14.8	16.3	15.1	12.6	13.4	14.0	13.0(DL,PE)
930	Charlotte	PI,(AA),XX	17.9	15.5	16.4	16.7	17.0	16.3	16.7	16.5	18.7	14.1(DL,PE)
985	Philadelphia	RC,NW,(AL,ML),XX	14.6	14.9	14.8	15.7	16.3	16.2	17.8	17.9	17.9	14.4
991	Salt Lake City	RC,WA,(CO),XX	12.7	15.2	14.9	13.8	14.0	13.9	13.3	12.2(FL)	12.4	11.0
1016	New York	RC,NW,PE,(ML),XX	13.9	13.7	13.8	14.8	15.3	11.1	9.0	8.8	9.2	10.9
1046	Houston	CO,(AA),XX	12.0	14.1	15.2	11.6	11.7	11.7	11.3	11.2	11.9	11.5
1124	Boston	RC,NW,(PE),XX	16.7	15.8	16.2	17.2	17.1	13.0	10.5	10.7	10.5	11.5
1175	Spokane	NW,(WA),XX	11.2	12.9	12.9	13.2	15.6	15.0	14.6	10.8(FL)	13.2	10.4
1276	Phoenix	RC,(CO),XX	8.7	11.5	12.9	11.9	11.4(CO)	11.6	11.1	10.2(FL)	9.8	9.7
1300	Las Vegas	RC,(FL,NW),XX	7.9	8.6	9.3	8.7	8.5	9.1	9.5	9.0	10.1	9.6
1306	Orlando	RC,(RC,NW),XX	7.4	8.6	9.6	9.8	10.1	10.6	11.0	10.1(ML)	9.1	9.2(DL,PE)
1311	Tampa	RC,NW,XX	8.0	9.4	11.8	11.5	11.8	12.1	12.0	11.5(ML)	8.2(PE)	9.8
1398	Seattle	RC,NW,(UA),XX	9.4	10.6	11.2	11.4	12.0	11.9(EA)	11.8	10.7(FL)	10.8	9.6
1426	Portland, OR	RC,NW,(CO),XX	9.1	9.8	11.6	12.1	12.2	11.6	11.4	10.5(FL)	10.1	8.9
1526	Los Angeles	RC,NW,(CO),XX	8.7	11.0	11.7	10.8	11.0	11.6	10.0	9.8(FL)	9.7	10.2
1526	Orange County	RC,XX	10.0	13.5	14.5	13.5	13.6	13.9	13.8	11.5(FL)	11.4	11.5
1532	San Diego	RC,NW,(FL,UA),XX	8.0	9.9	10.5	10.3	10.3	10.5	10.3	9.1	9.2	9.0
1587	San Francisco	RC,NW,XX	9.6	10.9	11.5	10.6	11.2	11.5	10.8	9.7(FL)	10.0	9.8

¹Based on June, 1985 OAG. XX indicates on-line connecting services listed. Carriers shown in ( ) have single-plane service with one or more stops. Other carriers shown have nonstop service.

Note: When yield data for a carrier appears for the first time in a given market this is indicated by identifying that carrier in ( ) beside the yield for the applicable period. In almost all instances, this indicates on-line connecting service.

Airline Codes:

UA = United	AA = American	DL = Delta	EA = Eastern	TW = TWA	WA = Western
CO = Continental	BN = Braniff	NA = National	NW = Northwest	AL = USAir	RW = Hughes Air West
FL = Frontier	PA = Pan American	NC = North Central	TI = Texas Int'l	PI = Piedmont	OZ = Ozark
SO = Southern	WN = Southwest	PS = PSA	OC = Air Cal	CL = Capitol	AS = Alaska
PE = People Express	HP = America West	MC = Muse/Transtar	EM = Empire	RU = Britt	HA = Hawaiian
ML = Midway	WO = World	RC = Republic			

Source: U.S. Department of Transportation.

EXHIBIT 9
MSP-DFW

The following is a time chronicle of a fare adjustment in the MSP-DFW market initiated by a connecting service carrier, TWA. This market is serviced by Republic, Northwest, and American Airlines on a nonstop basis.

    June 12, 1985: TW files MRG04IT = $238.00 RT. Comparable fare = $300.00 RT.
    June 15, 1985: OZ files QR = $238.00 RT. Comparable fare = $320.00 RT.
    June 16, 1985: RC files QR = $238.00 RT. Comparable fare = $380.00 RT.
    June 26, 1985: AA files MRG04IT = $238.00 RT. Comparable fare = $380.00 RT.
    June 26, 1985: OL files BR = $238.00 RT. Comparable fare = $380.00 RT.
    July 1, 1985: UA files MR = $238.00 RT. Comparable fare = $380.00 RT.
    July 19, 1985: NW files VR = $238.00 RT. Comparable fare = $340.00 RT.

These fares require a roundtrip purchase and are capacity controlled. The comparable fares are a gauge to what the passenger could buy using the same restrictions before the new fares were filed.

Notes: RT: roundtrip. TW, OZ, etc. are airline codes. MRG04IT, QR, etc. are fare codes indicating types of restrictions applying to fares.
Source: Northwest and Republic Airlines.

vantage of their concentration by enforcing a lower level of service or maintaining higher prices than carriers elsewhere.

In fact, the load factors of the dominant carriers at the three hubs ranked 11th, 14th, and 19th among the twenty-four (see Exhibit 10). Moreover, according to Randall Bennett, the DOT analyst who did this work, looking at all twenty-four hubs, in city pairs where dominant carriers had direct competition

their load factors were higher than other carriers' at seventeen hubs; in single-carrier markets the dominant carriers' load factors were higher than their own average load factors at only seven hubs (see Exhibit 11). "These data," the OPC wrote, "simply do not show that the dominance of city-pair markets by one carrier because of hub strength has produced a decline in service quality." Yields were broken down according to the length of flights for USAir, West-

EXHIBIT 10
Nonstop Segment Load Factors
Domestic Large Hubs

Third Quarter 1985		Fourth Quarter 1985	
Denver	68.34%	Las Vegas	61.27%
Seattle	66.76	Orlando	60.30
San Francisco	66.73	Phoenix	60.21
Los Angeles	66.26	San Francisco	59.82
St. Louis	63.45	San Diego	59.46
Boston	62.95	Los Angeles	59.36
San Diego	62.95	Dallas	59.22
New York	62.56	Miami	58.69
Chicago	62.30	Pittsburgh	58.49
Las Vegas	62.25	Denver	58.46
Pittsburgh	62.23	Tampa	57.91
Dallas	61.83	New York	57.48
Salt Lake City	61.29	Washington	57.26
Houston	61.05	Boston	57.07
Phoenix	60.71	Houston	56.22
Orlando	59.92	Chicago	55.98
Miami	59.33	Detroit	55.72
Washington	59.01	St. Louis	55.31
Minneapolis	57.90	Philadelphia	55.27
Detroit	57.63	Charlotte	55.07
Philadelphia	56.82	Seattle	55.00
Charlotte	56.41	Atlanta	54.90
Atlanta	56.36	Salt Lake City	54.17
Tampa	55.07	Minneapolis	52.91

Source: US Department of Transportation.

EXHIBIT 11

Nonstop Segment Load Factors
Domestic Large Hubs

	Third Quarter 1985			Fourth Quarter 1985		
	Multi-Carrier Markets	Single-Carrier Markets	Total Markets	Multi-Carrier Markets	Single-Carrier Markets	Total Markets
Atlanta:						
Total	56.07%	58.93%	56.36%	54.69%	56.81%	54.90%
Dominant carrier	54.20	58.01	54.60	54.54	57.02	54.80
Other carriers	58.00	—	—	54.85	—	—
Boston:						
Total	61.65	68.69	62.95	56.44	60.13	57.07
Dominant carrier	57.97	66.67	58.98	59.09	53.85	58.52
Other carriers	62.36	—	—	55.95	—	—
Chicago:						
Total	62.50	59.13	62.30	56.11	53.69	55.98
Dominant carrier	64.80	63.94	64.73	58.18	54.70	57.91
Other carriers	61.70	—	—	54.49	—	—
Charlotte:						
Total	55.86	57.54	56.41	53.05	58.13	55.07
Dominant carrier	58.02	57.54	57.79	58.38	58.13	58.24
Other carriers	53.19	—	—	47.03	—	—
Denver:						
Total	68.73	64.42	68.34	58.42	58.82	58.46
Dominant carrier	69.15	65.59	68.70	59.08	60.88	59.33
Other carriers	68.46	—	—	58.00	—	—
Dallas:						
Total	61.45	65.05	61.83	59.00	60.93	59.22
Dominant carrier	65.15	66.13	65.34	64.28	61.62	63.75
Other carriers	58.03	—	—	53.92	—	—
Detroit:						
Total	57.48	58.58	57.63	55.03	59.91	55.72
Dominant carrier	62.74	58.41	61.47	62.53	59.85	61.75
Other carriers	54.38	—	—	50.24	—	—
Houston:						
Total	61.26	60.26	61.05	56.54	54.99	56.22
Dominant carrier	67.15	65.78	66.79	60.15	56.99	59.37
Other carriers	57.48	—	—	54.13	—	—
Las Vegas:						
Total	63.37	55.87	62.25	61.17	61.60	61.27
Dominant carrier	55.76	59.67	56.63	54.45	60.57	56.21
Other carriers	63.81	—	—	61.41	—	—
Los Angeles:						
Total	66.37	65.52	66.26	59.23	60.16	59.36
Dominant carrier	66.51	60.47	66.08	57.87	64.54	58.30
Other carriers	66.32	—	—	59.63	—	—
Miami:						
Total	59.80	55.61	59.33	58.59	59.38	58.69
Dominant carrier	61.75	57.85	61.04	61.06	62.93	61.35
Other carriers	58.11	—	—	57.93	—	—
Minneapolis:						
Total	57.60	59.37	57.90	51.80	58.97	52.91
Dominant carrier	54.89	58.33	55.34	48.56	56.18	49.31
Other carriers	61.01	—	—	55.62	—	—
New York:						
Total	62.59	61.43	62.56	57.66	51.06	57.48
Dominant carrier	60.06	55.20	60.04	62.15	50.98	62.10
Other carriers	63.01	—	—	56.89	—	—
Orlando:						
Total	59.62	62.00	59.92	59.24	66.51	60.30
Dominant carrier	65.40	47.09	64.81	64.17	46.17	63.67
Other carriers	57.73	—	—	57.32	—	—

EXHIBIT 11

(continued)

	Third Quarter 1985			Fourth Quarter 1985		
	Multi-Carrier Markets	Single-Carrier Markets	Total Markets	Multi-Carrier Markets	Single-Carrier Markets	Total Markets
Philadelphia:						
Total	56.79%	56.95%	56.82%	55.16%	55.79%	55.27%
Dominant carrier	57.37	57.14	57.31	57.61	59.00	58.05
Other carriers	56.96	—	—	54.64	—	—
Phoenix:						
Total	60.99	59.72	60.71	61.45	56.31	60.21
Dominant carrier	66.31	59.40	63.24	63.86	53.76	59.51
Other carriers	59.93	—	—	60.93	—	—
Pittsburgh:						
Total	61.95	62.43	62.23	56.72	59.71	58.49
Dominant carrier	62.26	62.52	62.45	57.89	59.71	59.22
Other carriers	61.61	—	—	55.42	—	—
St. Louis:						
Total	60.32	68.78	63.45	53.88	57.36	55.31
Dominant carrier	63.20	70.11	66.68	55.62	57.85	56.84
Other carriers	57.08	—	—	51.71	—	—
Salt Lake City:						
Total	62.53	60.10	61.29	53.44	54.81	54.17
Dominant carrier	63.63	59.77	61.02	54.90	54.59	54.68
Other carriers	61.51	—	—	52.13	—	—
San Diego:						
Total	63.52	61.25	62.95	60.09	57.45	59.46
Dominant carrier	58.41	56.49	58.02	59.91	55.59	58.99
Other carriers	64.25	—	—	60.11	—	—
San Francisco:						
Total	66.42	68.35	66.73	59.69	60.53	59.82
Dominant carrier	72.21	66.61	71.47	63.22	58.98	62.70
Other carriers	64.10	—	—	58.18	—	—
Seattle:						
Total	66.77	66.72	66.76	55.13	54.08	55.00
Dominant carrier	73.71	50.21	73.25	60.27	45.88	59.96
Other carriers	64.71	—	—	53.50	—	—
Tampa:						
Total	54.42	59.19	55.07	57.18	60.79	57.91
Dominant carrier	58.43	49.59	57.87	64.44	49.18	63.31
Other carriers	53.43	—	—	55.35	—	—
Washington:						
Total	59.36	55.66	59.01	57.55	53.56	57.26
Dominant carrier	57.22	47.58	56.81	56.73	52.02	56.69
Other carriers	59.80	—	—	57.71	—	—
Total Large Hubs:						
Total	61.00	61.31	61.25	56.97	57.98	57.31
Dominant carrier	62.35	59.17	62.10	59.12	56.29	58.94
Other carriers	60.29	—	—	55.71	—	—

Source: US Department of Transportation.

ern, and Piedmont at their major hubs and compared with the yields of all other major airlines. "For both USAir and Piedmont," OPC wrote, "the yields at most mileage blocks are lower, or no more than five percent higher, than the average yields for all major carriers." OPC was silent on Western's yields, which

were consistently higher than average (see Exhibit 12).

The OPC saved its cruellest barbs for DOJ's emphasis on feed and feed ratios, by which it had attempted to demonstrate that a viable competitor would need to establish a Minneapolis/St. Paul hub.

EXHIBIT 12

Average Yield of Hub-Dominating Carriers,[1] Third Quarter 1985

Mileage Block	Total Majors	USAir	Western	Piedmont
0 – 99	54.53¢	—	—	51.26¢
100 – 149	45.10	42.05¢	39.56¢	44.30
150 – 199	32.72	42.75	41.63	35.30
200 – 249	31.38	34.45	22.14	30.46
250 – 299	28.26	27.67	35.19	19.99
300 – 349	25.15	25.27	31.05	25.29
350 – 399	22.65	21.28	28.82	21.66
400 – 449	21.45	21.79	24.07	17.51
450 – 499	19.59	20.06	22.83	15.63
500 – 599	19.83	18.83	22.29	16.37
600 – 699	17.68	16.36	21.13	13.59
700 – 799	15.08	13.50	18.50	14.09
800 – 899	14.44	14.00	13.82	13.71
900 – 999	13.19	13.38	13.34	12.78
1000 – 1499	11.56	12.23	11.54	11.76
1500 – 1999	9.94	9.25	11.06	9.06
2000 – 2499	9.21	10.18	10.38	9.13
2500+	7.57	8.09	8.59	—

[1]These yields are for the dominant carrier in each market. Yields that are five percent or more higher than the average for all the major carriers are underscored.

Source: US Department of Transportation.

"DOJ's feed ratio theory for measuring entry," read one of the section headings in its brief, "is unproven and meaningless." The methodology of calculating the ratios, OPC argued, was irredeemably flawed. Its position mirrored that of MIT economist Franklin Fisher, who had testified earlier on behalf of the applicant airlines:

> Perhaps an example will help here. Republic now serves the MSP-Cincinnati (CVG) city pair. Delta does not, but it does serve Cincinnati-Boston. When I and my family go to visit my in-laws in Cincinnati, we get counted in the "feed ratio" as though we were interested in going to Minneapolis. Such overcounting need not be in the numerator. When one of my colleagues flies Republic to Minneapolis to talk at the University of Minnesota, he or she gets counted in the denominator of the MSP-CVG "feed ratio," even though he or she has no interest whatever in visiting Cincinnati. At the same time, all those people who do have an interest in traveling over the MSP-CVG segment are already necessarily flying Republic. They are counted in the denominator of the "feed ratio."
>
> In a word, the "feed ratio" is a mess. In the example, it tells nothing about the likeli-

hood that Delta will enter MSP-CVG. More generally, it has nothing but its name to recommend it as an index telling us anything about entry.

Further, OPC wrote, if a competitor wanted or needed to create a hub at Minneapolis/St. Paul, the space could be leased or created.

Not, OPC thought, that they would need to do so. Other efficiencies, it argued, "make the establishment of a hub at Minneapolis by a potential entrant unnecessary." Those efficiencies were, in its view, such things as hubs at the far end of Minneapolis/St. Paul city pairs; hubs intermediate to Minneapolis/St. Paul and other cities, which could compete with the merged carrier with one-plane or connecting service (and which DOJ had ignored because of its focus on nonstop flight); and commuter and low-cost airlines. To see how competition might shape up if the merged carrier tried to exploit its new concentration in Minneapolis/St. Paul markets, OPC broke the markets at issue—the twenty-six in which a merger would eliminate the two carriers from competition, plus the twenty-one in which potential competition would be eliminated—down into four groups: six city pairs in which the merged carrier would have a market share of less than 50% and in which there was strong competition from other carriers; fifteen in which the merged carrier would have between 60% and 85% of the market but where there was other nonstop service; nineteen in which there were fewer than 200 passengers a day; and seven in which the merged carrier would have more than 85% of the market and there was little or no other nonstop or single-plane service (see Exhibit 13).

In the six city pairs for which the merged carrier would have less than 50%—markets like Atlanta and Chicago—OPC saw no real issue. In all six there were other nonstop carriers with a hub at the other end-point, several were served by carriers with a hub in between, and there was substantial single-plane and connecting service.

OPC saw little more of concern in the fifteen more concentrated city pairs, markets like Cleveland, Miami, and Las Vegas. In addition to some nonstop service, it wrote, "All have other single-plane or connecting service which attracts a significant amount of traffic. All but two of these cities have at least four carriers that serve both cities with a hub in between to provide feed. . . . The frequent on-line connecting services being offered in these city pairs would provide ample alternatives to passengers should Northwest attempt to raise fares or decrease service."

In all of the nineteen markets with fewer than 200 passengers a day—fourteen of them usually had fewer than 100—the merged carrier would be the sole carrier. Only three had competition at the time of writing, in each case between the merger applicants. Such markets—towns like Grand Rapids, Michigan, and Bozeman, Montana—were generally too small to sustain competition, OPC wrote. This would not mean there would be no competitive discipline, it went on; most of the traffic on those corridors was beyond traffic interested in Minneapolis only as a hub, and almost all the cities had connections to other hubs; still other hubs would or could soon compete for those beyond passengers. Some were close enough to Minneapolis that even bus transit was competitive.

Finally, there were seven city pairs in which the merged carrier would have more than 85% of the market, with little or no extant nonstop or single-plane competition. The Minneapolis/St. Paul-Boston corridor, OPC argued, was a large, 547 local passenger-a-day market, and if abused could easily be served by Delta and/or Eastern, which served both cities and had hubs in Boston. Five other airlines served both cities with hubs in between. Kansas City, Milwaukee, and Omaha were medium-sized hubs served by many carriers; OPC argued that they would fly to Minneapolis if the merged carrier exploited the route.

That left Bismarck, Fargo, and Grand Forks, North Dakota. Since these were small markets with little or no other service, current or potential, OPC had "less confidence than the joint applicants that potential competitive problems would be solved" by other carriers. But noting that the governor of North Dakota was on record as supporting the merger, that Northwest had promised to continue competitive service, and the general, nationwide benefits it expected from the merger, OPC recommended that it be approved.

EXHIBIT 13

Analysis of Cities Served by Republic and Northwest from Minneapolis (Summary)

City-Pair Markets in Which Joint Applicants' Combined Share Will Be Less Than 50% and Other Carriers Provide Alternative Service	*City-Pair Markets in Which Joint Applicants' Combined Market Share Will Be Less Than 85% and Alternative Service Is Available*	*City-Pair Markets in Which Joint Applicants' Combined Market Share Will Exceed 85% and Some Alternative Service May Be Available*	*City-Pair Markets That Generate Less Than 200 O&D Passengers per Day*
Atlanta	Detroit	Bismarck	Grand Rapids
Chicago	Los Angeles	Boston	Madison
Dallas/Ft. Worth	New York	Fargo	Rochester
Denver	Orlando	Grand Forks	
St. Louis	Philadelphia	Kansas City	
	Phoenix	Milwaukee	
	Portland	Omaha	
	San Diego		
	San Francisco		
	Seattle		
	Washington		

Source: U.S. Department of Transportation.

ASSIGNMENT FOR CLASS DISCUSSION

Come to class prepared to advise the administrative law judge whether the Northwest/Republic merger should be approved and why. In developing your recommendation and reasoning, please consider:

1. What are the potential costs and benefits of a merger to the economy as a whole?

2. Do you believe DOJ's contention that nonstop service is a market distinct from single-plane or on-line connecting service? What implications does your answer have for the analysis of this merger?

3. Do you believe DOJ's contention that a viable competitor would have to build a hub at MSP or DOT's contention that hubs are not an important barrier to competition? What implications does your answer have?

4. Do you believe the "contestability" theory applies to airlines? What implications does it have?

Competitive Bypass of Pacific Gas & Electric

In 1986, the world's largest private electric utility was facing the loss of many of its biggest and best customers. The threat came not from conservation, general economic depression, or competing utilities; rather, customers were beginning to self-generate, or operate their own, small scale power plants. According to a report by Pacific Gas & Electric (PG&E), a private utility company serving most of northern and central California:

> A great number of customers [have] already revealed their intention to bypass [PG&E]. If the cogeneration projects already identified were completed, about 6007 million kilowatt-hours (kwh) sales would be lost through on-site generation. This is equivalent to about 9.3 percent of PG&E's [1985] total sales.

Furthermore,

> PG&E estimated the extent to which various classes of its customers would find it cheaper to

generate power on-site than to pay PG&E rates. At present, 28 percent of sales were found to be at risk.

This prospect clearly frightened PG&E management. Not only current revenues were at risk, but long-run revenues as well, since customers who built their own generating facilities might never return to the PG&E system.

The situation also perplexed PG&E's regulators, the California Public Utilities Commission (CPUC). While current rates charged to industrial and commercial customers were clearly high enough to cause some bypass, it seemed that these could be lowered only at the expense of residential customers or the utility's financial health. Moreover, the region's surplus of generating capacity suggested that new power plants would only make a bad situation worse. Indeed, the CPUC was also struggling with an excess supply of third party generation, which utilities were required to buy under standard contracts set forth by the CPUC.

This case was written by Carl Danner, with direction from Professor John Meyer, for use at the John F. Kennedy School of Government, Harvard University. (0987)

COGENERATION ECONOMICS

Cogeneration involves the production of electricity along with heat for use in an industrial process. The thermal efficiency (the amount of useful heat and electricity produced per unit of fuel used) of cogeneration is generally greater than that achievable by producing either electricity or process heat alone. Recognizing this, Congress promoted cogeneration in the 1978 Public Utilities Regulatory Policy Act (PURPA): Utilities were required to pay (their own) full marginal or "avoided" cost to any cogenerator wishing to sell energy. PURPA also required utilities to provide cogenerators with backup electrical service ("standby service").

While avoided cost payments spurred an enormous increase in cogeneration in the late 1970s and early 1980s in California, most independent producers sold their electricity to PG&E and bought it back as needed. However, sharply falling oil and gas prices changed the situation dramatically by early 1986. For many industrial and commercial firms, the cost of cogenerated electricity fell below PG&E's average rates, while PURPA purchase prices (based on oil and gas prices) also fell. It became cheaper to construct and operate a new, small cogeneration facility than to continue to buy PG&E power over existing distribution lines. Further, the relative cleanliness of natural gas—the fuel generally used for self-generation—meant that environmental concerns would probably not limit most cogeneration projects.

Despite this, PG&E was convinced that most, if not all, self-generation would be wasteful. A report outlining PG&E calculations of bypass economics concluded, "that all of the potential bypass is uneconomic since even the lowest [bypass] cost ($.054 per kwh) exceeds PG&E's marginal operating cost . . . of about $.02 per kwh."

PUBLIC UTILITY RATEMAKING

The California Public Utilities Commission had responsibility for setting all rates, or prices, charged for PG&E electricity. This involved a two-step process. First, the CPUC determined PG&E's "revenue requirement" (RR), where:

$$RR = expenses + ROR \text{ (invested capital)}$$

To elaborate, operating expenses included fuel, labor, materials, taxes, depreciation, and so on. To these was added a rate of return (ROR) on invested capital judged adequate to compensate PG&E inves-

tors for the risk of the business. As of 1986, PG&E was allowed to recover its embedded cost of debt and preferred stock (10.38 percent and 9.38 percent, respectively) and up to 15.75 percent on equity (for various reasons, utilities rarely earn their full allowed return on equity). The sum of operating expenses and allowed rate of return on investment represented the total revenues permitted PG&E from sales of electricity.

The second step was "rate design." Roughly speaking,

$$Average\ rate = RR/expected\ sales$$

Sales were forecast for various classes of customers—most significantly, residential, industrial and commercial. The revenue requirement was then allocated among these customer classes. These allocations were always controversial, and usually ended up as a product of economic, equity and political considerations. Specific rates were set based on the expected sales and revenue allocation for each customer class.

Traditionally, residential customers had fared well in this process due to the political impact of residential rate increases. Industrial rates—offered to large firms—were higher, while commercial rates—paid largely by small businesses—were the highest. However, a variety of specialized rate schedules were available for industrial and commercial customers.

NEW GENERATING CAPACITY

As of the mid-1980s, power producers throughout California had a significant surplus of electric generating capacity. While estimates varied, it appeared that the state would need no new generating capacity until the mid to late 1990s.

Several factors had contributed to this surplus. High energy prices and conservation programs had cut demand growth substantially—from 5–7 percent annually in the 1960s to 1–2 percent in the mid-1980s. Four long-delayed nuclear power plants had recently begun operations: PG&E's Diablo Canyon Units 1 and 2 and Southern California Edison's San Onofre Units 2 and 3, totaling about 4000 megawatts (mw). The same two factors—reduced demand growth and new power plants—had created surpluses in the Pacific Northwest and desert Southwest, both connected to California utilities by high voltage transmission lines, or "grids." Furthermore, falling oil and gas prices were making less fuel-efficient, semi-retired generating plants economical to run again.

Finally, California's PURPA alternative generation program had produced an unexpected wealth of new power, which utilities were required to purchase under long-term contracts. By the end of 1985, alternative generators had 2800 mw of power generation on line, and held signed contracts to supply 12,000 mw more (only some of which would materialize). Statewide, 43 percent of such contracts were for cogeneration.

To make matters worse for PG&E, its new Diablo Canyon nuclear plants were the most expensive it had ever constructed: projections put the final cost at $5.8 billion, nearly a third of the company's total assets. Present rates reflected roughly 30 percent of this capital cost, but those rates were in place only on an interim basis.

The CPUC still needed to review the plants' construction costs; only those judged "prudent" would be allowed in rates. Several well-publicized mishaps had delayed the plants' construction and dramatically raised their cost. (Most notably, PG&E installed the Diablo Canyon plant's earthquake reinforcements backwards and had to rip out and reinstall them.) The CPUC's Public Staff Division was expected to recommend a substantial penalty—possibly as much as $3 billion—for "imprudence." PG&E insisted that all construction expenditures had been prudent.

The previous summer, the Public Staff Division, PG&E, and various consumer groups had negotiated about a "value of service" alternative to a prudency review for Diablo Canyon. Under this scheme, the utility would be paid for the power a plant produced—negotiations had centered around a rate of 7 to 9 cents per kilowatt-hour—and the CPUC would not guarantee any particular level of cost recovery. However, the subsequent drop in oil and gas prices had reduced the value of the fuel savings that the nuclear plants would create. Consequently, it was expected that the Public Staff Division would try to drive a much tougher bargain.

The alternative for PG&E and the CPUC, of course, was to conduct the prudency review and live with the outcome. Future rates depended on both Diablo Canyon and trends in fossil fuel prices; while much was uncertain, PG&E expected at least a 1–2 percent real annual increase in average rates for the foreseeable future.

In late 1986, as the time for a decision approached, PG&E and the CPUC considered this range of problems. The regulators worried about the efficiency of bypass and the potential impact on residential ratepayers. To these concerns, PG&E added the prospect of creating entrenched competitors and, in turn, failing to recover its investments in providing electric service.

ASSIGNMENT FOR CLASS DISCUSSION

Come to class prepared to explain whether you think the CPUC should continue to encourage cogeneration or, as PG&E has requested, discourage the practice. In formulating your position please consider:

1. What are the major arguments in favor of encouraging cogeneration? What are the major arguments against encouraging cogeneration?

2. Use the evidence from the case to evaluate these arguments in the case of PG&E.

3. What avoided costs rates should PG&E pay to cogenerators? Would your answer change if you expected a surge in demand for electricity?

EXHIBIT 1

PG&E Balance Sheet (EOY; $000)

	1985	1984
Assets:		
Utility plant	$16,199,897	$11,746,267
Construction work in progress	2,850,443	5,464,519
Total utility plant	$19,050,341	$17,210,786
Accumulated depreciation	(4,540,542)	(4,073,454)
Nuclear fuel	423,873	437,492
Net utility plant	$14,933,671	$13,574,824
Investments in subsidiaries	294,774	295,328
Special funds	67,892	29,189
Other property and investments	19,952	11,748
Total other property and investments	$382,618	$336,265
Working funds and cash	$330,051	$ 47,793
Customer accounts receivable	721,606	705,197
Other receivables	260,030	200,228
Fuel stock	257,405	290,431
Plant material and oper. supplies	147,376	102,324
Gas stored underground	329,205	347,822
Prepayments	156,638	148,426
Miscellaneous	385,224	418,018
Total current and accrued assets	$2,548,804	$2,260,239
Deferred debits	$667,714	$451,999
Total assets	$18,571,538	$16,623,327
Liabilities:		
Common stock issued	$1,686,741	$1,584,542
Preferred stock issued	1,679,951	1,687,451
Premium on capital stock	1,879,527	1,607,597
Other paid-in capital	4,341	4,341
Discounts on capital stock	(7,796)	(7,796)
Capital stock expense	(85,850)	(85,179)
Retained earnings	2,365,785	2,115,444
Unappropriated undistributed subsidiary earnings	244,727	224,597
Total proprietary capital	$7,767,426	$7,130,997
Long-term debt	$ 7,101,328	$6,225,424
Capital leases	$360,396	$392,426
Provision for injuries and damages	92,678	94,431
Total other noncurrent liabilities	$453,074	$486,857
Notes and accounts payable	$1,133,759	$1,060,136
Accrued taxes, dividends, interest, etc.	503,861	477,747
Total current and accrued liabilities	$1,637,620	$1,537,883
Deferred investment tax credits	$502,990	$397,631
Deferred income taxes	904,887	571,538
Other deferred credits	204,674	270,616
Total deferred credits	$1,612,551	$1,239,785
Total liabilities	$18,571,999	$16,620,946

Source: California Public Utilities Commission.

EXHIBIT 2
PG&E Income Statement ($000)

	1985	1984
Total company		
Operating revenues	$8,150,552	$7,479,718
Operating expenses		
Operation expenses	5,254,001	5,033,406
Maintenance expenses	309,358	285,480
Depreciation expense	502,667	404,463
Amortization of various losses	1,871	31
Taxes other than income taxes	162,227	132,887
Income taxes—federal	147,707	92,359
other	94,508	62,970
Provision for deferred inc. taxes	300,273	371,354
Provision for deferred income taxes—cr.	(28,586)	(6,908)
Investment tax credit adj.—net	116,879	92,608
Gains from disposal of util. plant	—	(3)
Losses from utility plant	—	5
Total utility operating expenses	$6,860,905	$6,468,652
Net utility operating income	$1,289,647	$1,011,066
Electric Operations Only ($000)		
Operating revenues	$5,822,572	$5,158,530
Operating expenses		
Operation expenses	$3,501,926	$3,271,737
Maintenance expenses	266,048	245,129
Depreciation expense	399,640	310,163
Amortization of various losses	1,871	31
Taxes other than income taxes	130,833	102,605
Income taxes—federal	(44,456)	(62,560)
other	43,969	25,040
Provision for deferred income taxes	397,504	408,806
Provision for deferred income taxes—cr.	(28,525)	(6,886)
Investment tax credit adj.—net	96,844	82,893
Gains from disposal of util. plant	—	(3)
Losses from utility plant	—	5
Total utility operating expenses	$4,765,654	$4,376,960
Net utility operating income	$1,056,918	$ 781,570

Source: California Public Utilities Commission.

EXHIBIT 3

Electric Sales, Revenues and Fuel Costs (Million Kwh, $000)

	1985	*1984*	*1983*	*1982*	*1981*
Residential					
Sales	21,068	20,730	19,779	19,107	19,575
Revenues	$1,659,401	1,400,148	1,192,997	1,401,267	1,128,851
Customers	3,224,837	3,161,430	3,097,264	3,056,448	3,016,632
Commercial					
Sales	21,453	20,627	19,259	18,662	18,723
Revenues	$1,952,531	1,580,192	1,326,406	1,530,542	1,233,564
Customers	385,499	376,521	365,725	358,146	351,997
Industrial					
Sales	17,042	16,109	14,987	15,844	16,402
Revenues	$1,381,346	1,105,750	914,786	1,078,493	860,577
Customers	1,194	1,118	1,065	992	920
Other					
Sales	5,165	5,868	5,986	6,833	6,969
Revenues	$427,696	380,984	335,840	461,207	400,510
Customers	113,358	113,014	112,239	112,478	112,543
Regulatory					
Balancing accts.	$300,967	567,948	87,545	(687,171)	204,964
Avg. fuel cost					
($/mBtu)					
Natural gas	$4.38	5.40	5.38	5.07	4.21
Fuel oil	$4.69	6.04	6.33	6.26	5.85
wtd. avg.	$4.39	5.40	5.43	5.10	4.47

Source: California Public Utilities Commission.

EXHIBIT 4

PG&E Electric Plant

Generation	*Hydro*	*Gas and Oil*	*Geothermal*	*Nuclear*	*Purchased*
Capacity (mw)	3694	7790	1135	1073[a]	2931
1985 Output[1] (mkwh)[2]	11,372	25,897	8456	6528	24,771
1985 O&M ($ 000)	$37,199	— 504,983 —		46,409	—
1985 Fuel ($ 000)	$0	1,433,311	346,281	48,314	—
Cost of purchases ($ 000)					$718,967
Original cost of plant ($ 000)	$1,818,962	— 2,014,821 —		3,238,425	
Depreciation to date ($ 000)	$342,827	— 784,724 —		72,037	

[a]Not including Diablo Canyon Unit 2, approximately 1073 mw, at $2.1 billion original cost.

Transmission	$1,452,066	original cost
	474,376	accumulated depreciation
Distribution	$4,345,501	original cost
	1,501,730	accumulated depreciation

[1]Output exceeds sales (see Exhibit 3) due to power lost in transmission and generation.

[2]Million kilowatt hours.

Source: California Public Utilities Commisssion.

EXHIBIT 5

Selected PG&E Residential Rates

Tier	Basic I	Basic II	Basic III	Electric Heat I	Electric Heat II	Electric Heat III
Summer	0–358 kwh	359–622	623+	0–661	662–1056	1057+
Winter	0–339	340–569	570+	0–1191	1192–1890	1891+

Tier I: $.06976/kwh   Tier 2: $.09069/kwh   Tier 3: $.11789/kwh

Example: An electric heating customer uses 1200 kwh in summer. He pays:

$$661 \text{ kwh} \times \$.06976 = \$46.11$$
$$395 \text{ kwh} \times \$.09069 = 35.82$$
$$144 \text{ kwh} \times \$.11789 = \underline{16.98}$$
$$\text{Total bill} \quad \$98.91$$

1. Customers with installed electric heat pay electric heat rates; all others pay basic rates.
2. For electric rates purposes, California is divided into ten different climate zones, each with different quantities of consumption within each rate tier. For simplicity, the above figures are simple averages of the number of kwh contained in each tier (for all climate zones).
3. PG&E employees receive a 25 percent discount.

Source: California Public Utilities Commission.

EXHIBIT 6

Selected PG&E Commercial and Industrial Rates

Rate	Service Charge	Per Kwh	Peak	Partial Peak	Off Peak	Min. Bill	Demand Charge per Kw[1]
A-1	$1.50	$.09971	—	—	—	$1.75	—
A-10[2]	—	.08569	—	—	—	750.00	1.70
A-18[3]	715.	—	.07148	.06744	.05814	—	—
A-21[4]	20.	—[5]	.13220	.07806	.06562	—	1.70
		—[6]	.10759	.08277	.07404	—	1.70
A-22[7]	20.	—[5]	.11288	.09255	.06423	—	1.70
		—[6]	.10810	.08316	.06950	—	1.70
AS-18[8]	—	.04759	—	—	—	—	—
AS-23[9]	—	.06057	—	—	—	—	—
S-1[10]	—	.80/kw[11]				5.00	
		1.00/kw[12]				5.00	

	Summer May 1 – Sept. 30	Winter Oct. 1 – Apr. 30	
On peak	12:30 pm – 6:30 pm	4:30 pm – 8:30 pm	M–F ex. hol.
Partial peak	8:30 am – 12:30 pm	8:30 am – 4:30 pm	M–F ex. hol.
	6:30 pm – 10:30 pm	8:30 pm –10:30 pm	M–F ex. hol.
	8:30 am – 10:30 pm	8:30 am – 10:30 pm	Sat. ex. hol.
Off peak	10:30 pm – 8:30 am	10:30 pm –8:30 am	M–S ex. hol.
	All day	All day	Sundays and holidays

[1]Based on maximum kilowatt demand each month; measured over 15 minute intervals.

[2]Available at customer option if customer's maximum demand is less than 500 kw; for customers otherwise on A-1.

[3]For high voltage customers of at least 500 kw demand, willing to be interrupted up to 40 times per year up to 8 hours each time, with 10 minutes notice. Total capacity available for both A-18 and AS-18 is limited to 300,000 kw.

[4]Mandatory for customers with demand more than 500 kw but less than 1000 kw.

[5]Summer.

[6]Winter.

[7]Mandatory for customers with 1000 kw or more demand.

[8]Interruptible rate available only to large California steel producers per State law.

[9]Firm rate available only to large California steel producers per State law.

[10]Standby rate, based on capacity. To be paid in addition to applicable tariff for energy used.

[11]For a cogenerator.

[12]For non-cogenerators.

Source: California Public Utilities Commission.

EXHIBIT 7

Fuel Prices

	1986	1985			
	Jan	Oct	Jul	Apr	Jan
Gas to PG&E[1]	4.00	4.22	4.42	4.82	4.72
Spot gas[2]	2.40	2.40	—	—	—
Gas to cogenerator[3]	$3.6942	—	—	—	—
Oil[4]	21.13	24.18	21.73	25.58	23.38

[1]Average price of natural gas delivered to California electric utilities (dollars per million Btu).

[2]Estimate of price spot gas available to California utilities.

[3]PG&E tariff price for natural gas delivered to a cogenerator (dollars per million Btu).

[4]Low sulfur waxy residual at Singapore (per barrel). Does not include transportation to California.

Source: California Public Utilities Commission

EXHIBIT 8

PG&E Estimates of Bypass Potential, by Industry

Question:

In Exhibit 112 (Response to Issues from Commissioner Duda's Office), PG&E presented estimates of bypass potential based on lists of customers that had revealed their intent to self-generate. Please disaggregate "Total Projected Generation" and "On-site Use" by general types of business such as Refineries, Enhanced Oil Recovery, and other major categories.

Answer:

Five types of business which accounted for 68 percent of "On-site Use" were identified as follows:

Type of Business	On-site Use		Projected Generation	
	mkwh[1]	%	mkwh[1]	%
Refinery/chemical	1,939	32	2,606	7
Enhanced oil recovery	905	15	7,302	21
Hospitals, hotels Schools, office bldg.	336	6	910	3
Paper/lumber	751	13	1,754	5
Food	179	3	4,116	12
All other	1,897	32	18,349	52
Total	6,007	100	35,037	100

[1]Million kilowatt hours.

Source: California Public Utilities Commission.

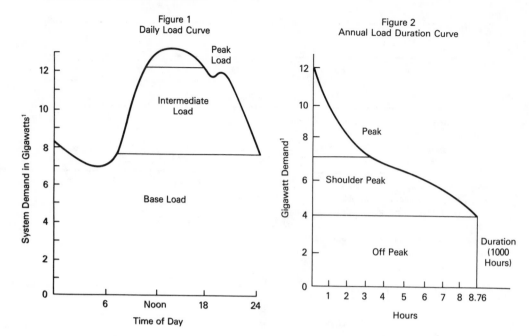

¹Gigawatt = million kilowatts.

EXHIBIT 9

Typical Electric Demand Patterns

¹Gigawatt = million kilowatts.
Source: California Energy Commission.

Figure 1 illustrates a typical California daily load curve. Daily load curves can be summed to yield annual load duration curves, shown in Figure 2. Load duration curves indicate the relationship between constant demand (base) and fluctuating (intermediate and peak) demand. The significance of such distinctions is that electrical generation technologies and fuels vary according to their effectiveness in meeting the various loads. Depending on the unique shape of each curve for a given utility and given time, certain power plants which rely on natural gas may be dispatched only a few hours in a year. Electricity from resources, such as most gas-fired cogeneration, which a utility is contractually obligated to take, then may replace nongas generation at other times of the year.

APPENDIX 1: COGENERATION EFFICIENCY AND ECONOMICS

Cogeneration produces both process heat (for some industrial purposes) and electricity from one fuel (usually natural gas). In thermodynamic terms, cogeneration is usually quite efficient.

Energy inputs and outputs are often measured in British thermal units, or Btu. For cogeneration, thermodynamic efficiency is defined as:

$$\frac{\text{Btus of electricty} + \text{Btus of process heat}}{\text{Btus of fuel used}}$$

Where conventional oil and gas utility plants are only 30 to 35 percent efficient, cogeneration efficiencies of 60 percent or more are often achieved, with some projects approaching 75 or 80 percent.

One kilowatt-hour (kwh) of electricity is equivalent to 3,414 Btu. The heat rate of a generating unit is the number of Btu of fuel needed to produce a kwh of electricity; for a typical utility plant, this figure is 9,500 to 10,000.

A cogenerator can calculate the marginal efficiency of generating electricity given an existing need for process heat, which depends somewhat on the temperature required for the process heat:

Temperature	Heat Rate
371 (F)	5,460
655	6,600
755	7,054
830	7,439

Under some conditions, even lower heat rates can be achieved. Of course, it is also possible to cogenerate less efficiently (with higher heat rates). The

Typical Cogeneration Plant Capacity	Temperature (F)	Application
Less than 20 mw	200–300	Heating and cooling: schools, office buildings, hospitals
20 to 50 mw	200–300	Large heating and cooling
	400	Lumber (wood chip burning)
	600–1,100	Small oil refinery
50 mw or more	105–450	Food processors
	600–1,100	Large oil refinery
	800–1,600	Chemical plant
	500–900	Enhanced oil recovery
	500–1,200	Cement
	1,200	Glass

required temperature for process heat varies depending on its industrial application (see above).

Incremental capital costs for cogeneration range from about $1,200 per kilowatt for a small (5–10) megawatt plant down to about $750 per kilowatt for a 200 mw or larger plant. Cogeneration plants can run up to an 85 percent capacity factor, depending on the need for process heat (which can be day-time only or can extend over two or three shifts for some industries). In addition to the fuel, an additional center per kwh can be expected as an operation and maintenance expense.

Finally, electricity not used by a bypassing customer can always be sold back to PG&E under PURPA rates.

APPENDIX 2: PG&E PURPA OFFERS TO INDEPENDENT GENERATORS

Because PG&E must buy electricity under PURPA, a cogenerator has the choice of selling to PG&E, using the electricity, or some combination of the two (using some and selling the rest).

PG&E pays cogenerators in two ways:

1. An energy payment to cover the fuel savings PG&E obtains by reducing its own production, and

2. A capacity payment to represent the value of the generating capacity provided by the purchased power. Most of these payments apply to summer peak times.

Cogenerators can choose whether to be paid on a time-of-day basis or on an averaged basis (not varying with the time of day).

Capacity payments are the confusing part of this little puzzle. While they are intended to pay for capacity (in other words, the number of *kilowatts* reliably provided by the cogenerator), they are actually paid on a production or output basis (the number of *kilowatt-hours* provided to the utility).

Ideally, a cogenerator would agree to provide capacity to PG&E under a long-term contract, thereby allowing PG&E to avoid the fixed cost of building its own additional capacity in the future. With such a contract, a fixed annual capacity payment (per kilowatt) to a cogenerator would be appropriate.

However, the CPUC has suspended (and is attempting to revise) its process for approving such long-term contracts. Therefore, new cogenerators can only sell electricity on an "as available" basis

Energy Price Offers to Cogenerators (Cents per Kilowatt-hour)

	January 1986	October 1985	July 1985
Non-time-of-day	5.324	6.314	5.551
Time-of-day			
On peak	6.334	7.513	6.423
Mid peak	6.036	6.000	6.000
Off peak	4.569	4.978	4.978

Capacity Price Offers to Cogenerators (Cents per Kilowatt-hour)

	Summer	Winter
Non-time-of-day	.699	.040
Time-of-day		
On peak	6.001	.496
Mid peak	1.138	.060
Off peak	.001	.001

(the utility receives only what the cogenerator chooses to supply, and the cogenerator has no obligation to provide any specific amount of electricity). So, per kilowatt-hour capacity, payments are an approximation of what a cogenerator's supply might be saving PG&E in new construction costs.

One additional complication relates to a subsidy paid from PG&E's electric customers to PG&E's natural gas customers. PG&E sells itself natural gas for use in its own electric generation. However, the price paid by the electric department for gas is far above what the gas department pays to obtain the gas. This intracompany price is then reflected in final utility rates; the result is higher electric rates and lower natural gas rates.

The electric department uses the cost of gas to the company in deciding which generating plants to run at any given time. However, the "avoided cost" cogenerator payments for energy are set based on the price paid by the electric department to the gas department.

Note on Competitive Bypass

The changes in utility industry structure and regulation that occurred during the late 1970s and early 1980s spawned a wide range of new language. Among the most widely used and emotion-laden of these terms is "bypass."

Bypass usually refers to competition with a firm regulated as a franchise monopoly. This competition can take many forms. Large utility customers can self-provide—e.g., through telecommunications links between plants, or on-site electricity generation. As another example, smaller customers may form a consortium to share a common investment. Some regulated firms have assisted their large customers in avoiding other, vertically integrated utility services (such as when a long distance company connects directly to customers, bypassing local telephone company charges).

The firms being "bypassed" typically employ large public networks to provide service (such as local telephone companies, electric, and gas utilities). The customer (or competitor) often avoids the use of existing capacity, instead constructing or acquiring new facilities that parallel those he is no longer using.

Many of the traditional participants in public utility regulation are greatly concerned by bypass, and seek to reduce or prevent it. At first glance, it may appear puzzling that such increased competition would be seen as harmful, as public utility commissions have often sought the efficiency that (at least in theory) is routinely provided by more competitive markets. To understand why, it is necessary to review some of the traditional rationales for public utility regulation along with some of the economics of networks.

THE NATURAL MONOPOLY THEORY

While many rationales have been used to support public utility regulation, the most important has been the theory of natural monopoly.

A natural monopoly is an industry in which economies of scale (and, for multiproduct firms, economies of scope) are so large that it is efficient for a single firm to satisfy the entire market demand for a good or a set of goods (such as electric or telephone service). Since one firm can minimize the production costs of a utility service, the existence of additional firms would be duplicative, or wasteful to society. To avoid this wasteful competition—and to prevent inefficient and unfair pricing—proponents of natural monopoly theory argue for establishing a legal monopoly along with a regulatory agency to monitor utility operations and prices.

In practice, agencies assigned the task of overseeing regulated utilities use a cost of service approach for setting prices, or rates: the utility's revenues are set equal to an estimate of its costs, including a return on invested capital. This "cost plus" approach to rate-setting inevitably reduces the monopolist's incentive for efficient production, a fact often cited by critics of the regulated monopoly as an institution.

Beyond the observation that electric, natural gas and telephone utilities feature large fixed and often low variable costs, there is little or no evidence about whether such firms have genuine natural monopoly cost structures. In theory, a natural monopoly's marginal cost is usually less than its average cost (hence the existence of unlimited economies of scale).

This note was written by Carl Danner, with direction from Professor John Meyer, for use at the John F. Kennedy School of Government, Harvard University. (1087)

Therefore, strict marginal cost pricing does not produce enough revenue to cover the firm's total costs. "Ramsey pricing" is economists' term for the approach that most efficiently makes up for such a shortfall: basically, higher rates are charged to customers with more inelastic demands (although such inelasticities are often unstable, and difficult to measure).

THE FRANCHISE, AND THE OBLIGATION TO SERVE

In return for protection from competition, regulation generally requires the utility to provide service to all who desire it—what's known as the "common-carrier obligation" or "obligation to serve." This arrangement can be thought of as an informal contract between regulator and regulated. The regulator's constituents are assured reliable and available service, while the firm can invest with the assurance of a protected market.

The resulting fixed investments have been enormous by any standard. Utility stocks have been called an ideal "widows and orphans" investment, offering steady if modest dividends and capital appreciation.

These investments have also been long-lived, with many assets depreciated over thirty or forty years. Utility assets are carried on the books at their original cost for rate-setting purposes. Historically, this has often led to significant gaps between the depreciated original cost of old equipment and the current cost of new, replacement equipment. For example, technological change has reduced the current value of some older telephone equipment; on the other hand, hydroelectric power plants are now worth much more than their book value due to increases in the cost of generating electricity by other means. However, explicit asset write-ups or write-offs (to reflect these capital gains or losses) are quite rare under regulation. These changing asset values are another factor affecting the relationship between utility rates and current marginal costs.

FIXED AND VARIABLE COSTS

As noted above, electric, gas and telephone utilities are capital intensive and feature large fixed costs. The need to recover these costs is an important ingredient in the bypass story.

The larger the gap between the utility's marginal cost and average rate, the greater the possible gains for customers who can self-produce at a similar marginal cost. As self-producers decrease their purchases, the utility loses the markup or contribution it made from them. Rates to remaining customers must then be raised to make up those margins, thus encouraging further bypass.

Thus, issues of price discrimination are central for a utility and its regulators. Customers who would bypass at typical rates might stay on the system at a lower rate (above utility marginal cost) that would still produce some utility contribution. In the short run, all remaining customers might be made better off by such selective price reductions to potential bypassers.

However, fixed cost recovery has become a hotly contested equity issue in regulatory proceedings. For example, many residential customers have long resented the lower electric rates paid by industrial and commercial customers for a near-commodity service; they are uninterested in paying more to fund additional "breaks" for business. As a result, consumer advocates have questioned the efficiency of the utilities and the quality of their regulatory oversight. And some regulators make explicit efforts to reduce the markups paid by certain customers in an effort to fulfill redistributive goals.

SHORT- AND LONG-RUN EFFICIENCY

Bypass is both a consequence and cause of excess capacity. To elaborate, when excess capacity exists, economic theory says that it should be utilized at a price close to zero; that's so because idle plant—which is appropriately priced at direct operating costs in the short run—has no opportunity cost. In reality, however, regulators often permit the utility to cover the costs of excess capacity through (cost-based) rates. Ironically, that increases the economic appeal of bypass; bypass, in turn, leads to additional excess capacity, and can even feature marginal costs higher than those of the utility (but, capital and marginal costs considered, still lower than the utility's margin-generating price). Thus, short-run efficiency losses may occur with bypass.

On the other hand, excess capacity is in itself wasteful, and perhaps indicative of utility incompetence. One can also argue that bypass enhances long-run efficiency, because competitive firms (bypassers) will make better investment decisions than will cost-plus regulated utilities. By this logic, eventual needs for new capacity are better satisfied with bypassers in the market; arguments to scuttle bypass on short-run efficiency grounds may ironically miss the broader lesson of how the excess capacity came about. Also, competitive firms may operate more cheaply than regulated utilities, leading even to some short-run savings. Self-production can sometimes be better tailored to a customer's needs, creating a better product than the utility may supply.

In sum, bypass is a complex and controversial development, and the question of whether bypass is efficient or wasteful has no easy answer. The economics of bypass vary from case to case, and from the short run to the long run.

Controlling Acid Rain, 1986

INTRODUCTION

Throughout the first six years of the Reagan administration, the issue of whether to control acid rain had been extremely divisive politically. Acid rain was generally thought to be caused, not entirely but most significantly, by sulfur dioxide (SO_2) emissions from midwestern utilities which were carried by prevailing weather patterns into the eastern U.S. and Canada, and deposited there (acid rain was, technically, "acid deposition," since emissions came down in snow and in gaseous and dry form as well as in rain). (See Exhibit 1.) According to a 1984 General Accounting Office (GAO) report, utilities were responsible for almost 16 million tons of such emissions, or about 67% of the 23.7 million tons of SO_2 emitted in the U.S. in 1980 (see Exhibit 2). According to a 1986 Congressional Budget Office (CBO) study, Missouri, Illinois, Indiana, Ohio, and Pennsylvania alone accounted for over 40% of U.S. annual utility SO_2 emissions. While uncertainty remained as to the exact mechanisms that governed acid rain's formation and transport, and which caused any environmental damage, environmentalists and such prestigious groups as the National Academy of Sciences were in general accord that the phenomenon was real and environmentally significant. Control, however, would have been expensive, and the environmental results uncertain.

The Reagan administration consistently aligned itself with the industry position that without a more detailed understanding of whether and how acid rain was really a problem, regulation would be premature: the president called repeatedly for additional research into the science of acid rain, and on one occasion Office of Management and Budget (OMB) chief David Stockman scuttled an experimental control program proposed by Environmental Protection Administration (EPA) chief William Ruckelshaus on the basis that it would cost $6,000 for every fish saved (see *Ruckelshaus and Acid Rain,* KSG case # C16-86-658.0). The issue was hotly de-

bated in Congress, but with no greater movement than in the administration. There, calls for control pitted midwestern politicians—whose constituents feared bearing the costs, to no personal advantage—against northeastern ones, whose constituents desired control's benefits without noticeable enthusiasm for paying the bill (see Exhibit 3). The result was legislative stalemate.

The administration took the first major step. Ironically, it apparently did so in response not to domestic environmental concern but to pressure from Canada, which had long been deeply concerned over U.S. "exports" of acid rain into its eastern parts. In March, 1985, the president appointed the politically savvy former Transportation Secretary Drew Lewis as special envoy on acid rain. In January, 1986, Lewis issued a joint report with his Canadian counterpart stating unequivocally that acid rain was dangerous. The president himself endorsed the report, reversing his stance that the jury was still out on the issue by calling acid rain "a serious problem."[1] The envoys eschewed immediate regulation and called instead for a joint $5 billion research program on control technology, but the political import of the report, and of Reagan's endorsement, went beyond any formal recommendations; it made favoring doing something about acid rain considerably more politically credible. In particular, as David K. Baker, legislative representative for the League of Women Voters of the U.S., told the *National Journal,* it "gave a lot of Republican members who had been reluctant to embrace acid rain control the freedom to go ahead and do that."

Congress made its own move on May 20, 1986,

[1] Lewis' selection for the job, and the switch in administration policy, became key issues in the influence-peddling scandal that grew around Reagan aide Michael Deaver, who was in the White House when Lewis was chosen but left shortly after to form a private lobbying business with Canada a major client.

This case was written by David M. Kennedy under the direction of Professors José A. Gomez-Ibañez and Joseph Kalt for use at the John F. Kennedy School of Government, Harvard University. (1286)

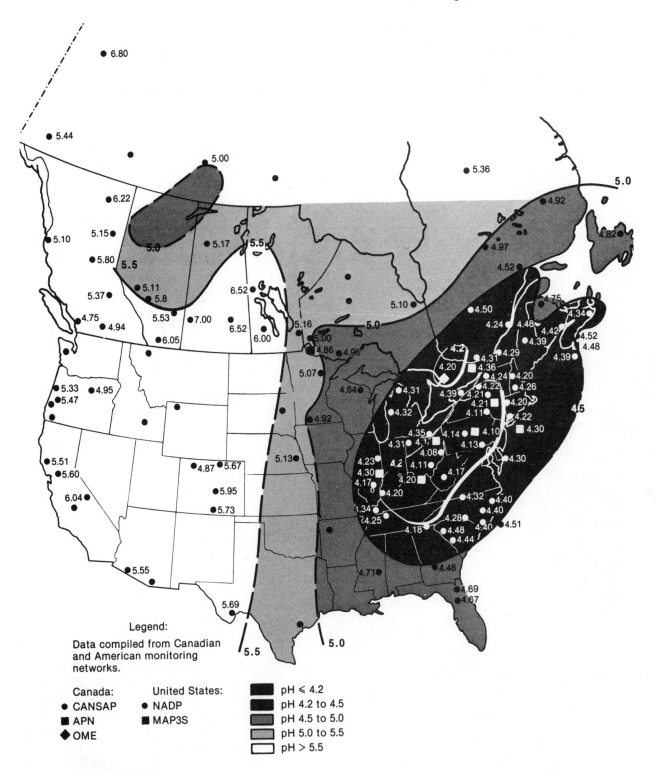

EXHIBIT 1

Precipitation Acidity—Annual Average pH for 1980, Weighted by Precipitation Amount

Note: Acidity is measured in pH units. Decreasing pH corresponds to increasing acidity, but in a nonlinear (logarithmic) way. Across the United States, average annual rainfall pH varies between about 4 and 6. Compared to a pH of 6, a pH 5 is 10 times more acidic; pH 4 is 100 times more acidic; and so on. Referring to the shading, pH 4.2 is twice as acidic as pH 4.5; about 6 times more acidic than pH 5; and about 20 times more acidic than pH 5.5.

Source: Reprinted in *Acid Rain and Transported Air Pollutants: Implications for Public Policy* (Washington, D.C.: U.S. Congress, Office of Technology Assessment, OTA-O-204, June 1984). *Impact Assessment,* Work Group 1, United States-Canada Memorandum of Intent on Transboundary Air Pollution, final report, January 1983.

EXHIBIT 2

Estimates of SO_2 Emissions in the United States, 1940–80

	1940	1950	1960	1970	1980
			(Millions of Metric Tonnes)		
Combustion					
Industry	4.5	4.4	3.3	3.9	2.3
Residential/commercial	3.1	3.3	2.0	1.3	0.8
Transportation	2.9	2.3	0.4	0.6	0.9
Electric utilities	2.2	4.2	7.4	15.6	15.9
Total	12.7	14.2	13.1	21.4	19.9
Smelters	3.3	3.5	3.8	4.1	1.8
Others[1]	1.4	1.9	2.3	2.4	2.0
Total	17.4	19.6	19.2	27.9	23.7

[1]Includes other industrial processes and miscellaneous burning.

Source: National Air Pollutant Emission Estimates, 1940–1980, U.S. EPA Report 450/4-82-001 (January 1982), table 3.

when the House Energy and Commerce Subcommittee on Health and the Environment voted out, 16–9, HR 4567, generally called the Waxman–Sikorski bill. The bill required utilities to limit their SO_2 emissions to 2.0 lbs/SO_2 per million British thermal units (BTUs) of fuel burned by 1993; this amounted to a national reduction of some 8 million tons annually from 1980 levels (a joint U.S./Canadian governmental working group predicted in 1982 that U.S. utility emissions of SO_2 would be 16.4 million tons annually by the year 2000, with total U.S. emissions that year of 26.8 million tons). The bill set a second round of cuts, to 1.2 lbs./SO_2 per million BTU's, amounting to a nearly ten million ton annual reduction, for 1997, unless "Congress enacts legislation providing that such requirements shall not take effect." Emissions were to be calculated on a statewide "bubble" system, meaning that individual plants in the same state could have differing levels of emissions, as long as the state met the required level. Other control proposals had specified that all power plants—old or new, dirty or clean—meet a single emissions ceiling; the bubble system gave state governors, who were accorded the authority to prepare plans for complying with the bill (subject to approval by the EPA's administrator), a free hand to assign different power plants different emissions targets, for theoretically more efficient regulation. Only if a state failed to file an acceptable plan did the bill—under a "default" provision—impose the 1.2 million pounds/SO_2 ceiling on each plant in the offending state. If a control scheme chosen by a state led to more than a 10% increase in utility rates, the bill provided for a subsidy to defray the costs to residential ratepayers, paid for by an eight-year nationwide electricity tax set at 1/2 mill per kilowatt hour (a mill is one thousandth

of a dollar; the average residential rate in 1984 was about $0.076/kwhr). Costs incurred by states under default provisions were not eligible for subsidies.

HR 4567 was widely regarded as the first politically credible piece of acid rain control legislation; by summer of 1986 it had garnered 160 cosponsors and the support of 21 out of 42 members of the Energy and Commerce Committee. Much of this was due to its two-step design. "Our group favors a phased approach that allows you to look at how you're doing environmentally at midcourse to decide if you're going to make the second cut," said Ned Helme, executive director of the Alliance for Acid Rain Control, a coalition of governors and corporate and public interest figures interested in the passage of cost-effective acid rain legislation. "We don't know enough environmentally to know if nine million tons or twelve million tons, or whatever, is the right number; the scientific side is very uncertain. But I'd opt for the lesser number initially because the marginal cost is so much more as you make larger reductions and we don't know that it's worth it." Its passage was by no means certain; among other things, it would have to get through the full Energy and Commerce Committee before floor action would be possible, and the committee's powerful chairman, John Dingell (D-MI), opposed it. Still, the conjunction of the change in the administration's stance and the Waxman-Sikorski bill gave control advocates real hope. "The clock is ticking and the end of this session [of Congress] is nearing," Helme told the *National Journal.* "The tactic of the opponents is to stall, delay the debate, make everything move slowly. The clock is working in their favor, but I think we have a shot at" getting control legislation through both Houses before the end of the session. As a result—whether

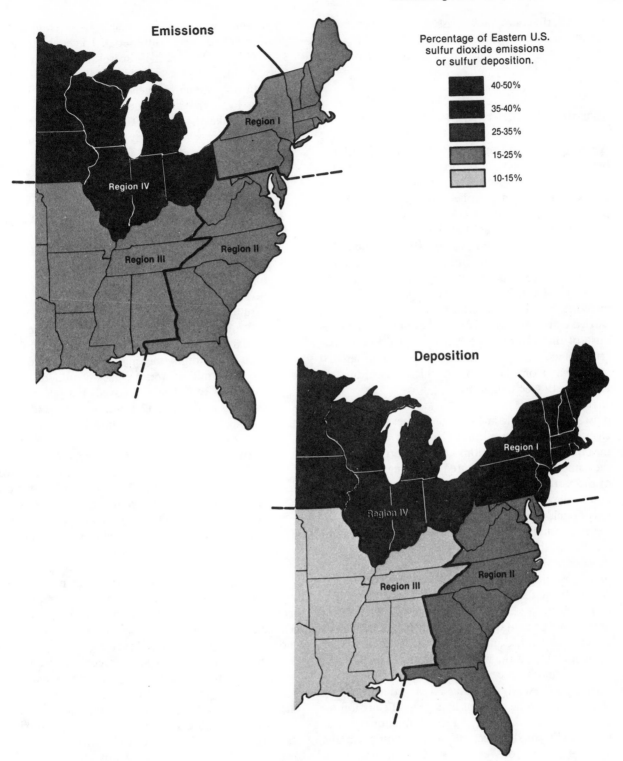

Emissions

Deposition

Percentage of Eastern U.S.
sulfur dioxide emissions
or sulfur deposition.

40-50%

35-40%

25-35%

15-25%

10-15%

Region I

Region IV

Region III

Region II

EXHIBIT 3

1979 Sulfur Dioxide Emissions and Estimated Sulfur Deposition—Percent Contributed
and Received in Four Subregions Covering the Eastern Half of the United States

Source: J. Shannon, personal communication, Argonne National Laboratory and E. H. Pechan & Associates, Inc.,
1982, as reprinted in *Acid Rain and Transported Air Pollutants: Implications for Public Policy* (Washington, D.C.:
U.S. Congress, Office of Technology Assessment, OTA-O-204, June 1984).

the legislation ultimately passed or not—members would for the first time have to grapple with a real accounting of the costs and benefits of controlling acid rain.

GENERATION AND TRANSPORT

According to a 1984 congressional Office of Technology Assessment (OTA) report, SO_2 emitted into the atmosphere can return to the ground quite quickly or can remain in the atmosphere, being carried east by prevailing winds, for a week or more (another concern about utilities was that they had been encouraged by the 1970 Clean Air Act to avoid polluting their immediate surroundings by building very tall smokestacks to disperse emissions over a large area; smokestacks which seemed almost made to order for injecting SO_2 into the atmospheric currents which carried emissions east). The OTA estimated that one-third of the sulfur compounds deposited in the eastern United States come from sources more than 300 miles away from the region in which they ultimately fall to earth (see Exhibit 4).

Sulfur emissions as such are not acidic; they must first be transformed, by one of several complex chemical routes, to sulfuric acid. This can occur in the atmosphere as emissions are transported (in much the same way smog is created) or along the surface of the earth after sulfur compounds are deposited in non-acidic form. While the chemical and physical details of acid formation from sulfur emissions are extremely complex, there is a general scientific consensus that, as the GAO put it, "on the average, regional [acid] deposition would be reduced essentially proportionally to decreases in regional SO_2 emissions. . . . A percentage decrease of SO_2 emissions applied uniformly over Eastern North America is likely to result in the same percentage reduction of [acid] deposition throughout the region." At the same time, the GAO made it clear that the weather patterns that transport acid rain and its precursors were so complex that it wasn't clear exactly how any given region receiving acid rain would be affected by a general emission reduction: across the eastern U.S., reductions in acid rain would equal reductions in emissions, but the acid rain reductions could be very unequal from place to place.

THE COST OF CONTROL

There was no question that utilities could in fact reduce emissions considerably. To get low and moderate levels of reduction, they could burn low-sulfur coal, which was readily available if generally more expensive than higher-sulfur coal. To get either moderate or quite high levels—up to around 12 million tons of SO_2/yr—they could install devices called "scrubbers" which cleaned smokestack gas before venting it to the atmosphere (newer coal-burning plants regulated under 1977 amendments to the Clean Air Act were already required to use scrubbers). The capital-intensive scrubbers were generally more expensive still. The most basic fact governing the cost of control was that it rose steeply at higher levels of SO_2 reduction, particularly if scrubbers were used. Looking at one simple reduction scheme very similar to Waxman–Sikorski, the CBO said that

> the results show costs would be $270 per ton of SO_2 abated at the 8 million ton rollback level . . . rising to $360 per ton at the ten million ton rollback level, and reaching $779 per ton at the 12 million ton rollback level. In fact, the marginal cost of achieving an additional 2 million ton reduction by moving from an 8 million ton to a 10 million ton rollback would be about $720 per ton of SO_2 removed. Further increasing this rollback to 12.1 million tons would cost about $2,775 for each additional ton abated.

> Costs would rise much more steeply at the stricter levels of SO_2 control because switching to low-sulfur coal—a relatively cost-effective option at [the 8 and 10 million ton] reduction levels—would be supplanted by scrubber use as control targets became more ambitious. In effect, scrubber use would become mandated at high levels of emission reduction.

There was no environmental difference between the two approaches: fuel-switching and scrubbing could both attain the reductions Waxman–Sikorski called for. There was a very significant structural economic difference, however: fuel-switching would cost mining jobs in high-sulfur coal fields, which were concentrated in Illinois, Indiana, Ohio, and Pennsylvania, and shift them to low-sulfur fields, largely in West Virginia, Wyoming, and Colorado. According to the CBO report, a 10 million ton/year SO_2 reduction met entirely through fuel switching would eliminate almost 22,000 jobs in the four states, relative to a projected no-regulation 1995 base case (the 1995 base case represents 275,172 mining jobs nationwide, substantially more than 1985's 207,992 jobs). West Virginia, Wyoming, and Colorado would gain 19,777 jobs, more than 16,000 of them falling in West Virginia alone. When the effects for all mining states were summed, almost 7,000 mining jobs were lost nationwide, largely because low-sulfur coal is

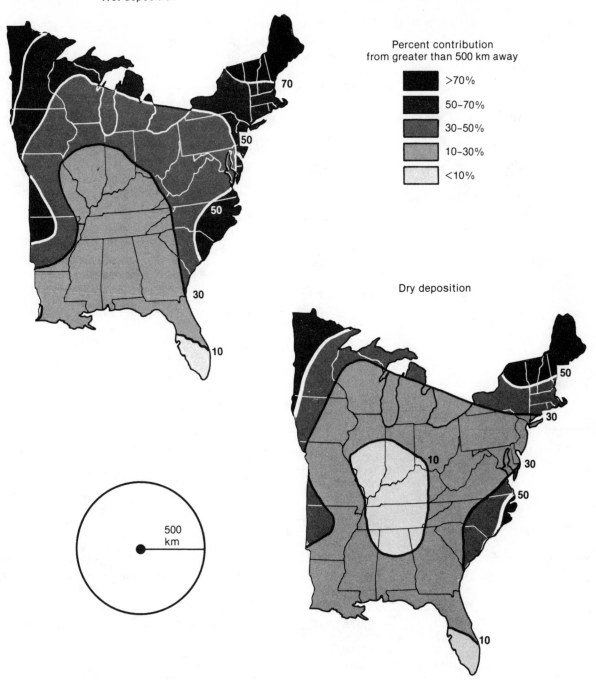

Wet deposition

Dry deposition

Percent contribution
from greater than 500 km away

>70%

50–70%

30–50%

10–30%

<10%

500 km

EXHIBIT 4

Estimated Percentage of Sulfur Deposition from Emissions over 500 km (300 Miles) Away (Summer 1980)

Source: J. Shannon, personal communication, Argonne National Laboratory, 1982, as reprinted in *Acid Rain and Transported Air Pollutants: Implications for Public Policy* (Washington, D.C.: U.S. Congress, Office of Technology Assessment, OTA-O-204, June 1984).

often surface mined, which is less labor-intensive than tunnel-mined coal (see Exhibit 5). Relying heavily on low-sulfur coal would still end up costing more than the current mix of fuels. The additional demand for low-sulfur coal would drive prices up, and the coal would often have to be transported long distances. (Coal prices vary widely across the country; according to the Edison Electric Institute, a national utility group generally opposed to acid rain regulation, low-sulfur coal presently commands a price premium of $3–6/ton over high-sulfur coal. Transporting low-sulfur coal from western coal fields to midwestern utilities can double its price.) Moreover, much western low-sulfur coal has a lesser heat content than other coals, and some utilities would have to both buy more and invest in boiler modifications in order to burn it.

The 1977 Clean Air Act amendments, which set emissions targets for new power plants at roughly the same level as Waxman–Sikorski's default option, had required that they be met with scrubbers instead of fuel switching in order to prevent unemployment in high-sulfur states. Many pre-Waxman–Sikorski acid rain control proposals—including an earlier Waxman bill—had followed suit. The CBO analyzed the effect of such provisions by looking at the impact, in 1995, of a 10 million-ton SO_2 reduction with 80% of 1985 coal purchases maintained, a picture compatible with a plan that relied mainly on scrubbers. The cost per ton of SO_2 removed jumped to $528, with considerable preservation of jobs in high-sulfur coal producing states.[2]

The subsidy Waxman–Sikorski provided to de-

[2] The CBO study actually showed fairly large national mining job losses relative to the 1995 base case (the losses were much less severe in high-sulfur coal producing states), but when pressed were inclined to dismiss the losses as a modelling aberration.

EXHIBIT 5

Coal Mining Employment Changes as of 1995 under 10 Million-Ton SO_2 Coal Switching Rollback, by Coal-Producing State

State	Number of Jobs			Difference from 1985		Difference from 1995
	Base Case 1984	Base Case 1995	Under Rollback	Base Case 1995	Under Rollback	Base Case Under Rollback
Alabama	9,077	8,124	7,543	−953	−1,534	−581
Arizona	855	1,177	1,155	322	300	−22
Colorado	2,927	3,288	4,062	360	1,135	775
Illinois	16,228	14,733	9,823	−1,495	−6,405	−4,910
Indiana	6,694	5,342	3,611	−1,352	−3,083	−1,732
Iowa	136	344	110	208	−27	−234
Kansas	306	753	129	447	−177	−624
Kentucky	47,753	63,014	59,098	15,261	11,345	−3,916
Maryland	923	695	417	−228	−505	−278
Missouri	1,348	1,948	1,276	600	−72	−672
Montana	1,209	1,251	955	42	−254	−296
New Mexico	1,741	2,846	2,846	1,104	1,104	0
North Dakota	1,570	1,375	1,374	−195	−196	−1
Ohio	9,797	7,136	1,183	−2,662	−8,614	−5,953
Oklahoma	1,377	2,344	2,146	967	770	−197
Pennsylvania	23,134	29,299	20,042	6,165	−3,092	−9,257
Tennessee	2,685	2,010	1,859	−675	−826	−151
Texas	2,851	6,890	6,854	4,039	4,004	−36
Utah	3,283	7,978	8,282	4,695	4,998	304
Virginia	16,803	19,339	21,375	2,536	4,572	2,036
Washington	426	48	48	−378	−378	0
West Virginia	50,893	89,473	105,792	38,580	54,899	16,319
Wyoming	5,975	5,768	8,451	−207	2,476	2,683
U.S. Total	207,992	275,172	268,431	67,181	60,439	−6,741

Source: Data taken from *Curbing Acid Rain: Cost, Budget, and Coal-Market Effects* (Washington D.C.: U.S. Congress, Congressional Budget Office, June 1986).

fray possible increases in residential electric rates was intended expressly to allow states to choose to protect high-sulfur coal mining by mandating scrubbers rather than fuel-switching, with the country as a whole footing the bill. Given that four of the five high-utility-emissions states—Illinois, Indiana, Ohio, and Pennsylvania, or all but Missouri—were also high-sulfur-coal producing states, it was entirely possible that some or all would avail themselves of the option. Estimating the bill's cost was greatly complicated by the latitude allowed states to decide how to comply; several studies were available, but their different assumptions gave markedly different results.

The CBO report already mentioned, for instance, looked at two possibilities based on Waxman–Sikorski: that each state met its "bubble" requirement, by the least costly method; and that all states were forced to meet the requirements of the "default" provision of the bill, again by the least costly method (the CBO study was based on coal market and utility models unable to accommodate Waxman–Sikorski's phased reduction scheme; instead it simply assumed all changes were made by 1995). In either case, CBO found, "virtually all of the reductions [in emissions] obtained . . . would occur as a result of utilities' switching to lower-sulfur coal." The report did not present its calculations of the amount, or cost, of such fuel switching, giving only aggregate bottom-line numbers: the bubble option cost $25.9 billion, 1986–2015, at $299 per ton of SO_2 removed; the default option $34.9 billion, at $368 per ton of SO_2 removed.[3] Electricity rates under the bubble option would generally rise from 2–4%, with only Utah breaking the 10% subsidy barrier. Under the default option rates tended to increase 3–6%; Wisconsin hit 11%, and West Virginia 23%. The rate figures were statewide averages, however, and not calculated for individual utilities.

Not all analysts were so sanguine. The Edison Electric Institute made a much different case with an evaluation of Waxman–Sikorski prepared by Temple, Barker, and Sloane, Inc. (TBS), a Massachusetts consulting firm. It was difficult to compare the TBS findings directly to the CBO's, since the two compared somewhat different options based on different financial and implementation assumptions, but there were indications from TBS that the legislation could be far costlier than the CBO thought. The key difference was TBS's prediction that many utilities would

be forced to or would choose to comply through scrubbers rather than fuel switching. According to TBS researcher Annette Hulse, some boiler designs in common use were not suitable for burning low-sulfur coal; moreover, said Hulse, when utilities could anticipate thirty years or more of operation from a power plant, the capital costs of installing scrubbers became less than the variable costs of fuel switching.

TBS calculated post-compliance rates for each U.S. utility, and predicted that the effect on utilities utilizing scrubbers could be profound. Kentucky Power Company, for example, was a utility with two generators that was predicted to comply with the bill by fitting a scrubber to the larger of them (the TBS analysis allowed intrautility bubbling, but not—as Waxman–Sikorsky did—intrastate bubbling). Fitting and operating the scrubber was anticipated to force Kentucky Power Company to raise residential rates more than 30%. Moreover, TBS interpreted the Waxman–Sikorski subsidy provisions to apply only to the costs of compliance-related debt financing; TBS argued that for no utility would such financing cause more than 10% of even large rate increases, and that the subsidy would thus not defray any part of control's cost to utility customers.

The Congressional Research Service (CRS) issued a prompt rejoinder to the TBS analysis, arguing that the utility-sponsored work did "not take advantage of the flexibility or the opportunities for cost-effective or imaginative responses provided by HR 4567." Looking specifically at the Kentucky Power Company example, CRS argued that the scrubber TBS assumed would be used on the larger generator—one which treated all of the generator's smokestack gas, at 90% efficiency—would remove more than half again as much SO_2 as required under Waxman–Sikorski, and that because the TBS analysis forbade intrastate bubbling the possibility that Kentucky Power Company might sell the resulting emission credit to a dirty utility was ignored out of hand. If the utility scrubbed only the amount of smokestack gas necessary to meet the Waxman–Sikorski target, CRS argued, the first-year rate increase would be only 10.4%, and "levelized" over twenty years only 4.0%. Moreover, CRS argued, there was no reason the utility could not meet its targets by fuel switching, with rate increases of 7.8% the first year and 6.5% over twenty years. TBS stuck by its work. "We did an aggregate, nationwide analysis," Huse said. "For individual plants, we may well have been off one way or another. Those mistakes will balance out; at a national level we did a really good job."

---

[3]All CBO cost estimates are the present value of the sum of annual utility costs incurred over the 1986–2015 period, using a real discount rate of 3.7%, and are presented in 1985 dollars.

DAMAGES

Almost coincidentally, a new assessment of the economic impact of acid rain became available at roughly the same time Waxman–Sikorski became a live political issue. The federal National Acid Precipitation Assessment Program (NAPAP), begun in 1980 under EPA auspices and carried out largely by academic and consulting-firm scientists and economists, was intended to be the first comprehensive look at the economic impact of acid rain-related damages in four areas: commercial agriculture, forests, recreational fishing, and selected types of materials. A preliminary round of assessments had been made in 1985, with a second round—to build on and refine the first—due in 1987, and a "final round scheduled for 1989. Early versions of the 1985 findings were circulating as the debate on Waxman–Sikorski developed.

As NAPAP participants were quick to point out, the assessment program was far from being either definitive or comprehensive. As one preliminary summary of the 1985 work put it,

> Several comments about the extent of coverage in each of . . . [the four damage assessment] areas are necessary. First, the treatment of economic damages in each of these areas is confined largely to the economic agents who actually use the services provided by the resources at risk in a particular receptor system, such as fishermen, timber owners, anglers and homeowners. The analyses do not take into account damages to non-users who would, in fact, be willing to pay some amount of money to preserve resources at risk for their own future use or for future generations. Second, only damages in the United States were evaluated. Finally, the ancillary [health and environmental] effects which the precursors of acid deposition may have . . . have also been omitted. . . . [citations omitted]

AGRICULTURE

This was not to say that the NAPAP research didn't contain some interesting revelations. Chief among them was the idea that acid rain might actually be good for farmers, unless they grew soybeans. According to controlled NAPAP field experiments only soybeans, and of soybeans only certain strains, were injured by acid rain: corn, wheat, and other crops seemed unaffected. Furthermore, crops need nitrogen and sulfur, and the NAPAP analysts believed that acid rain acted as a fertilizer by introducing additional nitrogen and sulfur compounds into cultivated land (except, again, for soybeans, which unlike most crops were biologically incapable of benefitting from the added compounds).

Using information on soybeans' response to acidity derived from the field experiments, and a mathematical agricultural model originally developed to assess the economic import of atmospheric ozone (which was known to be harmful to crops), NAPAP simulated the impact on soybean cultivation of increases in acid rain of 10%, 30%, and 50%, measured against a hypothetical base case set at 50% of 1980's actual acid deposition. Damages to producers and consumers together totalled more than $150 million for the 50% increase (all NAPAP analyses were performed in 1984 dollars). "These damages," the report noted, "are a small fraction (never more than 0.002) of the estimated $144 billion [profit] for the agricultural sector in 1982." When the beneficial effect of acid rain's hypothetical fertilization of other crops was incorporated, however, producers reaped a surplus of $161 million relative to the base case. Consumers still suffered losses of almost $110 million because lessened soybean production drove up prices for that crop, while farmers failed to pass along savings from fertilization effects for other crops. The model assumed that farmers bought less fertilizer instead of expanding production. "The net result," the NAPAP analysts wrote, "is a small increase in the value of total surplus, suggesting that economic agents in the U.S. agricultural sector may be benefited, rather than damaged, by current levels of acid deposition." (See Exhibit 6.)

FORESTS

One of the most significant and disturbing effects of acid rain, many thought, was harm to forests. "The damages," National Resources Defense Council attorney David G. Hawkins had written in 1985, "are potentially enormous in their scale."

> Studies in Vermont have shown reductions of 19% in forest growth at low elevations between 1965 and 1983, and reductions of 41% at higher altitudes. Recent studies of tree rings have documented growth declines in the Southeast too, including declines in red spruce, shortleaf pine, hemlock, hickory, yellow birch, pitch pine, and Fraser fir in the Smokies.

EXHIBIT 6

Agriculture: Estimated Annual Changes in Economic Surplus Due to Simulated Changes in Crop Yields, Passive Fertilization, and Liming (Millions of 1984 Dollars)

Case	Change in Economic Surplus		
	Consumers	Producers	Total
Direct effects			
−10%	−17.2	−3.2	−20.4
−30%	−66.5	−8.6	−75.1
−50%	−184.6	−32.2	−152.4
Direct[1] plus indirect effects[2]	−109.5	161.0	51.5

[1]Yield reduction consistent with −50% case

[2]Direct effects are yield reductions from acid rain; indirect effects are from fertilization.

Source: Callaway, Darwin, and Nesse, "Economic Valuation of Acidic Deposition Damages: Preliminary Results from the 1985 NAPAP Assessment," *Water, Air and Soil Pollution*, vol. 31, no. 3–4, (1986). Reprinted by permission of Kluwer Academic Publications.

The NAPAP report, however, said unequivocally that "no empirical relationships between variations in wet and dry deposition and recently observed episodes of forest dieback or decreases in forest growth have been found." (References omitted.) This was a half-empty scientific glass others tended to view as half-full: there was no definitive link between the troubling forest phenomena and acid rain, wrote Hawkins, but "other causes are being steadily ruled out by scientists studying the problem." This was essentially the Canadian position as well. The Canadian special envoy on acid rain, William Davis, had argued that the contribution of acidic pollutants to forest damage observed in North America and Europe (where Germany's famed Black Forest was suffering grievously) "has not been satisfactorily determined but is generally perceived in the scientific community to be a contributing factor. . . ."

However, the NAPAP study went on to straddle the analytic fence by assessing the economic effects of harm to forests, while explicitly not attributing any such harm to acid rain. "[T]his portion of the Assessment does not estimate the economic damages of current levels of acid deposition or of any form of air pollution," it said. "The analysis is designed to show, instead, the range of economic effects that could occur due to a wide range of growth slowdowns, regardless of the source of those slowdowns." It did so by simply positing 10%, 15%, and 20% reductions from current hardwood and softwood growth rates in northeastern and southeastern forests, using existing "forest sector market models" called TAMMSOFT and TAMMHARD. Those who believed acid rain was harmful to woodlands criticized these incremental assumptions, arguing that

many forests thought to have been affected by acid rain were simply dying or dead.

The results were presented as annualized changes in the present value of the economic benefit to timber owners, producers, and consumers (the NAPAP analysts emphasized that these models were not programmed to incorporate possible changes in investment or forest management which might be spurred by growth reductions). The net economic effect was negative for all three degrees of reduced growth; damage ranged from $342.4 million a year for the 10% reduction to $510.1 million a year for the 20% reduction. The effect was not the same for all parties, however: timber owners always benefited from reduced growth, consumers were always harmed, and producers were harmed until the reduction reached 20%, when their position improved by almost $150 million (it wasn't clear to the NAPAP analysts that this last result wasn't merely a modeling aberration). (See Exhibit 7.) Nor was it regionally homogeneous: timber owners in the southeast, the analysts said, would "suffer economic damages due to all growth slowdowns." Moreover, southeastern producers were hit much harder than their northeastern counterparts, who, the analysts said, "actually experience slight benefits."

FISHING

The NAPAP study's examination of acid rain's impact on recreational fishing was restricted to New York's Adirondack region. The analysts used two different methods, a participation model and a travel cost model, to assess economic effects from incremental damage to the area's lakes. The participation

EXHIBIT 7

Commercial Forests: Estimated Annualized Changes in the Present Value[1] of Economic Surplus Due to Hypothetical Reductions in Radial Growth for Selected Years (Millions of 1984 Dollars)

	Change in Economic Surplus			
Case	Timber Owners	Producers	Consumers	Total
− 10%[2]	63.4	− 63.4	− 342.4	− 342.4
− 15%[2]	109.9	− 40.4	− 516.3	− 446.8
− 20%[2]	220.7	148.0	− 878.8	− 510.1

[1]For the period 1985–2030.

[2]Indicates percent reduction in radial growth rates in Northeast and Southeast.

Source: Callaway, Darwin and Nesse, "Economic Valuation of Acidic Deposition Damages: Preliminary Results from the 1985 NAPAP Assessment," *Water, Air and Soil Pollution,* vol. 31, no. 3–4, (1986). Reprinted by permission of Kluwer Academic Publications.

model used statistical techniques to relate variation in the time anglers spent fishing at 24 multiple-lake sites to certain characteristics of the sites, such as fishable areas and catch rates (this information was obtained from the Adirondack Lake and Pond Survey, a 1984 survey of the Adirondack area performed by New York state). Information about the effect of acid deposition on these characteristics was used to calculate how different levels of acid deposition would affect the number of days anglers would fish at the different sites, and economic impact assessed by setting the value of a fishing day at $30.00 (this figure was obtained from the travel cost model). The travel cost model relied on the New York Angler Survey, which provided information on how far anglers came to fish, how much it cost them, and the quantity of fish they caught, as the basis for a statistical analysis of the value of fishing as a function of how much anglers in fact paid to catch fish at a given rate. The NAPAP study's assumption that lakes suffered incremental damage from acid rain was a sore point with environmentalists who pointed out that some lakes apparently affected by acid rain supported no fish at all. "It's much more of an over-the-edge phenomenon," said the National Resources Defense Council's Dick Ayres. "As the lake gets more acid the ecosystem unravels until it just falls apart." The ecological complexity of lakes made it extremely difficult to relate given levels of acid rain to degrees of change in their "fishability," or to predict how reductions in acid rain might improve the situation.

The NAPAP analysts themselves underscored several weaknesses in their recreational fishing analysis.

First of all, the estimates apply only to Adirondack lakes and do not include streams for which key data were unavailable. [The OTA, by contrast, had estimated that 9,400 lakes and 60,000 miles of streams were at risk throughout the eastern US.] Second, the aggregation procedure used to combine sites may not have captured important localized impacts, such as in high altitude lakes [which are thought to be particularly susceptible to acid rain damage]. Third, the damage estimates do not include changes in the non-use values. . . . Fourth, the treatment of fishing behavior in the travel cost model also does not account for the ability of anglers to switch to substitute fishing locations, which would presumably result in lower total economic damages. Finally . . . the estimated changes in fishable area and catch rates used in the analysis contain unquantified uncertainties that have not been incorporated into the economic damage estimates.

The calculated damages for the 24 multiple-lake sites, thus qualified, ranged from $1.7 million for the participation model's assessment of a 3.2% reduction in fishable area but no change in catch rates (the travel cost model gave damages of $0.7 million), to $12 million for the travel cost model's assessment of a 10% reduction in both fishable area and catch rates ($10.2 million for the participation model). (See Exhibit 8.)

MATERIALS

The last part of the NAPAP study, which assessed damages to the materials making up buildings and other structures, initially made the sums calculated for biological harm—be it to fish or forest—pale by comparison. When the NAPAP estimates, performed by the Brookhaven National Laboratory and the

EXHIBIT 8

Adirondack Lakes: Estimated Annual Differences in Economic Surplus Due to
Simulated Reductions in Fishable Area and Catch Rates (Millions of 1984 Dollars)

Model Type	Case	Physical Effect 3.2% Damage	Physical Effect 10% Damage
Participation	A	−1.7	− 5.2
	B	−3.2	−10.2
Travel Cost	A	−0.7	− 4.6
	B	−4.8	−12.0

Case A change in fishable area only.
Case B change in fishable area and average catch.

Source: Callaway, Darwin, and Nesse, ''Economic Valuation of Acidic Deposition Damages: Preliminary Results from the 1985 NAPAP Assessment,'' *Water, Air and Soil Pollution,* vol. 31, no. 3–4 (1986). Reprinted by permission of Kluwer Academic Publications.

Army Corps of Engineers, were first circulated for review in mid-1985, the *New York Times* announced the findings with a headline that read ''Draft study puts acid rain damage at $5 billion for 17 states.'' The figure represented the Brookhaven/Army estimate of annual damages to common building materials in an eastern block of the country bounded in the south by Kentucky, in the west by Illinois, and Maine in the northeast. It had the potential to affect the acid rain debate markedly. ''Its political significance is that it shows that everybody has a stake in this problem,'' the *Times* story quoted Frederick W. Lipfert, a scientist at Brookhaven. ''It is not just a question of a few high-altitude lakes in the Adirondacks.''

The Brookhaven/Army materials damage estimates were based on assessments of harm to three categories of materials: those used in ordinary buildings; those used in cultural structures; and those used in the nation's ''infrastructure.'' Common building materials included such things as steel, copper, aluminum, paint, and mortar; cultural materials included bronze, marble, and limestone, as used in statuary and as trim on historic buildings; infrastructural materials were restricted in the study to those used in transmission towers. The analysts compiled inventories of structures and the materials which comprised them, based for common building materials on a survey of four cities (New Haven, Pittsburgh, Cincinnati, and Portland, Maine), which was then generalized to the 17-state area, and for statues and monuments on the National Register of Historic Places. Utilities were surveyed directly to obtain an inventory of transmission towers. ''Damage functions,'' representing the proportion of a given material's mass lost over time at a given level of acid disposition, were calculated for the different metals, stones, paints, and other materials, and damage estimates calculated based on the damage functions and

simulated acid deposition patterns. Finally, the damage estimates were combined with estimated costs of repair to arrive at economic damage figures.

The Brookhaven/Army results were presented in the 1985 preliminary NAPAP report as annualized changes in maintenance costs. Statues and monuments were predicted to cost an additional $5–7 million annually, compared to the ''pristine'' base case, and historical buildings $17–100; transmission towers, the study said, would cost an extra $2 million (see Exhibit 9.) The NAPAP report did not present the $5 billion estimate for common building materials; the results, the report said ''could be criticized on both theoretical and empirical grounds.''

It might as truthfully have said that the results in fact had been so criticized, and to devastating effect. When the EPA circulated the analysis of common building materials for review, it had come under censorious scrutiny by such figures as Norbert S. Baer, a materials specialist from New York University who had served as a peer reviewer for EPA on similar matters and who was brought in by TBS to

EXHIBIT 9

Materials: Estimated Differences in Annualized
Maintenance Costs for Cultural Materials
and Transmission Towers in the Northeast
(Millions of 1984 Dollars)

Material Component	Annualized Change in Maintenance Cost
Cultural Materials	
Statues and monuments	5–7
Historical buildings	17–100
Transmission towers	2

Source: Callaway, Darwin, and Nesse, ''Economic Valuation of Acidic Deposition Damages: Preliminary Results from the 1985 NAPAP Assessment,'' *Water, Air and Soil Pollution,* vol. 31, no. 3–4, (1986). Reprinted by permission of Kluwer Academic Publications.

help it look at the Brookhaven/Army work. The city survey was questioned on the grounds that two of the four test sites were coastal, and thus quite possibly subject to distinctive weathering and environmental phenomena, while the bulk of the 17-state area study was not. The damage functions were criticized as flawed for various reasons—the mortar function, for instance, was based simply on a fraction of the limestone function, despite marked differences in composition—and irrelevant to boot. Property owners, the critics said, don't care whether layers of paint become thinner, as they would if they lost mass as described in the damage functions; they care if paint peels, bubbles, or separates from its substrate, phenomena which mass loss functions do not address and which the Brookhaven/Army analysis did not consider separately. Similarly, critics argued that for metals, mass loss as such—erosion over the whole of a surface or structure—matters less than the failure thresholds of critical components like brackets and fasteners.

The critics went on to argue that even if the surveys and damage functions had been satisfactory, the protocols for applying one to the other were not. This was a particular problem with estimated damages to paint, which accounted for roughly three-quarters of total damages to common building materials and which critics charged relied on questionable assumptions, such as that all wood and aluminum surfaces in the study area were painted, and once damaged would have to be stripped bare and repainted at commercial rates (this worked out to almost $6,000 a year for an average house, or the same as one of David Stockman's fish). Nobody disputed that acid rain could damage materials, but faced with these, and other, criticisms, NAPAP decided that the common building materials estimates were too questionable to stand up and declined to present them in the 1985 round.

VISIBILITY

Had NAPAP attempted, as it expressly did not, to assess one of the "ancillary" damages of acid rain, it might well have introduced a value comparable to the value for paint it rejected as unfounded. Visibility—how far people can see through the atmosphere—was hampered by the same emissions that cause acid rain, just as it was by smog, and it was widely accepted that controlling utility emissions would improve visibility. In work partially funded by the EPA, Oregon State University economist Richard

M. Adams surveyed the literature on the benefits of air pollution control and concluded that "the benefits from visibility improvement appear to be at least equal to those for agriculture, forestry, and materials categories." Adams noted that there was substantial uncertainty in the results of studies valuing visibility improvements, which relied on surveying or estimating the willingness of "consumers"—meaning, presumably, people who can and do look at things—to pay for increased visibility. (One similar study aimed at estimating the value of a scenic vista relied on showing tourists pictures of the area with and without a smoke plume from a contemplated powerplant, then asking the amount they'd be willing to pay to keep the vista plumeless.) He argued nonetheless that since the studies showed such consumers willing to pay $10 to $30 annually for each mile of improved visibility, "the potential benefits of visibility improvements are quite large." One study he cited calculated a benefit of almost $2 billion annually from a 12 million-ton reduction in SO_2 emissions.

THE PRESSURES OF TIME

It was far from clear just how helpful the NAPAP work could be when it came to weighing the costs and benefits of control programs. NAPAP's methodology was generally to assess, by various means, the effects of damage caused or posited to be caused by contemporary levels of acid rain. The resulting values were implicitly relative to a hypothetical "pristine" environment with no acid rain; as the summary said with gentle understatement, "Control policies would probably not achieve these conditions." Others, such as the National Resource Defense Council's Ayres, offered more fundamental criticisms. "The benefits of acid rain control are broader than the ones NAPAP has looked at," Ayres said. "Some of the most important ones, such as visibility and human health, aren't really measurable in economic terms."[4] Nonetheless, the Waxman–Sikorski bill was a live political issue, and the debate over the bill was unlikely to wait for NAPAP's uncertainties to be fully resolved.

[4]Elevated levels of atmospheric sulfur compounds have been linked, albeit very tenuously, to premature human mortality. There is no consensus among scientists on the matter; the OTA writes that "[w]hether [sulfur compounds are] actually linked to premature mortality, or merely indicates other harmful agents (e.g., other particulates) associated with [sulfur compounds], is unknown." The range in current scientific positions, the OTA estimated, would make airborne pollution to which sulfur compounds contribute responsible for from zero to five percent of annual U.S. mortality.

ASSIGNMENT FOR CLASS DISCUSSION

Imagine that you are an aide to a Western senator or representative (whose constituents' interests are not directly affected by acid rain). Come to class prepared to recommend how your boss should vote on the Waxman–Sikorski bill and why.

In developing your recommendation, please consider:

1. What are the costs of acid rain control?
2. What are the principal sources of uncertainty in forecasting the benefits of acid rain control?
3. Did the NAPAP study evaluate the appropriate benefits of control and place the correct dollar values on those benefits?
4. Based on the current information, what controls on acid rain would you recommend?
5. Is future research (e.g., the next phases of NAPAP) likely to resolve the uncertainties?

Rescission of the Passive Restraints Standard: Costs and Benefits

On October 23, 1981, the head of the National Highway Traffic Safety Administration (NHTSA) announced the rescission of those sections of Federal Motor Vehicle Safety Standard (FMVSS) 208 that would have required the installation of passive occupant restraint systems—either airbags or automatic seat belts—starting with 1984 model year cars. Eight months later, in response to a suit from the automobile insurance industry, a federal judge ordered NHTSA to reconsider, arguing that the rescission was arbitrary and capricious since the agency "drew conclusions that were unsupported by evidence on the record and then artificially narrowed the range of alternatives available to it under its legislative mandate."

The court action reopened a fifteen-year-long debate between the federal government, the auto industry, and the insurance companies on the merits of passive restraint systems. NHTSA had been investigating passive restraint systems since the late 1960s,

largely because of the failure of the driving public to use regular manual seat belts in large numbers. High usage of seat belts or other passenger restraint systems holds the promise of substantially reducing traffic fatalities and injuries, since belted passengers have approximately 50 percent lower fatality and serious injury rates.

REGULATORY HISTORY

One of NHTSA's first actions after it was created in 1966 was to require the installation of seat belts in all new cars starting with the 1968 model year. (Several states had required seat belts in new cars as early as 1964.) In a later attempt to increase seat belt use, NHTSA mandated that all new 1972 and 1973 model year cars be equipped with a warning buzzer that would sound continuously if the car were operated with seat belts unfastened. Starting with the 1974

This case was written by Professor José A. Gomez-Ibañez on the basis of public documents and an earlier case prepared by David M. Kennedy ("Rescission of the Passive Restraints Standard," Kennedy School of Government case #C16-82-455, 1982). (0589)

model year, NHTSA also required an ignition inter-lock system that prevented the car from being started unless the seat belts were fastened. Motorists quickly learned how to defeat or disconnect the continuous buzzer, but the public furor over the ignition inter-lock was so strong that in 1975 Congress ordered NHTSA to rescind the requirement and specifically prohibited the agency from mandating either inter-locks or any buzzer lasting longer than eight seconds.

NHTSA had proposed rules requiring passive restraint systems instead of regular seat belts as early as 1969, although these first proposals were delayed and modified in part because passive restraint tech-nology was still under development. (For a complete history of NHTSA rulemakings on passive restraints see *The Rescission of the Passive Restraints Stan-dard,* KSG case #C16-82-455.0.) In the late 1960s and early 1970s, the most promising passive restraint technology was the airbag. Airbag systems consist of deflated bags mounted in the glove compartment area and steering wheel that inflate virtually instanta-neously when on-board sensors detect crash forces. NHTSA regulations for the 1974 model year allowed automakers the option of installing airbags instead of an ignition interlock system, but all but one of the manufacturers opted for the ignition interlock be-cause of concerns about the reliability and cost of bags. General Motors offered the airbag as an option on several luxury models (Oldsmobiles, Buicks, Cad-illacs) during the 1974–1976 model years but only 10,000 were sold. Although airbag proponents criti-cized General Motors for not promoting the airbag more aggressively, the buyer response was still re-markably low given the heavily subsidized price ($225 per car) and the unattractive alternative (an ignition interlock).

The "modern" history of passive restraint reg-ulations began in 1976, when, in the wake of the in-terlock debacle, Secretary of Transportation William Coleman announced a major review of the evidence on passive restraints. In January of 1977, during the last days of the Ford administration, Secretary Cole-man issued new regulations that postponed, perhaps indefinitely, passive restraint requirements pending a test of their cost, reliability, and consumer accept-ance. Under the threat of requiring passive restraints in all cars, Secretary Coleman pressured Ford and General Motors into signing an agreement to manu-facture and market 60,000 airbag equipped cars start-ing with the 1979 model year. In a separate negotia-tion, Volkswagen also agreed to produce at least 125,000 more cars with a new kind of passive re-straint that it had introduced on its 1975 Rabbit: the

automatic seat belt. The VW system included a shoulder belt that was fastened to the outer edge of the door at one end and in the middle of the front seat at the other; closing the door wrapped the belt around the passenger. VW eliminated the need for a lap belt by redesigning the front dashboard to include a padded knee bar that prevented the passenger from sliding out from under the shoulder belt in a crash.

Less than two months later, in March 1977, President Carter's new transportation secretary, Brock Adams, gave notice that he was reviewing Sec-retary Coleman's decision. In July of that year, Sec-retary Adams announced yet another final rule, this time requiring passive restraints in all large cars as of model year 1982, mid-size cars as of model year 1983, and small cars in model year 1984. Although the standard was written so that either airbags or auto-matic seat belts would comply, NHTSA expected that manufacturers would opt for airbags on most models since airbags were more acceptable to motorists and, according to its projections, only slightly more costly. Ford and GM argue that this policy reversal released them from their agreement to sell 60,000 air-bag equipped cars. VW continued to offer automatic belts as an option on the Rabbit and GM began to experiment with an automatic seat belt option on its Chevrolet Chevette.

The Reagan administration took office in 1981 promising, as one of the four key elements in its eco-nomic program, to remove burdensome and unneces-sary government regulations. The passive restraint regulation was an obvious target for action because the auto industry was in a severe recession and the phasing of large cars first disadvantaged the U.S. manufacturers. In April of 1981, Transportation Sec-retary Drew Lewis announced a one-year delay of the implementation of the passive restraint requirement to allow the government to review the regulation once again. The secretary delegated responsibility for this decision to his NHTSA administrator, Ray Peck. By October 1981 Peck announced that he was re-scinding the requirement, largely because it now ap-peared that the manufacturer would rely almost ex-clusively on automatic belts rather than airbags to meet the standard. Automatic belts had proven to be much cheaper than bags, or at least so the manufac-turers argued. But both Peck and the automakers ex-pected that most motorists would find the automatic belts uncomfortable and disconnect them, thereby substantially reducing any safety benefits from the standard.

The insurance agency, which had long sup-ported airbags and other traffic safety measures, appealed Peck's decision to the courts, arguing that he had little basis to predict that automatic belts would not be used. The industry also argued that Peck had narrowed his options unduly by considering only two alternatives: no standard at all or a standard that could only be met with either bags or belts. Administrator Peck should have considered a standard that required only airbags, the industry contended. In agreeing with the insurance companies, the federal judge forced NHTSA to reconsider the entire passive restraint issue from scratch.

THE TRAFFIC SAFETY PROBLEM

Traffic safety is a serious problem in the United States. Every year approximately 50,000 persons die in traffic accidents, an annual death toll nearly equal to the number of U.S. servicemen killed in ten years of combat in Vietnam. For every traffic death, moreover, there are approximately 100 non-fatal injuries, 40 of which are serious enough to result in permanent or temporary disability.[1] Traffic accidents impose heavy economic costs in addition to death and suffering; in 1980 accidents cost the economy $57.5 billion in lost wages and in legal, medical, hospital, funeral,

[1] The National Safety Council reports only injuries serious enough to be fatal or cause permanent or temporary disability. The Insurance Information Institute reports injuries that are less serious as well.

property damage, and insurance administration expenses.[2]

For the past twenty years, the number of traffic fatalities has been held roughly constant at 50,000 per year which, because of the steady increase in the numbers of motorists and the volume of travel, has actually meant a decline in the accident rate (Exhibit 1). The gradual urbanization of the population accounts for part of the reduction in accident rates, since death rates are lower on urban than rural roads. Highway improvements, such as the construction of the Interstate Highway System and other controlled access expressways, were also an important factor, as was the imposition of the nationwide 55 mph speed limit in 1974. Finally, since 1966 NHTSA has issued new car safety standards designed both to improve vehicle crashworthiness and increase crash avoidance: standards include safety glass, padded dashboards, rear and side mirrors, side marker lights, and energy-absorbing steering columns as well as manual lap and shoulder belts.[3]

Without continued efforts to reduce accident

[2] Insurance Information Institute data as reported at Phillip S. Coonley and Carol Gurvitz, *Assessment of Insurance Incentives for Safety Belt Usage,* U.S. Department of Transportation, Transportation Systems Center, Cambridge, Mass., July 1983, p. 2-7.

[3] Some analysts have argued that requiring safety features in automobiles is self-defeating since it encourages motorists to drive more aggressively; see Sam Peltzman, "The Effects of Automobile Safety Regulation," *Journal of Political Economy* 83 (1975): 677-725.

EXHIBIT 1

Motor Vehicle Death Rates, 1950–1981

Year	No. of Deaths	No. of Vehicles (Millions)	Vehicle Miles (Billions)	No. of Drivers (Millions)	Deaths 10,000 Motor Vehicles	Deaths 100,000,000 Vehicle Miles	Per 100,000 Population
1950	34,763	49.2	458	62.2	7.07	7.59	23.0
1960	38,137	74.5	719	87.4	5.12	5.31	21.2
1970	54,633	111.2	1,120	111.5	4.92	4.88	26.8
1971	54,381	116.3	1,186	114.4	4.68	4.57	26.4
1972	56,278	122.3	1,268	118.4	4.60	4.43	27.0
1973	55,511	129.8	1,309	121.6	4.28	4.24	26.5
1974	46,402	134.9	1,290	125.6	3.44	3.59	22.0
1975	45,853	137.9	1,330	129.8	3.33	3.45	21.5
1976	47,038	143.5	1,412	133.9	3.28	3.33	21.9
1977	49,510	148.8	1,477	138.1	3.33	3.35	22.9
1978	52,411	153.6	1,548	140.8	3.41	3.39	24.0
1979	52,800	159.6	1,529	143.3	3.31	3.45	24.0
1980	52,600	161.6	1,521	145.3	3.25	3.46	23.2
1981	50,800	165.7	1,544	148.0	3.07	3.29	22.2

Source: National Safety Council, *Accident Facts, 1982* (Chicago, Ill.: National Safety Council, 1982), p. 59.

rates, however, safety experts fear that the annual traffic death toll will rise sharply in future years. Although the 1973–1974 and 1979 oil price shocks halted the growth in highway travel temporarily, traffic has continued to increase and most analysts project a two percent annual growth rate during the 1980s. Motorists have responded to higher energy prices by buying smaller and more fuel efficient cars, moreover, so the average car is projected to become lighter and, all other things being equal, substantially less crashworthy. In collisions between a small (2000 lb.) car and a large (4000 lb.) car, the occupants of the small car have three to four times the serious injury rates as the occupants of the larger car. Even when a small car collides with another small car, the injury rates are about twice as high as when a large car collides with another large car.[4] Although there is some evidence that small car drivers understand the higher risk they face and compensate by driving more cautiously and using seat belts more often, safety experts fear that they may not compensate enough to prevent traffic fatality rates from rising.

RESTRAINT DESIGN: BELTS, BUCKLES AND BAGS

There are three types of passenger restraint systems: active seat belts, automatic seat belts, and airbags. Active or manual seat belts are the most common form, and are so called because the motorists must fasten the belts themselves. The National Highway Traffic Safety Administration (NHTSA) required that all new cars sold in the United States be equipped with lap belts in the front seating positions starting with the model year 1968. NHTSA later upgraded its regulations to require the installation of both lap and shoulder belts (so-called three-point belts) in the front seats and lap belts in the back.

Automatic seat belts fasten automatically, without active assistance from the driver. Close to half a million seat belt systems have been sold, almost all of them as options offered since 1975 on the VW Rabbit or between 1978 and 1980 on the Chevrolet Chevette. In the last few years Cadillac and Toyota have also offered automatic belt options on several models, but relatively few have been sold so far. A variety of automatic belt designs have been developed since the initial VW model. General Motors designed a three-point belt that wraps around the occu-

pant when the door closes, for example, thereby eliminating the need for a padded knee bar. Toyota's design uses a motor instead of the closing car door to wrap the belt around the passenger and is therefore more expensive (Exhibit 2).

All automatic belt designs must provide some way for the passenger to quickly unfasten the belt in the event he or she is trapped in the car after an accident. Almost all the existing belt designs include a quick release button or buckle which can be used to detach or separate the belt. (An alternative solution is to wind one end of the belt on a special inertial reel which is designed to lock in response to a sudden tug on the belt, such as occurs in a crash, but to play out the belt in response to slow and steady pull. Both the manufacturers and NHTSA believe that a detachable or separate belt design is easier for a panicked passenger to use than an inertial reel design.)

Although automatic belts work well for the outboard passengers in the front seat, they are nearly impossible to design for the middle passenger. This problem is less serious for small than large cars (since small cars usually seat only two in front) and it may account for the fact that foreign rather than U.S. manufacturers first developed automatic belts.

Most airbag designs are essentially the same, varying only in details such as the inflation medium or propellant. The 10,000 airbag-equipped cars General Motors built and sold during the 1974–1976 model years have proven to be exceptionally reliable. With over a billion miles of accumulated experience, these bags have never inflated unnecessarily when the car was in motion and only failed to inflate in two out of 350 crashes (once after a mechanic mistakenly disconnected the sensor).

EFFECTS OF RESTRAINTS ON FATALITY AND INJURY RATES

At best, passenger restraints can reduce only a fraction of all traffic deaths, since occupants of passenger cars account for slightly more than half of all traffic deaths (the remainder being pedestrians, motorcyclists, truck occupants, and bicyclists). In 1980, for example, approximately 27,387 out of 52,800 traffic fatalities were passenger car occupants and 25,200 (92 percent) were front seat occupants.[5] Most car passengers are killed in collisions with other cars

[4]John R. Meyer and José A. Gomez-Ibañez, *Autos, Transit and Cities* (Cambridge, Mass.: Harvard University Press, 1983), p. 264.

[5]National Highway Traffic Safety Administration, *Final Regulatory Impact Analysis, Amendment to FMVSS 208, Occupant Crash Protection,* October 1981, p. IV-3.

EXHIBIT 2

Available Automatic Belt Systems, 1975–1981

Manufacturer and Model	Model Years	Option Price	Description	Separable	Ignition Interlock
VW Rabbit	1975–1981	$33–50	2-point automatic shoulder belt with knee bolster	yes	yes
Chevrolet Chevette	1978–1979	$65	2-point automatic shoulder belt with knee bolster and manual lap belt	yes	yes
Chevrolet Chevette	1980	$65	3-point automatic shoulder-lap belt	no	no
Toyota Corona and Cressida	1980–1981	$350	automatic motor-driven shoulder belt with knee bolster and manual lap belt	yes	no[1]
Cadillac	1981	$150	3-point automatic shoulder-lap belt	yes	no

[1]When the belt is detached a continuous buzzer sounds and red lights flash on the dash.

Source: NHTSA, *Final Regulatory Impact Analysis, Amendment to FMVSS 208 Occupant Crash Protection, Rescission of Automatic Occupant Protection Requirements,* October 1981.

or in accidents where the car runs off the road and turns over (Exhibit 3).

Passenger restraint systems do not protect car occupants perfectly against fatalities and injuries, and the effectiveness of bags and belts differs. Neither bags nor belts are much help in rear end collisions, for example, and belts are more useful in side collisions than bags since the bags don't always inflate on side impact and, without the use of a lap belt, don't provide protection from sideways forces. The airbag also loses effectiveness as accident severity decreases, since the airbag rarely deploys in minor accidents. Without a lap belt or a knee pad, more-

over, airbags are less effective because passengers may slide under the bag. If the bag deploys, however, it provides more protection against flying glass than a belt. The airbag's greatest advantage over belts is that it is activated automatically when needed, whereas belts, even of automatic design, may often be disconnected by the motorist.

NHTSA safety experts estimate the effectiveness of passenger restraints in reducing fatality and injury rates by analyzing actual crash data gathered as part of the National Accident Sampling System (NASS) and the National Crash Severity Study (NCSS). The NASS and NCSS accident data include

EXHIBIT 3

Motor Vehicle Deaths and Injuries by Type of Accident, 1977

Type of Accident	Deaths			Serious Nonfatal Injuries		
	Total	Urban	Rural	Total	Urban	Rural
Total	50,800	19,100	31,700	1,900,000	1,100,000	800,000
Collision with:						
Pedestrian	9,000	6,500	2,500	100,000	85,000	15,000
Other motor vehicle	20,700	5,500	15,200	1,340,000	830,000	510,000
Railroad train	900	500	400	4,000	2,000	2,000
Pedal-cycle	1,200	900	300	60,000	50,000	10,000
Animal or animal-drawn vehicle	100	*	100	6,000	3,000	3,000
Fixed object	3,800	2,300	1,500	80,000	50,000	30,000
Noncollision[1]	15,100	3,400	11,700	310,000	80,000	230,000

[1]Noncollision accidents are largely those in which the car overturns without hitting another vehicle or fixed object.

*Less than five.

Source: National Safety Council, *Accident Facts, 1982* (Chicago, Ill.: National Safety Council, 1982), p. 45.

the severity of the injuries and whether seat belts or other forms of occupant restraint were used. Injuries are rated on an Abbreviated Injury Scale (AIS) from zero to six, with zero being no injury and six an un-survivable injury (Exhibit 4). Most fatalities occur because of injuries of AIS 5 (critical) or 6, although persons who are older or who have special medical problems may die from injuries with an AIS of three (serious) or four (severe).

NHTSA's analyses of the NCSS and NASS crash data show that occupants with either a shoulder belt and a lower torso restraint (i.e., a knee pad) or a three-point belt have a 50 percent lower fatality rate and a 65 percent lower injury rate for AIS 2-5 injuries. Although the small number of accidents involving airbags precludes a definitive conclusion, crash data suggest that an airbag with either a lap belt or knee bar reduces AIS 4-6 injuries by 66 percent while an airbag alone reduces injuries by 40 percent.[6]

The auto manufacturers and others argue that crash data may exaggerate the potential effectiveness of more widespread use of passenger restraints. Present (voluntary) safety belt users may drive more cautiously and have less severe crashes than non-users.[7] In addition, there is some evidence that mandatory seat belts or airbags may make motorists feel safer

and, as a result, encourage them to drive more aggressively and get into more accidents.[8] Finally, the auto manufacturers argue that the airbag crash data is far too limited to support a reliable estimate and that larger samples would show that the airbag was perhaps only half as effective as a three-point belt.[9]

CURRENT SEAT BELT USAGE

Despite the fact that almost all cars on the road today are equipped with manual lap or lap-shoulder belts, only about 11 percent of all motorists wear their manual belts. Usage rates appear to have fallen in recent years, perhaps because the 1974 and 1975 model year cars with ignition lock systems are gradually being scrapped. Usage rates are higher in small cars than large, reflecting the greater risk that drivers perceive from driving a small car (Exhibit 5). Drivers who wear belts differ in several respects from those who do not, including being more averse to risks. Belted drivers are better educated, smoke less, are less likely to be involved in serious accidents, and fol-

[6]Coonley and Gurvitz, *Incentives for Safety Belt Usage*, p. 2-4, and National Highway Traffic Safety Administration, *Final Regulatory Impact Analysis*, p. IV-9.

[7]S. Partyka, "NCSS—The Analyst's Companion," National Highway Traffic Safety Administration, report no. DOT-HS-805-871, October 1981 as cited in Coonley and Gurvitz, *Incentives for Safety Belt Usage*, p. 2-4.

[8]This argument has been made about past NHTSA safety regulations, most forcefully by Peltzman, "The Effects of Automobile Safety Regulation."

[9]In the mid-1970s before extensive crash data with belts was available, General Motors estimated the potential effectiveness of airbags and belts based on extensive engineering analysis of a sample of 706 accidents. This analysis suggested that both bags and belts would reduce fatality rates by only about 20 percent. The extensive crash data conflicts sharply with General Motor's earlier results for belts, but General Motors argues that the crash data is too limited to be conclusive on airbags.

EXHIBIT 4
Abbreviated Injury Scale (AIS) Definition and Rates

AIS Injury Level	Definition	Estimated Number of Front Seat Passenger Car Occupant Injuries, 1979 (Excluding Fatalities)
0	no injury	10,700,000
1	minor (e.g., simple cuts and bruises)	2,410,000
2	moderate (e.g., simple fracture)	260,000
3	serious (e.g., compound fracture or dislocated joints)	110,000
4	severe (e.g., amputated limbs, depressed skull fracture, survivable organ injuries)	16,000
5	critical (e.g., major spinal cord injuries, critical organ injuries)	6,000
6	maximum, currently untreatable	1[1]

[1]Fatalities excluded.

Source: National Highway Traffic Safety Administration, *Final Regulatory Impact Analysis, Amendment to FMVSS 208 Occupant Crash Protection, Rescission of Automatic Occupant Protection Requirements,* October 1981.

EXHIBIT 5

Observed Proportion of Automobile Occupants Wearing Seat Belts

	Percent Using Seat Belts			Number of Observations		
Auto Size	1964–1977	1977–1978	1979	1964–1979	1977–1978	1979
Subcompact	18.8	19.5	17.3	17,600	7,755	8,463
Compact	14.6	12.6	10.4	14,435	6,414	9,303
Intermediate	11.3	10.3	8.5	10,887	10,266	11,768
Full-size	11.2	9.7	7.9	13,234	3,046	3,210
Total	14.6	13.4	13.4	56,156	27,481	32,744

Source: Opinion Research, Inc., *Safety Belt Usage—Survey of Cars in the Traffic Population,* interim report prepared for the National Highway Traffic Safety Administration, 1978; and National Highway Traffic Safety Administration, *Final Regulatory Impact Analysis, Amendment to FMVSS 208 Occupant Crash Protection, Rescission of Automatic Occupant Protection Requirements,* October 1981.

low the cars in front of them at a greater distance, for example. Conversely, belt use is lowest among the drivers most at risk—including young males and drunk drivers.[10]

Motorists surveyed cite inconvenience and discomfort as the primary reasons for not using manual seat belts. In a survey conducted for NHTSA, for example, 68 percent of non-users gave the reason that belts were bothersome, inconvenient, or that they forgot to use them, while 14 percent explained that the belts were uncomfortable, and eight percent expressed a fear that they might be trapped by the belts in the event of a crash. Only four percent cited doubt about claims that seat belts reduce injury rates.[11]

An alternative explanation is that while motorists recognize that "seat belts save lives" they systematically underestimate their probability of involvement in an auto accident, perhaps because they do not want to acknowledge the real risks of driving. For the average motorist, the probability of being injured in an auto accident is about 1 in 1000 per year and 1 in 100,000 per auto trip; the probability of dying in an auto accident is about 1 in 10,000 per year or 1 in 10,000,000 per auto trip.[12] Three quarters of motorists surveyed estimated their risk of accident involvement at less than the actual probability.[13]

Seat belt usage in the several hundred thousand

Rabbits and Chevettes equipped with automatic belts is substantially higher than both the national average or usage in the same models equipped with manual belts. Exhibit 6 shows, for example, that 79 percent of all passengers used the automatic belts in VW Rabbits while only 35 percent used the manual belts. The percentage of Rabbit passengers using automatic belts declines rapidly with the age of the vehicle, however, while manual belt usage is relatively constant across vehicle age. Automatic belt usage may decline because many cars are ultimately sold to second owners who find the belts less attractive. Belt usage rates are slightly lower in Chevettes than in Rabbits but, as with the Rabbits, the automatic belts are used more frequently than manual belts.

FORECASTING AUTOMATIC BELT USE AND LIVES SAVED

A key issue in the debate over mandatory passive restraints is the likely usage rates for automatic seat belts. The current experience with Rabbit or Chevette automatic belts probably provides a misleading guide for mandatory automatic belts for several reasons. In the first place, the Rabbit and Chevette designs encourage high use because they include either ignition interlocks or non-detachable belts. (Both the Rabbit and early [pre-1980] Chevette belts are detachable in an emergency, but include an ignition interlock to prevent the operation of the car when the belt is unbuckled. The late (1980) Chevette belt is not detachable.) Ignition interlocks can be offered as optional equipment but, under the recent congressional prohibition, they cannot be part of a mandatory belt system. If passive belts are mandatory, moreover, automakers are likely to insist on detachable or separable belts to ease passenger fears over being trapped in a car.

[10]Data cited by Kenneth E. Warner, "Bags, Buckles, and Belts: The Debate over Mandatory Passive Restraints in Automobiles," *Journal of Health Politics, Policy and Law* 8 (1983): 49-50.

[11]National Highway Traffic Safety Administration, *Final Regulatory Impact Analysis,* p. IV-25.

[12]Probabilities per auto trip are for a one-way 8.3 mile trip and are calculated at Coonley and Gurvitz, *Incentives for Safety Belt Usage,* pp. 2-13 and 2-20.

[13]Surveys cited by R. Arnould and H. Grabowski, "Auto Safety Regulation: An Analysis of Market Failure," *Bell Journal of Economics* 12 (Spring 1981): 27.

EXHIBIT 6

Observed Seat Belt Usage in VW Rabbits during 1978–1979

Model Year	Percent Using Automatic Belts	Number of Observations	Percent Using Manual Belts	Number of Observations
1979	97%	38	35%	97
1978	87%	178	39%	348
1977	74%	132	35%	372
1976	73%	103	35%	333
1975	59%	39	31%	257
Total	79%	490	35%	1,407

Source: National Highway Traffic Safety Administration, *Final Regulatory Impact Analysis, Amendment to FMVSS 208 Occupant Crash Protection, Rescission of Automatic Occupant Protection Requirements,* October 1981.

Rabbit and Chevette usage may also be unrepresentative because the automatic belts were offered as part of options packages. Surveys reveal that approximately half of the buyers of Rabbits and Chevettes with automatic belts either did not know they were getting automatic belts when they bought the car or accepted the automatic belt-equipped car because it was the only car available with other options they wanted.[14] Nevertheless, for most owners there was at least some voluntary aspect of the purchase decision which probably biases usage rates upward.

Finally, since Rabbit owners have higher than average education levels and both Rabbits and Chevettes are subcompacts, it may not be accurate to project Rabbit and Chevette usage to all cars and owners.

In the "regulatory impact analysis" issued to support its 1981 rescission of the passive restraint standard, NHTSA recognized the great uncertainty in forecasting automatic belt use. The agency implied, however, that mandatory automatic belts would most likely cause the same or slightly lower proportional increase in belt usage in other kinds of cars as they did in Rabbits. Since Rabbit rates were approximately twice as high for automatic than manual belts (79 vs. 35 percent), mandatory automatic belts could double existing overall usage rates from 11.4 to 22.8 percent. NHTSA also tested the implications of a variety of other usage assumptions ranging from no change (i.e., 11.4 percent) to an increase to 60 percent.[15]

If all 1984 model year cars were equipped with automatic belts, NHTSA calculated that between 2050 (22.8 percent usage) and 8750 (60 percent usage) fewer traffic fatalities would occur in those cars dur-

ing their expected useful lives. The reduction in serious injuries would range from 41,500 to 176,600 over the lifetime of the 1984 cars (Exhibit 7). One hundred percent usage, which is extremely unlikely with automatic belts but might occur with airbags, would result in a saving of 16,970 lives and 259,250 injuries in accidents involving model year 1984 automobiles.

The agency received numerous comments from interested parties on automatic belt usage during its rulemaking. The insurance industry and the American Seat Belt Council contended that automatic belt usage could easily be as high as 50 to 60 percent, based on Rabbit use, although they conceded that it probably could not go much higher since surveys suggested that 15 to 25 percent of the population were hard-core non-users. Many of the auto manufacturers, including Ford and General Motors, argued that usage rates would not increase above current levels because the automatic belts would be detachable and an interlock system could not be required. (Unfortunately, the only detachable, non-interlock automatic belts to be offered as an option so far were on the model year 1981 and later Cadillac Sedan Deville, and too few have been sold to provide reliable data on usage.[16])

Any reduction in fatalities and injuries would be of enormous benefit to society. According to estimates made by NHTSA, in 1980 the average traffic fatality cost society about $274,000 in medical expenses, lost wages or productivity, and property damage; the average cost of an AIS 4 or 5 injury amounted to approximately $43,729 to $190,010 in that same year (Exhibit 8).

These NHTSA estimates do not include the pain and suffering of accident victims and their families. Many studies have estimated the value individ-

[14]National Highway Traffic Safety Administration, *Final Regulatory Impact Analysis,* p. IV-35.

[15]National Highway Traffic Safety Administration, *Final Regulatory Impact Analysis,* pp. IV-49 to IV-57, esp. p. IV-57.

[16]National Highway Traffic Safety Administration, *Final Regulatory Impact Analysis,* pp. IV-50 to IV-51.

EXHIBIT 7

NHTSA Estimates of the Number of Fatalities and Injuries Averted over a Ten-Year Vehicle Lifetime from Requiring Automatic Belts in Model Year 1984 Cars[1]

	Front Seat Fatalities	Savings Due to Automatic Belts	Front Seat AIS 2-5 Injuries	Savings Due to Automatic Belts
If no belts used	35,990	—	560,000	—
With current manual belts (11.4% usage)	33,940	—	518,500	—
With automatic belts and usage rate of				
22.8%	31,890	2,050	477,000	41,500
30%	30,590	3,350	450,800	67,700
40%	28,790	5,150	414,400	104,100
50%	26,990	6,950	378,000	140,500
60%	25,190	8,750	341,600	176,600

[1]Estimates assume automatic and manual belts reduce traffic fatalities and injuries by 50 percent when used.

Source: National Highway Traffic Safety Administration, *Final Regulatory Impact Analysis, Amendment to FMVSS 208 Occupant Crash Protection, Rescission of Automatic Occupant Protection Requirements,* October 1981.

uals place on their lives, usually by examining their willingness to pay to reduce their risks of fatal accidents. Studies of the relative wage rates in more and less risky occupations suggest that workers value their lives at between $200,000 and $2,500,000 (in 1980 dollars). Surveys of the willingness of individuals to pay for subscription emergency medical services or other risk reducing programs suggest a similar range of values placed on life.[17] The cost per life

[17]For a review of estimates of the value of life see Martin J. Bailey, *Reducing Risks to Life: Measurement of the Benefits* (Washington, DC: American Enterprise Institute, 1980).

saved in other existing government health and safety programs varies widely, as shown in Exhibit 9.

MANUFACTURING COSTS OF PASSIVE RESTRAINTS

Estimates of the costs of passive restraint systems vary almost as much as estimates of their potential use. In its 1981 rulemaking, NHTSA calculated that the current manual seat belts cost manufacturers and consumers $50 to $75 per car, and that automatic belts would increase those costs between $50 and

EXHIBIT 8

NHTSA Estimates of the Social Costs of Motor Vehicle Accidents in 1980[1]. Costs for All Accidents in $ Millions

Type of Accident	Medical Costs	Productivity Losses (Wages)	Property Losses	Other Losses	Total	Number of Fatalities or Injuries	Cost per Fatality or Injury
Property damage only	0	0	16,984	4,127	21,111	—	$419
Injury, AIS							
1	543	319	2,656	3,933	7,451	—	$2,276
2	622	251	612	590	2,075	—	$4,592
3	631	313	424	684	2,052	—	$10,260
4	335	451	100	640	1,526	—	$43,729
5	1,125	801	33	245	2,204	—	$190,010
Fatality	70	12,602	174	306	13,730	50,200	$268,727
Other losses attributable to death and injuries	3.3	14.2	0	7.5	25.0		
Total losses	3,326	14,237	20,983	18,653	57,199		

[1]All costs in 1980 dollars.

Source: National Highway Traffic Safety Administration, *The Economic Cost to Society of Motor Vehicle Accidents,* DOT-HS-806-342, January 1983.

EXHIBIT 9

Estimates of the Cost per Life Saved in Programs Supported, Operated, or Mandated by Government

Program	Cost per Life Saved (Dollars)
Medical expenditure	
Kidney transplant	72,000
Dialysis in hospital	270,000
Dialysis at home	99,000
Traffic safety	
Recommended for benefit-cost analysis by the National Safety Council	37,500
Estimate for elimination of all railroad grade crossings	100,000
Military policies	
Instructions to pilots on when to crash-land airplanes	270,000
Decision to produce a special ejector seat in a jet plane	4,500,000
Mandated by regulation	
Coke oven emissions standard, OSHA	4,500,000 to 158,000,000
Proposed lawn mower safety standards, CPSC	240,000 to 1,920,000
Proposed standard for occupational exposure to acrylonitrile, OSHA	1,963,000 to 624,976,000

Source: From various sources as reported by Martin J. Bailey, *Reducing Risks to Life: Measurement of the Benefits* (Washington, D.C.: American Enterprise Institute, 1980), p. 26.

$150. The lower figure was for simple automatic belt systems offered in high volume subcompacts, such as the Rabbit, while the higher figure was for luxury cars with more comfortable belt systems or for models where the belts had to be fitted retroactively into existing vehicle designs. Given the mix of large and small cars and old and new designs anticipated in model year 1984, NHTSA expected that the average cost of automatic belts would be $105 per car.[18]

NHTSA's automatic belt cost estimates were reasonably consistent with those offered by other interested parties, including the manufacturers. The price of available automatic belt options ranged from $33 per car for early versions of the Rabbit to $150 for the Cadillac three-point system and $350 for the motorized Toyota belt (Exhibit 2). In response to the 1981 rulemaking, General Motors estimated an average cost of $70–$100 on its models, while Ford estimated $150 and Chrysler $100–$150.[19]

Cost estimates for airbags are much more controversial and varied. In the 1977 rulemaking which mandated passive restraints starting with 1983 model year cars, NHTSA estimated the additional costs of airbags at $112 per car (in 1977 dollars). These 1977 cost estimates assumed that most manufacturers would meet the passive restraint requirement with bags rather than belts and, when the manufacturers indicated their plans to rely largely on belts, NHTSA revised its unit bag costs upward to reflect the smaller volumes involved. In its 1981 rulemaking, for example, the agency indicated the price range would probably be approximately $285 per car for two front passenger systems and $335 for three front passenger systems, based on annual volumes of one million cars.[20]

Airbag manufacturers suggest the cost could be substantially lower than NHTSA predicted, although they acknowledge the importance of scale economies. With over two million units per year, for example, Talley Industries estimated an airbag cost to the consumer of $212 per car. At annual volumes of $500,000 Talley estimates costs at $280 per car, however, and at volumes of 10,000 or less the cost rises to $1200 per car.[21]

Vehicle manufacturers are significantly more pessimistic and argue that the Talley cost estimates do not take into account all the vehicle modifications necessary to accept airbags. GM estimates prices of

[18]This figure does not include $13 per car in added lifetime fuel consumption due to the weight of the belts; National Highway Traffic Safety Administration, *Final Regulatory Impact Analysis*, pp. IV-5 and VI-49.

[19]National Highway Traffic Safety Administration, *Final Regulatory Impact Analysis*, pp. VI-3 and VI-4.

[20]National Highway Traffic Safety Administration, *Final Regulatory Impact Analysis*, p. VI-7.

[21]National Highway Traffic Safety Administration *Final Regulatory Impact Analysis*, p. VI-8.

$650–$700 per car based on annual volumes of 400,000 units and $1100 per car with volumes of 100,000 units. Ford estimates $825 per car for 200,000 units per year.[22]

Between nine and 12 million cars are sold in each model year, depending largely on the strength of the economy (since automobiles are a durable good whose purchase can readily be postponed during economic downturns). Assuming 12 million units, as NHTSA does for model year 1984, the cost of installing passive restraints in every vehicle would be approximately $1.26 billion at $105 per unit (NHTSA's estimate for automatic belts) and $3.6 billion at $300 per unit (approximately NHTSA's latest estimate for airbags).

ALTERNATIVES TO MANDATING PASSIVE RESTRAINTS

Given the high cost of airbags and uncertain usage rates for automatic belts, a great deal of attention has been focused on alternative ways of persuading motorists to use seat belts, including educational campaigns, laws requiring seat belt use, and economic incentives.[23]

Educational Campaigns. Since its rescission of the passive restraint standard in 1981, NHTSA and the Reagan administration have favored educational publicity campaigns to encourage wider voluntary use of seat belts. Experience in the U.S., Canada, Great Britain and France, however, shows no detectable increase in seat belt use after major promotional campaigns. Several controlled experiments in providing motorists with information also have failed to produce increases in belt use.

Proponents argue that the educational approach has not been given a fair test. More research is needed on why people don't use seat belts, for example, so that more effective educational campaigns can be designed. Campaigns should be conducted over many years, they also argue, so that the messages are reinforced and non-users are gradually persuaded. But although educational campaigns almost certainly could be improved, many observers doubt that they will significantly increase belt use.

Seat Belt Use Laws. Some of the automobile manufacturers, most notably General Motors, favor laws that require motorists to use their seat belts. Since 1972, four provinces in Canada and over a dozen other foreign countries (including Australia, New Zealand, Sweden and West Germany) have enacted laws which require seat belt use. In Australia, New Zealand and Sweden, compliance is approximately 80 percent. In two of the Canadian provinces where lap but not shoulder belts are required (because of concern over discomfort), usage rates are 40 to 50 percent, presumably reflecting the added difficulty of enforcement.

In 1983, no mandatory seat belt use laws have been passed in the United States, perhaps because they conflict with the American ideal of individual freedom and the anti-regulatory climate of the 1980s. In a recent survey, for example, more than three-quarters of those polled opposed mandatory seat belt use laws. Although most states have adopted laws requiring that infants or young children be restrained in car seats when travelling in an automobile, compliance and enforcement are reportedly weak. The experience with motorcycle helmet laws is also instructive; over half the states recently repealed their helmet laws despite the substantial safety benefits of helmet use.

In 1983, only Michigan's state legislature is seriously considering a mandatory seat belt law, perhaps because of the traditional influence of the auto industry in that state. Although the law is strongly supported by both auto and insurance companies and there is little or no organized opposition, passage is in doubt because of legislators' concerns about driver reaction and traditional freedom of choice. To meet these concerns, the proposed Michigan law includes only a $10 fine and provides that individual citizens can petition the government for an exemption (the legislation offers no guidelines for granting the exemptions). Some auto industry officials hope that passage of this admittedly weak statute will lead to more widespread public acceptance of seat belt laws and the eventual enactment of tougher statues in Michigan and other states.

Economic Incentives. A final possibility that has not been used extensively is to provide economic incentives for the use of manual belts or the purchase of cars equipped with passive restraints. About one-quarter of the auto insurance companies offer discounts of up to 30 percent on medical and personal injury coverage for owners of cars equipped with passive restraints.[24] Several employers have experi-

---

[22]Op. *cit.*

[23]This section is largely based on the discussion in Warner, "Bags, Buckles, and Belts," pp. 50–53.

[24]See Coonley and Gurvitz, *Incentives for Safety Belt Use;* and National Highway Traffic Safety Administration, *Final Regulatory Impact Analysis.*

mented with economic incentives to encourage their workers to use seat belts more often as well.[25]

One potential problem with economic incentives is verifying or ensuring compliance. This problem is obviously most serious for cars equipped with either manual belts or detachable automatic belts and no ignition interlocks. A solution already used by at least one insurer is to condition insurance payments and benefits on belt use at the time of an accident. Mechanical systems for verifying belt use are also possible, although little has been done to develop them.

A more serious difficulty may be the size of the economic incentive necessary to induce significant increases in usage. Based on medical insurance claims by owners of automatic and manual belt cars, Nationwide Insurance Company estimates the annual insurance premium saving at at least $20 per year for each automatic belt car, or approximately $150 in discounted present value over the expected lifetime of the car.[26] Although this discount may be significant for many motorists, it probably would not be enough to promote increases in usage on the scale hoped for by proponents of mandatory passive restraints.

[25]Coonley and Gurvitz, *Incentives for Safety Belt Use.*

[26]As reported in Warner, ''Bags, Belts, and Buckles,'' p. 53.

ASSIGNMENT FOR CLASS DISCUSSION

Students should come to class prepared to explain whether and why (or why not) they would recommend that the U.S. Department of Transportation require that all new cars be equipped with passive restraints. In developing your recommendations, please consider:

1. What are the arguments for and against the government requiring that cars be equipped with passive restraints?
2. Using the evidence in the case, how compelling or persuasive are these arguments pro and con?
3. Do some of these arguments in favor of restraints support other government policies besides or instead of a requirement that all cars be equipped with passive restraints?

---

chapter 3

Social Justice in Economic Policy

When it is attempting to describe the way things are or predict the way things will be, economic analysis strives to be "value free." That is, economic theory cannot say how things *ought* to be—only how things are or will be. It makes no difference whether we think it is ethically proper or not; if bad weather destroys 80 percent of the world's wheat supply, economics predicts that the price of wheat will most likely rise if market forces are not prevented from operating. In the public policy arena, economic analysis (if not economists) can play a value-free role. Economics can, for example, provide ethically neutral guides to the *consequences* of alternative public policies: An excise tax on alcoholic beverages will tend to reduce consumption; a cut in farm price supports will tend to reduce farmers' land values.

When actual decision makers rely on economics as one of the justifications for the policies they promote or oppose, the claims of economics to ethical neutrality are tenuous, at best. Most fundamentally, this is true because virtually every economic policy decision affects the distribution of resources in society. A tax or regulatory impediment on one industry, for example, tends to shrink that sector, to the detriment of producers and consumers in that industry but to the benefit of producers and consumers in other sectors of the economy who absorb freed-up resources. Investment in public projects, such as roads or education, tends to benefit the consumers of roads and education but impose burdens on taxpayers who may not care for either.

In short, all else equal, those whose access to resources improves as a result of a public policy decision are better off and those whose access to resources is made more difficult are worse off. Are the implied redistributions of wealth morally acceptable according to defensible standards of social justice? Does the decision maker—voter, politician, bureaucrat—have the right to redistribute wealth from one class of citizen to another? If the government does not intervene in markets at all, it is still imposing an implicit economic policy (of laissez-faire). Are the resulting transactions that people engage in always morally proper? Is the distribution of income that people spend in the marketplace equitable? The answers to these kinds of questions are the province of the philosophical fields of social ethics and political theory, rather than economics. Nevertheless, it is important for the economic analyst to understand the implications of the economic consequences of alternative public policy choices for various standards of social justice.

Discussions by economists of social justice, or "equity," commonly equate the concept with standards of *distributional fairness.* In its most narrow presentation, equity is equated to equality in the distribution of income or wealth. Corresponding economic analyses of equity focus upon the progressivity or regressivity of alternative economic policy choices, where policies are denoted as "progressive" when redistribution is from the relatively wealthy toward the relatively less wealthy and "regressive" when redistribution runs in the other direction. While this egalitarian standard of social justice is familiar, exclusive attention to it is inconsistent with the breadth of both philosophical theories of social ethics and the views actually expressed by participants in the political process.

One entry point into alternative standards of social justice is found in the distinction between *outcome-based* and *process-based* criteria of fairness. Criteria of economic efficiency (including cost-benefit analysis), for example, embody an *outcome* standard of social ethics. When relied upon as a guide to actual policy decisions, these criteria can amount to implicit endorsement of a form of utilitarianism in which the aggregate well-being of society is measured by the sum of individual well-being, and people are assumed to have equal capacity for happiness or well-being (at least at the margin). Thus, a policy move that is efficient has the attribute that the winners' gains exceed the losers' losses; with winners and losers having equal capacities for happiness, social welfare must be improved on net by a move toward economic efficiency.

Another outcome-based criteria of justice is a variant on strict egalitarianism. It posits the possibility of disincentives that could be expected to accompany any attempt to equalize perfectly people's incomes or wealth and assesses the fairness of society by how well it maximizes the welfare of its least well-off members. *

Process-based criteria of social justice assess the fairness of a society and its policies according to the fairness of the *process* of social interactions by which people reach any particular outcome (for example, a distribution of wealth or opportunity). The Jeffersonian-libertarian tra-

*One widely discussed version of this approach to social fairness is associated with John Rawls, *A Theory of Justice* (Cambridge, Mass.: Belknap Press, 1971).

dition, for example, endorses as "fair" processes of interaction (such as market transactions) that are free of coercion. Coercion here is defined as a situation in which one party to a transaction is threatened with being left worse off after the transaction than if that party had never entered into the transaction.[†] Interestingly, the Marxist tradition also contains significant elements of a process-based approach to social justice. While it obviously is concerned with inequality in the distribution of wealth, the Marxist viewpoint lays substantial weight on the proposition that capitalist *processes* of social organization are alienating and exploitative — and, therefore, unjust.

The cases of this section are not intended to resolve philosophical debates over alternative theories of social justice, or to interject any particular viewpoint on such matters. Rather, the cases seek to allow the reader to confront and articulate sensitive issues of social equity. In the process, the reader is encouraged to explore the limits of economics as a tool for at least isolating, if not redressing, the matters of social inequity that the cases introduce.

These cases examine concrete public policy choices aimed at promoting their proponents' concepts of social justice. In the case of *Matters of Life and Death: Defunding Organ Transplants in the State of Arizona,* advocated standards of social justice include the edict that "no one should be denied the opportunity to preserve life." The case of *Graduate Student Fee Differentials in California Public Higher Education* raises the claim that "access to the opportunities that higher education provides should not be allocated on the basis of ability to pay." The appropriate standards for provision of public sector output are addressed in *Funding Schools in Washington State.* This case confronts the assertion that "all children should be provided with education up to a minimum acceptable standard," as well as restrictions on certain communities' abilities to choose to raise the level of their spending on education. Finally, *The Urban League and the Youth Subminimum Wage* raises the familiar debate of whether the government ought to intervene in labor markets to ensure that all workers earn at least a minimum wage. More precisely, it raises the question of whether it is just that the government protect the wages of one class of citizen (low-skill workers) from competition by another class of worker (even lower-skilled, teenage workers).

---

†A modern version of this approach to social justice is associated with Robert Nozick, *Anarchy, State and Utopia* (New York: Basic Books, 1974).

Matters of Life and Death:
Defunding Organ Transplants in the State of Arizona

Dianna Brown, who will be buried this morning in Yuma, was the first person to die under Arizona's newest death penalty law. She was 43 years old. She had committed no murder. No conspiracy. No theft. No parking violation. No crime. Dianna Brown's only offense was to be poor and sick. Under Arizona law, that's now punishable by death.

E.J. Montini, *Arizona Republic*
Column, September 18, 1987

INTRODUCTION

In the spring of 1987, the Arizona state legislature voted to eliminate funding for most organ transplants from the state's health care program for the indigent, the Arizona Health Care Cost Containment System (AHCCCS—pronounced "access"). At the same time, however, the legislature voted to increase other kinds of health coverage provided by AHCCCS. The most controversial item was the extension of basic health service to pregnant women and to children between the ages of six and 13 in the so-called "notch group"[1]—families that earn too much to qualify for AHCCCS automatically, but still earn less than the federal poverty level.[2]

Although the decision to extend health coverage to these women and children was debated extensively, the decision to defund organ transplants slipped through the legislature with relatively little notice or attention. A few months later, however, the

[1] The legislature had already voted to cover notch group children under age six the year before.

[2] To qualify for AHCCCS, a family had to be receiving assistance from Aid to Families with Dependent Children (AFDC) or Supplemental Security Income (SSI) programs already, or to meet state income standards. In January 1987, the state's income eligibility cut-off for a family of four was $5354, while the federal poverty level for a family of four was $11,650. Advocates for low-income residents argued that as a result, many of Arizona's poor had no health coverage of any kind.

legislators had to confront the effect of their decision in the person of 43-year-old Dianna Brown, a Yuma woman suffering from terminal liver disease. In accordance with the new state policy, AHCCCS denied Brown's request for payment for a liver transplant in August 1987. A few weeks later, she died. In the flurry of news coverage attending her death, several legislators publicly questioned their decision to defund the transplants and called for reconsideration of the matter in the 1988 legislative session.

BACKGROUND

In a brief characterization of Arizona's political landscape, the 1988 *Almanac of American Politics* states, "Arizona citizens face squarely first questions—government or free enterprise, development or environment, regulation or freedom—and tend to come out squarely on one side or the other." More often than not, the *Almanac* adds, they come out squarely on the conservative side. Arizona is the only state to have voted Republican in every presidential election since 1948, and Republicans heavily dominate both chambers of the state legislature. The Grand Canyon State also prides itself on a certain independent spirit. For instance, Arizona has openly defied the federally mandated 55 mile per hour speed limit. It was the last state in the country to develop a state park system. And from 1972 to 1982, it was the only state which had not accepted the federal Medicaid program.

Although the Dianna Brown case may have taken the public and even some legislators by surprise, it did not spring from nowhere. It grew out of a several-year struggle within AHCCCS to establish and enforce an organ transplant policy. More broadly, the case arose in the context of longstanding controversy over the type and cost of health care provided to Arizona's poor.

The Birth of AHCCCS. Medicaid was created at the national level in 1966 as an optional program:

if a state met the federal standards established for health care of the poor, the federal government would pay a share of the costs (the percentage varied depending on the relative wealth of the state). Many states were quick to sign on, but Arizona legislators steered clear of the program. "State policymakers feared intrusive federal intervention, as well as the potential for fraud and abuse and the uncontrolled cost to the state," according to a June 1987 report on the program prepared by the federal Health Care Financing Administration (HCFA).[3] For the next 15 years, each county in Arizona continued to provide some measure of health care to the poor with its own dollars. Over time, however, the county system resulted in "unequal eligibility, uneven services [across the state], and, most important, an increasing cost burden on the counties," according to the HCFA report. In the seventies, as elsewhere in the country, health care costs began escalating dramatically in Arizona—from $49 million in 1974 to $106 million in 1979—until they consumed, on average, a quarter of each county's annual revenues, drawn primarily from property taxes. In 1980, when Arizonans passed a referendum limiting the property tax levy, the counties' budget squeeze became a flat-out crisis: "The counties faced the possibility of a complete fiscal breakdown in 1981," HCFA wrote.

It was under this kind of financial pressure that the state legislature began to talk of ushering in a Medicaid program as a way to tap into federal funds. But many legislators remained reluctant, and during the summer of 1981, they bargained with HCFA to set up a program significantly different from a conventional Medicaid system. The Arizona program would be "experimental," designed "to contain cost by encouraging cost competition among prepaid plans and discouraging overutilization of health care," according to HCFA. In each county, different health maintenance organizations (HMOs) would bid to provide an agreed-upon health care package to AHCCCS-eligible residents in return for a fixed payment per person per month from AHCCCS.[4] The goal was to create within each HMO an incentive to keep medical costs low for routine health care. Simi-

larly, the federal government would pay a fixed "capitation rate" per month to the state for each Medicaid-eligible person in the program (a departure from the usual method of reimbursement: paying a share of the actual medical costs incurred.[5]). For this reason, the state had an incentive to keep its own costs low and to push for low bids from HMOs.

The administrative set-up of the AHCCCS program was also to be different from conventional Medicaid in several respects. For one thing, the entire program was to be administered by a private firm. For another, AHCCCS would not cover the full array of Medicaid services (the state received a special waiver so that it would not have to provide skilled nursing facilities for long-term care,[6] home health care, family planning, or nurse midwife services). Within the state, the program was never even called "Medicaid." In fact, according to AHCCCS Deputy Director David Lowenberg:

> When we submit a budget [to the legislature], or make presentations, or talk about policy issues, it's in terms of "AHCCCS" or—the closest we'll get is "Title XIX programs." I've been asked not to put the word "Medicaid" in, because Medicaid brings up all the bad that [the legislators] have either heard personally or read about in other states. There is a high level of concern of the abuse, the fraud. They did not want to be a party to such a system in this state.

The legislature and governor approved the creation of AHCCCS in November of 1981, and the program took effect 11 months later. In retrospect, health care professionals tend to think this speedy implementation allowed too little time for program planning and development. In any event, in its first 18 months, AHCCCS was "beset with administrative and budgetary problems," according to the HCFA report. The legislature voted to shift administrative control of AHCCCS from the private firm to the state in March of 1984, and hired Dr. Donald F. Schaller to head the program. Schaller had had extensive administrative experience with health maintenance organizations ever since 1972, when he had left

---

[3]*Evaluation of the Arizona Health Care Cost Containment System,* by Nelda McCall, project director, and Paul Lichtenstein, federal project officer, Officer of Research and Demonstrations, HCFA, Department of Health and Human Services, June 1987.

[4]HMOs were not expected to finance catastrophic health care, however; thus the relatively exorbitant costs were assumed by AHCCCS. For instance, if any individual's costs exceeded a set amount per year—typically $20,000—then the HMO would be responsible for only a small percentage of the excess; the bulk of the cost would be paid by AHCCCS.

[5]Under conventional Medicaid, the federal government would have paid the state 62 percent of all medical costs for Medicaid-eligible residents. Under the AHCCCS program, the federal government paid a fixed "capitation rate" for each eligible resident, regardless of his/her actual costs. To arrive at this figure, HCFA projected what total Medicaid costs would have been in Arizona under a conventional program, took 95 percent of this figure, and paid the state 62 percent of the 95 percent figure.

[6]Long-term care was still to be provided county-by-county.

15 years of work in private practice to co-found the Arizona Health Plan—one of the oldest HMOs in the state. When he came to AHCCCS, Schaller had also spent a year as senior vice president and medical director of the CIGNA Healthplan, and a year as consultant to a consortium of four HMOs.

Although AHCCCS remained controversial within the state under Schaller's leadership, he is widely credited with bringing the agency under fiscal and administrative control. By early 1987, 200,469 people were covered by AHCCCS,[7] and the program had a year-long budget of $294 million. More than two thirds of Arizona's licensed physicians participated in the program directly or through an HMO, and 14 different private HMOs were contracted to provide health care for the program.

During its first shaky year-and-a-half of operation, AHCCCS had no policy about funding transplants per se, partly because the agency received few transplant requests. Before his arrival, Schaller says, "I'm not sure how many transplants were paid for or what happened. There may have been one or two."

The State of the Art in Transplantation.   The practice of transplanting organs to treat patients began to emerge in the US in the late 1950s and early 1960s—initially with dismal survival rates, which steadily improved. During the 1980s, transplantation became a more viable method of treatment, and was used for an increasing number of organs. By 1987, the simplest and most routine transplants available were cornea and bone transplants, followed by kidney transplants. Heart, liver, and bone marrow transplants were increasingly common, and pancreas, heart-and-lung, and other organ combinations, while rarer, were actively being developed.

But there was no question that these organ transplants were costly. According to a 1984 study,[8] the fully allocated one-year cost of a liver transplant averaged between $230,000 and $340,000, and of a heart transplant, between $170,000 and $200,000. "This is in the range of four to ten times the cost of the other most expensive currently employed medical technologies," the task force reported:

The costs of doing the transplant operation itself are relatively minor, whether the operation lasts three hours or 23 hours. The real costs come from the post-operative hospitalization and the frequent need to re-hospitalize transplant patients to treat various complications. These are very common (averaging more than one per case in most reports on the literature). They include rejection episodes, complications from the operation itself, and infections that develop because such patients take drugs to suppress their immune systems to fight organ rejection, making them more vulnerable to other infections. There are also significant costs in pre-operative work-ups, routine, post-operative hospitalization, organ procurement, etc.

The History of Transplant Funding in Arizona.   Arizona was home to one of the pioneers of the heart transplant field—a much-celebrated young surgeon named Jack Copeland, who built a nationally recognized heart transplant program at the University of Arizona Medical Center in Tucson. Dr. Timothy Icenogle, a surgeon on Copeland's team, says that progress in the heart transplant arena was swift and dramatic in the 1980s. "Back in 1981, there were very dark days and nights of trying to take care of transplants. Survivorship wasn't very good back then. It was back in the days when there were just a few brave souls venturing into this."

It was also back in the days when transplants were covered by virtually no private insurers. "What happened back in 1981, before anyone was paying for this, [the patients] all had to go out and fundraise. And if they had the money, or were able to fundraise enough money, then they came to the 'active' list."[9] If they couldn't come up with the money, he adds, "they died fundraising." By 1986, however, Icenogle said that "almost all private insurers paid for it and if they didn't want to pay for it, we [encouraged the patient] to sue them, [with] nearly 100 percent success."[10]

---

[7]Of those people, 127,983 were either AFDC or SSI recipients, and thus automatically eligible for federal reimbursement. Another 51,770 were in roughly the same income range, but were not AFDC or SSI recipients; these people were not eligible for federal reimbursement. In addition, 20,716 AHCCCS recipients were children under age six from notch group families.

[8]*Report of the Massachusetts Task Force on Organ Transplantation,* presented to the Massachusetts Commissioner of Public Health and the state's Secretary of Human Services in October 1984.

[9]Those waiting in line for a suitable donor organ, and ready for surgery at any time.

[10]AHCCCS did its own informal survey of some 12 HMOs and insurance companies in the state, and found that while many offered some kind of coverage for transplants, they sometimes imposed limits on them as well. For instance, eight of the companies surveyed offered coverage for heart transplants, but one of the eight had a "cap" on the total amount it would spend and one said its decisions would be based on its own assessment of the individual's case. Thus, in reality, half the companies offered unlimited coverage and half offered limited coverage or none at all.

Really, the insurers don't have a choice, because heart transplantation now is not experimental. It is an accepted therapeutic modality, and it is the treatment of choice. It is just as therapeutic as getting penicillin for your pneumonia.

Icenogle adds that some companies—especially HMOs competing for business—have been persuaded that the "public embarrassment" of a protracted battle over payment of a transplant is not worth the fight. "One of them we coerced into paying for a patient, because they realized that the fallout from the lawsuit—and having to go in front of the television cameras and say what schmucks they were—was going to cost them a great deal of money."

"We play a sort of an advocacy role," Icenogle adds. "I think society demands something more from physicians than [to be] just a glob of bureaucrats, and I think we have to take a stand now and then. Our role, essentially, as patient advocate, is to tell them, well, just because the insurance company says they're not going to pay, that is not the end of all the resources. We can help show them other resources that are available."

In the Context of Deregulation. The increasing number of organ transplants, and the growing costs associated with them, coincided with another development in the state's health care system: the deregulation of medical facilities in March 1985. Before deregulation, hospitals were required to seek permission to make capital investments in their facilities. Regulation proponents argued that without such a process, hospitals would begin to perform more and more glamorous high tech, high-dollar medical procedures—like transplants—and that costs would escalate while quality of care would decline.[11] Says Rep. Cindy Resnick (D-Tucson), a member of the House Health Committee, the transplant units "get a great deal of PR and they get a great deal of money."

---

[11]By fall of 1987, no one had traced the impact of deregulation on transplants per se, but a *Phoenix Gazette* reporter, Brad Patten, did a survey of hospitals performing by-pass surgery published on August 26, 1987, and found that: 10 hospitals had begun performing by-pass surgery since deregulation; the number of open heart surgeries was up 36 percent from 1983 to 1986, but the number performed per hospital was down 85 percent; hospitals performing a relatively low volume of by-pass operations had a death rate twice that of hospitals performing a high volume of such procedures; and that overall, the death rate for Medicare patients in by-pass procedures had increased 35 percent in Arizona between 1984 and 1986.

It is a money-making system. If it was just pure concern about the [medical] needs out there, we'd have far more burn units than we have transplant units. The reality is they make money on those units. You can bring in anywhere from a million to three million dollars on that service alone to a hospital a year.

"There's also a prestige factor," adds Phil Lopes, executive director of the regulatory Health Systems Agency of Southeast Arizona before it was dismantled. "You do all these fancy high tech things with somebody's ticker, and there's something sexy about that. Everybody wants to have one of those, wants to have that service. You're in the Big Time."

DON SCHALLER'S VIEW

Right from the start, Schaller was uncomfortable about AHCCCS funding of transplants for several reasons. For one, he questioned whether a program with tight resources should be spending its money on high-dollar, high-risk procedures. After all, AHCCCS was intended as a general health program for the genuinely poor. By contrast, many of AHCCCS's transplant recipients did not start out poor enough to qualify for the program, but—due to their illnesses or to the failure of their private insurance companies to cover their medical expenses—they had "spent down" their assets and become AHCCCS-eligible. Schaller worried that AHCCCS might, *de facto,* be swallowed up by such heavy dollar expenses and turn into a catastrophic health program for the general public. AHCCCS should provide "basic health care to poor people, not just cater to people who have real expensive health problems," he said in an interview aired May 29, 1986 on KAET-TV's "Horizon" program.

Schaller also had several fundamental concerns about the ethics and equity of the complex organ transplant system. For one, he questioned the fairness of the system by which scarce organs were allocated—namely, to those with money, media-appeal, or political support. For another, he objected to the high rates doctors and hospitals were charging for the procedures. When an organ was rejected, for instance, the doctors might re-transplant, substantially increasing the patient's cost: "The way things are set up, when the doctor re-operates, guess what? He gets another fee."

The charges, I think, are excessive. Most of the funding for these procedures goes to private individuals that charge full-bore and excessive fees. I would have less objection if the money went to the University of Arizona, and the University of Arizona had on its staff a physician that got only a salary for performing procedures, not a fee for each service. You could almost say that, since the surgeons charge a fee for service, they might even have a financial incentive to do more and more procedures.

Does Schaller think organ transplants have become a racket? "It's not a racket," he says, "but the financial part of it has come close to that."

Surgeons disagree with Schaller's characterization of the costs. In a September 15, 1987 television interview during KAET-TV's "Horizon" program, Dr. Lawrence Koep, a liver transplant surgeon in Phoenix, said:

The vast majority of the cost is hospital-incurred cost. Personnel, drugs, beds, those are where we spend the lion's share of the money. Time in the operating room—these are long operations—that's horribly expensive. The kind of technology available, particularly in the OR [operating room] and the intensive care unit, is just mind-boggling.

According to Icenogle, the University of Arizona actually provides one of the least expensive heart transplants in the country, but the basic truth, he says, is that "some health care is just more expensive than other health care."

If penicillin were more expensive, then the state legislature would not approve penicillin for pneumonias. Outpatient health care is less expensive than inpatient health care. But what it really comes down to is—is the health care proven, effective, and therapeutic?

In a few rare instances, he says, the University Medical Center has waived costs for patients, but he adds,

I don't think the University Medical Center can make it a policy to absorb the state's responsibility to take on transplantation. Those kind of dollars do not exist. The hospital is a small hospital, it's only 300 beds. This place does not have money to throw away.

AHCCCS' TRANSPLANT POLICY UNDER SCHALLER

When Schaller came on board, there was an established procedure for handling organ transplant requests. The patient would submit a request to AHCCCS which would eventually end up on the director's desk. The director would make the final decision either to grant or deny the request. There were, however, no clear criteria for the director to use in evaluating such requests. Before the mid-1980s, transplant decisions had been so infrequent that they had not caused much consternation within AHCCCS. But when Schaller became director, the number of transplants—and the amount of money spent on them—began to climb. (See Exhibit 1.)

EXHIBIT 1

Cost Information on AHCCCS—Funded Transplants by Organ, February 23, 1987

	Bone Marrow Transplant Recipients			
Date Performed	Total Claim Charges[1]	Date of Death	Member Code[2]	Age
11/86	$72,333.31	11/30/86	C	20
12/24/86	Not yet calculated			23
2/86	$204,150.59			24
2/13/86	$45,336.28	6/3/86		1
3/86	$49,235.71			1
3/86	$526,151.69	7/4/86		21
1/19/87	Not yet calculated			30
12/11/86	$98,826.18			20
1/6/87	Not yet calculated		C	20

Heart Transplant Recipients

Date Performed	Total Claim Charges[1]	Date of Death	Member Code[2]	Age
2/19/87	Not yet calculated			34
2/17/87	Not yet calculated			43
3/4/85	$107,357.10	3/8/85	C	35
1/21/86	$196,714.96			27
6/12/85	$126,931.17		C	41
3/84	$224,259.96			29

Liver Transplant Recipients

Date Performed	Total Claim Charges[1]	Date of Death	Member Code[2]	Age
10/30/84	$107,668.25		C	44
7/2/86	$133,730.13		C	47
1/20/87	Not yet calculated		C	46

Kidney Transplant Recipients

Date Performed	Total Claim Charges[1]	Date of Death	Member Code[2]	Age
7/3/86	$38,949.38		C	24
9/84	$13,580.41		C	34
3/29/84	$16,547.63			26
3/28/84	$92,703.51		C	26
4/86	$63,646.20		C	32
12/20/85	$97,830.64		C	43
1/17/86	$115,032.06			44
3/86	$53,551.94		C	18
7/8/85	$93,229.47			17
3/6/85	$69,309.77		C	26
4/8/86	$82,348.90			15
7/9/85	$46,946.78		C	36
9/85	$107,554.24		C	32
2/4/85	$56,212.46	10/4/85	C	49
7/10/86	$81,284.50			28
5/16/84	$41,759.07			34
4/86	$28,441.21			50
12/85	$54,727.32	8/30/86	C	44
6/5/85	$25,084.99			26
4/14/85	$23,425.26	4/30/85	C	47
1/6/86	$4,897.67			30
9/30/84	$20,176.38	9/30/84	C	41
5/86	$93,336.00		C	24
3/3/86	$119,233.17		C	37
2/4/85	$79,830.91		C	32
5/10/85	$27,442.53		C	25
8/2/85	$23,001.89	5/6/86		25
5/6/85	$19,918.56			39
7/3/85	$15,765.78		C	33
3/13/85	$60,443.36		C	45
5/31/85	$25,942.37		C	40
5/12/84	$68,780.43		C	40

[1] These costs do not include ongoing post-operative medical expenses for transplant patients, which, in some cases, come to $20,000 per year.

[2] When a "C" appears in this column, it means that the patient is "categorically" eligible for AHCCCS; these costs, therefore are eligible—directly, by special arrangement, or indirectly under the terms of the capitation plan—for federal reimbursement. All other patients are the sole responsibility of the state.

Source: Arizona Health Care Cost Containment System.

In 1984, AHCCCS paid for one heart, one liver, and four kidney transplants. In 1985, the program paid for two heart and 16 kidney transplants. The following year, it was one heart, one liver, seven bone marrow, and 12 kidney transplants.[12] Aggregate costs for heart, liver, bone marrow, and kidney transplants rose from $451,012 in 1984 to $1,060,954 in 1985 to $2,141,663 in 1986. In addition, transplant patients' medical expenses after surgery—even when successful—were chronically high as they needed to take immunosuppressant drugs, at an average cost of $500 per month, for the rest of their lives.

Schaller began to take a hard look at the transplant requests coming to AHCCCS, and to consider the merits of each. Rep. Resnick recalls:

> [There was] one instance—perhaps a rumor— that one of our patients, who ultimately had a liver transplant, needed a new liver because they'd used up the last one with alcohol. And they're quickly on the road to using up the second one. That's difficult for physicians in Dr. Schaller's position to see. First, the transplant is imposed on him, and then he's paying for something [and] perhaps—as he said before— the money could have been used much more wisely someplace else.

Schaller soon discovered, however, that he did not always have clear authority to make decisions about transplant requests. "You've got the legislature pushing on one end, the governor says something else, then you've got a judge that says, 'You've got to do this,'" says Schaller. "You know, we tried to have a policy, but it was hard to implement a single policy and apply it the same across every case." The reality was that AHCCCS made its decisions on a case-by-case basis. Before the state legislature took action on the matter—and before the Dianna Brown case surfaced—AHCCCS confronted several controversial transplant cases. Two, in particular, contributed to the development of the legislature's policy.

Sharon Brierley: A Case of Political Pressure. Whenever he did deny a transplant request, Schaller found himself engulfed in a whirlwind of political pressure, sometimes from the legislature, sometimes from the governor, and sometimes even from the White House. In 1984, for example, Schaller ran into trouble when he initially refused the request of 41-year-old Sharon Brierley for a liver

transplant. Brierley had moved to Tucson four years earlier from Vermont after an unhappy marriage, and before she had established a new career, she began to suffer from cirrhosis of the liver, reportedly caused by a previous bout with hepatitis. When Brierley learned she needed a liver transplant, she appealed to AHCCCS. After reviewing the particulars of her case, Schaller refused Brierley's request.

In large part, Schaller's decision had to do with a dispute between AHCCCS and HCFA over transplant funding. AHCCCS took the view that such an extraordinary expense should receive a 62 percent federal reimbursement above and beyond the capitation rate. HCFA argued that, under the terms of its agreement with AHCCCS, the agency should receive no money beyond the capitation rate. Politicians "from the State House to the White House," lobbied both AHCCCS and HCFA on Brierley's behalf.[13] Even First Lady Nancy Reagan voiced concern about the case, according to Schaller. In the end, HCFA agreed to fund a share of the costs, and Schaller authorized AHCCCS payment for the procedure as well—partly because HCFA had agreed to contribute, and partly because, in the absence of clear criteria for making transplant decisions, Schaller knew he was potentially vulnerable to "fairness questions."

After the Brierley case, Schaller decided to formalize his transplant policy. Following the lead of the Medicare system,[14] Schaller decided that AHCCCS— again, using its own administrative discretion to determine appropriateness—would cover heart and bone marrow transplants, but would cover liver transplants only for patients under the age of 18, for whom survival rates were higher. For patients 18 and older, Schaller argued, liver transplants were still "experimental" procedures, and thus AHCCCS was under no obligation to provide them.

Barbara Brillo: A Case of Judicial Pressure. This policy soon received a legal challenge, however. Barbara Brillo, a 46-year-old woman, requested a liver transplant early in 1986 and was denied by AHCCCS on grounds that she was too old. Brillo's husband, Jerome, frantically tried to reverse the decision—an effort which ended with several state legislators and a White House aide exerting pressure on AHCCCS. At the same time, he tried to fundraise for his wife. By April, still without the requisite

---

[13]*Arizona Daily Star*, May 29, 1986.

[14]Medicare tends to be a standard-bearer for states in determining which procedures are considered "experimental" and which are regarded as standard medical care. Health care providers and insurers are under no obligation to provide "experimental" care to patients.

[12]Of the 45 patients to receive these transplants between 1984 and 1986, nine died within a few months of surgery.

$50,000 needed for preliminary tests at the liver transplant center at Phoenix's Good Samaritan Hospital, and with Barbara Brillo's life expectancy down to one or two months, Jerome Brillo arranged for his wife to travel to a Pittsburgh center. "Down deep, I really thought they would come through for us eventually," he told the *Arizona Star* (April 11, 1986). "But, as the weeks went by, my hopes got dimmer. Yes, I'm bitter, because you know what? This could happen to anyone. And believe me, if you don't have the $50,000 (down payment), you're nowhere."

Schaller continued to defend his decision, and to feel the heat for it. In a July 7, 1986 interview on KAET-TV's "Horizon" program, Brillo's attorney, Howard Baldwin, asked, "Why should we pay $110,000 for Don Schaller's salary when we could use that money to provide medical care? Or why should we have a PR man for AHCCCS? It always troubles me to find people fighting for principles over other people's bodies."

After a rancorous court battle, Brillo won her case in the summer of 1986 on grounds that the surgery was medically necessary and was not properly considered experimental. AHCCCS was forced to fund her liver transplant, which had been carried out in Pittsburgh in the interim. Within AHCCCS, "the [Brillo] court decision really precipitated a lot of discussion," says Lowenberg.

> I think what that did is showed us how vulnerable we were going to be to make policy on what's covered and not—and just from the real practical standpoint, as an agency—how do you budget that? What you soon learn is that you really don't have control, because [if you deny patients], they're going to take it to court, and you don't know how the judge is going to rule. In this case, we lost.

In fact, as AHCCCS would write in a report to the legislature the following spring:

> Although the courts, including the Supreme Court, have stated that the states have wide discretion in determining the scope of benefits that they will provide under Medicaid,[15] several courts have held that a particular organ transplant must be covered, since it was determined to be medically necessary under the circumstances.

[15]AHCCCS administrators found that, by 1986, 33 states were paying for liver transplants, 24 for hearts, 13 for hearts-and-lungs, and three for pancreases.

The report also stated that although no state policy would be "fool proof in the absence of federal law," AHCCCS's counsel advised that at the least, "a statutory amendment will be required to effectively exclude coverage of organ transplants for medically needy persons, indigent persons, and eligible children." Thus, AHCCCS decided to ask the legislature to enact a state transplant policy into law. The next question: exactly what kind of law did AHCCCS want to recommend to the legislature?

CREATING THE NEW POLICY

During the summer of 1986, Schaller and a group of his top administrators began to discuss various policy options. These discussions were fairly freewheeling, according to Lowenberg, with administrators tossing out a number of possibilities. He recalls:

> We started to get into [ideas like], "Well, we'll cover *one* heart transplant, but we won't cover *two* heart transplants"—in other words, if the [first transplant fails and the] person needs another one. [But] what's the rationale for drawing the line [there]?

So early on, the AHCCCS team began to consider a blanket policy: no transplants, period, a position also favored initially by the governor's staff. But, Lowenberg says, the AHCCCS administrators soon convinced themselves that this approach did not really make any sense either:

> Initially it was—either you have transplants or you don't—because when you start making exceptions, then it becomes more and more difficult to draw the line. . . . Then, of course, we began to look at the kidney and say, "Well, wait a minute, that doesn't make sense for the kidney or the cornea."

So Schaller and the AHCCCS team began to consider a policy to fund kidney, cornea and bone transplants, but no other kind of organ transplants. This, they argued, was easily defensible, because kidney, cornea, and bone transplants were significantly different medically and economically from transplant of heart, liver, and bone marrow. In the case of corneas and bone transplants, the procedures were simple, there was no issue of tissue match, and they could be performed at many health care establishments.

In addition, these procedures seemed to meet

the "cost-benefit" test: "For the eye implant, it was [a question:] do we allow the person to be on [the] SSI Disabled [list]? Is that in the best interests of the public, that the person becomes blind and cannot work and must be supported by either the state or the federal government?" says Lowenberg.

Kidneys were different from other major organs in that they did not require the donor's death, and were, in fact, often donated by relatives of the patients. Questions of speed, timing, and tissue match were therefore removed from the equation. What's more, though not cheap, kidney transplants were less expensive over time than the alternative— dialysis treatment. AHCCCS discovered that on average, dialysis cost $2500 per month while the average kidney transplant cost $68,000. Thus, "the 'break-even point' economically justifying kidney transplants may be after two years and three months," AHCCCS wrote in a report to the legislature. Heart, liver, and bone marrow transplants were in a whole different league, however, in terms of cost and complexity as were new transplant procedures for the pancreas or heart-and-lung.

After some consideration, AHCCCS did recommend, in the form of its budget request, that the legislature fund only kidney, cornea, and bone transplants—but, cautions Lowenberg, "I think it's real important to understand that we didn't present necessarily a 'policy.' We presented [that] this is an issue that you at the legislature and governor's office need to decide."

LEONARD KIRSCHNER'S VIEW

Schaller left AHCCCS to become a private consultant in January of 1987 and was succeeded the following month by Leonard Kirschner, a physician who, most recently, had served as the medical director of an HMO in Phoenix that treated AHCCCS patients.

Although Kirschner came to AHCCCS after the agency had already submitted a recommendation to the legislature, he quickly got behind the proposal: "Philosophically, I was already in agreement with them," he says. Kirschner's reasoning about the issue, however, was somewhat different from Schaller's. To the incoming director, "aggregate costs" were the major concern, and spending dollars where they would do the most good. A physician with 22 years of service in the military, Kirschner believed that—like the triage practiced on the battlefield—a public program with limited resources must establish clear priorities for treatment. Thus, he favored broad-based health care for the poor over organ transplant coverage. "You take a high risk population that gets no prenatal care—the teenage pregnancy out of the barrio, doesn't want anybody to know she's pregnant, doesn't take care of herself, is on alcohol, and tobacco, or maybe drugs—the risk of low birth weight is up to about 18 percent," he says.

What's the cost to society for that bad baby? Neonatal intensive care unit costs for that baby are probably going to be in the range of $40,000. And to boot, what you are met with on the outside as that child grows up frequently is residual damage from that premature birth: low IQ, low lifetime learning expectancy, won't be able to function, mental retardation, seizures—all the bad things that happen from low birth weight.

So where do you want to spend your money? Do I want to spend my money on doing eight heart transplants at a million and a half dollars? Or go out and get more of these poor people who are not getting prenatal care, and give them some prenatal care? That's about $2000 a case. What's $2000 into a million five? 700 cases? What about 700 deliveries for 8 heart transplants?

"This is probably going to make me sound like Atilla the Hun," Kirschner adds, but "when I have limited resources, it's women and children first. The 'Titanic' concept of medicine."

More broadly, Kirschner believes that—while positive in many ways—the trend toward high tech medicine has serious drawbacks, not just from a financial point of view but also from a human one. "A young man I was peripherally involved with a year ago had a bone marrow transplant and then went into bone marrow rejection, which is a horrible experience. He died a horrible death," he says. "Obviously spending all those resources, and causing him a death far worse than he would have had from the disease makes one sit there and say, 'Well, why in the world did I do that to that person?'"

Everytime we bring a new person into the world, we accept the fact that that person's going to die, and we're almost reaching the point in society where we want to repeal that biological fact.

Now if there's an individual who does have those resources and wants to purchase that, we live in a capitalist society. So be it. But in a public program, that has the widest range of responsibilities, and limited resources to handle those responsibilities, I think it's unacceptable to use those limited resources in a way that really doesn't further the public good.

LEGISLATIVE ACTION IN THE SPRING OF 1987

The legislature—which meets in regular session for only 100 days a year in Arizona—confronted major budget difficulties during its 1987 session. Conservative Republican Gov. Evan Mecham had just taken office and had come to the legislature with an extremely lean budget. At the same time, the state was dealing with a budget overrun from the preceding year, and the legislature was making some mid-year corrections to make up the difference. "So agencies, including ourselves, had to accept serious cutbacks," says AHCCCS's Lowenberg.

What's more, the legislature had to make a number of major budgetary decisions about the AHCCCS program in 1987. The whole program, enacted for five years as a "demonstration," was scheduled to end in October unless the legislature voted to extend it. In addition, the legislature was considering proposals to add services to AHCCCS, including long-term health care, provided at that time by county governments, and service to pregnant women and children between the ages of six and 13 in the notch group—at that time, not offered at all.

Health care committees in both the House and the Senate came up with versions of the omnibus AHCCCS bill. In the Senate discussion, the chair of the Health and Welfare Committee—Sen. Greg Lunn (R-Tucson)—played a significant role. Lunn was a moderate young Republican, especially interested in environmental matters, who had come to office in 1981 from a career in broadcast journalism. He was known as an articulate rising young star whose district included the University of Arizona and its Medical Center. Upon learning that the legislature might defund organ transplants, the Medical Center urged its state senator to preserve funding for heat transplants. Lunn found the university's arguments convincing, and, likewise, convinced his colleagues in the Senate to include funding for heart transplants—but not for liver or bone marrow transplants—in the AHCCCS budget. His reason, he says, was "basically twofold":

I thought that relative to the other major categories of transplantation that we were, in essence, precluding payment for in the future—

liver transplants and bone marrow transplants—that heart had shown a greater rate of success in terms of the success of the procedure itself, longevity, and the quality of life associated after a successful procedure was done.[16] Additionally, I was certainly persuaded by the fact that I believe we have one of the preeminent centers for heart transplantation here in the state at the University of Arizona Medical Center, and I thought it was in the interests of that facility and the research they were doing that AHCCCS continue to be a payer.

When the bill moved to the House Health Committee, the question of organ transplants received little consideration, however, and the committee opted for the AHCCCS administration recommendation. The two versions of the AHCCCS bill, with assorted differences, then went to the House-Senate conference committee on health care, also chaired by Lunn, for final negotiations.

The Conference Committee Resolution. When the AHCCCS bills reached the conference committee, the Senate bill included coverage for heart transplantation and also for psychotropic drugs, another expensive item. The House bill included neither of these items, but did include a significant expansion of coverage for the notch group.[17] "As in any conference committee procedure, you end up assuming that those elements that are consistent are in the bill, and then you argue about the differences," says Lunn. Within the conference committee, therefore, the transplant debate was narrowed to the question of whether or not to fund heart transplants.

Dr. Jack Copeland, the head of the U of A's heart transplant center, weighed in with a letter to the committee. The U of A had performed a total of 125 heart transplants, he wrote. During the past three years, AHCCCS had funded five heart transplants

---

[16]This view of transplants was not uniformly held. While cautioning that the procedures are very different from one another ("It is truly comparing apples, oranges, and tangerines"), Leonard Kirschner says that given limited resources, he would favor funding liver transplants for children and bone marrow transplants for children and young adults before funding heart transplants for the middle aged.

[17]According to Bill Merrick, assistant director of AHCCCS' Division of Financial Management, health care for some 26,200 notch group children under six between January 1, 1987 and June 30, 1987 was expected to total $6.8 million (with HCFA paying $1.2 million). He estimated that to serve 27,000 children aged six to 13 from October 1, 1987 to June 30, 1988 would cost $10 million—with HCFA picking up about $1.9 million. (See Exhibit 2.)

EXHIBIT 2

AHCCCS Statistics about Costs of Heart, Liver, and Bone Marrow Transplants in FY 1987 and Estimated Increase Needed to Cover Such Procedures in FY 1988.

	Arizona Health Care Cost Containment System Administration								
Human Organ Transplants	Fiscal 1986–1987[1]			Program Change			Fiscal 1987–1988 Request		
	Number	Cost per	Amount	Number	Cost per	Amount	Number	Cost per	Amount
Heart transplants	0	0	0	8	164,000	1,312,000	8	164,000	1,312,000
Liver transplants	1	134,000	134,000	5	134,000	670,000	6	268,000	804,000
Bone marrow transplants	1	230,000	230,000	7	230,000	1,610,000	8	460,000	1,840,000
Totals	2		364,000	20		3,592,000	22		3,956,000

[1]For fiscal 1986–1987 transplants are paid as inpatient hospital in the Fee-for-Services category. Number and costs are estimated as transplant bills have not been submitted at the date of this budget request.

Source: Arizona Health Care Cost Containment System

and post-operative costs of one artificial heart ("bridge-to-transplant") procedure. "Five of these patients are doing well and living a high quality of life, and the bridge-to-transplant patient has returned to full-time employment. We currently have two AHCCCS patients needing heart transplants who are being evaluated and we project there will be five or six AHCCCS patients per year." Copeland then offered some economic arguments for funding heart transplants:

> For most of our patients (married males, less than 50 years of age with pre-school or teenage children), the major reasons for undergoing cardiac transplantation were to maintain some semblance of family stability and to resume competitive employment. Our patients are generally referred for vocational rehabilitation and one third have returned to work within six months of transplantation.

Copeland argued that even if AHCCCS refused a patient a transplant, it would have to continue to provide some health care to the person while s/he continued to deteriorate and die. Heart transplants were only performed in dire cases—where the patient's life expectancy was less than 12 months—but those health care costs could still run quite high. He wrote that on average, "according to the National Heart Transplant Study, the cost difference between a patient who is transplanted and one who is not is approximately $6,100"—not much money in the scheme of things. Copeland added:

> Should the non-transplanted patient die leaving a wife and three children (aged 5, 10, and 15),

the family becomes eligible for monthly social security benefits approximating $1036 which payments continue until the youngest child reaches the age of 18 or until age 21 for all three children should they pursue college educations.

Copeland also included cost estimates for heart transplants ($65,000 to $80,000) in his letter, and mentioned that his center was likely to become one of 10 approved transplant centers across the country designated by Medicare as an approved treatment facility.

These last two points aroused the anger and concern of AHCCCS administrators. For one, they felt Copeland had vastly underestimated the true cost of an average heart transplant (which they calculated to be $165,000).[18] In addition, they saw the emergence of the U of A as a nationally recognized transplant center to be a double-edged sword: in increasing numbers, patients would move to the state to receive medical treatment, and if they established residency and were income eligible, AHCCCS would have to pay for them. Already, two such patients had surfaced, according to Schaller, who appeared before the conference committee as a consultant to the committee:

> We're finding ourselves as a state paying for patients who move in from Idaho and California with no ability to go back to those states

[18]In fact, the AHCCCS administrators showed the committee that in another context, the university itself had estimated the cost of a heart transplant at $153,000. That cost-estimate included hospitalization as well as 24 months of drugs and follow-up care, however.

and collect from their Medicaid agencies our costs. That's one of the reasons I don't think we ought to pay for this, because if we're going to be attracting people from all over the country who are so impressed with Dr. Copeland's ability, I'm wondering who's going to pay for 'em. If he wants to be a regional center, let him go out and collect his money from everybody in the region—not AHCCCS.

Furthermore, AHCCCS warned that if the program began to cover each transplant requested, "it would not be long before most health insurance carriers would cease to consider transplants as a covered benefit on the theory that AHCCCS (and the taxpayers) is the paying alternative."

AHCCCS also confronted the committee with another problem: the Health Care Financing Administration. While in the past, HCFA had reluctantly provided extra funding for transplants on a case-by-case basis, the federal agency decided in 1986 that this arrangement was not in keeping with the spirit or ground rules of the AHCCCS-Medicaid experiment. Thus, HCFA insisted that the costs of the transplants be covered the way any other medical costs were covered—out of the basic capitation rate given to the state. In a letter to AHCCCS dated October 17, 1986, HCFA wrote that "the state will include all organ transplant costs in the base computations used to determine capitation rates for categorically eligible AHCCCS recipients, and HCFA will not provide a regular federal match based on actual organ transplant costs for these procedures on an individual basis." Paul Lichtenstein, federal project officer for AHCCCS under HCFA's Office of Research and Development, says that HCFA would have been more than willing to increase the capitation rate to reflect the cost of transplants for Medicaid-eligible people. But according to Lowenberg, it is not reasonable to try to work such changeable and erratic costs into a standard formula: "It's our viewpoint that with such a low-volume, high price type of incident, i.e., transplant, it doesn't make sense to attempt to include it in a capitation. . . . Capitation is never going to cover all the costs. Never."

This legislative tug-of-war over funding for heart transplants ended with a decision that heart transplants *might* be funded in part, but only if HCFA relented and agreed to share the costs on a case-by-case basis. Says Lunn:

It ended in a compromise. A lot of people would have just as soon not had [heart transplants] in there at all. I would have just as soon had [them] in there [unconditionally] as an AHCCCS-covered service. So—just tire people out, that's the way—we never finished the bill. When we *abandoned* the bill, that's what it looked like.

Ultimately, everything [in dispute between House and Senate committees] went in the bill, but modified. The way hearts got modified was squirrelly language about "if HCFA agrees to paying for it the way we would like them to participate, then we'll go ahead and do it." Psychotropics got modified by saying, "subject to legislative appropriation," so it wasn't an entitlement—it was, we'll fight that out when we come to the Appropriations Committee next year. And the notch group stuff was modified by putting if off a year, to a later effective date. It was like trying to fit an elephant through a keyhole. You had to push it in different places to get it to fit.

My recollection is that [the heart transplant compromise] was proposed by AHCCCS itself. I think they probably were much more aware than I at the time of the chances of convincing Health Care Financing Administration to go along on that basis were pretty damned small, because that seems to be the case now. So I think, in retrospect, I may have been snookered.

Another member of the conference committee—Rep. Resnick—characterizes the legislature's negotiations over AHCCCS as "raw politics," primarily focused on the question of funding for pregnant women and children in the notch group. Resnick, who had been in the legislature since 1983, was a liberal Democrat from Tucson who had become active in health policy matters in 1980, when she joined a coalition working to bring Medicaid to Arizona. Like most Democrats, Resnick had initially opposed establishment of AHCCCS in favor of a more comprehensive, conventional Medicaid program. Once the AHCCCS program was in place, however, she and other Democrats had worked to make it as comprehensive as possible. During the 1987 session, the Democrats drew a line in the sand: without the notch group expansion, they would vote against extending AHCCCS beyond October. The strategy, says Resnick, ultimately worked; the notch group expansion was included.

The legislative vote on the final omnibus AHCCCS bill—including both the notch group coverage and the transplant policy—was overwhelming: 44 to

EXHIBIT 3

Memo Estimating Costs of Notch Group Expansion under Legislature Consideration in Spring, 1987

Arizona Health Care Cost Containment System
MEMORANDUM

TO: Leonard J. Kirschner, M.S., M.P.H.
           Director

FROM: Bill Merrick, Assistant Director
           Division of Financial Management

SUBJECT: Expansion of the Children's Program to Include Ages Six (6) through Thirteen (13)

DATE: March 23, 1987

Before going on to the numbers, I calculated the fiscal impact for nine (9) months beginning October 1, 1987, and six (6) months beginning on January 1, 1988. These breaks logically follow our contracting cycle. In my opinion, it would not be cost effective to start the program on July 1, 1987 as AHCCCS would need to bid this population for the period July 1, 1987 to September 30, 1987.

Now the numbers:

	Number of Children	Total	State	Federal
Nine (9) months beginning October 1, 1987	27,000	$10,304,400	$8,449,800	$1,854,600
Six (6) months beginning January 1, 1988	26,200	$ 6,800,500	$5,576,400	$1,224,100

For the purpose of comparison, I also calculated the fiscal impact of just adding the six (6) year olds by the nine (9) and six (6) month breaks.

	Number of Children	Total	State	Federal
Nine (9) months beginning October 1, 1987	4,250	$ 1,708,628	$1,401,075	$ 307,553
Six (6) months beginning January 1, 1988	4,023	$ 1,078,155	$ 895,009	$ 183,146

Should you have any questions, just give me a buzz.

BM/rc

Source: Arizona Health Care Cost Containment System.

6, with 10 not voting in the House; 23 to 2 with 5 not voting in the Senate. But, with so much emphasis on the notch group coverage and the general extension of AHCCCS, this vote did not reflect legislative opinion on the transplant issue per se, according to Resnick:

There is such a select group in the legislature that actually dealt with the AHCCCS issues—

there were probably eight of us at the most, and then probably only three to four of us who were intimately involved with the discussion. I don't think [the others] considered [transplants one way or the other]. In the broad scheme of things, the bill looked okay.

In any event, under the terms of the AHCCCS bill, the new transplant policy took effect August 18,

1987. Within the month, the case of Dianna Brown surfaced.

DIANNA BROWN'S STORY

Dianna Brown, 43, was a woman from the city of Yuma with lupoid hepatitis, an ailment which had shrunk her liver so that she could not process liquids properly. She had been nearly incapacitated since January of 1985, when her illness forced her to quit her job as manager of a doughnut shop. "I noticed I couldn't pick up anything from counters," she told the *Arizona Republic.*[19] At one point, she remembers, "I nearly fell into the fryer."

"I said, 'I'm going to have to take a leave of absence until I get better.' But then I never got better. I only got worse."

Born in Texas, Brown had quit school at a young age to support her family, and by the summer of 1987, virtually everyone in her immediate family had serious health problems. Her mother was living in a nursing home. Brown had been caring for her niece's two children ever since her niece had suffered brain damage in a car accident. Her sister had recently suffered a heart attack.

Brown applied for AHCCCS funding for a liver transplant in late August, but under the terms of the new law, was clearly ineligible. "If a transplant isn't necessary, I don't want it," Brown told the *Arizona Republic* in an interview printed September 7, 1987. "But if it is the only solution, I would like a chance for a chance." She said that she hoped "to work again": "That is a dream off in the future. Surely there is something I can do. I might not be able to work with my hands like I used to, but I'm sure I still could do something.

"I can understand that you have to look at the overall picture. I always try to understand. I can't say I always do—Lord knows I don't—but I try."

Four days later, the *Republic* reported that the husband of a woman who had undergone a successful liver transplant had started a transplant fund for Brown with $35,000 left over from their family's fundraising effort. A radio talk-show host joined the effort, and within a few days had increased the sum to $37,000. But it was too little too late. On September 11, Brown's kidneys began to fail, preventing her body from eliminating toxins. This led to brain damage, coma, and eventual liver failure. On September

14, she died. Even if AHCCCS had approved Brown's request, there is some question about whether a transplant could have been arranged in time to save her. But her personal physician, Dr. George Burdick, told the *Republic* the next day that he believed she could have been helped. "I don't think her death was unreasonably painful or prolonged," he said, "but in my mind it was unnecessary."

Brown's family did not even have enough money for her funeral.

THE AFTERMATH OF DIANNA BROWN'S DEATH

When Dianna Brown died, the press began to reconstruct the legislature's policy decision of the previous spring, and in general, reporters and some legislators characterized it as a conscious "trade-off" between transplants and the notch group expansion. Some observers and participants, however, believe this represents a rewriting of history. "That argument is just a whitewash," says Icenogle. "What we're talking about here is a legislature that just doesn't want to come up with the money, period. And this is their way of trying to defuse the issue."

Rep. Resnick agrees that the legislature was not really trading services. "That's how the press perceived it, and maybe they were not totally wrong, but from my perspective, we weren't making a trade." Instead, she says, dropping funding for transplants was a quick way to respond to Schaller's concern "that the thing was out of control." Other legislators agreed that they relied heavily on AHCCCS's recommendation in making their transplant policy. Says Lunn, "You try to listen to medical experts in terms of what is reasonable and what is cost-effective and what makes sense from a medical standpoint."

"Our legislative session is only 100 days," adds Resnick, "so it's difficult to say, 'Let's talk about it during the session.' It was easier just to say, 'Let's drop authority for AHCCCS to provide these transplants and then let's re-look at the issue.' No one ever thought that we would just drop it and never deal with transplants."

Resnick saw the transplant debate as part of a larger set of issues. Rather than make an "up" or "down" decision on funding organ transplants under AHCCCS, she believed the legislature should stand back, take a broader view, and "deal with the issue of catastrophic health care."

We ought to make the health system responsive to those kinds of needs, but it isn't necessarily the AHCCCS system. It isn't necessarily a pro-

---

[19]"Patient doomed by policy; AHCCCS refuses to fund transplant," by Martin Van Der Werf, *Arizona Republic,* September 7, 1987.

gram for the poor that ought to be responding to that. What I don't want to see is that we change state policy, allowing more flexibility in the AHCCCS program, without addressing all the other issues related to that decision, without discussing the ramifications of having too many hospitals doing heart transplants, without discussing ramifications related to the insurance industry, which will—if there's somebody out there who's going to pay for these services—back down real quick in providing those for their own clients. So my preference would be that we discuss it all at the same time. Otherwise you get a really bad decision.

Other legislators focused primarily on the financial aspect of the question, and the issue of fairness to individuals in need of transplants. AHCCCS's refusal to fund Brown's transplant was "asinine," "grossly discriminating," and "embarrassing," according to Rep. Earl Wilcox (D-Phoenix), a member of the House Health Committee. "If we don't make taking care of this problem a priority in our next session, we'll be remiss as legislators."[20]

"It's not a comfortable decision that we had to make," says Senate Minority Leader Alan Stephens (D-Phoenix). "Unfortunately, you have to look at it in the context of Arizona state government."

It's been a battle in this state, in a conservative era, to increase services. And we do it on a piecemeal basis. If you want to look at people's deaths, and the case of Mrs. Brown obviously comes to mind in this situation, but if you went back, I'm sure you could find a lot of people that died in this state as a result of not getting care that's routinely given in other states, because we didn't provide the service that other states provide.

But other legislators stood by their decision. "None of us can live forever," said Sen. Doug Todd (R-Tempe). "I think it was a decision that was made by the legislative body to benefit the most residents of the state of Arizona."[21]

"The public generally is not willing to, say, double the taxes in this state to insure that everyone got the maximum possible health care—the public isn't willing to accept that," stated Rep. Bill English (R-Sierra Vista) in an interview aired September 15, 1987 on KAET-TV's "Horizon" program. While he defended the legislature's decision to defund transplants, however, he left open the possibility of changing the decision in the future:

I'm going to say that next year, the decision may very appropriately be a different decision, with progress in the state of the art [of transplantation]. What is the right decision for today may not be the right decision for tomorrow.

---

[20]*Arizona Republic,* September 16, 1987.　　　　[21]*Arizona Republic,* September 16, 1987.

ASSIGNMENT FOR CLASS DISCUSSION

Come to class prepared to explain whether or not you think the Arizona legislature was right in deciding not to fund certain kinds of organ transplants under the state's health care program for the indigent. In preparing your answer, please consider:

1. What principles are helpful to you in deciding what the state of Arizona's responsibility is? Do you regard health care as a right, for example, and if so why?
2. Does economic analysis have anything to contribute to your position on what the state's responsibilities are?

Graduate Student Fee Differentials in California Public Higher Education

One of the most deeply ingrained tenets of state support for higher education in California has been the "no-tuition" principle—the view that students should not be charged for any direct instructional costs. For over a century, strong supporters of state subsidies to the University of California (UC) and the California State University (CSU) had upheld the principle that revenues from student charges could not be used to meet direct instructional expenses—California would remain a "tuition-free state." Students were, however, expected to make some contributions in the form of student activities fees. In the early 1980s, after several years of cutbacks in state programs and sharp and unpredictable increases in student fees by the California legislature, the "no-tuition" principle appeared to be under indirect attack. The California Postsecondary Education Commission (CPEC) was charged in 1984 to convene a committee of interested parties and develop a long-term statutory formula for setting student fees.

The Legislative Analyst's Office (LAO) had long challenged the distinction between fees and tuition as arbitrary and even counterproductive. However, the committee's deliberations led to a sharp dispute over the LAO's contention that undergraduate and graduate students' contributions should be differentiated on the basis of the relative cost of instruction at each level. Representatives of student organizations and university administrations contended that the higher cost of graduate education was more than offset by greater social benefits, and that the institution of a graduate fee differential would contravene the principle that students would remain immune from the burden of direct costs of instruction. The committee would, ultimately, have to decide.

CALIFORNIA SUPPORT FOR HIGHER EDUCATION

The commitment to public higher education in California has enjoyed a historical level of support that rivals that of any other state in the nation. Since the founding of the University of Santa Clara in 1851, the number of public higher education institutions has grown to 137, divided among three segments: UC, CSU, and the California Community Colleges (CCC). By the early 1980s, California, a state with 10.4 percent of the nation's population, accounted for 16.9 percent of the nation's public college and university students and 13.4 percent of national public expenditures for such institutions.

This generous support was founded on two widely shared beliefs: that the state's prosperity was closely related to the level of investment in higher education; and, that the state bore a responsibility to ensure universal access to institutions of higher learning. In the most recent of a series of studies entitled *The Wealth of Knowledge,* the CPEC calculated that the benefits from direct expenditures on higher education in California, including a multiplier effect, amounted to $28.3 billion in 1981-82—about 7.9 percent of the gross state product. Of this total, about $20.6 billion was accounted for by public institutions. (See Exhibits 1-4.) In addition, the study listed a number of unquantifiable benefits derived from investments in "human capital," ranging from increases in workers' skills and earning power (see Exhibits 5-6), to the effect that exposure to education has on the character of the state's citizens. Howard Bowen, whose works are often quoted in publications on California public higher education, summarized the latter category of beneficial changes:

> Higher education tends to make people more open to change, more flexible in their thinking, less prejudiced toward others, and more cognizant of humane values and social responsibility.

As for the overall balance between investments and returns from higher education, Bowen concluded:

> First, the monetary returns from higher education alone are probably sufficient to offset all the costs. Second, the nonmonetary returns are

This case was written by Vlad Jenkins under the direction of Professor José A. Gomez-Ibañez for use at the Kennedy School of Government, Harvard University. This case was made possible in part by funds from the Parker Gilbert Montgomery Endowment for Public Policy. (0388)

EXHIBIT 1

Economic Impact of California State University Expenditures, 1981–82

Source of Expenditure	Direct Expenditures	Added Impact of Multiplier	Total Economic Impact
Institution	$ 313,040,618	$ 428,865,647	$ 741,906,260
Faculty and staff	581,597,858	796,789,065	1,378,386,923
Students	1,237,322,626	1,605,131,997	2,932,454,623
Visitors	28,000,000	38,360,000	66,360,000
Total	$2,159,961,102	$2,959,146,709	$5,119,107,811

Source: The Wealth of Knowledge. California Postsecondary Education Commission Report 84-1. Adopted January 30, 1984.

EXHIBIT 2

Economic Impact of University of California Expenditures, 1981–82

Source of Expenditure	Direct Expenditures	Added Impact of Multiplier	Total Economic Impact
Institution	$1,970,000,000	$3,506,600,000	$5,476,600,000
Employees	1,140,000,000	2,029,200,000	3,169,200,000
Total	$3,110,000,000	$5,535,800,000	$8,645,800,000

Source: The Wealth of Knowledge. California Postsecondary Education Commission Report 84-1. Adopted January 30, 1984.

EXHIBIT 3

Economic Impact of California Community College Expenditures, 1981–82

Source of Expenditure	Direct Expenditures	Added Impact of Multiplier	Total Economic Impact
Institutional	$ 218,511,081	$ 477,766,621	$ 769,227,702
Faculty and staff	1,401,662,096	2,102,493,144	3,504,155,240
Students	1,043,394,660	1,565,091,990	2,680,486,650
Total	$2,763,562,837	$4,145,351,755	$6,909,919,592

Source: The Wealth of Knowledge. California Postsecondary Education Commission Report 84-1. Adopted January 30, 1984.

EXHIBIT 4

Economic Impact of 60 Independent California Colleges and Universities, 1981–82

Source of Expenditure	Direct Expenditures	Added Impact of Multiplier	Total Economic Impact
Institutional (less payroll)	$1,367,700,000	$2,051,550,000	$3,419,250,000
Faculty and staff	879,700,000	1,319,550,000	2,199,250,000
Students	789,700,000	1,184,550,000	1,974,250,000
Visitors	54,700,000	82,050,000	136,750,000
Total	$3,091,800,000	$4,637,700,000	$7,729,500,000

Source: The Wealth of Knowledge. California Postsecondary Education Commission Report 84-1. Adopted January 30, 1984.

EXHIBIT 5

Income Ratios of Males Based on Different Levels of Educational Attainment, 1979

	Age of Worker			
Educational Level	*25–34*	*35–44*	*45–54*	*55–64*
One to three years of college compared to a high school graduate	1.05	1.12	1.14	1.23
Four years of college compared to a high school graduate	1.21	1.49	1.56	1.68
Five or more years of college compared to a high school graduate	1.38	1.72	1.77	1.90
Four years of college compared to three or fewer years of college	1.15	1.33	1.36	1.37
Five or more years of college compared to three or fewer years	1.31	1.48	1.55	1.55
Five or more years of college compared to four years	1.13	1.15	1.13	1.13

Source: The Wealth of Knowledge. California Postsecondary Education Commission Report 84-1. Adopted January 30, 1984.

several times as valuable as the monetary returns. And third, the total returns from higher education in all its aspects exceed the cost by several times.

The second article of faith in California public higher education was that universal access depends on the maintenance of a no-tuition policy. This principle, articulated as early as 1863, in the Organic Statutes which set up the University of California, had been inviolably preserved. UC and CSU students remained in the unique position of not having to pay tuition; their yearly payments of $1,387 and $692, at UC and CSU respectively in 1983-84, were defined as student activities fees and could not be used to cover direct educational expenses. According to the 1960 Master Plan for Higher Education "tuition is defined generally as student charges for teaching expense, whereas fees are charged to students, either collectively or individually, for services not directly related to instruction, such as health, special clinical services, job placement, housing and recreation."

The no-tuition philosophy and policy were challenged most forcefully during Ronald Reagan's

EXHIBIT 6

California State University Costs of Instruction of Students at Various Levels, and Estimated Extra Income Taxes Paid by These Students during Their Lifetimes above Those of High School Graduates, Based on 1979–80 Costs and Tax Rates

	Cost of Instruction to the State	Extra Taxes	
Years of College Completed		*Men*	*Women*
Three years of college	$ 5,588		
Federal income taxes		$ 4,446	$ 2,889
State income taxes		1,278	206
Total additional income taxes		$ 5,274	$ 3,095
Four years of college	$13,008		
Federal income taxes		$15,428	$ 5,323
State income taxes		3,715	661
Total additional income taxes		$19,143	$ 5,984
Five and one-half years of college	$22,835		
Federal income taxes		$18,157	$12,303
State income taxes		5,438	2,407
Total additional income taxes		$23,595	$14,710

Source: The Wealth of Knowledge. California Postsecondary Education Commission Report 84-1. Adopted January 30, 1984.

EXHIBIT 7

Student Fees in California Public Higher Education Institutions Selected Years

	1979–80	1981–82	1983–84			1984–85 (Proposed)		
			Fee Level	Change from 1979–80		Fee Level	Change from 1983–84	
				Amount	Percent		Amount	Percent
University of California:								
Undergraduate	$ 736	$ 997	$1,387	$ 653	89%	$1,317	–$70	–5.0%
Graduate	784	1,043	1,434	650	83	1,364	–70	–4.9
California State University:								
Undergraduate (full-time)	204	320	692	488	239	650	–42	–6.1
Graduate (full-time)	204	320	728	524	257	686	–42	–5.8
Hastings College of the Law	752	985	1,430	678	90	1,131	–108	–9.5
California Maritime Academy	886	1,183	1,259	373	42	1,277	18	1.4

Source: Analysis of the Budget Bill for FY July 1, 1984 to June 30, 1985, Report of the Legislative Analyst to the Joint Legislative Budget Committee, California Legislature.

term as governor of California. During those turbulent years on California's campuses, the Reagan administration pointed to an ongoing academic debate and challenged the existing policy toward public higher education. A series of papers in the *Journal of Human Resources* by Prof. B. Weisbrod started with the casual observation that the average family income of students at UC Berkeley was higher than that of students at Stanford. Weisbrod then calculated that support for higher education out of General Fund tax revenues amounted to a subsidy for a group of families whose average income was substantially higher than that of the average taxpayer. (Responses to the article published in the same journal included calculations demonstrating that expenditures on higher education actually had a progressive impact on income distribution.) The Reagan administration tried and failed to institute a tuition, but it did leave in place new and higher student activities fees, as well as a graduate fee differential—student fees that were $60 higher for graduate students than for undergraduates at UC.

Following the passage of Proposition 13, budgetary considerations became the primary determinant in the process of setting annual student fees. After years of relative stability, students suddenly faced successive increases in fees as the state tried to balance its budget and offset losses in property taxes. (See Exhibit 7.) Student fees—one of the last items on the agenda of the assembly's budget conference committee—were not determined until late July and were often also increased at mid-year.

The haphazard manner of determining fee levels left nobody satisfied. Student organizations

sought ways to avoid large fee increases, mid-year fee increases, and last minute decisions about fee levels in the budget. To this end, UC and CSU students' lobby organizations initiated, in 1982 and 1983, resolutions calling for the establishment of a "graduate, moderate, and predictable" policy regarding fees and limitations on the uses of student fee revenues. Nonetheless, in 1982-83, fees increased by about 30 percent and 60 percent at UC and CSU, respectively.

The following year, Republican Governor George Deukmejian was inaugurated and issued an immediate call for a two percent cut in the state operations budget. As a further budget reduction measure, Governor Deukmejian also introduced a $64 graduate fee differential at CSU for the school year 1983-84. The legislature—confronted with a $1.5 billion deficit—agreed to additional mid-year increases that brought the increase in UC and CSU fees for 1983-84 to eight percent and 40 percent, respectively. Outraged by the results of two consecutive years of large mid-year fee increases, students launched a legal challenge to the governor's authority to increase fees at CSU and built a strong bipartisan coalition in the legislature to oppose further fee increases for 1984-85. The Deukmejian administration reacted with proposals in the 1984-85 Governor's Budget to reduce fee levels at UC (by $79, to $1,317) and CSU (by $42, to $650).

During budget testimony, the LAO and the CPEC noted that 1984 would be a propitious time to establish a consistent, long-term policy for fees at UC and CSU. Student organizations—which had long sought ways to establish a formula for fees in a statute—and most legislators—who sought to dispel the

EXHIBIT 8

Hypothetical Fees Calculated as Different Percentages of Segmental Cost in 1984–85[1]

Segment	Current Fee (1983–84)	Fee Proposed for 1984–85 in Governor's Budget	Hypothetical Fees in 1984–85 Using Different Percentages of Total Cost					
			12%	13%	14%	15%	16%	17%
UC	$1,387	$1,317	$1,284	$1,385	$1,487	$1,588	$1,689	$1,789
CSU	692	650	659	708	757	804	853	901
Hastings	1,430	1,131	765	822	880	938	996	1,053
Maritime	1,259	1,277	1,160	1,256	1,353	1,449	1,547	1,643

[1]Fee based on percentage of state appropriation and student fees in 1983–84, adjusted for the average annual change in state appropriations and student fees during the three prior years. Campus-based fees ($72 for UC and $80 for CSU) are added to total after percentage calculation.

Source: Analysis of the Budget Bill for FY July 1, 1984 to June 30, 1985, Report of the Legislative Analyst to the Joint Legislative Budget Committee, California Legislature.

perception that they were balancing the budget by increasing student fees—welcomed the initiative.

THE LAO AND GRADUATE FEE DIFFERENTIALS

A fundamental dispute had separated the position of the students' organizations from that of the LAO and the CPEC, who had been arguing for years that the distinction between student fees and tuition was moot and even counterproductive. In a statement to the Senate Education Committee in October 1983, the LAO explained:

First, [the current policy] tends to put emphasis on what students pay for, rather than how much they pay. California's "no-tuition" policy has led to excessive concern with terminology and budget accounting. Meanwhile, many students and their parents believe they are paying tuition. At the time they must make their check to UC or CSU, the distinction between "fees" and "tuition" is lost.

Second, by creating a set of protected categorical programs, the current policy reduces the flexibility of the legislature and the segments to the point where it can produce unintended and undesirable results. Since reducing expenditures in fee-funded programs does not permit General Fund budget reductions, these programs have fared better than instructional programs during the past two years when significant budget reductions were made at each segment.

These concerns were not shared by either the segments' administrations or students, and the LAO and CPEC appeared willing to concede to the almost unanimous support in California politics for the no-tuition principle. The LAO also continued to disagree with the students' organizations on the question of what share of the total costs student contributions should occur.

A compromise on these issues appeared possible. However, the question of whether the formula for determining student fees should differentiate between the fees of graduate and undergraduate students remained to be one of the most divisive aspects of the upcoming debate. In its yearly analyses of the budget between 1978 and 1984, the LAO had submitted proposals for raising the differential between undergraduate and graduate student fees. In addition, that office also proposed that non-resident health science (medicine, dentistry, and veterinary science) students be charged an additional annual tuition of $1,000. The LAO contended that its recommendations would make the system both more equitable and more efficient.

The LAO based its recommendations, first, on the principle suggested by the Carnegie Commission on Higher Education:

Public colleges and universities should carefully study their educational costs per student and consider restructuring their tuition charges at upper-division and graduate levels to reflect the real differences in the cost of education per student, eventually reaching a general level equal to about one-third of educational costs.

In its most recent analysis of the budget, the LAO had first noted that graduate programs cost more per student than undergraduate programs, "due to the specialized nature of the instruction and the typically low faculty-student ratio." At CSU, for example, the cost of instruction per undergraduate

EXHIBIT 9

Comparison of Marginal Cost per Student
in Selected Disciplines

Medical curriculum	$32,936
Dentistry curriculum	22,494
Health science graduate academic	7,552
Health science graduate professional	7,552
General campus undergraduate	3,573

Source: Analysis of the Budget Bill for FY July 1, 1984 to June 30, 1985, Report of the Legislative Analyst to the Joint Legislative Budget Committee, California Legislature.

EXHIBIT 10

	Student/Faculty Ratio
Medicine	3.5 to 1
Dentistry	4.0 to 1
Veterinary medicine	5.4 to 1
General campus	17.45 to 1

Source: Analysis of the Budget Bill for FY July 1, 1984 to June 30, 1985, Report of the Legislative Analyst to the Joint Legislative Budget Committee, California Legislature.

was $3,766 while the cost per graduate student was $7,587 in 1980-81. Although a similar breakdown of costs was not available from UC, the LAO estimated that the cost of graduate instruction there was as much as four times greater than that of undergraduate instruction. The LAO's analysis focused in particular on students in the health sciences, who have lower faculty-student ratios and higher incremental costs for an additional student than general campus students. (See Exhibits 9–10.)

Second, the LAO observed that "a greater proportion of the benefits from education accrues to the individual [graduate student] directly, because specialized knowledge is more likely to translate into a higher income than is the general knowledge acquired as an undergraduate." Again, the LAO presented statistics for the average net incomes of graduates from health science graduate programs. According to professional organizations, the average starting salaries in 1976 were $58,584 for physicians, $44,706 for dentists, and $30,000 for veterinarians.

The use of this argument was related to the perception of LAO analysts that a considerable share of private benefits from education were accruing to students who would not only have the ability to pay for their education by virtue of their higher earning power, but also to students who already had the ability to pay by virtue of their high family incomes. Students at UC, the LAO observed, had much higher family incomes than students at either CSU or private institutions, and yet the state was providing them a total subsidy twice that provided CSU students ($7,535 versus $3,873 in 1980-81). (See Exhibits 11–12.)

Finally, the LAO warned that "many economists maintain that minimal tuition charges at the graduate level lead to an inefficient over-investment in graduate education," and a "proliferation of workers who are over-educated for the jobs to which they are hired." The LAO noted that state contributions to meeting the rising cost of higher education had risen faster than student fees. During the early

EXHIBIT 11

Total Family Income of Dependent Undergraduates by Higher Education Segment, 1980[1]

Family Income	Higher Education Segment			
	UC[2]	CSUC[3]	CCC[4]	Private[5]
Less than $12,000	12.0%	17.6%	39.7%	16.5%
$12,000–$23,999	23.9	27.5	30.0	27.3
$24,000–$35,999	27.8	29.7	18.8	26.5
$36,000–$47,999	14.8	12.3	6.0	10.3
$48,000 or more	21.5	12.8	5.5	19.4
Totals	100.0%	99.9%[6]	100.0%	100.0%

[1]As determined by California definition of dependency; figures for students reporting total family income only.
[2]University of California.
[3]California State University and Colleges.
[4]California Community Colleges.
[5]Private colleges and universities in California (does not include proprietary institutions).
[6]Details do not sum to 100 percent due to rounding.
Source: Analysis of the Budget Bill for FY July 1, 1984 to June 30, 1985, Report of the Legislative Analyst to the Joint Legislative Budget Committee, California Legislature.

EXHIBIT 12

Percentage of Undergraduate/Graduate Students Enrolled by Ethnicity and Sex
Fall 1979

	CSUC		UC		CCC	
	Male	Female	Male	Female	Male	Female
Undergraduate:						
White	50.5%	53.1%	68.6%	70.5%	60.9%	64.9%
Black	4.6	6.5	3.0	4.3	8.5	8.3
Hispanic	6.8	6.5	5.5	5.0	10.5	9.0
Asian	6.7	6.7	11.7	11.6	5.7	4.6
American Indian	1.0	1.0	0.5	0.5	1.3	1.2
Other	2.4	2.4	1.3	1.0	2.6	2.1
Nonresident alien	4.1	1.5	3.4	1.8	2.4	1.4
No response	23.9	22.3	6.1	5.3	8.0	8.5
Graduate:						
White	47.1%	53.2%	60.8%	65.7%	—	—
Black	3.0	4.1	2.3	4.1	—	—
Hispanic	4.9	4.6	4.0	4.0	—	—
Asian	6.0	4.5	5.8	6.0	—	—
American Indian	0.8	0.8	0.3	0.4	—	—
Other	2.2	2.0	0.8	0.7	—	—
Nonresident alien	5.9	2.2	14.0	7.5	—	—
No response	30.1	28.6	11.9	11.6	—	—

Source: CPEC, *Postsecondary Education in California Information Digest* (1980), p. 53.

1980s, the state was subsidizing an even greater share of the cost of education than a decade before, and student charges in California had fallen even farther behind those at comparable public institutions in other states. In particular, California had become a unique example by virtue of its minimal graduate differential and unusually low tuition for health science students. (See Exhibits 13–15.)

The combination of these concerns, the LAO concluded, warranted the establishment of a graduate student fee differential by increasing charges in 1983-84 by $600 for all graduate students. In addition, the LAO recommended that the legislature request the regents of UC to charge an annual health science resident tuition in 1983-84 of $2,500 for medicine, $2,000 for dentistry, and $600 for all other

EXHIBIT 13

UC Resident Charges Falling Further Behind Comparison Universities[1]

	Comparison Group Average	UC	Difference
Graduate			
1979–80	$1,393	$ 795	$ 598
1981–82	1,720	1,018	702
Dollar increase	327	223	104
Medicine			
1979–80	2,764	781	1,983
1981–82	3,888	1,015	2,873
Dollar increase	1,124	234	890
Dentistry			
1979–80	2,545	773	1,772
1981–82	3,359	1,024	2,335
Dollar increase	814	251	563

[1]UC public university comparison group includes the University of Michigan (Ann Arbor), University of Wisconsin (Madison), State University of New York (Buffalo), and University of Illinois (Champaign-Urbana). The comparison group average for dentistry is the average of three universities, because the University of Wisconsin does not have a dentistry program.
Source: Analysis of the Budget Bill for FY July 1, 1984 to June 30, 1985, Report of the Legislative Analyst to the Joint Legislative Budget Committee, California Legislature.

EXHIBIT 14

Health Science Tuition and Fees at UC Comparison Institutions 1978-79

	Undergraduate		Medicine		Dentistry		Veterinary Medicine	
	Resident	Non-resident	Resident	Non-resident	Resident	Non-resident	Resident	Non-resident
Stanford	$5,130	$5,130	$5,388	$5,388	—	—	—	—
Yale	5,150	5,150	5,480	5,480	—	—	—	—
Harvard	4,850	4,850	6,060	6,060	$5,000	$5,000	—	—
SUNY, Buffalo	930	1,380	3,167	4,367	3,000	4,000	—	—
Cornell	4,850	4,850	5,500	5,500	—	—	$2,800	$4,500
Michigan	1,020[1]	3,244[1]	2,790	5,390	2,080	4,160	—	—
Wisconsin, Madison	705[1]	2,565[1]	2,425	4,117	—	—	—	—
Illinois	814[1]	1,986[1]	2,256	5,840	1,317	2,907	—	—
Average	$2,931	$3,644	$4,133	$5,268	$2,849	$4,017	$2,800	$4,500
UC	825	2,730	825	2,730	825	2,730	825	2,730

[1]Data are for 1977-78.

Health Science Tuition and Fees

	Average Tuition and Student Fees	
	Resident	Nonresident
Medical Schools[1]		
All—121 schools	$3,603	$4,722
Public (72)	1,772	3,653
Private (49)	6,293	6,293
Dental Schools[2]		
All—59 schools	3,020	4,078
Public (36)	1,773	3,348
Private (23)	4,972	5,220
Veterinary Medical Schools[2]		
All—21 schools	1,363	2,507
Public (19)	1,146	2,331
Private (2)	3,425	4,175
UC Medical, Veterinary, and Dental Schools[1]	825	2,730

[1]1978-79 tuition and fees.

[2]1977-78 tuition and fees.

Source: Analysis of the Budget Bill for FY July 1, 1984 to June 30, 1985, Report of the Legislative Analyst to the Joint Legislative Budget Committee, California Legislature.

health science graduate students. According to the LAO proposal, a portion of the additional revenue could be set aside for use as financial aid to offset possible effects on enrollment.

THE STUDENTS' AND ADMINISTRATIONS' OPPOSITION

The UC and CSU students' organizations opposed graduate student fee differentials as a matter of principle and sought the elimination of the small differentials already in place. Jim Lofgren, president of the

UC Students Lobby, explained that graduate student fee differentials—which have their conceptual basis in the difference between the instructional costs of different programs—violate the spirit of the no-tuition philosophy—which holds that students should not be responsible for covering any direct instructional costs. The students' organizations, with the support of the UC and CSU administrations, had already rebutted the LAO's arguments in a series of letters to legislators and a *Report of the Student Fee Advisory Committee* issued by CSU in August 1984.

The students conceded that both the costs of instruction and the private benefits derived from edu-

EXHIBIT 15

Resident Tuitition and Fees Charged by UC and CSUC Public Comparison Institutions (Undergraduate and Graduate), 1979–80

	Undergraduate	Graduate
I. University of California Comparison Institutions		
State University of New York (Buffalo)	$ 929[1]	$1,504
University of Illinois	916	962
University of Michigan (Ann Arbor)	1,372	1,868
University of Wisconsin at Madison	870	1,237
Average, UC Comparison Institutions	$1,022	$1,393
University of California	$ 735	$ 795

	Undergraduate	Graduate
II. California State University and Colleges Comparison Institutions		
State University of New York (Albany)	$1,035[1]	$1,610
SUNY College, Buffalo	1,005	1,510
University of Hawaii	475	578
University of Wisconsin (Milwaukee)	898	1,258
University of Nevada	690	720
University of Oregon	860	1,295
Portland State University	780	1,197
University of Colorado	892	926
Illinois State University	788	804
Northern Illinois University	847	780
Southern Illinois University	753	747
Indiana State University	975	960
Iowa State University	816	951
Wayne State University	1,121[1]	1,425
Western Michigan University	892	948
Bowling Green State University	1,086	1,431
Virginia Polytechnic Institute	792	852
Miami University (Ohio)	1,190	1,340
Average, CSUC Comparison Institutions	$ 883	$1,074
California State University and Colleges	$ 207	$ 207

[1]Average of lower division and upper division fees.

Source: Analysis of the Budget Bill for FY July 1, 1984 to June 30, 1985, Report of the Legislative Analyst to the Joint Legislative Budget Committee, California Legislature.

cation are higher at the graduate level; however, they continued, this imbalance was more than offset by the additional benefits that both the universities and the state derive from graduate programs. Undergraduate education, the CSU report observed, benefited from the "higher quality faculty who are attracted by the opportunity to participate in graduate programs" and from the instructional role performed by graduate students. The universities, UC in particular, had been able to attract considerable federal research grants to their graduate programs. And, finally, the state benefited from "the availability of an adequate supply of appropriately trained persons beyond the bachelor's level," and from "the relationship between the economic well-being of the state and the ability to produce technological advances due to the availability of highly educated individuals and research."

The CSU report also argued that while it was difficult to differentiate fees on the basis of level of instruction, it was even more difficult and inappropriate to differentiate by type of program. The CSU students and administration attacked the LAO proposal to charge higher fees to medical students as the first step towards even further differentiation (e.g., engineering versus English). Such an approach, they wrote, would create an administrative nightmare and might "inappropriately influence a student's choice of program in terms of student fees."

Finally, the UC Students Lobby challenged the consideration of the students' present or future ability to pay for their education as a criterion for determining a segment's or a program's charges. To use average future earnings as a determinant of student charges would be unfair to all those students, such as public health physicians and public interest lawyers, who choose less well paying positions in that field, the students argued. Also, to increase the charges of a segment of students on the basis of their higher family income would jeopardize the access of less privileged students within that segment. Even if the higher fees were accompanied by a substantial increase in financial aid, the students argued, some applicants would still be deterred by the "administrative and psychological barriers of financial aid."

THE STUDENT FEE POLICY COMMITTEE

In October 1984, the California legislature charged the CPEC with organizing a committee to design a long-term formula for setting student fees at UC and CSU. CPEC, whose reports on higher education had been attacked in the past by legislators and students' organizations, appointed Dr. Frank Bowen, an independent consultant, to run the committee. Over the following three months, the committee's members—including representatives from the students' organizations, the administrations of UC and CSU, the LAO, the Department of Finance, various committees of the legislature, and CPEC—would have to devise a methodology for calculating student fees. The question of whether a graduate fee differential should be included was one of the issues that most separated the LAO from the university administrations and student organizations.

ASSIGNMENT FOR CLASS DISCUSSION

Come to class prepared to explain whether or not you would support a significantly higher fee for graduate than undergraduate students in California's public higher education system. In preparing your position, please consider:

1. What are the circumstances under which users of a public service should be charged a fee equal to the cost of serving them?

2. Do these circumstances or assumptions apply in the case of California public higher education? Do they apply equally to graduate and undergraduate students? Be specific where possible, using the numbers and other information in the case and exhibits.

3. Is the distinction between fees and tuition a useful one?

4. Do low fees and no tuition in California redistribute income toward the poor or the rich? Be specific where possible.

Funding Schools in Washington State

In 1986, an 18-member advisory council to Washington state Governor Booth Gardner was grappling with a dual challenge. It had been charged with finding a way to ensure adequate and equitable educational opportunities in the state's widely varied public school districts while at the same time it tried to head off a looming fiscal crisis in public education. Washington's state legislature had assumed primary responsibility for local education costs in 1977, after the state supreme court ruled that local school districts' previous reliance on property taxes violated the state constitution. In an effort to equalize educational opportunities between districts, the 1977 reforms also had capped the amount of local property tax money school districts could raise to supplement their state grants. School districts whose local levies exceeded the cap in 1977 were supposed to phase down their reliance on local funds. But that would

This case was written by Linda Kincaid under the direction of Professors José A. Gomez-Ibañez and Joseph Kalt for use at the Kennedy School of Government, Harvard University. (0388)

have required high-levy school districts—principally the large urban and suburban districts in the populous Puget Sound region—to cut more than $125 million (in 1986 dollars) from their budgets between 1982 and 1990. After forcing a first round of local levy cuts in 1985, the legislature stalled the cuts for three years while Gardner's advisory council searched for a way to keep the phasedown from decimating school programs in levy-dependent districts.

At its July meeting, the council reviewed three alternative solutions to the school funding problem. In the process, it faced some hard questions. Was the state's basic education funding adequate? How much more could Washington afford, especially given that it had no income tax and one of the highest sales taxes in the nation? And how far could Washington go toward equalizing educational opportunities between school districts, without forcing some of its best school programs to sacrifice quality? Parents, teachers and school board directors in the highest-levy districts were not anxious to give up the flexibility that came with their ability to raise extra dollars

through local taxes. But education advocates in poorer districts were frustrated that their children might be left behind, simply because their voters didn't have such lofty expectations or such deep pockets. As Ginny DeForest, school board member for the wealthy Seattle suburb of Mercer Island, saw it: "I know, and I think a number of other people on Mercer Island know . . . that there's no way we're going to be allowed to do all the things that we want to do without some help for districts who can't [afford] some of the things that they might want to do. It's a political problem, and it's also an educational problem. You really do want to be sure that kids get a good education across the state." (For a map of Washington State, see Exhibit 1.)

WASHINGTON EDUCATION FINANCE AND THE COURTS

Washington's responsibility for public education is driven by a state constitutional mandate that "it is

EXHIBIT 1
State of Washington Metropolitan Statistical Areas, Counties and Selected Places

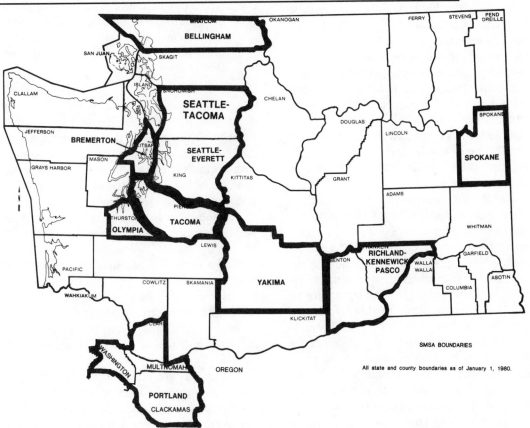

Source: State of Washington, *Washington State Data Book,* 1983.

the paramount duty of the state to make ample provision for the education of all children within its borders . . . The legislature shall provide for a general and uniform system of public schools." But until 1977, the state's local school districts had shouldered a major—and growing—share of the costs of education; in fact, by 1977 more than half of some school districts' yearly budgets were underwritten by local voter-approved property tax levies, referred to as "special levies."

The outcome of these levy votes became increasingly important to Washington's local school districts in the late sixties and early seventies. Beginning in 1965, Washington's state funding for schools failed to keep up with rising education costs, and the state share of local school budgets decreased from 59.2 percent to 42.5 percent between the 1964-65 and 1974-75 school years. That left school districts more dependent on local levies, increased the educational disparity between property-poor and property-rich districts, and exposed up to 60 percent of some districts' education budgets to voter veto in the annual levy elections. And veto they did, with increasing frequency in the 1970s, as tightened assessing practices and a rapid rise in property values pushed property taxes up. Things came to a head in 1975, when Seattle voters rejected their school board's levy request. With a 20 percent budget shortfall for the 1975-76 school year, Washington's largest school district made a legal run at the education finance system, arguing that the state was not meeting its constitutional obligation to make "ample provision" for education if up to half a local school budget could be held hostage to the whims of the voters.

In early 1977, Thurston County Superior Court Judge Robert Doran found in favor of the school district, ruling that the state constitution required the legislature to define a program of basic education "which will equip our children to live as productive citizens of the state and nation," and then provide a "regular and dependable" source of full funding for this program in the local districts. Although the Doran decision was appealed to—and ultimately upheld by—the state supreme court, it is a matter of some pride to Washingtonians that the legislature began crafting the state's education finance reforms before the supreme court mandate. That June, lawmakers passed two bills which together transferred the burden of education funding primarily to the state. The Basic Education Act set up a formula for distributing state funds to local school districts, while the Levy Lid Act placed strict limits on the amount of local funds school districts could raise to supplement their state grants.

THE BASIC EDUCATION ACT

The 1977 Basic Education Act defined a minimum program of basic skills (reading, math, etc.), work skills and electives that each school district had to offer, required certain percentages of those subjects in elementary, junior high and senior high school, and prescribed minimum hours of instruction per year for various grade levels. To pay for that program, the legislature was required to fund at least these costs in the state's biennial budget:

- **Salary costs:** full funding of each district's annual average salary costs (including benefits) to maintain a ratio of 50 "certificated" staff members (teachers, administrators and others who hold a teaching certificate) per 1,000 full-time-equivalent (FTE) students, and one "classified" staff member (custodians, bus drivers, etc.) for each three "certificated" staff
- **Non-salary costs:** a flat amount per pupil designed to cover the district's annual average expenditures for energy, books, and equipment
- **Adjustments for the extra costs of small and remote schools.** For example, each small district which operated a high school was guaranteed a minimum of 9 1/2 high school teachers regardless of enrollment, since the state's basic program standards for high school required at least that many teachers.

This formula produced about 75 percent of the state's biennial contribution to local school district budgets. The remainder came through categorical grants for student transportation, and special education programs for the districts' handicapped, bilingual, remedial and gifted students and vocational training. Over the years, the legislature tinkered with its formulas, but in general, the method of allocating basic education funds changed very little between 1977 and 1986.

Washington's formula approach did not produce a uniform grant-per-pupil statewide, because of the difference in salary costs between districts, and a wide variation in school district size. (While the bulk of Washington's public school students are served by the 75 largest school districts, the rest of the state, particularly the vast desert and forest areas east of the Cascades, are dotted with tiny school districts, some serving fewer than 25 children.) The average state expenditure-per-student was $3,077 in 1984-85, but Washington spent far more on students in its smallest school districts. The highest expenditure-per-pupil was in the tiny Hazelmere district, located in northeast Washington's Ferry County, where the state spent $36,303 for each of its 3.14 FTE pupils. Other high-expenditure districts were Shaw ($12,644/FTE), a remote school district of 8.44 FTE pupils in the San Juan Islands; and North River ($11,107/FTE), a southwestern Washington district of 47.82 FTE pupils. State grants were also above average in the urban and suburban Puget Sound districts, such as Seattle ($3,889/FTE), and Tacoma ($3,551/FTE), where salary costs were higher than average. Below average state expenditures-per-pupil were found in mid-size school districts in rural or poorer areas—where salary and other costs were lower—such as Evergreen ($2,834/FTE) in southwestern Washington, and Toppenish ($2,740/FTE) in agricultural Yakima County.

Even though the state's allocation formula was based on specific staff/student ratios, the legislature actually sent basic education funds out to the districts with very few strings attached. Thus, districts were free to allocate resources between students as they wished, so long as they met the program requirements of the Basic Education Act, and spent categorical grants on the programs for which they were designed. But the legislature's efforts to preserve local spending control left it with another dilemma: how to tie the money to good management, so the state didn't just send money out into the districts based on what they spent. Those conflicting goals were focused in a long-running controversy over state control of employee salaries, which accounted for about 68 percent of the state grant to local districts. Beginning in 1981—to the dismay of the state teachers' union—the legislature prohibited local school districts from granting pay raises greater than the salary increases the legislature built into the local district's state grant.

The legislature had also taken action in each biennium since 1977 to equalize teachers' salaries, by granting larger raises to teachers in districts with below-average salaries, and by establishing (in 1986) a statewide minimum salary of $16,500. In general, teachers were better-paid in the urbanized Puget Sound counties and in the smaller cities of Vancouver, Yakima and Spokane, while rural districts in eastern and southwest Washington typically paid below-average salaries. By 1984-85 the state had narrowed the salary gap, but differences remained—teachers in the wealthy Seattle suburb of Bellevue were the highest paid in the state, commanding $29,663 ($30,662 for certificated staff overall), while the small, rural northeast Washington district of Orient paid the least—$15,597 for teachers ($17,210 for

certificated staff). As the controversy over salary control continued, Washington teachers' salaries lagged behind education reform-inspired salary increases in other states, dropping from fifth in the nation in 1979-80 to 17th by 1985-86 (Exhibit 2).

SQUEEZING STATE REVENUES

In 1983, a second court ruling effectively gave K-12 education first claim to state funds. Midway through the 1981-83 biennium, Washington's state revenues fell far short of projections, thanks to a severe national recession and drastic federal aid cutbacks. When the legislature prepared to cut all state services, the Seattle school district returned to Thurston County Superior Court to challenge the constitutionality of education budget cuts. The school district argued that once the state had defined basic education, the constitution's "paramount duty" clause required it to fully fund the program, regardless of Washington's larger fiscal problems. Judge Doran essentially agreed. In a 1983 decision, dubbed Doran II, he held that the legislature had the latitude to redefine "basic education" through new legislation. But once the legislature had defined the basic education program for any one year, Doran said, it had to provide 100 percent of the dollars required to fund it. The judge also ruled that the state must fully fund its defined handicapped, bilingual and remedial education programs, and student transportation, because lawmakers had recognized those programs as part of the state's constitutional responsibility.

After a decade of reform, K-12 education was Washington's largest single state expenditure, and the state ranked second in the nation in state support of public K-12 education (Exhibit 3). The Doran decisions had stabilized state funding for local school districts by protecting state grants to local districts from any mid-year cuts, and ensuring that—short of rewriting the basic education law—the legislature would make only marginal cuts in programs when preparing its biennial budget. "K-12 education is sacrosanct," said Anne Carlson Hallett, who was chief lobbyist for Citizens for Fair School Funding. "If cuts are made, they tend not to be made in K-12 education."

On the downside, though, K-12 education was putting the squeeze on other state services, largely because hard economic times had combined with Washington's unpredictable tax structure to limit tax revenue growth. Washington had suffered more than other states in the national recession of 1981-82, and by 1986 its recovery was still lagging behind the na-

EXHIBIT 2

Average Teacher Salaries[1]

Where Washington Ranks among States

	Amount	Percent of Ntl Average	Ntl Rank
1985–86 (est.)	$27,166	102.3%	17th
1984–85	$26,633	107.3%	9th
1983–84	$25,428	111.0%	8th
1982–83	$24,519	112.5%	7th
1981–82	$23,990	119.1%	4th
1980–81	$22,277	121.2%	3rd
1979–80	$19,735	117.6%	5th

[1]Includes teachers, principals, counselors, librarians, and other instructional personnel.

Comparison with Selected States

	1977–78	1979–80	1981–82	1983–84	1985–86
Washington	$16,114	$18,820	$22,954	$24,780	$26,015
Alaska	22,544	26,604	31,924	36,564	41,480
California	17,149	18,020	22,755	26,403	29,750
Hawaii	17,722	19,920	22,542	24,357	25,845
Idaho	11,724	13,610	16,401	18,640	20,969
Minnesota	14,167	15,912	19,907	24,480	26,970
Oregon	13,832	16,266	20,305	22,833	25,788
Wisconsin	14,053	16,002	19,387	23,000	26,800
National average	$14,247	$15,966	$19,142	$22,019	$25,257

Source: National Education Association, *Estimates of School Statistics,* selected years.

tion's. Unemployment, which peaked at 12.1 percent in 1982, was still above the national average in 1986, and the only portion of personal income which had grown in the eighties was income from interest, dividends and rents. One of only five states in the nation without an income tax, Washington raised nearly half its state revenue from a retail sales tax—one of the highest in the nation—and from a tax on the gross revenues of all businesses.[1] Other state revenues were derived from the nation's highest liquor tax, the nation's second highest gasoline tax, and a relatively low-rate state property tax (Exhibits 4, 5 and 6). Critics complained that these consumption-based taxes were most vulnerable and unpredictable in times of economic recession, and were unable to tap the growth in unearned income.

Meanwhile, the pressure on the state budget from the K-12 program promised to increase after 1986, when public school enrollments were expected to end their long decline and begin climbing again (Exhibit 7). At the Basic Education Act's standard allocation of 50 certificated staff per thousand students, the projected enrollment increase would require an additional 4,000 staff by 1990. The Washington Roundtable, a group of representatives from Washington's thirty largest corporations, had estimated that new students could cost the system an additional $300 million by 1990.

THE LEVY LID LAW

Passed in tandem with the Basic Education Act, the Levy Lid Act was intended to cap each school district's special levy for schools at 10 percent of its previous year's state funding allocation. While neither Doran decision had explicitly required the legislature to cap local school levies, levy lid advocates were convinced that the cap would keep pressure on the legislature to provide adequate funds for basic educational programs. The lid also allowed legislators to

---

[1]Food and drugs have been exempt from Washington's sales tax since July 1983. The so-called "business occupations" tax was levied at three rates: 0.4 percent for wholesaling, 0.471 percent for retailing, and 1.5 percent for service industries.

EXHIBIT 3

Percent of School Revenues from State Funds

Where Washington Ranks among States

	Percent State Funded[1]	National Rank
1985–86 (est.)	75.6%	2nd
1984–85	74.5%	4th
1983–84	75.2%	4th
1982–83	75.0%	3rd
1981–82	77.9%	3rd
1980–81	74.9%	2nd
1979–80	70.8%	3rd
1978–79	61.3%	9th

[1]These figures do not reflect state funding for the Teachers' Retirement System.

Comparison with Selected States	*1977–78*	*1979–80*	*1981–82*	*1983–84*	*1985–86*
Hawaii	78.5	85.2	89.7	90.7	90.6
Alaska	66.9	70.2	80.1	83.1	74.6
Washington	59.2	70.8	77.9	75.1	75.6
California	38.1	71.2	74.3	67.0	68.7
Idaho	45.3	55.0	61.7	64.1	65.6
Minnesota	55.0	56.6	63.1	54.1	54.4
Wisconsin	34.9	37.6	36.6	37.9	39.8
Oregon	29.5	35.5	33.6	28.8	27.9

Source: National Education Association, *Estimates of School Statistics,* selected years.

EXHIBIT 4

Washington Public School System Levy Data by School Year

School Year	Excess Levy Dollars per School Year ($ in Millions)	Excess Levies as a Percent of Total Expenditures	State Average Rate/$1,000 Property Valuation
1972–73	$176.1	22.5%	$5.51
1973–74	210.8	23.0%	5.70
1974–75	257.9	26.0%	7.15
1975–76	226.9	20.7%	3.66
1976–77	250.8	21.4%	6.30
1977–78	329.0	23.7%	5.66
1978–79	319.7	20.6%	4.37
1979–80	210.0	11.5%	1.83
1980–81	152.7	8.0%	1.39
1981–82	172.5	8.9%	1.65
1982–83	222.9	11.0%	1.73
1983–84	254.2	11.5%	1.83
1984–85	254.4[1]	10.6%[1]	1.83[1]

[1]Estimated.

Source: Governor's Advisory Council on Education Funding.

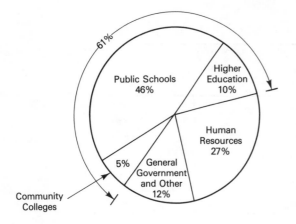

State of Washington
1985–87 Revenue Forecast

EXHIBIT 5

Washington State Budget, 1985–87 (General Fund)
(Dollars in Millions)

Higher education	933	10%
Public schools	4,222	46%
Community colleges	483	5%
Natural resources	204	2%
General government	122	1%
Human resources	2,472	27%
Transportation	28	%
Special Approp	623	7%
All other	163	2%
1985–87 Total	9,249	100%

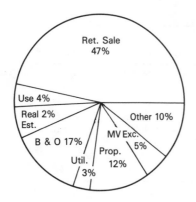

State of Washington 1985–87 Revenue Forecast

Retail Sales	4,336.5	47%
Use Tax	362.4	4%
Real Estate Excise	221.2	2%
B & O	1,540.8	17%
Public Utility	291.0	3%
Property Tax	1,121.6	12%
Motor Vehicle Excise	448.6	5%
All Other	967.5	10%
1985–87 Forecast	9,289.6	100%

Source: State of Washington House of Representatives, Ways and Means Committee.

guarantee their constituents local property tax relief in return for the increased state taxes needed to underwrite the state's growing financial responsibility for public schools. On average, that shift in tax burdens did occur; between 1980 and 1986, the average property tax rate for schools dropped seventy percent, from a high of over $7.15 per $1,000 of assessed valuation to less than $2.00 per $1,000. And many education activists and legislators who represented poorer school districts hoped the levy lid would make school funding more equitable, by reducing expenditure disparities between rich and poor districts.

While the 1977 act put an immediate 10 percent cap on all school districts whose 1977 levies were at or below that level, it "grandfathered" 75 of the state's biggest districts, which at the time had levies ranging from 10–40 percent of their state grants. The grandfather clause was designed to protect high-levy districts until the legislature could find a way to reduce their dependence on local funds without cutting their educational programs. But as the state moved into the eighties and grappled with a devastating re-

cession and the increasing budget demands of K-12 education, the legislature consistently chose to deal with the problem by stalling. In fact, it put off clamping down on the 75 grandfathered districts four times between 1977 and 1986, and in the process allowed previously capped districts to exceed the 10 percent ceiling. In 1984, with no plan for replacing the grandfathered districts' $125 million in annual levy revenues above the 10 percent limit, the legislature forced them to take the first cut of a levy phasedown plan that was supposed to get all districts down to 10 percent by 1990. In the ensuing uproar—the high-levy districts tended to be large and urban, with considerable political clout—the legislature froze the phasedown in 1985 for three years, and then raised the cap for all 298 school districts[2] (Exhibit 8). But,

[2]The legislature's action allowed each district to choose the larger of (1) its own actual levy percentage; (2) the state average (18 percent in 1985); or (3) the average levy percentage for all districts in its Educational Service District—a regional grouping of school districts.

EXHIBIT 6

Tax Rates in Washington: Comparisons with Other States

Most of Washington's taxes are imposed at relatively high rates compared to other states. State liquor taxes are the highest in the country. State gas taxes are the second highest in the country; sales, cigarette, and motor vehicle excise taxes all rank third.

Tax	Rate	Rank	Description
Sales	7.5%	3rd	State and maximum local rates as of November 1985
Property	1.03%	28th	Effective tax rates for calendar year 1983
Gas	18 cents	2nd	State tax rate per gallon as of July 1986
Cigarette	31 cents	3rd	State tax rate per pack as of April 1986
Motor vehicle	$77	3rd	Average owner's motor vehicle fees and taxes as of September 1983
Liquor	$11.45	1st	Based on average price of $7 per fifth including liquor sales and liter taxes as of September 1983
Public utility[1]	3.9%	12th	Based on gas and electric utility revenue as of September 1983
Foreign insurance; other	2%	24th (tied w/22 states)	% of gross premiums on property and casualty insurance for both foreign and domestic companies for 1985
Domestic	2%	20th (tied w/14 other states)	

[1]Only 19 states impose public utility taxes on gas and electricity. Other states impose a corporate and/or sales tax.

Source: State of Washington House of Representatives, Ways and Means Committee.

beginning in calendar year 1989, all school districts would again have to start reducing their levies in yearly increments to meet the 10 percent goal by 1993. In the meantime, the legislature intended to settle the levy lid dilemma once and for all in the 1987 session.

THE SPECIAL LEVY PROBLEM

The 1985 levy freeze bill allowed Washington's local school districts to move even further from the 10 percent levy goal. Statewide, the average 1986 school levy was 18 percent, and 190 school districts had ap-

EXHIBIT 7

Washington State Demographic Trends

Year	Population	K-12 October Headcount Enrollment	K-12 Enrollment as % of State Population
1984–85	4,376,547	739,514	16.90%
1985–86	4,432,678	752,900	16.99%
1986–87	4,496,361	769,200	17.11%
1987–88	4,565,461	781,600	17.12%
1988–89	4,639,932	791,000	17.05%
1989–90	4,719,518	802,900	17.01%
1990–91	4,800,353	821,100	17.10%
1991–92	4,881,867	842,900	17.27%
1992–93	4,963,723	864,300	17.41%
1993–94	5,045,543	885,600	17.55%
1994–95	5,127,107	906,000	17.67%
1995–96	5,208,597	922,200	17.71%
1996–97	5,290,191	937,000	17.71%
1997–98	5,372,019	943,400	17.56%
1998–99	5,454,127	946,100	17.35%
1999–2000	5,536,595	947,200	17.11%
2000–01	5,619,407	948,100	16.87%

Source: Governor's Advisory Council on Education Funding.

EXHIBIT 8

Analysis of 1985 Levy Usage by School Districts

Dollar Levy per Fte Student	Number of Districts	Percent of Statewide Enrollment	Assessed Valuation per Fte Student
No levy	62	7.4	131,257
1–100	-0-	-0-	-0-
101–200	17	3.7	131,403
201–300	56	21.1	157,232
301–400	54	23.7	163,526
401–500	45	27.7	198,321
501–750	38	7.4	209,482
751–1,000	14	8.7	457,222
Over 1,000	13	0.4	425,812

Source: Governor's Advisory Council on Education Funding.

proved levies above 10 percent that year. Many school districts were heavily dependent on local levies, including the two largest—Seattle (28.73 percent) and Tacoma (24.72 percent), and wealthy districts like Mercer Island (31.32 percent) and Bellevue (27.36 percent).

Across the state, school districts raised dramatically different levy amounts per pupil, depending on the size of the community's tax base and the voters' willingness and ability to pay high taxes for schools. In Mercer Island, where real estate agents used the schools as a selling point to lure wealthy doctors, lawyers and Boeing executives, residents taxed themselves $2.31 per $1,000 of assessed valuation to raise $845/FTE in 1986. But, had voters in communities like Sunnyside—a small, largely Hispanic farming town southeast of Yakima—been willing to tax themselves at the same rate, their narrower tax base would have yielded just $258/FTE.

Statewide, the average assessed property value per FTE was $212,184; coupled with an average tax rate for schools of $1.87 per $1,000 of assessed valuation, that yielded an average levy of $400 per student. In property-rich King County—home to Seattle and much of the state's industrial and commercial base—the average 1986 levy was $552 per FTE; with an average assessed property value of $309,153, King County's average tax rate for schools was $1.79 per $1,000 of assessed value (Exhibit 9). Across the state in Yakima County, where Sunnyside was located, the average assessed property value was $129,755/FTE; to support an average 1986 levy of $239/FTE, Yakima County school districts required an average tax rate of $1.84 per thousand (Exhibit 10).

The amount of levy money a district raised per student also depended on the number of students in the district, and on who ultimately paid the tax bill.

Voters in the tiny Lopez Island district, a posh summer resort in the San Juan islands, raised $459 for each of its 193 students in 1986, knowing that the burden would fall largely on the owners of expensive summer homes, who voted elsewhere. At the other extreme, voters rarely approved a school levy in many of the small towns in northeast Washington's logging country, where unemployment soared after the area's timber industry collapsed in the early eighties. "People are out of work," said Ed Fleischer, an aide to House Speaker Wayne Ehlers. "And if they're not out of work, they're worried that they're going to be out of work, and they're not ready to vote for more property taxes."

While there was considerable support in the legislature and the districts for an increase in the levy lid, many argued that the statewide levy average of 18 percent proved that the state's basic education grants simply weren't enough. "A ten percent [levy] should be enough for locally desired programs," said Ben Edlund, associate director of the state school directors' association. "We maintain they have not funded basic education." Many local school directors could point to their own experience on that point. The Issaquah school district, located east of Seattle, had been trapped under the 10 percent cap until 1986, when the levy freeze bill allowed it to float up to its Educational Service District[3] average of 21.74 percent. In the years under the 10 percent cap, Issaquah voters had consistently approved the maximum 10 percent allowable levy. But the school board found itself using most of those funds to supplement state grants for transportation and special education, rather than for extra educational programs. "A major portion

---

[3]Issaquah was part of ESD #121, which included King and Pierce counties, and thus, most of the state's highest-levy districts.

EXHIBIT 9

1986 School Levy Analysis: King County

King County			Amount	Rank
Population (1985)			1,346,400	1
Incorporated			796,818	1
Unincorporated			549,582	1
Area (sq. mi.)			2,128	11
Density/sq. mi.			632.7	1
Assessed value (1984)				
(In millions)			56,979.4	1
Per capita			42,951.5	6
Personal income (1983)				
(In millions)			19,170.6	1
Per capita			14,577.0	4

County Seat—Seattle

King County School Districts	Oct. '85 FTE	Levy Lid %	Actual Levy %	Levy per FTE	AV per FTE[1]	Tax rate, $100/FTE[2]	Actual Tax Rate
Seattle	41,806	29.73	28.73	813	528,685	0.19	1.54
Lester							
Federal Way	14,376	21.74	10.26	254	189,578	0.53	1.34
Enumclaw	3,451	21.74	14.70	376	187,520	0.53	2.01
Mercer Island	3,203	31.32	31.32	845	365,635	0.27	2.31
Highline	14,815	21.74	17.43	463	241,786	0.41	1.92
Vashon Island	1,426	21.74	18.57	491	300,057	0.33	1.64
Renton	11,355	21.74	17.09	432	290,871	0.34	1.48
Skykomish	85	21.74			526,888	0.19	
Bellevue	15,060	27.36	27.36	781	422,207	0.24	1.85
South Central	1,451	49.91	40.84	992	462,705	0.22	2.14
Lower Snoqualmie	1,478	21.74	19.60	479	205,092	0.49	2.34
Auburn	8,580	21.74	14.12	343	189,656	0.53	1.81
Tahoma	2,990	21.74	12.65	323	170,058	0.59	1.90
Snoqualmie Valley	2,984	21.74	12.43	300	184,808	0.54	1.62
Issaquah	6,791	21.74	10.77	287	217,609	0.46	1.32
Shoreline	8,741	24.71	24.71	641	222,962	0.45	2.88
Lake Washington	18,124	21.74	20.21	497	251,165	0.40	1.98
Kent	16,551	21.74	19.52	480	203,841	0.49	2.36
Northshore	13,944	21.74	17.65	437	179,329	0.56	2.44
King	187,208			552	309,153	0.32	1.79
Total all districts	714,781	21.15	15.50	397	212,184	0.47	1.87
Levy districts only	658,449	21.29	16.86	431	217,420	0.46	1.98

[1]Assessed value per FTE.

[2]Tax rate required to raise $100 per FTE.

Source: Office of Financial Management, and Legislative Evaluation and Accountability Program (LEAP)

of our 10 percent levy money went to make up the difference between what the state said that we had to provide in the classrooms and what it cost to provide it," said Karen Taylor Sherman, an Issaquah school board member. "Our experience indicates that it is not possible to meet the needs of students in the suburban districts with a funding formula of 50 [certi-

fied staff] per thousand with a 10 percent levy lid. We were strangling. We were just drying up."

In 1986, Issaquah's voters approved the new maximum allowable levy of 21.74 percent. The school board spent some of that on "extras"—such as 20 new classroom teachers and a modest staff development program—but much of it went to make

EXHIBIT 10
1986 School Levy Analysis: Yakima County

Yakima County		Amount	Rank
Population (1985)		182,500	6
Incorporated		90,429	5
Unincorporated		92,071	7
Area (sq. mi.)		4,287	2
Density/sq. mi.		42.6	13
Assessed value (1984)			
(In millions)		4,333.6	7
Per capita		24,075.6	35
Personal Income (1983)			
(In millions)		1,775.5	7
Per capita		10,022.0	32

County Seat — Yakima

Yakima County School Districts	Oct. '85 FTE	Levy Lid %	Actual Levy %	Levy per FTE	AV per FTE[1]	Tax rate, $100/FTE[2]	Actual Tax Rate
Union Gap	470	19.05	16.22	447	211,194	0.47	2.12
Naches Valley	1,197	18.08	7.96	217	163,893	0.61	1.32
Yakima	10,576	18.08	16.99	426	141,847	0.70	3.00
Moxee	1,680	18.08	12.12	308	163,200	0.61	1.89
Selah	2,727	18.08	11.29	289	115,145	0.87	2.51
Mabton	546	18.08			98,522	1.02	
Grandview	2,021	18.08	8.22	204	120,562	0.83	1.70
Sunnyside	3,494	18.08			111,519	0.90	
Toppenish	2,338	18.08			78,447	1.27	
Highland	756	18.08	11.62	311	187,218	0.53	1.66
Granger	826	18.08	10.48	274	101,320	0.99	2.70
Zillah	788	18.08	7.12	178	132,056	0.76	1.35
Wapato	2,344	18.08			110,185	0.91	
West Valley	3,274	18.08	9.76	242	144,734	0.69	1.67
Mount Adams	776	18.08			92,357	1.08	
Yakima	33,811			239	129,755	0.77	1.84
Total all districts	714,781	21.15	15.50	397	212,184	0.47	1.87
Levy districts only	658,449	21.29	16.86	431	217,420	0.46	1.98

[1] Assessed value per FTE.

[2] Tax rate required to raise $100 per FTE.

Source: Office of Financial Management, and Legislative Evaluation and Accountability Program (LEAP).

long-deferred replacements of textbooks and classroom furniture, and to pay for a portion of teachers' pension costs that the state no longer funded.

It was harder to see precisely what programs were funded by levy dollars in districts like Seattle, which had consistently had high levies. But Seattle school officials maintained that if Seattle's levy was suddenly cut to 10 percent from its 1986 level of 28.7 percent, the district would have to cut staff in ancillary programs, and possibly in the classroom as well. Even in a district like Mercer Island, where histori-

cally high levies had helped fund the development of a challenging and innovative educational program, school board members complained that some of those local funds were used to underwrite deficiencies in the state's funding package, particularly for special education. And high-levy districts argued that parents in their districts were demanding some of the "extras" that increased local funds were able to pay for. "The expectations that people brought with them when they moved here are very high," said Issaquah's Sherman, and I think that if there was any action taken which would result in an appreciable diminishing of the revenues that we have now, we would experience in our district a serious migration to private schools. . . . The level of education that the middle class expects I think exceeds what the state's definition is of basic education. So there needs to be a source of revenue above basic education that allows school districts in this state to respond to those higher expectations.

THE GOVERNOR'S ADVISORY COUNCIL ON EDUCATION FUNDING

The 1985 levy freeze bill had provided for a joint select committee of the legislature to study alternative means of meeting Washington's public school funding responsibilities. Governor Gardner vetoed that part of the bill, promising to appoint his own study committee with a broader charge and membership. When Gardner's Advisory Council on Education Funding met for the first time in September 1985, it included most of the heavy-hitters in Washington's education community and legislature. Chairing the committee was Orin C. Smith, the governor's budget director; the group was asked to report back to Gardner in November 1986.

The governor's original charge to the council had called for a "comprehensive education funding study," but by spring 1986, Chairman Smith and several of the legislators on the council were pushing the group to make the levy lid—which would come before the legislature again in 1987—its first priority. Those who traveled in Washington's education and political circles had long discussed three possible reforms of the state's education funding system: some increase in the levy lid; an increase in the state's basic education grant to districts; and some form of "local effort assistance," a scheme using state funds to subsidize local school levies in districts with a below-average assessed value per student. State School Superintendent Frank Brouillet, a council member, proposed a combination of all three options. His plan would have increased the basic education formula to 55 certificated staff per thousand students, and raised the levy lid to 20 percent. State money would be used to subsidize the first 10 percent of levies in districts with below-average property tax bases. "Casual observation indicates that local constituencies are more than willing to tax themselves to support education, and they're willing to tax themselves beyond 10 percent," explained Brouillet's budget assistant, Bruce Mrkvicka. "They're more than willing

to go above 20 percent. We also feel that 20 percent doesn't violate the concept of a reliable source of revenue; it doesn't expose the essential part of the program of education to the vagaries of the voting behavior of the local school district."

At the July council meeting, Brouillet distributed computer runs showing how three different schemes for school funding—including his—would have changed the amount and distribution of state and local school funding in 1986. All three computer runs assumed 1986 enrollment levels, 1986 assessed property values, and the actual levy percent approved in each district in spring of 1986. Thus, if a district had no levy in 1986, it got no local effort assistance. Option 1 raised the levy lid to 25 percent and provided state funds to subsidize local levies up to 10 percent in property-poor districts. That solution would have added $42 million to the state's 1986 education spending. The assistance would go entirely to low-levy and property-poor districts, while requiring a revenue cut for districts that were above the 25 percent levy lid in 1986 (Exhibit 11).

Option 2 increased the levy lid to 20 percent, and enriched the basic education formula to 55 certificated staff per thousand students. That solution would have cost the state $174 million more, and would have meant an average of 6.4 percent more state funds for local school districts. Poorer districts would again benefit more, but it was essentially a wash for Seattle, which would trade a levy reduction for increased state funds. The increased state aid would not make up for the required levy reductions in some of the highest-levy districts, like King County's South Central or Mercer Island (Exhibit 12). Brouillet's proposal—option 3—would cost almost $208 million more. This alternative would help property-poor school districts while effectively holding Seattle harmless and requiring only modest budget cuts in the highest-levy districts (Exhibit 13).

The council weighed these three options against a backdrop of severe fiscal constraints. In June, the House Ways and Means Committee had estimated that adjustments for enrollment and salary increases in the K-12 budget would require an additional $211 million in the 1987-89 biennium. Carryforward adjustments and mandatory increases in overall state spending would require an additional $686 million in 1987-89 (Exhibits 14 and 15). The committee's best-case revenue estimate indicated the state would have only $392 million left over after covering those mandatory increases, while its worst-case estimate suggested only a $4 million balance (Exhibit 16). And, of course, not all of the state's revenue growth was likely to go toward public education. In fact, the

EXHIBIT 11

Option 1: 25% Levy Lid and 10% Local Effort Assistance

District Name	Total Resources (Current)	Additional State Funds (55/1000)	Reduction in Special Levy	Local Effort Assistance	Total Resources (Proposed)	Diff.	% Diff.
State Totals	2,383,552,962	0	(12,266,108)	42,386,673	2,413,673,527	30,120,565	1.26%
King County							
Seattle	166,095,931	0	(6,054,514)	0	168,041,417	(6,054,514)	−3.65%
Lester	0	0	0	0	0	0	0.00%
Federal Way	44,797,365	0	0	546,151	45,343,516	546,151	1.22%
Enumclaw	11,753,413	0	0	186,927	11,940,340	186,927	1.59%
Mercer Island	11,826,054	0	(570,145)	0	11,255,909	(570,145)	−4.82%
Highline	53,782,026	0	0	0	53,782,026	0	0.00%
Vashon Island	4,999,992	0	3,817	0	5,003,809	3,817	0.08%
Renton	38,193,412	0	81,765	0	38,275,177	81,765	0.21%
Skykomish	633,881	0	0	0	633,881	0	0.00%
Bellevue	57,828,509	0	(1,070,898)	0	56,757,611	(1,070,898)	−1.85%
South Central	5,943,601	0	(835,591)	0	5,108,010	(835,591)	−14.06%
Lower Snoqualmie	5,192,197	0	0	34,689	5,226,886	34,689	0.67%
Auburn	28,572,544	0	0	367,296	28,939,840	367,296	1.29%
Tahoma	9,690,858	0	0	196,431	9,887,289	196,431	2.03%
Snoqualmie Valley	9,238,566	0	0	106,039	9,344,605	106,039	1.15%
Issaquah	24,330,474	0	0	167,837	24,498,311	167,837	0.69%
Shoreline	31,196,776	0	(1,763)	74,337	31,269,350	72,574	0.23%
Lake Washington	61,679,583	0	489,951	0	62,169,534	489,951	0.79%
Kent	54,912,985	0	129,258	322,292	55,364,535	451,550	0.82%
Northshore	47,491,153	0	0	901,376	48,392,529	901,376	1.90%
Yakima County							
Union Gap	1,526,744	0	0	8,073	1,534,817	8,073	0.53%
Naches Valley	3,750,699	0	0	117,012	3,867,711	117,012	3.12%
Yakima	36,325,445	0	118,733	1,360,051	37,804,229	1,478,784	4.07%
Moxee	5,223,443	0	0	148,123	5,371,566	148,123	2.84%
Selah	8,231,515	0	0	401,569	8,633,084	401,569	4.08%
Mabton	1,626,874	0	0	0	1,626,874	0	0.00%
Grandview	5,818,806	0	0	270,072	6,088,878	270,072	4.64%
Sunnyside	9,352,485	0	0	0	9,352,485	0	0.00%
Toppenish	6,582,434	0	0	0	6,582,434	0	0.00%
Highland	2,544,602	0	0	62,776	2,607,378	62,776	2.47%
Granger	2,674,122	0	0	148,023	2,822,145	148,023	5.54%
Zillah	2,311,777	0	0	95,409	2,407,186	95,409	4.13%
Wapato	6,889,988	0	0	0	6,889,988	0	0.00%

Source: Office of the Superintendent of Public Instruction (OSPI).

committee had identified 11 areas where legislators or outside groups were likely to make spending increase requests—from up to $200 million to cover potential cuts in federal aid to the state to $30 million to restore dental care for adults on public assistance (Exhibit 17).

The revenue forecast wouldn't leave the governor or the legislature much room to increase state funding for education without a tax increase. Cynics had suspected the school funding crisis might be an ideal vehicle for carrying an income tax proposal, but Gardner quashed that speculation in June, when he told the Seattle City Club he would "take the income

tax off the table" for 1987. Instituting an income tax in Washington would require a constitutional amendment, and Gardner said he had reached the "inescapable conclusion" that he had neither the two-thirds of the legislature nor the majority of voters required to pass such an amendment. The governor's decision meant that any increased revenues for 1987-89 would have to come from traditional sources—changes in the base and/or rate of existing sales, excise and business income taxes—since there were no constitutional constraints on those taxes.

Meanwhile, some council members were frustrated that in its full-court press to solve the levy lid

EXHIBIT 12

Option 2: 20% Levy Lid and 55 'Certs' per Thousand Students

District Name	Total Resources (Current)	Additional State Funds (55/1000)	Reduction in Special Levy	Local Effort Assistance	Total Resources (Proposed)	Diff.	% Diff.
State Totals	2,383,552,962	173,602,583	(20,588,338)	0	2,536,567,213	153,014,251	6.42%
King County							
Seattle	166,095,931	10,702,642	(10,314,748)	0	166,483,825	387,894	0.23%
Lester	0	0	0	0	0	0	0.00%
Federal Way	44,797,365	3,489,538	0	0	48,286,903	3,489,538	7.79%
Enumclaw	11,753,413	862,236	0	0	12,615,650	862,237	7.34%
Mercer Island	11,826,054	825,321	(855,765)	0	11,795,610	(30,444)	−0.26%
Highline	53,782,026	3,771,136	0	0	57,553,162	3,771,136	7.01%
Vashon Island	4,999,992	348,511	(1,712)	0	5,346,792	346,800	6.94%
Renton	38,193,412	2,790,802	12,228	0	40,996,443	2,803,031	7.34%
Skykomish	633,881	18,434	0	0	652,314	18,433	2.91%
Bellevue	57,828,509	4,065,886	(2,527,222)	0	59,367,173	1,538,664	2.66%
South Central	5,943,601	373,400	(965,763)	0	5,351,238	(592,363)	9.97%
Lower Snoqualmie	5,192,197	359,098	0	0	5,551,295	359,098	6.92%
Auburn	28,572,544	2,069,112	0	0	30,641,656	2,069,112	7.24%
Tahoma	9,690,858	708,076	0	0	10,398,934	708,076	7.31%
Snoqualmie Valley	9,238,566	683,436	0	0	9,922,003	683,437	7.40%
Issaquah	24,330,474	1,708,160	0	0	26,038,634	1,708,160	7.02%
Shoreline	31,196,776	2,215,646	(735,349)	0	32,677,072	1,480,296	4.75%
Lake Washington	61,679,583	4,568,887	32,111	0	66,280,580	4,600,997	7.46%
Kent	54,912,985	3,932,222	965	0	58,846,171	3,933,186	7.16%
Northshore	47,491,153	3,447,968	0	0	50,939,121	3,447,968	7.26%
Yakima County							
Union Gap	1,526,744	115,597	0	0	1,642,340	115,596	7.57%
Naches Valley	3,750,699	297,180	0	0	4,047,886	297,187	7.92%
Yakima	36,325,445	2,654,357	118,733	0	39,098,535	2,773,090	7.63%
Moxee	5,223,443	411,806	0	0	5,635,248	411,805	7.88%
Selah	8,231,515	662,048	0	0	8,893,564	662,049	8.04%
Mabton	1,626,874	124,192	0	0	1,751,066	124,192	7.63%
Grandview	5,818,806	477,911	0	0	6,296,717	477,911	8.21%
Sunnyside	9,352,485	799,788	0	0	10,152,272	799,787	8.55%
Toppenish	6,582,434	558,570	0	0	7,141,005	558,571	8.49%
Highland	2,544,602	185,032	0	0	2,729,634	185,032	7.27%
Granger	2,674,122	191,226	0	0	2,865,348	191,226	7.15%
Zillah	2,311,777	181,770	0	0	2,493,547	181,770	7.86%
Wapato	6,889,988	578,995	0	0	7,468,983	578,995	8.40%

Source: Office of the Superintendent of Public Instruction (OSPI).

147

EXHIBIT 13

Option 3: 20% Levy Lid, 10% Local Effort Assistance, and 55 'Certs' per 1,000

District Name	Total Resources (Current)	Additional State Funds (55/1000)	Reduction in Special Levy	Local Effort Assistance	Total Resources (Proposed)	Diff.	% Diff.
State Totals	2,383,552,962	173,602,583	(25,455,080)	33,617,890	2,565,318,380	181,765,418	7.63%
King County							
Seattle	166,095,931	10,702,642	(10,314,748)	0	166,483,825	387,894	0.23%
Lester	0	0	0	0	0	0	0.00%
Federal Way	44,797,365	3,489,538	0	230,384	48,517,287	3,719,922	8.30%
Enumclaw	11,753,413	862,236	0	112,326	12,727,976	974,563	8.29%
Mercer Island	11,826,054	825,321	(855,765)	0	11,795,610	(30,444)	−0.26%
Highline	53,782,026	3,771,136	0	0	57,553,162	3,771,136	7.01%
Vashon Island	4,999,992	348,511	(1,712)	0	5,346,792	346,800	6.94%
Renton	38,193,412	2,790,802	12,228	0	40,996,443	2,803,031	7.34%
Skykomish	633,881	18,434	0	0	652,314	18,433	2.91%
Bellevue	57,828,509	4,065,886	(2,527,222)	0	59,367,173	1,538,664	2.66%
South Central	5,943,601	373,400	(965,763)	0	5,351,238	(592,363)	−9.97%
Lower Snoqualmie	5,192,197	359,098	0	0	5,551,295	359,098	6.92%
Auburn	28,572,544	2,069,112	0	178,728	30,820,384	2,247,840	7.87%
Tahoma	9,690,858	708,076	0	137,277	10,536,211	845,353	8.72%
Snoqualmie Valley	9,238,566	683,436	0	41,917	9,963,920	725,354	7.85%
Issaquah	24,330,474	1,708,160	0	0	26,038,634	1,708,160	7.02%
Shoreline	31,196,776	2,215,646	(735,349)	0	32,677,072	1,480,296	4.75%
Lake Washington	61,679,583	4,568,887	32,111	0	66,280,580	4,600,997	7.46%
Kent	54,912,985	3,932,222	965	0	58,846,171	3,933,186	7.16%
Northshore	47,491,153	3,447,968	(506,035)	615,561	51,048,647	3,557,494	7.49%
Yakima County							
Union Gap	1,526,744	115,597	0	0	1,642,340	115,596	7.57%
Naches Valley	3,750,699	297,188	0	94,694	4,142,580	391,881	10.45%
Yakima	36,325,445	2,654,357	(86,532)	1,190,407	40,083,677	3,758,232	10.35%
Moxee	5,223,443	411,806	0	117,115	5,752,363	528,920	10.13%
Selah	8,231,515	662,048	0	366,064	9,259,638	1,028,113	12.49%
Mabton	1,626,874	124,192	0	0	1,751,066	124,192	7.63%
Grandview	5,818,806	477,911	0	242,527	6,539,244	720,438	12.38%
Sunnyside	9,352,485	799,788	0	0	10,152,272	799,787	8.55%
Toppenish	6,582,434	558,570	0	0	7,141,005	558,571	8.49%
Highland	2,544,602	185,032	0	46,732	2,776,366	231,764	9.11%
Granger	2,674,122	191,226	0	138,559	3,003,907	329,785	12.33%
Zillah	2,311,777	181,770	0	83,649	2,577,196	265,419	11.48%
Wapato	6,889,988	578,995	0	0	7,468,983	578,995	8.40%

Source: Office of the Superintendent of Public Instruction (OSPI).

EXHIBIT 14

Preliminary 1987–89 "Current Services" Level Projections State General Fund
(Dollars in Millions)

1985–87 authorized expenditure level		$9,249
Carry forward adjustments and mandatory increases		
K-12		
K-12 enrollment growth	$ 78	
Remediation enrollment	27	
Non-employee related costs	43	
K-3, voc formula enrichment	14	
Staff mix, OASI, salary equalization	65	
TRS adjustment for non-state staff	(16)	
Total K-12	211	
Human Services		
Income assistance caseloads	65	
Medical assistance caseloads	81	
Corrections caseloads	10	
Other human services[1]	84	
Total human services	240	
Other		
September 1986 salary increase	98	
Comparable worth	33	
General inflation[2]	90	
Other adjustments[3]	14	
Total other	235	
Total all adjustments		686
Projected 1987–89 baseline budget		$9,935

[1]Includes long-term care (nursing homes), mental health, children and family services, other.

[2]1987–89 general inflation other than K-12, includes state revenues for distribution.

[3]Includes adjustments for one-time costs and transfers.

Source: State of Washington, House of Representatives Ways and Means Committee.

EXHIBIT 15

Major Reasons for the Increase between 1985–87 and 1987–89 Base Line Budget

The general fund budget for 1985–87 is $9.249 billion. The cost of extending that budget into the next biennium will be $9.935 billion, an increase of $686 million. How can it end up costing so much more to do only what we're doing now? The following are the major components of the increased spending level.

1. Workload increases $261 Million

 Enrollment in our public schools is projected to increase from the current level of 708,560 to 729,740 in the next biennium. The number of people qualifying for nursing home care, public assistance, mental health care, etc., under *existing* eligibility standards will continue to increase as well. Simply extending current educational and social services to these people will cost an additional $261 million.

2. Compensation increases $185 Million

 Salary increases granted to employees this year must be extended through the entire 1987–89 biennium. The same is true for the federally mandated social security premium increases. Additional cost: $185 million.

3. Inflation increases $133 Million

 The cost of goods and services in K-12, higher education, and all other state government is subject to inflation. Goods and services include everything from office leases to paper supplies. Inflation in the 1987–89 biennium is projected to be 3.7% and 3.6%. Increased cost: $133 million.

4. Other increases $107 Million

 The cost of continuing program improvements implemented only in the second year of the current biennium is a major source of additional appropriations for the next two years. Examples include the formula enrichment for K-3 and vocational students. Increased cost: $107 million.

Source: State of Washington, House of Representatives Ways and Means Committee.

EXHIBIT 16

1987–89 Revenue and Economic Forecast

The official revenue forecast for the 1987–89 biennium will not be available until November 1986. In the meantime, the Economic and Revenue Forecasting Council staff have prepared preliminary forecasts which will be refined in June and September.

There are three sets of assumptions for projecting a range of revenues for the 1987–89 biennium:

Assumption 1   Control or baseline $9.939 billion

The initial forecast developed by the Council staff for 1987–89 is $9.939 billion. It assumes a better than 50 percent chance the economy will stagnate in late 1988. Historical data indicates the average duration of economic expansions from 1945–1982 has been 45 months. The current expansion began in December 1982 and if it continues until July 1988, it will have lasted 66 months, the second longest period of expansion since World War II. The longest expansion was 105 months and took place during the Vietnam War era (1961–1969).

Assumption 2   Constant growth $10.173 billion

A second approach used by the Council staff simply assumes the same growth rate in 1987–89 that is estimated for 1985–87. Using this assumption results in a revenue estimate of $10.173 billion for 1987–89.

Assumption 3   Optimistic $10.327 billion

The most optimistic projection is based on the Data Resources Incorporated (DRI) forecast. DRI assumes continued and improved economic growth throughout the next biennium and results in a revenue estimate of $10.327 billion for 1987–89.

Following are comparisons of the three revenue assumptions and the projected "current services" budget for 1987–89.

	Control	*Growth*	*Optimistic*
	($ in Millions)		
Revenue forecasts	$9,939	$10,173	$10,327
Current svcs projection	9,935	9,935	9,935
Balance	4	230	392

Source: State of Washington, House of Representatives Ways and Means Committee.

EXHIBIT 17

Potential Requests for Enhancements to Base Line Budget

Gramm-Rudman   *Up to $200 Million*

Federal budget cuts resulting from Gramm-Rudman are subject to speculation. However, *if* Congress allows Gramm-Rudman to be implemented or takes comparable action and the state were to replace the major program cuts, the annual cost could be as high as $200 million. The biggest cuts would likely be in Social Service Block Grants (e.g., chore services, mental health) and education (e.g., remediation, handicapped).

Salary Increases   *$665 Million*

The following are the three major categories of employees paid by the state budget and the potential cost of likely salary increase requests.

State employees—Full implementation of the salary survey is projected to require an average increase of 17% effective July 1, 1987. Phasing in the increases over two years would cost $176 million.

College faculty—Attaining salary levels equivalent to the peer averages would require increases ranging from 20% at the UW to 11% at the regional universities. A two year phase-in would cost $88 million.

School teachers and staff—Salary increases comparable to the likely requests for state employees and college faculty would require a 17% increase. Phased in over two years, the cost would be $401 million.

EXHIBIT 17
(continued)

For reference, the cost of a 1% across the board salary increase on July 1, 1987 is $57 million. Based upon this number, one can calculate the cost of various salary increase alternatives. For example, a 5% salary increase on July 1, 1987 would cost $285 million ($57 million × 5). If given on July 1, 1988, the cost would be about one-half that amount or $142.5 million ($57 million × 5 × $\frac{1}{2}$).

| *K-12 Class Size Improvements* | *$53 Million* |

Increasing the current 50/1000 teacher/student ratio to 55/1000 would cost $219 million. The first two years of a five year phase-in of the 55/1000 ratio would cost $53 million.

| *Preschool Education* | *$45 Million* |

The passage of HB 1078 in 1985 set up a pre-school program for "at risk" children. Full implementation of the program in 1987–89 would cost $132 million. The first two years of a five year phase-in would cost $45 million.

| *Higher Education Support Levels* | *$100 Million* |

State funding for instructional support at our colleges and universities (e.g., support staff, equipment, supplies) lags behind funding made available to comparable institutions in other states. Attaining the national "peer average" would cost $100 million. The University of Washington would account for $63 million of the total.

| *Hospital Reimbursement* | *$49 Million* |

The state is currently paying hospitals 62% of the cost of the medical treatment they provide to state patients. 100% reimbursement in the next biennium would cost $49 million.

| *Vendor Rate Increasess* | *$33 Million* |

The legislature generally provides inflation adjustments to nursing homes and other vendors. With inflation projected at 3.7% and 3.6% over the next biennium, cost of the adjustments would be $33 million.

| *Income Assistance Grant Increases* | *$60 Million* |

Similar to vendor rate increases, annual inflation adjustments for public assistance recipients would cost $60 million in 1987–89.

| *Adult Dental Services* | *$30 Million* |

Dental care for adults on public assistance was eliminated in 1981. Restoring the program would cost $30 million in 1987–89.

| *Health Care for the Uninsured* | *$40 Million* |

Some 200,000 to 600,000 people in this state do not have health care insurance. Senator McDermott's basic health care plan that was introduced but not enacted earlier this year (SB 4777) would cost about $20 million per year to provide health care for 30,000 of these people.

| *Budget Reserve* | *$200 Million* |

A budget reserve is essential to cover fluctuations in revenues and unforseen emergencies requiring supplemental appropriations. A reserve of 2% is approximately $200 million.

Source: State of Washington, House of Representatives Ways and Means Committee.

problem, the council had prematurely narrowed both its goal and the range of options available to it. Representatives from the Washington Roundtable and the group Citizens Education Center Northwest believed the council needed to make a careful study of why some districts spent so much more than others, in order to craft a cost-effective and fair solution to the problem. "We're making a decision without information," complained Citizens Education Center representative Diana Gale in August. "I don't see a rational justification for pouring millions into school districts and increasing funding for most of the small districts." And Terry Bergeson, president of the state teachers' union, feared that the governor and legislature were rushing the council to come up "with a quick and clean solution that won't cost a whole bunch of money. . . ."

The thing that I want is to have a solution that's a real solution. And if we don't have the money to fund it, then by God, let's figure out why we don't have the money to fund it and let's deal with that. We don't have to deal with that on the commission. . . . But at least we should come out with something that will work for the education system in this state, and stop messing around with all these little band-aid things that really create more of a mess for educators, principals, teachers, superintendents, and don't allow us to do what we want to do.

ASSIGNMENT FOR CLASS DISCUSSION

Come to class prepared to explain whether or not you would support a relaxation of the 10 percent lid on local levies for education to allow more decentralized decision making about school funding. If so, why and in what form? If not, why not? In formulating your answer, please consider:

1. What are the economic efficiency arguments for centralized versus decentralized finance of, and decision making about, government services? To what degree do they apply in this case?
2. What other considerations influence the decision about relaxing the levy lid?
3. Do you recommend any one of State School Superintendent Frank Brouillet's three options? If so, why?

The Urban League and the Youth Subminimum Wage

Several writers have termed black youths an "endangered species" because of the escalating numbers . . . who have been frustrated in their attempts to find work.

National Urban League,
Youth Employment in American Industry

By the spring of 1984, the US economy had witnessed a spectacular recovery from its worst recession in 50 years. The gross national product, which had declined 1.9 percent during 1982, grew 3.3 percent in 1983, leading to the sharpest recorded drop in unemployment figures since the government began compiling such data in 1948—from 10.7 percent of the labor force in November 1982 to 8.2 percent in December 1983. Despite this improvement in overall employment, 19.4 percent of all teenagers, and 44.8 percent of black youth, remained jobless. As the end of the school year approached, press reports described thousands of teenagers show-

This case was written by Vlad Jenkins under the direction of Professors Dorothy Robyn and Joseph Kalt for use at the John F. Kennedy School of Government, Harvard University. (0288)

ing up to apply for occasional summer job openings.

In keeping with its free market philosophy, the Reagan administration had been seeking a greater role for private industry in reducing the problem of youth unemployment. Arguing that the minimum wage, by acting as a barrier to the employment of low-skilled workers, had "caused more misery and unemployment than anything since the Great Depression," President Reagan sought to lower the minimum wage, at least for teenagers. Efforts to establish a youth subminimum wage had died in congressional committee in 1981 and again in 1983, but in 1984, the White House was preparing to wage a new offensive. As part of their efforts to rally support for the controversial youth subminimum wage, administration officials contacted members of the National Urban League in the hopes of winning an endorsement from the highly respected black organization.

THE HISTORY OF MINIMUM WAGE LEGISLATION

The Supreme Court ended decades of judicial opposition to state minimum wages for children and women when it reversed itself in 1937, with Chief Justice Hughes declaring that:

> The exploitation of a class of workers who are in an unequal position with respect to bargaining power and are thus relatively defenseless against the denial of a living wage is not only detrimental to their health and well-being, but casts a direct burden for their support upon the community. What these workers lose in wages the taxpayers are called upon to pay. The bare cost of living must be met.

At President Franklin Roosevelt's request, Congress enacted the first federal minimum wage through the Fair Labor Standards Act (FLSA) of 1938. The intent of the act, championed by organized labor, was to maintain a "minimum standard of living necessary for health, efficiency, and general well-being of workers," and to increase pay levels "without substantially curtailing employment."

Initially establishing a minimum wage of 25 cents per hour and applicable to a quarter of the work force, the FLSA was amended several times to raise the wage floor (see Exhibit 1) and to extend coverage to additional industries. The major extensions occurred in 1961 and 1966, when Congress brought service and retail workers under the minimum-wage

EXHIBIT 1
Growth of the Minimum Wage

	Minimum Wage	Value 1938 Dollars
1938	$0.25	$0.25
1939	0.30	0.30
1945	0.40	0.31
1950	0.75	0.45
1956	1.00	0.52
1961	1.15	0.54
1963	1.25	0.57
1967	1.40	0.60
1968	1.60	0.66
1974	2.00	0.58
1975	2.10	0.57
1976	2.30	0.58
1978	2.65	0.59
1979	2.90	0.59
1980	3.10	0.56
1981	3.35	0.57

Source: Labor Department.

umbrella. By 1981, almost 92 percent of nonsupervisory farm and nonfarm wage earners were effectively covered by the minimum wage, then $3.35 per hour.

From the beginning, businessmen had opposed the minimum wage on pocketbook grounds, and critics had argued that, by denying workers the flexibility to seek jobs at lower wages, the minimum wage hurt those whose skills were the most marginal. In the mid-sixties, as black youth unemployment became a severe problem (see Exhibits 2 and 3), conservatives were quick to fault the minimum wage.[1] Declared University of Chicago economist Milton Friedman in a 1966 paper:

> The minimum wage requires employers to discriminate against persons with low skills. The high rate of unemployment among teenagers, especially black teenagers, is both a scandal and a serious source of social unrest, largely as a result of minimum wage laws.
>
> We regard the minimum wage law as one of the most, if not the most, anti-black laws on the statute books. It penalizes them by preventing them from offering to work for low-wage jobs as a means of inducing employers to give them on-the-job training.

[1] In 1948, black youth unemployment did not differ significantly from that of whites: blacks aged 16-17 had an unemployment rate that year of 9.4%, compared to 10.2% for whites of the same age. Black teenagers continued to have a higher labor force participation rate than white teenagers into the early 1960s. (See Exhibits 4, 5 and 6.)

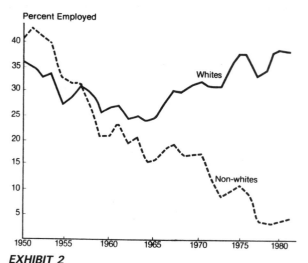

EXHIBIT 2

Employment-to-Population Ratios: 16–19-Year-Old Males

Source: Reprinted with permission from *The American Economic Review,* vol. 72, No. 4 (Sept. 1982).

While not all economists shared Friedman's view of the minimum wage as the major cause of black teenage unemployment, they were generally agreed that it contributed to the problem, and a steady stream of econometric studies during the late sixties and seventies confirmed theoretical predictions that the wage floor was a barrier to employment of teenagers and other low-skilled groups. One of the most outspoken economists was Walter Williams, a black Temple University professor who wrote in 1977 that the minimum wage served to encourage racial discrimination:

For example, suppose there are two groups of workers who are equally productive but differ in some other respect. Type X workers are willing to work for $2.00 per hour and type Y are willing to work for $2.65. The cost to the employer of discriminating against type X workers

EXHIBIT 3

The Minimum Wage and Jobs

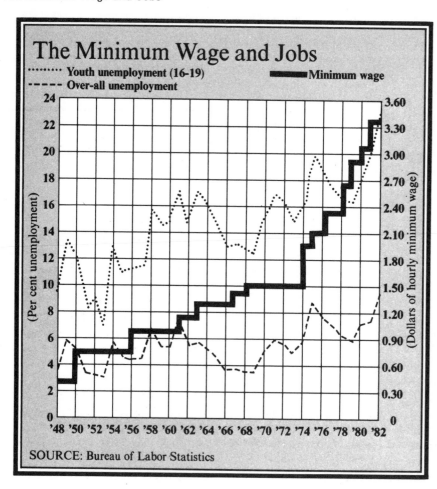

Source: Bureau of Labor Statistics. Reprinted with permission from *National Journal,* March 12, 1983.

EXHIBIT 4

Comparison of Youth and General Unemployment by Race (Males)

Year	General	White 16–17	Black 16–17	B/W Ratio	White 18–19	Black 18–19	B/W Ratio	White 20–24	Black 20–24	B/W Ratio
1948	3.8	10.2	9.4	.92	9.4	10.5	1.11	6.4	11.7	1.83
1949	5.9	13.4	15.8	1.18	14.2	17.1	1.20	9.8	15.8	1.61
1950[1]	5.3	13.4	12.1	.90	11.7	17.7	1.51	7.7	12.6	1.64
1951	3.3	9.5	8.7	.92	6.7	9.6	1.43	3.6	6.7	1.86
1952	3.0	10.9	8.0	.73	7.0	10.0	1.43	4.3	7.9	1.84
1953	2.9	8.9	8.3	.93	7.1	8.1	1.14	4.5	8.1	1.80
1954	5.5	14.0	13.4	.96	13.0	14.7	1.13	9.8	16.9	1.72
1955	4.4	12.2	14.8	1.21	10.4	12.9	1.24	7.0	12.4	1.77
1956[1]	4.1	11.2	15.7	1.40	9.7	14.9	1.54	6.1	12.0	1.97
1957	4.3	11.9	16.3	1.37	11.2	20.0	1.70	7.1	12.7	1.79
1958	6.8	14.9	27.1	1.81	16.5	26.7	1.62	11.7	19.5	1.66
1959	5.5	15.0	22.3	1.48	13.0	27.2	2.09	7.5	16.3	2.17
1960	5.5	14.6	22.7	1.55	13.5	25.1	1.86	8.3	13.1	1.58
1961[1]	6.7	16.5	31.0	1.89	15.1	23.9	1.58	10.0	15.3	1.53
1962	5.5	15.1	21.9	1.45	12.7	21.8	1.72	8.0	14.6	1.83
1963[1]	5.7	17.8	27.0	1.52	14.2	27.4	1.83	7.8	15.5	1.99
1964	5.2	16.1	25.9	1.61	13.4	23.1	1.72	7.4	12.6	1.70
1965	4.5	14.7	27.1	1.84	11.4	20.2	1.77	5.9	9.3	1.58
1966	3.8	12.5	22.5	1.80	8.9	20.5	2.30	4.1	7.9	1.93
1967[1]	3.8	12.7	28.9	2.26	9.0	20.1	2.23	4.2	8.0	1.90
1968[1]	3.6	12.3	26.6	2.16	8.2	19.0	2.31	4.6	8.3	1.80
1969	3.5	12.5	24.7	1.98	7.9	19.0	2.40	4.6	8.4	1.83
1970	4.9	15.7	27.8	1.77	12.0	23.1	1.93	7.8	12.6	1.62
1971	5.9	17.1	33.4	1.95	13.5	26.0	1.93	9.4	16.2	1.72
1972	5.6	16.4	35.1	2.14	12.4	26.2	2.11	8.5	14.7	1.73
1973	4.9	15.1	34.4	2.28	10.0	22.1	2.21	6.5	12.6	1.94
1974[1]	5.6	16.2	39.0	2.41	11.5	26.6	2.31	7.8	15.4	1.97
1975[1]	8.1	19.7	45.2	2.29	14.0	30.1	2.15	11.3	23.5	2.08
1976[1]	7.0	19.7	40.6	2.06	15.5	35.5	2.29	10.9	22.4	2.05

[1]Shows change in the Federal minimum wage law.

Source: Adapted from Department of Labor, Bureau of Labor Statistics, *Handbook of Labor Statistics* 1975—Reference Edition (Washington, D.C.: U.S. Government Printing Office, 1975), pp. 153–55; U.S. Department of Labor, Bureau of Labor Statistics, *Employment and Unemployment in 1976,* Special Labor Force Report 199 (Washington, D.C.: U.S. Government Printing Office, 1977), as printed in U.S. Senate, Committee on Labor and Human Resources, Hearing 99-347, May 22, 1985.

is 65 cents per hour per employee. If, however, there were a law requiring all employees to be paid a minimum wage of $2.65 per hour, the cost to the employer of discriminating against type X workers becomes zero. According to the law of demand, given a taste for racial discrimination, there will be more discrimination when its cost is lower.

Since the minimum wage also limits the availability of low-skilled labor as a substitute for high-skilled labor, it's not surprising that unions are its major proponent, Williams noted. He recalled that past black leaders—notably Booker T. Washington and W.E.B. DuBois—had been lifelong foes of trade unions, and that DuBois had called them "the greatest enemy of the black workingman."

Williams, like many other economists, sup-

ported a subminimum wage for teenagers, as one way of restoring the bottom rung on society's economic ladder. The idea was far from novel: The original FLSA of 1938 provided for a "sub-standard wage" for learners, apprentices and handicapped workers. As part of the 1961 FLSA amendments, Congress instituted a limited subminimum wage for full-time students working part-time, and in the years following the 1966 amendments, as the effects of expanded coverage were felt, discussion of a general youth subminimum wage began in earnest. President Richard Nixon endorsed the concept in a message to Congress accompanying his 1971 veto of legislation to increase the minimum wage, and bills to establish a subminimum wage were introduced in that session of Congress and two succeeding sessions. Strongly opposed by organized labor, the bills repeatedly failed in committee.

EXHIBIT 5

Civilian Unemployment Rate by Demographic Characteristic, 1948–83 (Percent;[1] Monthly Data Seasonally Adjusted)

Year or Month	All Civilian Workers Total	White							Black and Other						
		Total	Males			Females			Total	Males			Females		
			Total	16–19 Years	20 Years and Over	Total	16–19 Years	20 Years and Over		Total	16–19 Years	30 Years and Over	Total	16–19 Years	20 Years and Over
1948	3.8	3.5	3.4			3.8			5.9	5.8			6.1		
1949	5.9	5.6	5.6			5.7			8.9	9.6			7.9		
1950	5.3	4.9	4.7			5.3			9.0	9.4			8.4		
1951	3.3	3.1	2.6			4.2			5.3	4.9			6.1		
1952	3.0	2.8	2.5			3.3			5.4	5.2			5.7		
1953	2.9	2.7	2.5			3.1			4.5	4.8			4.1		
1954	5.5	5.0	4.8	13.4	4.4	5.5	10.4	5.1	9.9	10.3	14.4	9.9	9.2	20.6	8.4
1955	4.4	3.9	3.7	11.3	3.3	4.3	9.1	3.9	8.7	8.8	13.4	8.4	8.5	19.2	7.7
1956	4.1	3.6	3.4	10.5	3.0	4.2	9.7	3.7	8.3	7.9	15.0	7.4	8.9	22.8	7.8
1957	4.3	3.8	3.6	11.5	3.2	4.3	9.5	3.8	7.9	8.3	18.4	7.6	7.3	20.2	6.4
1958	6.8	6.1	6.1	15.7	5.5	6.2	12.7	5.6	12.6	13.7	26.8	12.7	10.8	28.4	9.5
1959	5.5	4.8	4.6	14.0	4.1	5.3	12.0	4.7	10.7	11.5	25.2	10.5	9.4	27.7	8.3
1960	5.5	5.0	4.8	14.0	4.2	5.3	12.7	4.6	10.2	10.7	24.0	9.6	9.4	24.8	8.3
1961	6.7	6.0	5.7	15.7	5.1	6.5	14.8	5.7	12.4	12.8	26.8	11.7	11.9	29.2	10.6
1962	5.5	4.9	4.6	13.7	4.0	5.5	12.8	4.7	10.9	10.9	22.0	10.0	11.0	30.2	9.6
1963	5.7	5.0	4.7	15.9	3.9	5.8	15.1	4.8	10.8	10.5	27.3	9.2	11.2	34.7	9.4
1964	5.2	4.6	4.1	14.7	3.4	5.5	14.9	4.6	9.6	8.9	24.3	7.7	10.7	31.6	9.0
1965	4.5	4.1	3.6	12.9	2.9	5.0	14.0	4.0	8.1	7.4	23.3	6.0	9.2	31.7	7.5
1966	3.8	3.4	2.8	10.5	2.2	4.3	12.1	3.3	7.3	6.3	21.3	4.9	8.7	31.3	6.6
1967	3.8	3.4	2.7	10.7	2.1	4.6	11.5	3.8	7.4	6.0	23.9	4.3	9.1	29.6	7.1
1968	3.6	3.2	2.6	10.1	2.0	4.3	12.1	3.4	6.7	5.6	22.1	3.9	8.3	28.7	6.3
1969	3.5	3.1	2.5	10.0	1.9	4.2	11.5	3.4	6.4	5.3	21.4	3.7	7.8	27.6	5.8
1970	4.9	4.5	4.0	13.7	3.2	5.4	13.4	4.4	8.2	7.3	25.0	5.6	9.3	34.5	6.9
1971	5.9	5.4	4.9	15.1	4.0	6.3	15.1	5.3	9.9	9.1	28.8	7.3	10.9	35.4	8.7
1972	5.6	5.1	4.5	14.2	3.6	5.9	14.2	4.9	10.0	8.9	29.7	6.9	11.4	38.4	8.8
1973	4.9	4.3	3.8	12.3	3.0	5.3	13.0	4.3	9.0	7.7	26.9	5.8	10.6	34.4	8.2
1974	5.6	5.0	4.4	13.5	3.5	6.1	14.5	5.1	9.9	9.2	31.5	6.9	10.8	34.5	8.5

1975	8.5	7.8	7.2	18.3	6.2	8.6	17.4	7.5	13.8	13.6	35.2	11.6	13.9	38.3	11.5
1976	7.7	7.0	6.4	17.3	5.4	7.9	16.4	6.8	13.1	12.7	35.1	10.6	13.6	38.8	11.3
1977	7.1	6.2	5.5	15.0	4.7	7.3	15.9	6.2	13.1	12.3	36.6	10.0	13.9	39.6	11.7
1978	6.1	5.2	4.6	13.5	3.7	6.2	14.4	5.2	11.9	11.0	34.0	8.7	13.0	38.1	10.6
1979	5.8	5.1	4.5	13.9	3.6	5.9	14.0	5.0	11.3	10.4	31.3	8.5	12.3	35.6	10.2
1980	7.1	6.3	6.1	16.2	5.3	6.5	14.8	5.6	13.1	13.2	34.4	11.3	13.1	36.5	11.1
1981	7.6	6.7	6.5	17.9	5.6	6.9	16.6	5.9	14.2	14.1	37.5	12.1	14.3	38.3	12.4
1982	9.7	8.6	8.8	21.7	7.8	8.3	19.0	7.3	17.3	18.2	44.0	16.2	16.4	43.8	14.3
1983	9.6	8.4	8.8	20.2	7.9	7.9	18.3	6.9	17.8	18.5	45.0	16.5	17.1	44.6	15.2
1982:															
Jan	8.6	7.6	7.7	20.8	6.7	7.5	18.4	6.5	15.4	16.2	36.3	14.7	14.5	42.6	12.4
Feb	8.9	7.8	7.8	20.5	6.8	7.8	19.4	6.6	16.1	16.7	40.3	14.7	15.6	42.1	13.4
Mar	9.0	8.0	8.0	20.2	7.1	7.9	17.8	6.9	16.6	17.5	45.6	15.2	15.7	42.3	13.7
Apr	9.4	8.3	8.3	21.8	7.3	8.2	18.9	7.2	16.7	17.2	43.1	15.2	16.2	41.1	14.4
May	9.4	8.2	8.3	21.0	7.3	8.2	18.6	7.1	17.0	17.5	43.9	15.4	16.5	46.7	14.2
June	9.5	8.4	8.7	21.7	7.8	8.0	17.6	7.1	16.9	17.9	47.6	15.7	15.8	41.5	14.1
July	9.9	8.8	9.1	22.5	8.1	8.4	19.1	7.4	17.5	17.8	44.7	15.8	17.0	48.0	14.6
Aug	9.9	8.7	9.1	22.1	8.1	8.2	18.7	7.3	17.5	18.2	41.8	16.2	16.8	49.8	14.2
Sept	10.2	9.0	9.4	22.2	8.5	8.4	19.1	7.4	18.1	19.5	44.5	17.5	16.6	43.8	14.5
Oct	10.4	9.2	9.7	22.6	8.7	8.7	19.9	7.6	18.6	20.1	44.3	18.1	16.9	41.3	15.1
Nov	10.7	9.6	10.0	22.7	9.0	9.0	19.8	7.9	18.7	19.8	48.6	17.6	17.5	43.2	15.6
Dec	10.7	9.6	10.0	22.8	9.1	9.2	20.4	8.1	18.9	20.3	47.0	18.2	17.3	42.5	15.4
1983:															
Jan	10.4	9.1	9.4	21.5	8.5	8.8	19.0	7.9	18.9	19.9	44.7	18.1	17.7	42.7	16.0
Feb	10.4	9.2	9.6	21.4	8.8	8.6	18.7	7.7	18.2	19.2	43.2	17.5	17.1	41.4	15.5
Mar	10.3	9.1	9.5	22.6	8.5	8.5	19.6	7.5	18.6	19.3	43.9	17.5	17.8	41.6	16.2
Apr	10.2	8.9	9.4	21.4	8.5	8.2	19.1	7.3	18.7	19.8	46.5	17.9	17.5	45.3	15.5
May	10.1	8.8	9.2	20.4	8.4	8.2	19.4	7.2	18.5	19.8	49.1	17.6	17.2	41.4	15.5
June	10.0	8.6	8.8	20.4	7.9	8.4	19.7	7.4	18.6	19.6	47.4	17.2	17.6	45.9	15.5
July	9.5	8.2	8.6	20.3	7.7	7.7	18.4	6.8	17.9	19.1	46.0	16.9	16.6	44.7	14.7
Aug	9.5	8.2	8.6	20.7	7.7	7.7	18.2	6.7	17.9	18.7	48.5	16.3	17.1	44.7	15.1
Sept	9.2	8.0	8.4	18.9	7.7	7.5	17.4	6.6	17.3	17.7	48.2	15.4	16.7	44.8	14.8
Oct	8.8	7.7	8.1	19.8	7.3	7.1	16.9	6.3	16.7	16.8	41.7	14.9	16.6	48.3	14.5
Nov	8.4	7.3	7.6	17.6	6.9	6.9	16.6	6.0	16.1	16.1	39.0	14.3	16.1	46.6	14.1
Dec	8.2	7.1	7.4	17.5	6.7	6.7	16.5	5.9	16.3	15.9	41.1	14.0	16.7	48.1	14.6

[1]Unemployment as percent of civilian labor force in group specified.

Source: Department of Labor, Bureau of Labor Statistics.

EXHIBIT 6

Male Civilian Labor Force Participation Ratio by Race, Age

		B/W Males 16–17	B/W Males 18–19	B/W Males 20–24	B/W Males 16 and Over
	1954	.99	1.11	1.05	1.00
	1955	1.00	1.01	1.05	1.00
1.00/hr	1956	.96	1.06	1.01	.99
	1957	.95	1.01	1.03	.99
	1958	.96	1.03	1.02	1.00
	1959	.92	1.02	1.04	1.00
	1960	.99	1.03	1.03	1.99
1.15/hr	1961	.96	1.06	1.02	.99
	1962	.93	1.04	1.03	.98
1.25/hr	1963	.87	1.02	1.04	.99
	1965	.88	1.01	1.05	.99
	1966	.87	.97	1.06	.98
1.40/hr	1967	.86	.95	1.04	.97
1.60/hr	1968	.79	.96	1.03	.97
	1969	.77	.95	1.02	.96
	1970	.71	.92	1.00	.96
	1971	.65	.87	.98	.94
	1972	.68	.85	.97	.93
	1973	.63	.85	.95	.93
2.00/hr	1974	.65	.85	.95	.92
2.10/hr	1975	.57	.79	.92	.91
2.30/hr	1976	.57	.77	.91	.90

Source: Computed from U.S. Department of Labor, Bureau of Labor Statistics, *Handbook of Labor Statistics 1975—Reference Edition* (Washington, D.C.: U.S. Government Printing Office, 1975), pp. 36–37; U.S. Department of Labor, Bureau of Labor Statistics, *Employment and Unemployment in 1976:* Special Labor Force Report 199 (Washington, D.C.: U.S. Government Printing Office, 1977), as printed in U.S. Senate Committee on Labor and Human Resources, Hearing 99-347, May 22, 1985.

Comparable legislation in 1977 came close to passage, however. Offered as an offset to legislation raising the minimum wage from its existing $2.30 to $3.35 by 1981, the subminimum wage proposal lacked only five votes in the Senate and one vote in the House. Congress did, however, agree to establish a commission to study various aspects of the minimum wage, including the likely effects of a youth exemption.

SUBMINIMUM WAGE PROPOSALS: 1981

Even before the Minimum Wage Study Commission had completed its work, proposals for a subminimum wage surfaced again. In February 1981, at a White House meeting of mayors, Tom Bradley of Los Angeles and Edward Koch of New York volunteered their cities for an experiment with a youth differential. A recently inaugurated Ronald Reagan was favorable to the idea but noncommittal, on the ad-

vice of David Stockman, director of the Office of Management and Budget, who had warned the president to defer antagonizing organized labor until after he had lobbied for budget reductions. Even without Reagan's explicit backing, three Republican senators, including Orrin K. Hatch, newly appointed chairman of the Senate Labor and Resources Committee, introduced separate bills to establish a youth subminimum wage, and prospects for passage in the most conservative Congress in years looked good.[2]

In late March, the Senate Subcommittee on Labor met to consider these three bills and to explore what Chairman Don Nickles (R-Okla.) termed "a national burden of unparalleled magnitude—youth unemployment." During two days of hearings before a standing-room-only crowd, business leaders told the

[2]The three GOP-sponsored bills included one to eliminate the minimum wage altogether for workers under 18. Another proposed to slice 25 percent off the minimum for persons under 20, and the third sought to cut the wage rate by 15 percent for those under 20.

subcommittee that a "youth opportunity wage" would create jobs for the young and restore employers' incentive to provide on-the-job training. Labor and civil rights leaders countered that a youth subminimum wage would create few new jobs: rather, it would bring about large windfall profits to employers and the displacement of adult workers—a phenomenon described as "fire dad to hire junior."

Testifying on behalf of the legislation were representatives of a variety of small business groups, primarily from the retail and services sector. The National Restaurant Association submitted studies commissioned from Chase Econometrics and Data Resources which revealed that every 10 percent increase in the minimum wage reduced employment in that industry by 2.5 percent, or about 112,000 full-time jobs. The association, which claimed that 16 percent of all working teenagers—1.5 million in all—were employed by the food service industry, estimated that 500,000 full-time jobs in that industry were lost as a result of the 1977 FLSA amendments.

Addressing the concern that a youth differential wage would cause adult minimum wage workers to be displaced, representatives of retail grocers' organizations argued that the jobs that would be created for teenagers were ones that had been priced out of the market by the minimum wage:

> In ours and other service industries, there are plenty of jobs to be done, many that are no longer done because the minimum wage has made their cost prohibitive. Service station attendants, grocery store bag boys, soda fountain workers, carhops, all manner of errand-runners and clerks have been greatly reduced in number or eliminated entirely because of the higher minimum wage. Since we have grown accustomed to the self-service salad bar, gas station or retail store, we tend to forget that they represent the loss of jobs once performed by others.

Moreover, they maintained, employers were too sensitive to the high costs of turnover and retraining to engage in wanton substitution of workers.

Representatives of various social service and civil rights organizations joined organized labor, represented by Lane Kirkland, president of the AFL-CIO, to testify against the legislation. Speaking on behalf of the National Urban League was Maudine R. Cooper, vice president for Washington operations:

> The National Urban League has opposed an expanded youth differential since it was first dis-

cussed seriously in the 91st Congress [1969-70]. Although subminimum wage legislation has been introduced in each Congress since 1971, none of it has become law—for reasons we believe are still relevant and sound.

Cooper argued that since jobs were moving in great numbers from central cities to suburban areas, minority teenagers would not benefit from any newly created positions.[3] Moreover, the gains to white suburban youth from a subminimum wage would come at the expense of black adult primary earners.[4] Citing the results of a Department of Labor survey which showed that black subminimum wage workers were older and more likely to be primary earners than white subminimum wage workers, Cooper concluded that "since [a youth differential] would legalize the payment of subminimum wages to most young people, black adults who are currently being paid subminimum wages would be the group most likely to be displaced first by young people or, at the very least, continue to be paid illegal subminimum wages."

Cooper also testified that employers were fundamentally reluctant to hire chronically unemployed youths, and hence did not take advantage of existing minimum wage exemptions or generous wage subsidy programs. Echoing her warning was William Grinker, president of the Manpower Demonstration Research Corporation, a non-profit organization set up to oversee and test new social policy initiatives. As part of the Youth Incentive Entitlement Pilot Projects, set up in 1977, MDRC had offered employers generous subsidies to hire economically disadvantaged youths aged 16 to 19—80% of them black and Hispanic—who met school performance and attendance standards. Even though MDRC handled all paperwork (thought to be a disincentive in other employment training programs), relatively few employers were interested: only 5% of eligible firms participated when the wage subsidy level was 50%, 10% when the subsidy was 75%, and 18% when the wage subsidy was 100%.

---

[3]In a 1977 paper, Walter Williams disputed the "myth" that high unemployment of inner city blacks is due to jobs moving to the suburbs. "The ratio of black to white unemployment in suburban areas (those that have large black populations) is very similar to the ratio of black to white unemployment in the cities," Williams wrote.

[4]A study of the characteristics of workers paid in violation of the federal minimum wage, conducted by the US Department of Labor during 1969-70, revealed that of black subminimum wage earners, 83% were older than 19 and 56% were primary earners, compared to the white subminimum wage earners, of whom only 63% were over 19 and 35% were primary earners.

One of the most colorful combatants in the war of words and statistics was Sol C. "Chick" Chaikin, president of the International Ladies Garment Workers Union, who recommended that the subcommittee rename the youth wage proposals the "McDonald's Windfall Gifts Amendments."[5]

The McDonald's near the ILGWU headquarters is open 18 hours a day, 363 days a year. The approximately 12 teenagers who work there at any given time would lose, as a result of a 75 percent youth subminimum, 84 cents an hour each. In total wages, that single McDonald's would be saving $10.06 an hour, $181.44 a day, $65,862.72 a year. Multiply that by the 5000 McDonald's across the country and you discover that the McDonald's Corporation stands to gain roughly $329 million. McDonald's shareholders get a break, too. The firm of Dean Witter estimates that if a youth subminimum is passed, the value of McDonald's stock will jump 31 cents a share.

Althea T.L. Simmons, director of the Washington Bureau of the NAACP, echoed Chaikin's message that "the group with the most to gain . . . is the employer who could make high profits as a result of cheap labor." Least likely to benefit from a wage differential, Simmons cautioned, were blacks and other minority youth, "since there is rampant discrimination on the basis of race . . . even in the fast food industry in this country."

Blacks know what it is like to be exploited, to be unhired, and to be denied opportunity. You have heard persons testify with reference to what the minimum wage is worth today. For those persons who believe that black teenagers work for pin money or pocket change, we suggest as a demonstration that they just "walk a while in the shoes" of the have-nots who must make every penny count in order to survive.

Simmons pointed out that black employment increased more rapidly than that of whites in periods of expansion and declined more rapidly than white employment in periods of recession (see Exhibit 7). Thus economic growth was a key to improving the well-being of blacks. The black unemployment rate was even worse than it appeared, Simmons also noted, because it was rising in the face of declining labor force participation (that is, even though increasing numbers of blacks had given up looking for work and were thus not counted as unemployed).

While the hearings were dominated by interest group spokesmen, economists—many serving as consultants to the Minimum Wage Study Commission—took an active part in the debate, in the media if not in subcommittee. However, their ranks were far more divided by the subminimum wage than by the minimum wage. Consistent with his earlier stand, Temple economist Walter Williams disputed the displacement argument:

---

[5]No one from McDonald's testified at the two-day hearing. The Food Service and Lodging Institute, which represents McDonald's, Burger King, Kentucky Fried Chicken and other multistate restaurant and hotel chains, decided not to testify, at least in part so as to undercut the efforts of union organizers, who were trying to enlist members by charging that fast-food chains were seeking authority to pay a subminimum wage. Also absent from the hearings was the US Chamber of Commerce, which feared a counterpunch to the youth subminimum wage in the form of a higher minimum wage for everyone else. "We're not talking about the multinational oil companies," said chamber lobbyist Mark DeBernardo in a Washington Post story (March 21, 1981). "In the retail trades, we shoot for a three percent profit margin. . . . Holding the line on the minimum wage is the No. 1 priority, and No. 2, No. 3, No. 4 and No. 5. . . . The question is what is there that's worth opening up the Fair Labor Standards Act to amendment? The youth differential is not."

EXHIBIT 7

Economic Growth and Unemployment (Percent Change from the Preceding Year)

Year	Real GNP (1972 Dollars)	Employment	
		Black	White
55	6.70	3.11	3.48
56	2.14	3.06	2.55
57	1.81	1.29	0.33
58	−0.21	−2.98	−1.46
59	6.02	3.15	2.46
60	2.28	4.57	1.46
61	2.51	−1.37	0.11
62	5.80	2.52	1.33
63	3.95	1.94	1.55
64	5.26	3.40	2.14
65	5.89	3.52	2.46
66	5.95	3.04	2.48
67	2.72	1.73	2.06
68	4.38	1.97	2.09
69	2.57	2.63	2.61
70	−0.32	0.73	0.96
71	2.99	−0.50	0.76
72	5.74	2.68	3.33
73	5.46	5.83	3.02
74	−1.39	2.03	1.78
75	−1.27	−2.64	−1.18
76	5.88	4.34	3.05
77	5.30	3.68	3.48
78	4.38	7.39	3.84
79	2.28	3.63	2.61
80	−0.20	−1.90	−1.70

Source: Economic Report of the President, 1981. Bureau of Labor Statistics, Department of Labor.

The lump of labor theory, which says there are only a finite number of jobs in the economy, is nonsense. For the most part, teenagers hired at a subminimum wage would fill new jobs or old jobs that would be reinstated. There might be ushers at movies again, for example, and hotels might decide to keep their corridors and windows cleaner.

But MIT economist Michael Piore predicted that few teenagers—particularly black teenagers—would want to take jobs paying less than the minimum wage:[6]

White teenagers might well work for subminimum wages because they would know the jobs would be temporary and their identity would not be bound up in the work. Young blacks, however, would see the jobs as the same kind their fathers and grandfathers had and would view them as a symbol of their degradation in American society. It's not that young blacks don't want to work. What they are unwilling to do is accept the kind of status in American society that their parents had. And that's why their unemployment rate is high and rising.

Paul Osterman, a Boston University economist and collaborator with Piore, testified that "astronomical rates" of black teenage unemployment were also due to "growing job competition from adult women, illegal aliens, and white youth; the poor quality of inner city schools; and racial discrimination." These same adult women would be the group most vulnerable to layoffs resulting from a subminimum wage, Osterman cautioned. Displacement aside, the hiring of black teenagers would not appreciably reduce youth unemployment rates, since more black youth would enter the labor market in response to the new jobs. "Most seriously," Osterman warned, "school dropout rates would certainly rise since there is a widely accepted and unambiguous relationship between youth job availability and school leaving."

MINIMUM WAGE STUDY COMMISSION

Following the two-day hearings, the youth subminimum wage bills lost in subcommittee, when proponents failed to win the votes of swing Republicans.

Crucial to their defeat was the Reagan administration's failure to endorse specific legislation. Labor Secretary Raymond Donovan had testified that while he supported the idea in principle, further research—such as that being done by the Minimum Wage Study Commission—would have to precede administration support of a particular legislative approach. The commission staff had in fact largely completed its work by that time, though the panel's six-volume report was not issued until May 1981. In the end, that report did little to resolve differing views among the eight commissioners.[7]

Employment Effects. The economic findings most relevant to the subminimum wage debate concerned the employment effects of the minimum wage on teenagers.[8] Commission staff economists found a consensus in the existing literature of time-series studies that a 10 percent increase in the minimum wage would reduce teenage employment by 1.0 to 2.5 percent. Staff efforts to update these studies produced a more precise estimate of 1.0 percent drop due to a 10 percent minimum wage hike. (See Exhibits 9 and 10.) (When part-time workers were converted to full-time equivalents, the estimated effect on teenage employment was increased 0.5 percent.) A commissioned study by Michigan State economist Daniel Hamermesh, which sought to improve on previous methodologies, produced a consistent and robust estimate: regardless of the choice of wage measures, time periods or statistical models, a 10 percent increase in the minimum wage reduces teenage employment by 1.0 percent.

The employment effects are likely to be more accurate than unemployment effects as an indication of the impact of the minimum wage. Unemployment increases will understate employment losses if some individuals respond to reduced employment opportunities by withdrawing from the labor force altogether. Such individuals have given up the search for a job and hence are not officially counted among the unemployed. It is also possible, of course, that a new minimum wage level will induce some persons to enter the labor force who otherwise would have remained out of the job market.

Based on these figures, Hamermesh estimated that a permanent 25 percent youth differential would increase teenage employment by about 3.0 percent or 250,000 jobs (total teenage employment was about

[6]Both the Piore and Williams quotes are from the *National Journal* (January 24, 1981).

[7]For a list of the commissioners appointed by the Carter administration secretaries of labor, commerce, agriculture, and health, education and welfare, see Exhibit 8.

[8]While the commission staff looked at unemployment as well as employment effects, they concentrated on the latter.

EXHIBIT 8

Minimum Wage Study Commission

James G. O'Hara, Chairman
Attorney at Law, Patton, Boggs, and Blow
Washington, D.C.
Appointed by the Secretary of Health, Education, and Welfare

William D. Byrum
Grain and Pork Producer
Onondaga, Michigan
Appointed by the Secretary of Agriculture

Jay H. Foreman[1]
International Vice President, Executive Assistant to the President
United Food and Commercial Workers International Union
Washington, D.C.
Appointed by the Secretary of Labor

S. Warne Robinson
Chairman of the Board, G. C. Murphy Company
McKeesport, Pennsylvania
Appointed by the Secretary of Commerce

Clara F. Schloss
Consultant, AFL-CIO
Washington, D.C.
Appointed by the Secretary of Labor

Michael L. Wachter
Professor of Economics, University of Pennsylvania
Philadelphia, Pennsylvania
Appointed by the Secretary of Commerce

Phyllis Ann Wallace
Professor of Management
Sloan School of Management, Massachusetts Institute of Technology
Cambridge, Massachusetts
Appointed by the Secretary of Health, Education, and Welfare

Sandra L. Willett
Executive Vice President, National Consumers League
Washington, D.C.
Appointed by the Secretary of Agriculture

[1]Succeeded Gerald M. Feder who resigned May 1979.
Source: Report of the Minimum Wage Study Commission, Vol. V (June 1981).

eight million). Although he did not calculate adult employment effects, his estimates implied that adults would not suffer a net decline in employment as a result of increased "employment of teenagers. Using Hamermesh's work, commission staff performed an alternative calculation which showed a larger teenage employment gain of 4.0 to 5.0 percent, or 400,000 to 450,000 jobs, at a cost of 50,000 to 150,000 adult jobs.

Additional evidence came from analyses of existing youth differentials and wage subsidies. A commissioned study by Harvard economist Richard Freeman, et al., looked at the FLSA exemption allowing employers in retail, service and higher education to hire full-time high school and college students on a part-time basis at 85 percent of the minimum wage. Freeman found that the program increased hours worked by students for certified employers (largely colleges and universities) by about 11 percent, with less than a 1.0 percent reduction in the hours worked by non-students. In addition, the commission staff examined the Targeted Jobs Tax Credit (TJTC), a federal program begun in 1979 which provided an 18 month, 50 percent wage subsidy to employers of economically disadvantaged youth aged 18 to 24. Most striking was the limited use made of the generous subsidy: between March 1979 and July 1980, only 70,000 of some 2.8 million eligible youths were hired or certified under TJTC.

Income Distribution Effects. Neither the data on the TJTC nor the economists' studies revealed whether a 15 or 25 percent wage differential would yield significant benefits for disadvantaged

EXHIBIT 9

Estimated Impact of a 10 Percent Change in the Minimum Wage by Sex, Age, and Race

	Per Cent Change in Employment (10 x Elasticity)								Change in Unemployment Rate (In Percentage Points)							
	White Males		Nonwhite Males		White Females		Nonwhite Females		White Males		Nonwhite Males		White Females		Nonwhite Females	
	16–17	18–19	16–17	18–19	16–17	18–19	16–17	18–19	16–17	18–19	16–17	18–19	16–17	18–19	16–17	18–19
Kaltz (1970)	-1.700[1] (2.9)	-.814[1] (2.0)	-.075 (0.1)	1.988 (1.9)	-2.072[1] (2.3)	.077 (0.2)	1.236 (0.7)	.002 (0.0)	.344[2]	.073[2]	-1.445[2]	-1.529[2]	.181[2]	-.226[2]	.609[2]	.457[2]
Lovell (1972)[3]	—	—	—	—	—	—	—	—	-.043 (0.3)	-.087 (1.0)	-.191 (0.5)	-.224 (0.7)	.049 (0.3)	.019 (0.1)	.165 (0.3)	1.147[1] (2.5)
Lovell (1973)[3]	—	—	—	—	—	—	—	—	-.381 (1.1)	-.555[1] (2.0)	-.824 (0.8)	1.152 (1.2)	-.839 (1.6)	.225 (0.6)	1.567 (1.1)	.701 (0.6)
Kelly (1975)	-2.185[1] (4.3)	-1.164[1] (3.6)	-3.957 (3.5)	-.326 (0.4)	-1.548[1] (2.1)	-.174 (0.4)	-.149 (0.9)	.069 (0.0)	—	—	—	—	—	—	—	—
Kelly (1976)[4]	.07 (0.21)	-.76[1] (5.10)	—	—	-1.33[1] (2.65)	-.59[1] (2.19)	—	—	—	—	—	—	—	—	—	—
Ragan (1977)	-.71[2]	-.89[2]	-5.14[2]	-2.47[2]	-.13[2]	-.07[2]	-2.57[2]	1.15[2]	1.19[2]	.68[2]	.98[2]	.73[2]	.36[2]	.79[2]	.84[2]	-.31[2]
Mattila (1978)[4]	-.73[2]	-.71[2]	—	—	-1.17[2]	-.90[2]	—	—	-.06[2]	.04[2]	—	—	.32[2]	.17[2]	—	—
Mattila (1979)[4]	—	-1.23[2]	—	—	—	-.22[2]	—	—	—	.14[2]	—	—	—	-.02[2]	—	—
Ragan (1979)	.06[2]	-.78[2]	-4.40[2]	-2.97[2]	.42[2]	-.30[2]	-.32[2]	.92[2]	.611[2]	.304[2]	-.901[2]	1.159[2]	.628[2]	.099[2]	3.171[2]	1.153[2]
Wachter-Kim (1979)	-2.777[1] (2.3)	-1.192 (1.2)	-4.458 (1.2)	-2.566 (1.1)	-3.578[1] (2.4)	-2.166 (1.8)	-13.39[1] (2.5)	-4.784 (1.7)	—	—	—	—	—	—	—	—

Notes:

[1] Statistically significant (t-statistics in parentheses below coefficients).

[2] No significance tests available because reported coefficients were calculated from disaggregated data or (for unemployment effects) from employment and labor-force effects.

[3] Equations are based on the unemployment/population ratio; while they have been converted to unemployment rate impacts, they are not strictly comparable.

[4] Estimates are not disaggregated by race; impacts shown in "white" columns are for all members of that column's age-sex group.

Source: Report of the Minimum Wage Study Commission, Vol. V (June 1981).

EXHIBIT 10

Estimated Impact of a 10 Percent Change in the Minimum Wage on Teenagers 16–19 Years, by Sex and Race

	Per Cent Change in Employment (10 × Elasticity)					Change in Unemployment Rate (in Percentage Points)				
	White Males	White Females	Nonwhite Males	Nonwhite Females	All Workers	White Males	White Females	Nonwhite Males	Nonwhite Females	All Workers
Kaltz (1970)	-1.210[2]	-.746[2]	1.165[2]	.438[2]	-.98[1] (2.3)	.190[2]	-.034[2]	-1.556[2]	.519[2]	-.006[2]
Adle (1971)	—	—	—	—	—	.731[2]	3.256[2]	5.793[2]	12.761[2]	2.525[2]
Moore (1971)	—	—	—	—	—	2.960[1] (4.8)		8.901[1] (6.0)		3.649[2]
Kosters-Welch (1972)	-3.31[1]	-2.41[1]	-3.56[1]	-3.01[1]	-2.96[2]					
Lovell (1972)[3]	-1.620[2]	-.700[2]	-1.775[2]	-.080[2]	-1.204[2]	-.067[2]	.030[2]	-.210[2]	.793[2]	-.001[2]
Adle (1973)	-.35[2]	-.96[2]	—	—	-.66[2]	.160 (1.3)	.700[1] (3.4)	1.925[1] (4.5)	2.787[1] (6.1)	.518[1] (3.3)
Lovell (1973)[3]	—	—	—	—	-.94[2]	-.475[2]	-.181[2]	.494[2]	.505[2]	.249[2]
Kelly (1975)	—	—	—	—	-2.31[2]					
Kelly (1976)[4]	—	—	—	—						
Gramlich (1976)	—	—	—	—						
Hashimoto-Mincer (1970) & Mincer (1976)	-2.05[1]	—	-4.65	—	-1.78[1] (2.2)	.412[2]		.693[2]		.445[2]
Welch (1976)	—	—	—	—						
Ragan (1977)	-.81[2]	-.09[2]	-.350[2]	-.10[2]	-.65[2]	.91[2]	.62[2]	.83[2]	.10[2]	.75[2]
Mattila (1978)[4]	-.72[2]	-1.00[2]	—	—	-.84[2]	.00[2]	.23[2]	—	—	.10[2]
Al-Salam, Quester & Welch (1979)	—	—	—	—	-1.19[2]	—	—	—	—	—
Freeman (1979)	—	—	—	—	-2.46[2]	—	—	—	—	.00[2]
Ragan (1979)	-.41[2]	-.35[2]	-3.51[2]	.51[2]	-.52[2]	—	—	—	—	—
Wachter-Kim (1979)	-1.883[2]	-2.722[2]	-3.290[2]	-7.710[2]	-2.519[2]	.431[2]	.306[2]	.265[2]	1.814[2]	.512[2]

Notes:

[1] Statistically significant (t-statistics in parentheses below coefficients).

[2] No significance tests available because reported coefficients were calculated from disaggregated data or (for unemployment effects) from employment and labor-force effects.

[3] Equations are based on the unemployment/population ratio; while they have been converted to unemployment rate impacts, they are not strictly comparable.

[4] Estimates are not disaggregated by race; impacts shown in "white" columns are for all members of that column's age-sex group.

Source: Report of the Minimum Wage Study Commission, Vol. V. (June 1981).

teenagers. While no direct evidence on that score existed, evidence on the economic status of low-wage wage workers and the income distribution effects of the minimum wage was indirectly relevant.

A demographic profile revealed that black women of all ages had the greatest likelihood of working at or below the minimum wage. Nearly one quarter of the country's four million black women workers earned the minimum wage or less, although they accounted for only nine percent of the minimum wage population. While half of all black male teen-

agers earned the minimum or less (for white male teens, the figure was 37 percent), they represented only eight percent of minimum-wage workers (see Exhibit 11).

Data on family income revealed that the proportion of minimum-wage workers accounted for by teenagers increased dramatically as family income rose: Over 70 percent of teenage minimum-wage workers were in families with incomes of $15,000 or more, and over one third were in families with incomes of $25,000 and up (see Exhibit 12).

EXHIBIT 11

Wage and Salary Employment of Persons at or below the Minimum Wage by Sex, Age, and Race/Ethnicity, Second Quarter 1980
(Numbers in Thousands)

| Age, Sex, and Race/ Ethnicity | All Employed Workers | Minimum Wage Workers | | | | | | As % of All Minimum Wage Workers |
| | | Total | | Below Minimum | | At Minimum | | |
		Number	Percent	Number	Percent	Number	Percent	
All workers	83,535	10,293	12.3	5,178	6.2	5,116	6.1	100.0
White								
Total	69,015	7,825	11.3	4,050	5.9	3,776	5.5	76.0
Men, 16 years								
and over	38,652	2,792	7.2	1,451	3.8	1,341	3.5	27.1
16–19 years	3,205	1,202	37.5	508	15.8	694	21.6	11.7
20–24 years	5,457	537	9.8	252	4.6	285	5.2	5.2
25–64 years	29,012	815	2.8	542	1.9	273	0.9	7.9
65 years & over	978	238	24.3	149	15.2	89	9.1	2.3
Women, 16 years								
and over	30,363	5,033	16.6	2,599	8.6	2,435	8.0	48.9
16–19 years	2,940	1,497	51.0	734	25.0	763	26.0	14.5
20–24 years	4,892	798	16.3	388	7.9	410	8.4	7.8
25–64 years	21,772	2,456	11.3	1,299	6.0	1,157	5.3	23.9
65 years & over	759	282	37.2	177	23.3	105	13.8	2.7
Black								
Total	8,485	1,540	18.1	722	8.5	818	9.6	15.0
Men, 16 years								
and over	4,361	593	13.6	273	6.3	320	7.3	5.8
16–19 years	286	143	50.0	56	19.6	87	30.4	1.4
20–24 years	659	141	21.4	42	6.4	99	15.0	1.4
25–64 years	3,304	250	7.6	146	4.4	104	3.2	2.4
65 years & over	112	59	52.7	29	25.9	30	26.8	0.6
Women, 16 years								
and over	4,124	948	23.0	449	10.9	499	12.1	9.2
16–19 years	217	112	51.6	36	16.6	76	35.0	1.1
20–24 years	593	149	25.1	61	10.3	88	14.8	1.4
25–64 years	3,212	623	19.4	308	9.6	315	9.8	6.1
65 years & over	102	63	61.8	44	43.1	19	18.6	0.6
Spanish								
Total	4,529	718	15.8	293	6.5	425	9.4	7.0
Men, 16 years								
and over	2,711	310	11.4	109	4.0	201	7.4	3.0
16–19 years	286	94	32.9	23	8.0	71	24.8	0.9
20–24 years	498	70	14.0	19	3.8	51	10.2	0.7
25–64 years	1,904	141	7.4	62	3.3	79	4.2	1.4
65 years & over	23	5	21.7	5	21.7	0	—	.1

EXHIBIT 11 (continued)

Age, Sex, and Race/ Ethnicity	All Employed Workers	Minimum Wage Workers						As % of All Minimum Wage Workers
		Total		Below Minimum		At Minimum		
		Number	Percent	Number	Percent	Number	Percent	
Women, 16 years and over	1,818	408	22.4	184	10.1	224	12.3	4.0
16–19 years	162	81	50.0	40	24.7	41.	25.3	0.8
20–24 years	340	67	19.7	20	5.9	47	13.8	0.6
25–64 years	1,303	253	19.4	117	9.0	136	10.4	2.5
65 years & over	13	7	53.9	7	53.9	0	—	.1
Other								
Total	1,506	210	13.9	113	7.5	97	6.4	2.0
Men, 16 years and over	758	78	10.3	49	6.5	29	3.8	0.8
16–19 years	46	22	47.8	6	13.0	16	34.8	0.2
20–24 years	113	17	15.0	10	8.8	7	6.2	0.2
25–64 years	581	30	5.2	24	4.1	6	1.0	0.3
65 years & over	18	9	50.0	9	50.0	0	—	0.1
Women, 16 years and over	748	132	17.6	64	8.6	68	9.1	1.3
16–19 years	59	30	50.9	13	22.0	17	28.8	0.3
20–24 years	107	19	17.8	11	10.3	8	7.5	0.2
25–64 years	578	82	14.2	40	6.9	42	7.3	0.8
65 years & over	4	1	25.0	0	—	1	25.0	—

Note: Individual items may not add to totals because of rounding.
Source: Current Population Survey.

EXHIBIT 12

Wage and Salary Employment of Persons at or below the Minimum Wage by Family Income and Household Relationship, March/May 1978
(Numbers in Thousands)

Family Income and Household Relationship	Total	All Employment Workers			
		At or below the Minimum Wage			
		Number	Percent		As Percent of All Minimum Wage Workers
Total	17,108	2,257	13.2	100.0	100.0
Household head	9,989	636	6.4	28.2	100.0
Spouse of head	4,191	635	15.2	28.1	100.0
Children	2,235	849	38.0	37.6	100.0
Other	693	136	19.6	6.0	100.0
Less than $6,000	1,056	412	39.0	100.0	18.3
Household head	758	288	38.0	69.9	45.3
Spouse of head	78	34	43.6	8.3	5.3
Children	47	30	63.8	7.3	3.5
Other	173	60	34.7	14.6	44.1
$6,000–$9,999	1,986	404	20.4	100.0	17.9
Household head	1,368	171	12.5	42.3	26.9
Spouse of head	295	122	41.4	30.2	19.2
Children	159	88	55.3	21.8	10.4
Other	163	23	14.1	5.7	16.9

EXHIBIT 12   (continued)

Family Income and Household Relationship	Total	All Employment Workers			
		At or below the Minimum Wage			
		Number	Percent	As Percent of All Minimum Wage Workers	
$10,000–$14,999	3,212	409	12.7	100.0	18.2
Household head	2,119	91	4.3	22.2	14.3
Spouse of head	696	169	24.3	41.3	26.6
Children	258	126	48.8	30.8	14.8
Other	139	23	16.5	5.6	16.9
$15,000–$24,999	6,261	619	9.9	100.0	27.4
Household head	3,637	73	2.0	11.8	11.5
Spouse of head	1,766	236	13.4	38.1	37.2
Children	741	295	39.8	47.7	34.7
Other	117	15	12.8	2.4	11.0
$25,000–$49,999	4,246	382	9.0	100.0	16.9
Household head	1,947	12	0.6	3.1	1.9
Spouse of head	1,273	71	5.6	18.6	11.2
Children	939	288	30.7	75.4	33.9
Other	87	11	12.6	2.9	8.1
$50,000 and over	347	30	8.7	100.0	1.3
Household head	160	1	0.6	3.3	0.2
Spouse of head	83	3	3.6	10.0	0.5
Children	91	22	24.2	73.3	2.6
Other	13	4	30.8	13.3	2.9

Note: Numbers may not add to totals because of rounding.
Source: Current Population Survey.

Proportion of Employed Wage and Salary Workers at or below the Minimum Wage, by Family Income and Household Relationship, March/May 1978

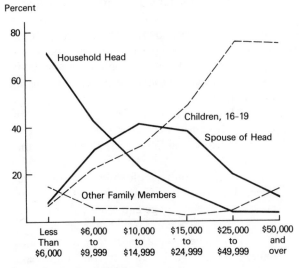

Proportion of Employed Wage and Salary Workers at or below the Minimum Wage, by Family Income and Household Relationship, March/May 1978

Source: Current Population Survey.

A commissioned study by Linda Datcher and Glenn Loury examined the effect of the minimum wage on the distribution of earnings among blacks and whites. The authors concluded that the effect of the minimum wage was positive on both full-time and part-time white male teenagers, but for part-time black male and white female teenagers (about 93 percent of workers in both groups were part-time), the effect was negative (see Exhibit 13). When Datcher and Loury examined family earnings, they found more evidence that the minimum wage was "not an egalitarian policy." A hypothetical 20 percent increase in the minimum raised white earnings by a little more than one percent on average, while the gain for blacks was less than one fifth as large. The percentage gain for all white families in the first quintile was over 33 times larger than that for blacks (see Exhibit 14).

The staff concluded that, despite the gaps and inconsistencies in the data, "a fairly clear message stands out":

The minimum wage has caused a small but real improvement in the personal well-being of those near the poverty level. Equally clear,

168 *Social Justice in Economic Policy*

EXHIBIT 13

Regression Estimates of the Effects of the Minimum Wage on Ln Annual Earnings by Full-Time and Part-Time Status

| | Men | | | | | | Women | | | | | |
| | Ages 25 and Over | | Ages 20–24 | | Ages 16–19 | | Ages 25 and Over | | Ages 20–24 | | Ages 16–19 | |
	Black	White	Black	White	Black	White	Black	White	Black	White	Black	White
Ln coverage adjusted minimum— full-time workers	−.054 (.042)	.048[1] (.019)	−.183 (.136)	.200[2] (.052)	.005 (.114)	.174[1] (.064)	−.019 (.106)	−.106[2] (.017)	.086 (.081)	−.044 (.046)	.016 (.107)	.174[1] (.082)
Ln coverage adjusted minimum— part-time workers	.106[2] (.041)	.103[2] (.020)	−.028 (.132)	.205[2] (.048)	−.271[1] (.122)	.068[2] (.033)	.024+ (.014)	.039[2] (.015)	.133[1] (.067)	.101[2] (.037)	.085 (.081)	−.052[2] (.019)

Standard errors are in parentheses. The other variables included in the regressions were years of schooling, years after schooling, year after schooling squared, number of children less than 18, in nonlabor income, dummy variables for completed high school only, completed college, married, no children less than 18, region, metropolitan residence, detailed industry, and full-time as well as separate time trend variables for each industry. The coefficients of most of these variables were constrained to be the same for blacks and whites. A full-time worker is defined as an individual who worked 50–52 weeks during the year annual earnings is reported *and* who worked at least 35 hours during the survey week.

[1]Denotes significant at the 5% level.

[2]Denotes significant at the 1% level.

Source: Linda Datcher and Glenn Loury, "The Effect of Minimum Wage Legislation on the Distribution of Family Earnings among Blacks and Whites," in *Report of the Minimum Wage Study Commission,* Vol. VII, 1981.

however, is the message that other mechanisms such as direct government transfer payments or some variant of a negative income tax would be more effective tools for fighting poverty, no matter how it is defined.

Commission Recommendations. Even before the staff had completed its work, it was clear that the commission's recommendations would reflect politics as well as analysis. In January 1981, several months before its three-year study was released, the commission majority noted in a preliminary report that "the moral and political premises that underlie a question have more to do with shaping the answer than do the nuggets of fact that merely provide the foundation for the road between." Referring to the commissioned studies nearing completion, the report concluded that "what justice demands will not emerge from a computer."

In March, 1981, following completion of the staff's work, the commission voted six to one (with one member voting present) to recommend that Congress not enact a national youth differential. (Panel members also voted to recommend indexation of the minimum wage and elimination of the full-time stu-

dent exemption for college but not high school students.) The majority acknowledged the consensus among economists that the minimum wage had reduced teenage employment, but they found no justification for a youth subminimum, even on a local experimental basis:

Several considerations led us to this recommendation: First, available estimates suggest that a youth differential has a limited potential for reducing the unemployment rate among teenagers, because teenage employment increases probably would be modest and a differential is likely to attract additional teenagers into the labor market.

Also, there is no evidence that areas with the highest youth unemployment rates would be the most likely beneficiaries of a youth subminimum.

Second, adult employment would be reduced by a youth differential, and forced to choose between teenage and adult employment, the latter seems a considerably higher priority.

Third, there is reason to hope that teenage unemployment will lessen in the not-too-distant

EXHIBIT 14

Means of 1976 Actual Family Earnings and Hypothetical Family Earnings with Twenty Percent Increase in the Minimum Wage[1]

	Means of Actual Family Earnings		Means of Hypothetical Family Earnings		Absolute Change from Actual Mean to Hypothetical Mean		Percentage Change from Actual Mean to Hypothetical Mean	
	Black	*White*	*Black*	*White*	*Black*	*White*	*Black*	*White*
All Families	10844	15434	10868	15618	24	184	0.22	1.19
1st quintile	2997	3146	2998	3178	1	32	0.03	1.01
2nd quintile	8544	8713	8552	8813	8	102	0.09	1.17
3rd quintile	13441	13460	13481	13627	40	167	0.30	1.24
4th quintile	18531	18714	18579	18941	48	227	0.26	1.21
5th quintile	29032	31279	29116	31651	84	372	0.29	1.19
Two-Person Families	10076	14141	10099	14308	23	162	0.23	1.15
1st quintile	2418	2534	2421	2556	3	22	0.12	0.87
2nd quintile	7464	7714	7469	7798	5	84	0.07	1.09
3rd quintile	12503	12460	12520	12613	17	153	0.14	1.23
4th quintile	17465	17503	17517	17715	52	212	0.30	1.21
5th quintile	27059	29151	27163	29473	104	322	0.38	1.10
Four-Person Families	13162	18181	13194	18405	32	224	0.24	1.23
1st quintile	4982	5776	4979	5851	−3	75	−0.06	1.30
2nd quintile	11985	11989	12027	12145	42	156	0.35	1.30
3rd quintile	16089	16419	16135	16627	46	208	0.29	1.27
4th quintile	21137	21264	21212	21515	75	251	0.35	1.18
5th quintile	30925	33811	30997	34220	72	409	0.23	1.21

[1]Only families with earnings greater than $100 are included.
Source: Linda Datcher and Glenn Loury, ''The Effect of Minimum Wage Legislation on the Distribution of Family Earnings among Blacks and Whites,'' in *Report of the Minimum Wage Study Commission,* Vol. VII, 1981.

future as the large group of baby-boom teenagers passes into young adulthood.

Fourth, a youth differential would represent a departure from the principle that there should be equal pay for equal work regardless of accidents of birth, such as race, sex, ethnic or national origin, or age. If suggestions were made that the very real employment problems of women or members of minority groups be solved by paying them less for their labor, such a proposal would be rejected out of hand as fundamentally unjust. We can see no difference in principle between such proposals and those based on age.

In view of the fourth consideration, the proposal ''ought to be rejected as a policy option even if we thought it would substantially reduce youth un-

employment,'' concluded commission chairman James O'Hara, a former congressman from Macomb County, Michigan, an affluent blue collar suburb of Detroit.

Commissioner S. Warne Robinson, chairman of the board of G.C. Murphy Co., wrote a lengthy and scathing minority report which faulted the majority for its refusal to hold public hearings and its ''cynical disregard for the conscientious, painstaking findings of our economic research.''

Clearly this willingness by the Commission's majority to enshrine personal preference in place of the hard facts means that the majority report will consistently fail to answer the questions Congress asked in creating the Commission. If Congress intended this Commission to vote on the basis of its opinions rather than the evidence, this Commission should have been retitled the Minimum Wage Opinion Commission. It could have then reached its conclusions three years ago and avoided the time and trouble of undertaking extensive—and expensive—economic research.

REAGAN ADMINISTRATION INITIATIVES: 1983-84

Publication of the commission's report in May 1981 was followed by a period of silence from within the Reagan administration. By the summer of 1982, however, administration figures were again speaking out for a youth subminimum wage.[9] Clarence Pendleton, Jr., controversial chairman of the US Commission on Civil Rights and former president of the San Diego chapter of the Urban League, called for an emergency jobs program to reduce teenage unemployment. "This would require our suspending the minimum wage for a minimum of six months to create new jobs in the private sector," Pendleton advised. During a meeting with editorial writers in February 1983, President Reagan explained that the minimum wage "is really based in mind of the mature employee" and "should never have been applied to young people." Although "the right thing to do" would be to eliminate the minimum wage for teenagers, the president explained, sending such a proposal to Congress would be "hopeless."

Recognizing the futility of such a drastic step, Rep. Barber Conable Jr. (R-NY) and Sen. Robert Dole (R-Kan.) introduced joint legislation to conduct a three-year national experiment with a 25 percent youth wage differential. Titled the "Youth Employment Opportunity Wage Act of 1983," the Conable-Dole legislation also included provisions for penalties to employers who lowered the wages of teenagers already employed, or replaced minimum-wage adults with subminimum-wage teenagers. In addition, the program was limited to May 1 through September 30.

Supporters of the legislation stressed that it would not affect the wages of teenagers already employed. "There is no constraint on the teenager to

---

[9]Advocacy took a variety of forms. The September 1982 issue of *The American Economic Review* featured an article by John Cogan, assistant secretary for policy, evaluation and research in the Labor Department, which tried to pinpoint the causes of rising black teenage unemployment from 1950 to 1970. Cogan cited increased minimum wage rates and coverage as a major factor. However, Cogan concluded, "My principal finding is that the primary source of the fall in black teenage employment is the substantial decline in the demand for low-skilled agricultural labor," particularly in the rural South.

accept a job at the new minimum if his or her skills, experience, or record of dependability can command a higher wage," maintained Senate Labor Committee chairman Orrin Hatch. Hatch's insistence that valued workers had bargaining power seemed to be supported by casual observations that, by 1983, the starting wage for traditional minimum-wage positions in the services sector was about $4.50 per hour—well above the minimum wage.

But organized labor found far more to object to (the AFL-CIO ridiculed the proposal as the "Youth Discrimination and Displacement Act"), and key House Democrats such as George Miller, chairman of the Education and Labor Subcommittee on Labor Standards, regarded it as "a sorry response to a serious situation." Miller labeled the approach another example of "Faginomics," referring to the character in Charles Dickens' Oliver Twist who trained children in crime.

Despite strong backing from the Reagan administration, the bill generated little enthusiasm even from natural allies, who felt that it would be "dead on arrival" in Congress. Past supporters such as the National Restaurant Association opted to put their limited resources into more promising initiatives—for example, elimination of the 1982 tax law provision requiring income tax withholding on employees' tips.

The Conable-Dole bill died quietly, without so much as a committee hearing. But President Reagan vowed to "keep trying," and in the spring of 1984, the administration planned to have a modified version of the Conable-Dole proposal introduced in Hatch's Labor Committee. Sen. Edward Kennedy, the ranking Democrat on that panel, had meanwhile paired up with Augustus F. Hawkins, chairman of the House Labor Committee and a member of the Black Congressional Caucus, to promote an alternative approach. Their "Youth Incentive Employment Act of 1984" was a $2 billion proposal calling for subsidized employment and training for economically disadvantaged teenagers who agreed to remain in school.

Observers speculated that if the Hawkins-Kennedy bill passed in the House, and the administration bill passed in the Senate, there could be a move to reach a compromise between the two bills in conference committee. In view of that prospect, some Republican members of Congress contemplated drafting the subminimum wage bill to apply to economically disadvantaged youth only. Others regarded either alternative as absurd, given the irreconcilability of the two bills, House antagonism toward the subminimum wage concept, and the unacceptability of different minimum wages for minority and white youth.

THE URBAN LEAGUE'S DILEMMA

One thing was certain: the subminimum wage proposal would get nowhere without black support. The issue posed a particular dilemma for the National Urban League, a community service organization that came to prominence during the civil rights activism of the 1960s, under the leadership of Whitney Young Jr. and later Vernon Jordan Jr. Since its founding in 1911, the Urban League had been committed to seeking "equal opportunities for the poor and minorities in all sectors of our society." While the League had long opposed a youth subminimum wage, by 1984, as the group approached its 75th anniversary, still-rising black unemployment and drastic cutbacks in federal funding challenged it to find new ways to help the disadvantaged.

The black community itself had become divided over the subminimum wage issue. Key black organizations such as the NAACP remained steadfastly opposed, but others—most notably the National Conference of Black Mayors—had endorsed a limited test of the idea.

The Conference was composed of over 250 mayors, most of them from small southern towns. The president of the organization, Mayor Johnny Ford of Tuskegee, Alabama, had been a supporter of the youth subminimum wage for several years; Mayor Marion Barry of Washington, DC, who was likely to succeed Ford later in 1984, was also sympathetic to the idea and had characterized the reluctance to experiment with new approaches as "mushy-headed liberalism." At its annual convention, on April 19, 1984, the mayors endorsed almost unanimously the Reagan administration's proposal to establish, as a three-year experiment, a special $2.50 minimum wage for youth aged 16–20, effective between May and September. The alarming rise in teenage unemployment had created "a compelling need to develop new solutions to get minority youth off the streets," a position paper released after the convention explained. "We want this program not to displace youth or adults currently employed at or above the minimum wage," said Sam Tucker, a director of the Conference. "We will be the first out there raising hell if it doesn't work."

The endorsement sent waves of excitement through Washington. Sen. Hatch called the mayors'

decision "an act of bravery in an election year." "They are closer to the problems of black unemployment than are most elected officials in Washington," said Hatch, "and we ought to pay attention to what they say about subminimum wages. I am hopeful the resolution by the black mayors will change some minds in Congress."

In deciding to support the administration's position, Mayor Barry exposed himself to considerable criticism from traditional liberals. Aware of the risks Mayor Barry had taken, Deputy Mayor Tom Downs explained that

> The national government felt that it probably ought to do something for the mayor 'cause he took a lot of grief in doing it. There was a quid pro quo inasmuch as after the mayor found the position to be reasonable, and after he got the Conference of Black Mayors to agree to try this experiment . . . the Secretary of Labor found it in his heart and in his budget to fund an additional 1500 summer youth employment slots for the District [of Columbia].

Jobs had long been a priority of the Urban League as well. During the Carter administration, the Urban League and its 116 affiliates had become involved in the development and administration of employment training programs funded under the Comprehensive Employment and Training Act (CETA). When the Reagan administration slashed CETA funding in 1982, and then replaced the program with the Jobs Training Partnership Act (JTPA), the League and its affiliates lost over a third of their permanent employees. In this new environment, the League found itself dealing frequently with representatives of private industry, whose contributions now accounted for about half its budget, and who, under JTPA, had been given control over the allocation of funds for employment training programs. JTPA funds were allocated to states in the form of block grants to be administered locally by Private Industry Councils (PICs), on which businessmen and women had majority representation. Perhaps as a result of this change, the League began to counsel its affiliates on how to lobby PICs for funding in a manner more sensitive to "businessmen's return-on-investment mentality."

Despite the fact that most businesspeople on PICs with which the Urban League was dealing were joining in the "loud hue and cry about the youth subminimum wage," James Reed, Jr., deputy director of the League's Community Based Organization Pro-

EXHIBIT 15

Employers' Attitudes toward the Submission Wage Differential, by Type of Business (Percentage Distribution)

Attitude toward Subminimum Wage	Business				
	Manufacturing	*Trade*	*Finance*	*Service*	*Other[1]*
Increase jobs for youths	48	63	43	61	48
Decrease jobs for youths	1	5	2	1	—[2]
Have no effect	51	33	55	38	52
Total	100	100	100	100	100
Sample size	(83)	(126)	(44)	(141)	(31)

[1]Other businesses include agriculture, mining, construction, and transportation.
[2] There were no answers in this category.

Source: Published by permission of Transaction Publishers, from *Youth Employment in American Industry,* by Robert B. Hill and Regina Nixon. Copyright © 1984 by Transaction Publishers.

gram, was suspicious about the plan, seeing it as a "ploy by the Reagan administration to take away (job training) money from youth to reduce the deficit." Others in the organization were even more vehement; one employee observed that "even talking about the youth subminimum wage [was] like talking about bringing back segregation." Nevertheless, the League had included several questions concerning the youth subminimum wage in a recent national survey of employers (see Exhibits 15 and 16).

Douglas Glasgow, who had replaced Maudine Cooper as vice-president for Washington operations in the fall of 1983, was also concerned about the consequences of "the changed format of youth training programs from CETA to PICs. And we were very leery about . . . the PIC councils' willingness to seriously go after the needs of the poor, long-term unemployed, or those who had no skills. We had a feeling that they were going to be bypassed in the new training programs." This fear, together with the tragic rate of unemployment among minority youth, convinced Glasgow of "the need to experiment wherever possible if the administration supported an issue."

TAKING A STAND

In May 1984, the White House launched its formal campaign for the youth subminimum wage. During his weekly paid political radio broadcast, speaking of the high rate of teenage unemployment, President Reagan proclaimed that "if the dream of America is to be preserved, we must not waste the genius of one mind, the strength of one body or the spirit of one soul." The president attacked the minimum wage for youth, "because the cruel truth is, while everyone must be assured a fair wage, there's no compassion in mandating $3.35 an hour for start-up jobs that simply aren't worth that much in the marketplace."

As part of its campaign, the White House

EXHIBIT 16

Employers' Attitudes toward the Subminimum Wage Differential, by Proportion of Teenage Hires (Percentage Distribution)

Attitude toward Subminimum Wage Differential	Proportion of Teenage Hires		
	Low (0–1%)	*Moderate (2–9%)*	*High (10% & Over)*
Increase jobs for youths	54	59	58
Decrease jobs for youths	3	1	4
Have no effect	43	40	38
Total	100	100	100
Sample size	(143)	(157)	(186)

Note: Percentages may not add to 100 due to rounding.

Source: Published by permission of Transaction Publishers, from *Youth Employment in American Industry,* by Robert B. Hill and Regina Nixon. Copyright © 1984 by Transaction Publishers.

planned to host a reception in the Rose Garden for representatives of the National Conference of Black Mayors and other supporters of the youth subminimum wage. The event was sure to be highly visible.

"The issue began to gain a certain amount of momentum," Douglas Glasgow recalled, "which we felt forced us to make it clear where we were on the issue."

ASSIGNMENT FOR CLASS DISCUSSION

As the Urban League is positioned in the case, it faces the decision of whether or not it should come out in favor of a youth subminimum wage. If the decision were yours to make for the Urban League, what would it be? In addressing the problem before you, please consider the following:

1. What is your assessment of the weight of empirical evidence regarding the effects of the minimum wage? The effects of a youth subminimum wage? What effects are you looking for?

2. What impact would a youth subminimum wage have on constituencies other than your own (e.g., organized labor, employers in various size categories and industries, nonunionized labor, consumers of industrial products)? In what ways does your analysis here affect the decision you face?

3. What weight should be given in your decision to the past positions of the Urban League regarding similar proposals? If you decide that the Urban League should reverse its previous stance, how should the inconsistency be handled in public discussions?

chapter 4

Public Sector Investment and Pricing

It goes without saying that the resources devoted to public projects are not free: Public projects divert resources from other productive uses. The economic problem posed by public sector investment lies in deciding whether particular projects are worth the cost, where cost is measured in terms of foregone delivery to consumers of output in other sectors of the economy. When considering a public investment, how can we determine whether the resources at issue contribute more to people's well-being as a public project than they would if they stayed in their alternative employments? A related question concerns the ranking of alternative public uses of resources: Is it a better use of public funds to build a new highway or a new school? The techniques of project evaluation and cost-benefit analysis are intended to permit quantitative assessment of these kinds of questions. The first three cases of this section illustrate these techniques.

Closely related to the question of appropriate investment by the public sector is the question of the appropriate pricing of goods and services produced by the public sector. The prices charged by a government clearly can serve the function of raising revenue, perhaps to cover costs of production. Public sector prices, however, can also influence consumers' choices and, thereby, ration governmentally provided goods and services across the public. What standards might guide public sector pricing? This issue is taken up in the final case of this section.

The case of New York City's *West Side Highway Proposal* addresses the question of what is a cost and what is a benefit when the public sector undertakes investment in social infrastructure, such as a highway. This seemingly straightforward issue is clouded by the distinction between the viewpoint of the individual and the viewpoint of society as a whole. This distinction, in turn, influences the language of political discussion on a matter such as a large highway project. Are the jobs that are created by a program of highway construction a cost or a benefit? Should the tax revenues that result from the economic activity generated by a large public project be counted as costs, benefits, or just transfers between one group of citizens and another? Are there multiplier effects on regional economic activity when the public sector undertakes a major expenditure? If a project such as a major highway system changes the character of a city or a neighborhood, is that a cost or a benefit? If the federal government will cover a sizable portion of a state or local government's project costs, is the project less expensive? From whose standpoint?

Saving the Tuolumne illustrates the problems and principles of project evaluation when a project has significant impacts on things that people care about but that are not traded in the marketplace (such as the quality of the environment). In this case, hydroelectric dam development on California's Tuolumne River would reduce the river's attraction as a site for whitewater rafting, wilderness recreation, and aesthetic beauty. The absence of markets in which to observe the value of these kinds of goods and services forces the analyst to resort to surrogate means of measurement. The interest group performing the measurement in the Tuolumne case, the Environmental Defense Fund, is insistent upon a quantitative cost-benefit analysis. The resulting effort drives home the point that project evaluation and cost-benefit analyses are not cookbook exercises. Their worth as decision tools depends crucially upon the quality of the economic judgment and evidence employed by the analyst.

The standard economic (i.e., efficiency) justification for public provision of a good or service flows from the theory of public goods, which has been discussed in Chapter 2. In the absence of economical methods for making free riders pay for their use of a public good, the private sector is likely to underproduce that good, or not produce it at all. But are there circumstances in which public ownership could produce regular nonpublic goods more efficiently than the private sector? This question of privatization versus public ownership is taken up in *The Sawhill Commission: Weighing a State Takeover of LILCO.* This case documents the state of New York's recent interest in purchasing a large, private electric power company, the Long Island Lighting Company (LILCO). It is clear that resources are not made less socially costly under public ownership, but the public sector may have tax advantages or the capacity to shift the risks of an enterprise onto customers or taxpayers. If public ownership of an electric utility can cut the company's tax bill or cut its risks, is a state takeover justified? Would a takeover therefore constitute sound public policy?

When public sector enterprises sell their output in the marketplace, they are typically not permitted to earn returns above costs. Pricing by such enterprises then primarily serves the function of cost recovery. In so doing, the role of prices as devices for determining who gets what is commonly overlooked. *The Department of Transportation and Airport Landing Slots* looks at a situation in which the public sector provides a public good—airport facilities—under pricing policies that leave substantial excess demands at some airports. The result is extreme congestion and delay for passengers during rush hour periods of high demand. While the airports' recorded accounting costs may be recovered by their pricing, the rates charged for landing slots during periods of high demand fail to cover the costs of inconvenience and aggravation that passengers suffer. Such costs may not be as apparent as the cost of concrete for runways; but just as concrete has other beneficial uses that it could be put to, so passengers have better uses for their time than sitting in airport lounges or juggling their arrival and departure arrangements. In the face of these costs of overcrowding, the U.S. Department of Transportation has been considering auctions of tradable property rights in landing slots. The case examines the implications this would have for the profits of airlines, the welfare of passengers, and the fate of airline competition.

The West Side Highway Proposal (Abridged)

For most of the 1970s, New York City debated the future of its dilapidated West Side Highway. Planners suggested that it be replaced with a below-grade highway built on infill extending into the Hudson River. Construction of the 4.2 mile highway, known as Westway, and of the infill land surrounding it, was estimated at $1.2 billion. Under the terms of the Federal-Aid Highway Trust Fund, the government would pay up to 90 percent of the cost, once the project was approved.

As final approval looked imminent in early 1978, opinion remained sharply divided in New York. Supporters of Westway heralded it as the best hope of the beleaguered city, "the twentieth century equivalent of Central Park." It would, they argued, revitalize Manhattan's West Side by getting some of the traffic off its congested streets, opening up the waterfront, and creating additional housing. More importantly, the billion federal dollars that would finance Westway was money the bankrupt city could not afford to turn down.

But its opponents claimed that rather than revitalizing the West Side, Westway would destroy it. A bigger highway, they argued, could only lead to more traffic and worse pollution. Furthermore, the hous-

ing it would produce wasn't needed, and the city would see only a small portion of that billion dollars.

All sides, however, seemed to agree on one thing: the decision on Westway was one of the most important the city faced about its future.

THE WEST SIDE HIGHWAY (WSH)

The West Side Highway, running from the southern tip of Manhattan to the New York City-Yonkers line, was built in the 1930s. Since that time, it has carried more vehicles into the city's central business district than any other highway, and more people daily than the area's largest commuter rail operation, the Long Island Railroad.

At its southern end, the WSH was an elevated structure running for four miles along the Hudson River, separating the waterfront and its piers and warehouses from the adjacent communities of Greenwich Village, Chelsea, Clinton, and Lower Manhattan. Because the WSH was restricted to automobiles, trucks were forced to use the streets in the neighboring communities, causing congestion and additional air pollution. In December 1973, after

This case was abridged by Professors José A. Gomez-Ibañez and Marc Roberts, of the Kennedy School of Government, from a previous case by Associate Professor R. E. Herzlinger of the Harvard Business School, with Arva Clark and Barbara Fried, research assistants. Copyright © 1977 and 1985 by the President and Fellows of Harvard College.

years of abuse and neglect, a portion of the elevated structure collapsed. Inspectors subsequently found much of the rest structurally unsound and closed the elevated portion to traffic for an indefinite period.

For years before the WSH's collapse, the state Department of Transportation (DOT) had been involved with the highway because of its frequent need for reconstruction. In 1969, the department recommended to the Federal Highway Administration (FHWA) that the WSH be designated as part of the National System of Interstate and Defense system which would make it eligible for 90 percent federal funding for any relocation or replacement project.

The FHWA accepted the WSH into their interstate system in 1971. The same year, the Urban Development Corporation (UDC), a state authority headed by Nelson Rockefeller's appointee, Edward Logue, recommended that the WSH be torn down and replaced with a new highway and mass transit system, both to be built on an elevated structure over the water beyond the existing shoreline.

Governor Rockefeller liked the UDC idea. This was another opportunity—like the South Mall in Albany and Radio City and Rockefeller Plaza in New York City—to change the face of the earth. New York's Mayor Lindsay was willing to go along with the project but was not anywhere as enthusiastic as the governor. He felt that something had to be done about the West Side Highway but he didn't know what, and he wanted the City Planning Commission rather than the highway department to control the project. A group of city, state and federal officials prepared a memorandum of understanding that established the West Side Highway Project (WSHP), under the guidance of a steering committee composed of representatives of 16 state and city agencies, but made it clear that the city of New York—not the state or a highway agency—would control the project and that the purpose of the highway was to act as a catalyst for the redevelopment of the west side of Manhattan.

THE WEST SIDE HIGHWAY PROJECT (WSHP)

During their early discussions in 1971, members of the informal planning group decided that the state DOT should hire a consultant to act as executive director of the WSHP. They wanted someone who could steer the project through the labyrinth of regulations governing the use of federal highway funds. They contacted Lowell Bridwell, head of a Washington, DC consulting firm that specialized in transpor-

tation projects. Bridwell, an intense and energetic man, had been a journalist, an adviser to a number of federal and state transportation agencies, and had served as FHWA administrator from 1961 to 1963, and later, undersecretary of the DOT.

When Bridwell met with the members of the informal WSH planning group in 1971, he made two suggestions. First, he recommended that a small "working group," rather than the larger steering committee, take responsibility for the project's ongoing work. Second, he recommended that preparation for public hearings become an immediate and continuing priority of the project team.

As a result of this meeting, the planning group asked Bridwell to serve as executive director of the WSHP. The project was formed as an independent organization by Bridwell and members of his firm on contract with the state DOT. It was not a legal entity or a government agency. Bridwell was given responsibility for the overall direction of the project and for all environmental analysis. He was also responsible for relations with the public and the press. Most observers agreed that Bridwell was the person most responsible for shaping the West Side Highway Project.

PREPARING THE DRAFT EIS

The staff's first task was to study the neighborhoods that would be most affected by any change in the WSH. Through statistics, interviews and other sources they developed a portrait of their "study corridor," which encompassed the western third of Manhattan below 59th Street, including the Hudson River waterfront; the residential communities of Clinton, Chelsea, and Greenwich Village; and the financial district of Lower Manhattan.

They found that the waterfront, once the hub of New York's economy, had in the last two decades become obsolete. As the shipping industry converted to containers, it had deserted Manhattan for roomier ports elsewhere and left behind empty and deteriorating piers and warehouses.

Clinton, an ethnically and economically mixed residential neighborhood at the northern end of the corridor, had long been under intense pressure from the Midtown central business district, which had singled it out as the "logical" area for future commercial expansion.

Lying to the south of Clinton was Chelsea, a neighborhood of brownstones and row houses, that had seen a renaissance in the 1960s, when upper income families had bought and rehabilitated its run-down brownstones. The cost had been the dislocation of many of the average and lower income families.

Greenwich Village, the wealthiest of the three neighborhoods in the study area, was one of the most sought-after residential communities in the city. Demand for housing in the village exceeded supply and the only area left for expansion was the waterfront where redevelopment was impeded by deteriorating piers, and the dilapidated WSH.

All three communities, as well as the commercial district of Lower Manhattan, shared with the rest of the island the burdens of being the nation's busiest city: air pollution, noise, congestion, and bumper-to-bumper rush hour traffic. But conditions appeared to be further exacerbated in the study corridor by the necessity for trucks, barred from the WSH, to use city streets.

THE SELECTION OF ALTERNATIVES

While all of this information was being assembled, the project staff began to generate alternative plans for the West Side Corridor. Their first job was to decide the scope of alternatives to be considered. Said one member of the steering committee:

> The FHWA said that the things that should be studied are the alternatives that can be funded and all other feasible alternatives. What they wanted to have included were other modes of transportation, such as mass transit. The city also wanted us to study every potential alternative for the West Side Corridor, but insisted we not go any further inboard than West Street. In other words, there was to be no West Side Highway in Greenwich Village. Since we had to have the city's approval, we agreed.

By the spring of 1974, the WSHP staff had generated from this list 17 alternative proposals for the West Side Highway Corridor which were delineated and described in a public document and released for public comment. With the advice of the City Planning Commission and further feedback from the community the WSHP staff then cut the list down to the following five alternatives:

- **Maintenance.** The existing WSH would be repaired and maintained as an operating facility.
- **Reconstruction.** Partial reconstruction of the existing WSH in order to correct major struc-

tural difficulties, to make the road safer, and to enable trucks to use it.

- **Arterial.** The existing WSH would be torn down and replaced with an at-grade (level with surrounding area) arterial roadway of lower traffic capacity, and a depressed (underground) mass transit facility.
- **Inboard.** The existing WSH would be torn down and replaced with a six-lane interstate highway with a public transit system in the median strip. Some parts of the highway and transit system would be depressed, and approximately 21 acres of new land would be created.
- **Outboard.** The existing WSH would be town down and replaced by a six-lane, limited-access interstate highway constructed in landfill beyond the existing shoreline and covered in sections, with an adjacent mass transit system and a reconstructed West Street-Twelfth Avenue. Most of the existing waterfront facilities would be replaced with 243 acres of new landfill. Approximately 40 acres would be used for transportation facilities, 75 for recreation and open space along the river's edge, and 128 for housing and other development.

Only the outboard and inboard alternatives would be built as expressways, and thus they were the only ones that would meet the standards for 90 percent federal funding under the interstate and defense system. The remaining highways would be eligible for up to 70 percent federal funding under the federal primary of secondary road grant programs. Unlike the interstate grants, which are awarded on a project-by-project basis, the primary and secondary grants are distributed to states according to a formula and can be used by the state DOT for any primary or secondary highway within the state.

COSTS AND BENEFITS OF THE ALTERNATIVES

The staff summarized its findings in the Draft Environmental Impact Statement (EIS), as required by federal law. The Draft EIS did not provide a cost-benefit analysis of the five alternatives, but it did describe the impacts of each alternative on the environment, the economy, and the performance of the highway and traffic system. For some impacts, specific dollar estimates of the costs and benefits were provided, notably highway user cost savings and construction costs. Exhibits 1 and 2 provide a compilation of the staff's findings for the five alternatives

EXHIBIT 1

West Side Highway Proposal

Costs and Benefits for Alternatives (Millions of Dollars)

Alternatives	Source of Funding	Total Construction and Right-of-Way Costs Undiscounted	Annual User Savings in 1995[3]	Annual Property Tax Gains in 1995[3]	Increase in Regional Income during Construction	One-Time Expenditures Avoided by City	Total Benefits Undiscounted
Maintenance[1]	70% federal 30% city or state	76	0	0	25×3=75	—	75
Reconstruction[1]	70% federal 30% city or state	227	26.2	0	65×3=195	—	1249.4
Arterial (with railway)[1]	70% federal 30% city or state	307	14.2	0	90×3=270	—	836.3
Inboard (with busway)[1]	90% federal (interstate) 10% state	1111	89.5	0	315×3=950	—	4529.8
Outboard (with busway)[2]	90% federal (interstate) 10% state	1415	86.5	76	400×3=1200	61.5	4658.4
Modified Outboard[2]	90% federal (interstate) 10% state	1356 (Row) 95 (Construction) 1009 (Ganesvoort) 52 Incinerator 200 (Maintenance 40 years)	69.2	76	285×3=855	61.5	6068

EXHIBIT 1
(continued)

Alternatives	New Housing	New Parkland	Morning Peak Hour Traffic (1995)	Local Street Traffic	Relocation	Air Pollution	Noise[4] Pollution	Water Pollution	Drivers Diverted to Transit Daily
Maintenance[1]	None	None	Volume exceeds capacity for most of highway Average speed hwy = 14.5 MPH Average speed streets = 6.0 MPH	No change	None	No change in CO, hydrocarbons, or NO	During const.—1 After const.—3	No change	None
Reconstruction[1] None	None	None	Volume exceeds capacity for 1/3 of highway Average speed hwy = 18.4 MPH Average speed streets = 6.0 MPH	Insignificant change in cars; 9% fewer trucks	4 bldgs (13 businesses)	Slight increase in CO levels; no change in others	During const.—2 After const.—5	No change	None
Arterial (with railway)[1]	None	2.81 inland acres; Improved access to Battery Pk.	Volume exceeds capacity for 1/3 of highway; near capacity for rest Average speed hwy = 12.1 MPH Average speed streets = 5.7 MPH	Insignificant change in cars; 6% fewer trucks	None	Largest increase in CO levels, exceeding federal standards	During const.—3 After const.—4	No change	9000
Inboard (with busway)[1]	none	21 acres of waterfront park	Volume exceeds capacity for 1/3 of highway Average speed hwy = 22.6 MPH Average speed streets = 6.8 MPH	Slightly fewer cars; 9% fewer trucks	48 bldgs. (89 residents 91 businesses) 18 pier tenants	Slight decrease in CO (by diverting truck traffic)	During const.—5 After const.—2	Slight improvement from smoothing shoreline	10,500
Outboard (with busway)[2]	128 acres for future development	75 acres of waterfront park	Volume exceeds capacity for 1/3 of highway Average speed hwy = 23.6 MPH Average speed streets = 6.8 MPH	Slightly fewer cars; 12% fewer trucks	46 bldgs. (89 residents & 101 businesses) 23 pier tenants	Slight decrease in CO (by diverting truck traffic)	During const.—4 After const.—1	Slight improvement from smoothing shoreline	10,500
Modified outboard[2]	101 acres for future development	93 acres of waterfront park	Same as Outboard	Same as Outboard	47 bldgs. (109 residents and 92 businesses) 15 pier tenants	Same as Outboard	Same as Outboard	Same as Outboard	Same as Outboard

[1]Based on construction to 72nd St.

[2]Based on construction to 42nd St., including transit system construction (without transit right-of-way costs).

[3]Annual benefits presumed to accrue for 40 years, the expected lifetime of the highway.

[4]1 = least pollution
5 = greatest pollution

EXHIBIT 2

West Side Highway Proposal

Coast and Benefits That Are Estimated in Dollars (Millions of Dollars)

	Maintenance	Reconstruction	Arterial (w/Railway)	Inboard (w/Busway)	Outboard (w/Busway)	Modified Outboard
(A) Construction and right of way costs (federal, state and city)						
Year 1	1	18	20	92	125	120
Year 2	22	14	25	123	159	152
Year 3	18	16	43	101	106	102
Year 4	11	19	40	119	144	138
Year 5	8	20	39	153	152	146
Year 6	8	23	34	157	209	200
Year 7		27	25	149	191	183
Year 8		19	28	141	165	158
Year 9		24	24	53	112	107
Year 10		19	29	23	52	50
Year 11		19				
Year 12		9				
Total:	76	227	307	1111	1415	1356
(B) Annual user savings in 1995	0	26.2	14.2	89.5	86.5	69.2
(C) Annual land value gain in 1995	0	0	0	0	76	76
(D) Regional income gains (one time, during construction)	75	195	270	950	1200	855
(E) City expenditures avoided (one time)	0	0	0	0	61.5	61.5
Undiscounted totals, 40 year life						
Construction cost	−76	−227	−307	−111	−1415	−1356
User savings	0	1048	568	3580	3460	2768
Property tax	0	0	0	0	3040	3040
Regional income	75	195	270	950	1200	855
City expenditures	0	0	0	0	62	62
	−1	1016	531	3419	6347	5369
Discounted totals (present values), 40 year life, 10 percent discount rate per year						
Construction cost	−56.9	−128.1	−189.1	−699.7	−877.9	−841.3
User savings	0.0	74.2	48.7	306.8	296.5	237.2
Property tax	0.0	0.0	0.0	0.0	260.5	260.5
Regional income	56.1	110.0	166.3	598.3	744.5	530.5
City expenditures	0.0	0.0	0.0	0.0	38.2	38.2
	−0.7	56.2	25.9	205.4	461.7	225.0
B/C ratio	0.99	1.99	1.14	1.29	1.53	1.27

described in the Draft EIS along with a sixth, a slightly modified version of the outboard, proposed in the Final EIS.

Costs and benefits were computed according to OMB procedures, which require that both be expressed in constant (in this case 1974) dollars, and then discounted at the rate of 10 percent per annum.[1] Annual benefits were accrued for 40 years, the assumed life span of the highway. The "user cost savings" represent the time savings, where one person-hour = $3.64, and operating and accident cost savings resulting from the faster and smoother flow of traffic.

The anticipated regional income is derived from the multiplier effect on direct construction wages by which one dollar of wages paid into a region generates additional expenditures, wages, and profits in other sections of the economy. Contemporary studies indicate that multipliers range from 2.0 for small metropolitan areas to 3.2 for larger areas. The multiplier the project staff used for New York City was 3.0, which they considered a conservative estimate.

The city's income from the 200 acres of developable land created by the modified outboard alternative was derived by assuming 200 dwelling units and associated commercial activities and parking per acre. As explained in the Final EIS:

> Utilizing current values for construction, financing, maintenance and rents, a market value of just over $1 million per acre was calculated. Each acre of land plus the more than $7.5 million worth of buildings assumed to be on it generated taxes of about $375,000 per acre annually, under the constrained development conditions [laid down by the city in agreement with local residents]. It has been assumed that each new acre of land created . . . (except those used for highway purposes) would have this value, including the park, industrial and community service landfill parcels. Since the decision to forego the monetary benefits of using the land for residential purposes is assumed to be a rational one, the non-monetary benefits received by society from the other uses are equal to or greater than, the benefits of residential development. (p. 153).

The traffic projections were produced after months of study by the project staff and technical con-

sultants, and were critical in the design and ultimate approval of a replacement for the WSH. The forecasts were based on the current volume, of all daily person-trips into the central business district (CBD), as well as the capacities of the existing road network. With that data, a computer program replicated existing traffic conditions, and the results were checked against observed conditions. Then, the staff projected the effect that future changes in land-use patterns would have on the total volume of vehicular traffic into the CBD. They predicted a seven percent increase by 1995, the project's target year, which they later revised to five percent when preparing the Final EIS. The program was changed to reflect that increase, and then was used to stimulate traffic conditions for 1995 on each alternative road network proposed.

It was not the purpose of the Draft EIS to select a particular alternative but rather to outline a number of alternatives so that public agencies and concerned individuals could comment on the analysis. Only in the Final EIS was a specific alternative to be recommended. Nevertheless, the evaluation of the Draft EIS seemed to suggest that the "inboard" and "outboard" alternatives were probably superior to all others. Although the physical environment of Manhattan had more problems than any one highway project could solve, the inboard and outboard alternatives were judged to add the least of its air, water, and noise pollution, largely because they would remove the most traffic from local streets and place the highway some distance from existing shorelines and the new highway, for parks and housing. The economy of the area would be stimulated the most by these two alternatives, since they would most improve the accessibility of the Manhattan CBD and would create the most jobs during construction. Finally, the inboard and outboard alternatives were estimated to provide greater reductions in highway user time, operating, and accident costs than the other alternatives. The inboard and outboard alternatives cost more to construct, but the benefits seemed to be larger too.

PROCESS OF SELECTING FINAL ALTERNATIVES

Several of the staff on the City Planning Commission who were most actively involved described the process leading up to the selection of the final alternatives in the Draft EIS:

> We took every community's concerns into account. At one point, we changed the highway design in the Outboard proposal in response to suggestions from the Greenwich Village people.

[1]Discounting accounts for the fact that a dollar in the future is worth less than a dollar in the present. This is true even if there is no inflation since today's dollars can be invested to produce more in the future. With a 10 percent interest rate, for example, 91 cents today would increase to $1.00 next year. Hence, the present value of receiving $1.00 a year from now using a discount rate (another term for an interest rate) of 10 percent is approximately 91 cents.

The project staff was appalled that nontechnical people were moving the road. But when we asked why it couldn't be changed, they couldn't come up with reasons. Then we were able to show people in the community that we had made the change they requested.

This was a political as well as a technical document. We went over every word for nuances. We were selling two things—a process and a vision.

We held more than 500 public meetings. Bridwell is a brilliant man. . . . He knows how to build a highway and all that is involved. That is essential for our credibility, which is always on the line. John Zuccotti (chairman of the New York City Planning Commission) knows how to work with people. He doesn't believe in big projects for their own sake, in "sacrificing for the greater good." To understand people's needs, he feels you should listen, work with them, become part of the process yourself. That's the key, that's what he did.

Graham Bailey, who replaced Russell Eckloff as area engineer in the FHWA division office in 1975 after completion and circulation of the Draft EIS, described his unit's role in its preparation:

Our office carefully reviewed the input and criteria used in the various technical studies that supported the conclusions of the Draft EIS in order to determine the reasonableness and accuracy of the data which is fed into the mathematical models as well as the propriety of the model itself. Many meetings and discussions were required before the necessary input data could be agreed upon.

THE APPROVAL PROCESS FOR THE DRAFT EIS

In accordance with standard practice at USDOT, the Draft EIS was sent up the chain of command in the FHWA and the USDOT for review, comment, and approval. Since the FHWA division office had been involved in the WSHP from its inception, its staff was able to approve and forward the Draft EIS quickly to the FHWA regional office for review. The FHWA regional office also acted quickly, since the division office had been so closely involved.

After review by FHWA's divisional and regional offices, the Draft EIS was sent to the Environmental Programs Division in the headquarters office of FHWA and to the assistant secretary for environment, safety, and consumer affairs in the USDOT.

Both offices made comments for consideration in the preparation of the Final EIS. At the national office, Robert Gausman, highway engineer for environmental programs, directed the review. His office, he claimed, had the agency's real expertise on the matter:

At the division and regional level, the people aren't generalists. They know the area, the city well, but aren't as expert in the particular technical fields as the people in Washington. Our office reviews the Draft EIS from a technical standpoint. We look at the results, to find out if the answers to technical questions are reasonable. Our technical people do not develop their own models during the review, to check the models used in the preparation of the draft, but they are in contact with people around the country who are developing models, and they know which models are relevant and which are not. This is true for air quality, noise, traffic—all the technical areas.

PUBLIC RESPONSE TO THE DRAFT EIS

To most observers, it seemed likely that the WSHP staff and the city might take only two alternatives seriously—the inboard and the outboard proposals—since these were the only two that would be funded at a 90 percent level by the federal government, and that required *no city* funds. Both proposals had large groups of supporters, including the construction industry, labor groups, and much of the city's financial community. Both proposals also engendered controversy.

Opposition came from several quarters, including environmentalists who were suspicious of the claim that larger highways would lead to cleaner air; mass transit advocates who felt that the billion dollars might be better invested in improving the city's public transit system; and community residents who feared a sudden large-scale redevelopment would fundamentally change the character of their neighborhoods.

Mass Transit Trade-In.   Mass transit advocates, among them Bella Abzug, congresswoman for part of the West Side, proposed that the city build a new subway system in the WSH Corridor. To do this, the city applies for an "interstate transfer," with the approval of the governor. If the secretary of USDOT determines that the section of highway in question is not essential for completion of a unified and connected interstate system, the federal share of the estimated cost to complete that section can be used to construct other roads or transit projects. For transit projects, an amount equal to that federal share is transferred to and administered under the jurisdiction of the Urban Mass Transportation Administration (UMTA). Participation by UMTA in transit projects is at the ratio of 80 percent federal and 20 percent others. This 20 percent can be a state contribution or shared by the state and city or other governmental entity.

The WSHP staff had in fact considered a trade-in for transit funds as another alternative to the 17 it presented, but had discarded the idea before the list was made final. One WSHP staffer explained:

> We did a lot of work on the possibility of a trade-in of Federal-Aid Highway Trust funds for mass transit funds. To get the same amount of money for mass transit as for a highway, the city would actually have to raise more money because the ration is 80 percent federal funds to 20 percent city funds. The main argument against mass transit was a fiscal one.

Others argued that experience showed that new subways did not divert people from using automobiles. Therefore new mass transit would not relieve the traffic congestion that was driving companies out of the area.

The Discount Rate. The most detailed critique of the Draft EIS on behalf of community residents was provided by several consultants working for "Combo," an alliance of community boards 2, 7, and 9—the local planning boards of the communities adjacent to the West Side Highway. The consultants were paid out of the budget of the WSH project. The Combo critique questioned virtually every aspect of the Draft EIS, but perhaps the most widely publicized criticism was that the Draft EIS's own figures showed that the benefit-cost ratios of the inboard and outboard alternatives were less than 1.0, while the ratio for the more modest "arterial" alternative was more than 1.7.

Combo argued that WSHP ignored the effects of the recent rapid inflation in construction costs by estimating all costs at 1974 prices and then using a 10 percent discount rate. Instead they proposed that construction costs should be inflated at 15 percent per year (the rate of construction price increases in recent years). All other benefits and costs (including the value of time and auto operating costs) would increase at about six percent per year, Combo argued, and the discount rate should be six percent. Combo

claimed that using their assumptions about inflation and the discount rate (but WSHP estimates of user benefits and capital costs), the large highways no longer had favorable benefit/cost ratios:[2]

Alternative	Combo Estimate of B–C Ratio	WSHP Estimate of B–C Ratio (Exhibit 3)
M(aintenance)	N.A.	.99
R(econstruction)	1.0	1.44
A(rterial)	1.70	1.14
I(nboard)	.89	1.29
O(utboard)	.64	1.53

Combo further argued that their computation is conservative (in favor of the big highways) since use benefits do not begin to occur at their full value until some 10 years after costs being incurred. Also, since the Draft EIS omitted highway maintenance costs, they were omitted from Combo's calculations too.

Travel Forecasts. Furthermore, Combo said, the Draft EIS may have overestimated benefits to users because of errors in travel and traffic forecasting methodology. Combo was particularly concerned that the amount and distribution of travel employment and population did not vary with highway alternatives—there was no induced travel. Combo argued that each of the proposed replacements for the WSH would generate additional traffic in proportion to the time/cost savings its increased capacity offered users. Because the WSHP staff failed to add this increase to the traffic growth they projected for 1995 for all five alternatives due to changes in land use, Combo argued that the staff had underestimated future traffic by as much as 200,000 vehicle miles traveled a day, and hence greatly underestimated noise and air pollution and greatly overestimated user savings. In conclusion, Combo said: "The travel forecasting methodology of the WSHP has only demonstrated that a fixed amount of highway travel can be better accommodated on a larger highway network than on a smaller highway network."

Quality of Life. In addition to the financial and forecasting arguments put forth by Combo,

---

[2]Combo used a capital recovery factor method to calculate annualized benefits and costs in a typical year (1995) assuming a 40-year life for the highways. The authors of this case were unable to reproduce the benefit/cost ratios that Combo reported, however.

community residents voiced concern about the effect the proposed highway would have on the quality of neighborhood life. Construction of either the inboard or outboard alternatives would take a minimum of 12 years, during which time traffic would be further disrupted, and noise and dirt continually generated by construction equipment. In addition, many feared that the development of large new tracts of land would draw too many residents and businesses out of adjacent communities. Others, pointing to the number of units in new housing developments such as West Village Housing that were still unoccupied, suggested that it might draw too few, thereby creating a wasteland of deserted or half-completed buildings.

But perhaps the central concern of residents was that, whatever the air, noise, and traffic analyses might show, the net result of building a larger highway was to make the city more hospitable to cars and less hospitable to people. Jane Jacobs, a well-known critic of urban master planning, voiced her concern in an interview in *New York Magazine:*[3]

> Westway [the modified outboard alternative proposed in the Final EIS] is only one small piece of a plan for an overwhelming highway network for Manhattan that would, piece by piece, Los-Angelize New York. It's an old plan that dates back to 1929, pieces of [which] keep surfacing every few years. Nobody would ever consent to . . . doing the whole thing, yet piece by piece it gets done.
>
> If Westway goes in, the Lower Manhattan Expressway proposal will be revived. . . . And that would create pressure to rebuild the rest of the West Side Highway north of Westway to interstate standards, . . . cutting into Riverside Park. And there would be new crosstown traffic routes like 34th Street and so on up the island. Westway will never be an isolated highway segment. It's like a tree trunk that has to grow branches.
>
> Furthermore, it's nonsense to say that this highway is going to remove traffic from the city's streets. It's got to have its ramps to draw traffic onto and off city streets, until the system has invaded the entire city. Plans like Westway are death sentences for neighborhoods. Before the first building falls, the plan enforces deterioration, stops investment in existing businesses.

Jacobs also argued that the new bankrupt city did not have the money to finish and maintain any newly created park land; that most of the much-touted construction money would actually go to jobs outside the region; and that the West Side, rather than deteriorating as proponents of the highway claimed, had begun a natural and self-financed revitalization that would continue unless the interstate were built.

Instead of building an interstate highway, Jacobs proposed a trade-in of the Westway money, for transit rehabilitation plus a modest rebuilding of the West Side Highway. According to a six-month Sierra Club study, it would deliver 103,000 man-years of employment, both inside and outside of New York City; Westway promises only 78,000 and most of those will be outside the region—in plants manufacturing the steel, cement, and other component parts and materials.

THE FINAL EIS

The project staff favored the outboard alternative. John Zuccotti (who had left the City Planning Commission to become deputy mayor in the Beame administration, but who remained an influential member of the "working group") was responsive to the concern of some neighborhoods that the outboard plan created too much new land. What evolved after an extensive series of meetings, studies and negotiating was a modified outboard that would create 110 acres of infill land for real estate development, rather than the 128 originally planned. The plan was endorsed by Gov. Hugh Carey and Mayor Abraham Beame in March 1975. According to Robert Bagt, assistant director of the New York State budget division:

> We supported the Westway proposal for several reasons, all obvious. One is economic development—absolutely vital. Jobs are crucial. If we didn't have a fiscal crisis in New York City, it might have been a more difficult decision to make, but given where the city is, I don't think we had any choice. There were other reasons— the flow of people in and out of the city—primarily we're talking about rehabilitating an area. We're talking about a government decision like many government decisions, involving many city and state agencies, but into that mix we're pouring something that is unique in the history of municipal government—New York City's financial crisis.

[3]"How Westway Will Destroy New York," February 16, 1978, *New York,* pp. 30-34.

The Final EIS was published in the summer of 1976, and contained the following description of Westway:

> Like the original Outboard, the Modified Outboard was planned as a catalyst for major physical changes on the West Side. It will function as a mechanism to transform the waterfront by eliminating the present barrier effect of the elevated highway structure, and by removing all existing deteriorating or inactive maritime facilities south of 34th Street. Its most dramatic feature will be the creation of 181 acres of new landfill, and the reconfiguration of 53 acres which presently exist between the pierhead and bulkhead lines. Of this, 31 acres will be utilized by transportation facilities, 93 acres will be public park land along the river from Lower Manhattan to Midtown, and the remaining 110 acres will be available for new development. (p. 146)

In the Final EIS the West Side Highway Project staff also responded to the criticisms of the Combo report. They argued that Combo made several errors in calculating its benefit-cost ratios:

> Although the Combo report asserts that their benefit cost calculations are conservative and "in favor of the big highways," in fact, the opposite is true, the calculations are biased against the big highway. Combo increased the construction costs for the alternatives by 15 percent per year to 1980 to account for inflation. In addition, the costs of the alternatives were increased by over 15 percent, and benefits were increased by only six percent per year. This approach seriously reduces benefits in comparison to costs.
>
> The [US] Office of Management and Budget in their circular #A-95 recommends that for nearly all federally funded projects the annual percentages applied to cost be the same as those applied to benefits. This approach assumes that inflation will affect both costs and benefits in the same manner. (FEIS, Section 6: "Comments and Responses on the DEIS," pp. 19–20.)

The project staff also responded to Combo's charges that they had failed to consider "induced traffic" in their forecasts. They agreed that the theory that highways generate their own demand was basically sound, and said that they had indeed considered the possibility of induced traffic when they did their original projections. However, they concluded that two factors unique to Manhattan made that potential so slight as to be insignificant: 1) that all traffic entering Manhattan had to use river crossings (bridges or tunnels) that are already used to capacity in peak hours, and 2) that on- and off-street parking in the CBD was already almost filled to capacity during the day, and the city intended to further limit future parking supply in an effort to relieve traffic congestion. Both factors, the staff argued, would put a ceiling on the volume of vehicular traffic in Manhattan whichever replacement was built for the WSH. The net effect of a larger highway, therefore, would be to decrease time and cost for the fixed volume of traffic that would use it.

With the publication of the Final EIS, Westway was ready to be sent through the layers of the FHWA, for final location approval by the secretary of DOT.

THE SECRETARY'S DECISION

President Ford appointed William Coleman to the post of secretary of transportation in 1974. (See Exhibit 3 for USDOT organization chart.) The Westway proposal reached his desk in December 1976, about one month before Jimmy Carter would become president. Coleman asked Judith Connor, his assistant secretary for environment, safety, and consumer affairs, to get ready to brief him on all details. Said Connor:

> I felt it wasn't right for the Office of the Secretary to get into technical analyses; we only had to be sure the analyses were done well. We shouldn't be second-guessing our highway people. I spent a great deal of time with Bridwell and his staff to be sure they had done the best possible job on predictions. I was satisfied that present congestion in the area, with the absence of a highway, made for worse pollution than the development of a highway would.
>
> Some of my staff had their doubts about the project's costs, but for years we had been pressuring FHWA to internalize the costs of making highways environmentally compatible. Here was the perfect example of how to do it in an urban area. A substantial portion of Westway's costs would be involved in doing so. They'd adopted every principle we'd advocated—dedicated lanes for heavy traffic, bridle paths, bicycle paths, parks, etc. The federal

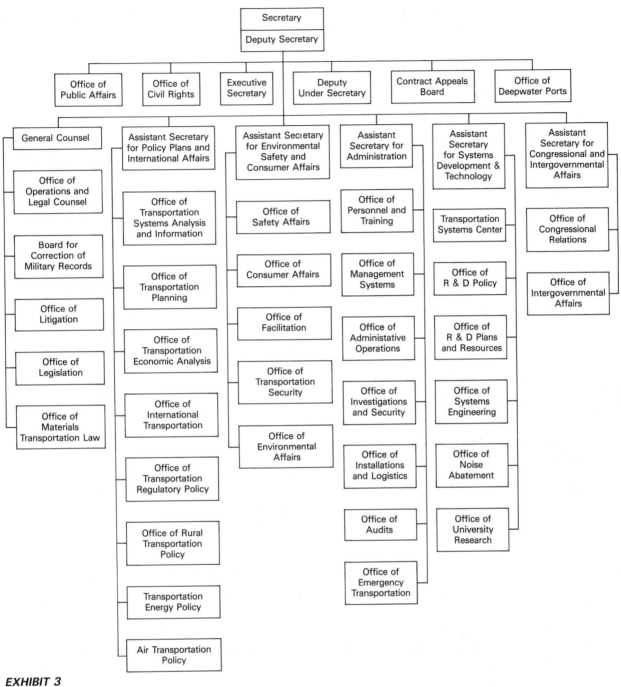

EXHIBIT 3
The West Side Highway Proposal
Present Organization
Department of Transportation
Office of the Secretary

government's policy was to make highways environmentally compatible. On that basis, I recommended to Secretary Coleman that he approve it. What else could we do?

Members of New York City's financial, labor, and political communities voiced their vigorous support of Westway in a number of meetings with the secretary. In 1975, David Rockefeller, chairman of the board of the Chase Manhattan Bank, and Harry Van Arsdale, president of the Central Labor Council of the AFL-CIO, had become co-chairmen of a group of 25 business, labor, education, and cultural leaders who acted as a lobby for the approval of

Westway. It was as spokesman for this group that Rockefeller and Van Arsdale had met on numerous occasions with Coleman. On December 30, 1976, the two men signed a letter to the secretary in which they identified 11 broad categories of private investment, for a total of $7.378 billion, that would accompany the development of the new land in the Westway proposal. In addition, Rockefeller and Van Arsdale promised—at Coleman's request—that apprenticeship opportunities, skilled training slots, and jobs would be open to minorities, including blacks, Hispanics, and unemployed youth, during the construction of Westway, if approved, and that the project would be completed without strikes or other work stoppages.

On January 4, 1977, Secretary Coleman came to New York City to announce his approval of the WSH proposal. His statement on Westway noted:

> I have based this decision on my review of the history documents submitted to me, including the Final Environmental Impact Statement, and the relevant policy and statutory considerations. In addition, an important factor in my decision is the strong support given to the proposed project by the governor of the state of New York, the mayor of the city of New York, many (although not all) of the local elected officials, and the leadership of the private business and labor communities. Finally, it is my judgment that the extensive opportunities for community participation in the planning process for this highway have resulted in the development of an alternative that best reflects, protects, and advances the concerns of the affected citizens.

Westway was now cleared for final design. In the fall of 1977, Ed Koch was elected mayor of New York City. During the campaign he had announced his opposition to Westway and promised it would never be built if he were elected. In its stead, Koch urged a trade-in for mass transit funds. As Koch took office in January 1978, everyone awaited his decision. If he were to give final design approval to Westway, only two obstacles would remain to its construc-

tion: an air-quality permit from the state Department of Environmental Conservation, and a permit for the landfill from the Army Corps of Engineers.

In the year since location approval had been given, neither Westway's supporters not its critics had lost their customary zeal. Said Lloyd Kaplan, chief aide to John Zuccotti:

> If the Westway project is killed, once-in-a-lifetime opportunities for spurring the economy and opening up the waterfront will be killed along with it.

Said Jane Jacobs:

> No mayor will make the difference to New York that this highway will make. If Koch does nothing more than kill Westway, he'll be one of the greatest mayors of the city.

Koch remained intransigent throughout the early spring. On April 14th, after a three-hour meeting in Albany, Koch and Gov. Carey held a news conference to announce that they had reached a settlement. Carey pledged to maintain the city's 50 cents transit fare through 1981, to make $80 million available for mass transit improvements, and to make the new waterfront area a state park, finished and maintained by state funds, in return for Koch's agreement that "The Westway shall proceed." Koch, in response to charges of betrayal, termed the decision "inevitable." "I am not able to change the governor's position," he said.

As news reached New York City, Sen. Moynihan said, "Well done!" and numerous union officials expressed their delight with the agreement. State Rep. Ted Weiss, nine members of the city council, and several other local elected officials charged Koch had "sold out to Carey," saying that the transit money Carey had promised would have been forthcoming to the city anyway under legislation pending in Congress. Other Westway opponents vowed that, if all else failed, they would delay its construction for years with litigation in courts.

ASSIGNMENT FOR CLASS DISCUSSION

Imagine that you are a staffer to Transportation Secretary William Coleman and that he has asked you to evaluate the benefit-cost analysis in the FEIS and explain to him whether it supports the recommendation to build the modified outboard expressway rather than one of the smaller and less expensive alternatives. In formulating your answer, please consider:

1. What categories of costs and benefits should be considered in deciding whether or not to build the West Side Highway? Are all the relevant costs and benefits listed in case Exhibit 2? Do any omissions of appropriate benefits or costs, or inclusions of inappropriate ones, bias the recommendations?
2. Are the benefits and costs in Exhibit 2 properly valued?

Saving the Tuolumne

From its origins high on Mount Lyell and Mount Dana in Yosemite National Park, the Tuolumne River flows 158 miles west to California's San Joaquin Valley. Despite hydroelectric developments at either end of the Tuolumne, the river still runs free in a 30-mile stretch through Tuolumne Canyon, between the O'Shaughnessy Dam in Yosemite and the headwaters of the New Don Pedro Reservoir. Here the Tuolumne hurtles down the western slope of the High Sierra, fed by four major tributaries—the Clavey River, Cherry Creek, and the Middle and South Forks. Only two roads wind into the isolated canyon, where the river courses between sheer granite cliffs and rugged slopes covered with digger pine, incense cedar and oak. Mink, screech owl, river otter and the endangered Southern Bald Eagle share the canyon with large deer herds that travel there each winter from Yosemite. The cold water pools of the Tuolumne and Clavey rivers harbor some of California's finest trout reserves—by one estimate two to three times more productive than the state's best flatwater fishing areas. Tuolumne Canyon also contains several historic and pre-historic sites, including ruins of abandoned gold mines and sites inhabited by the Miwok Indians, who lived in the canyon until the mid-1800s.

The Tuolumne's continuous succession of rapids and cataracts make it one of the nation's finest and most popular whitewater rafting rivers. Each year between March and October, thousands of rafting enthusiasts travel a single-lane dirt road into Lumsden's Landing to make the 18-mile trip downriver to Ward's Ferry. With 25 major rapids and a white-knuckle plunge over the eight-foot-high Clavey

Falls, this stretch of the Tuolumne is considered comparable only to the Colorado River through the Grand Canyon, or Idaho's Salmon River. More than 15,000 rafters from all over the country made this run in one-to-three-day trips in 1982, and a few hundred others braved the more treacherous stretch of the Tuolumne above Lumsden's Bridge. About 9,000 of those boaters ran the rapids on their own, while another 6,000 took trips arranged by one of ten commercial expedition firms. With government studies documenting an increasing demand over time for rafting on the Tuolumne, some expedition operators and environmental groups expect the number of Tuolumne rafters to double within the next decade.

While rafting is the Tuolumne's major attraction, others travel to the area to hunt, fish, hike, and camp. The US Forest Service recorded 22,000 visitor-days at its campgrounds on the Tuolumne in 1983, and total recreational use is estimated at 35,000 user-days annually. Tuolumne River Canyon is also home to three city-run family campgrounds, operated by the cities of Berkeley, San Jose, and San Francisco, which provide low-cost camping and recreation for city residents.

With its steep, narrow canyon walls and large volume of flowing water, the Tuolumne River Canyon is also an ideal site for hydroelectric development. In April 1983, the city and county of San Francisco and two irrigation districts in Merced and Stanislaus counties commissioned a feasibility study of their longstanding proposal to dam to Tuolumne for power and water. At the same time, a coalition of environmentalists, rafters, fishing enthusiasts and California residents known as the Tuolumne River

This case was written by Linda Kincaid under the direction of Professors Joseph Kalt and José A. Gomez-Ibañez for use at the Kennedy School of Government, Harvard University. (0388) Copyright © 1986 by the President and Fellows of Harvard College.

Preservation Trust was lobbying Congress to protect the river from further development under the federal Wild and Scenic Rivers Act. The dam proponents had already produced several favorable cost-benefit studies of their proposal; in June 1983 the Trust asked economists at the Environmental Defense Fund to respond to those studies with an economic assessment of the proposed dam's environmental costs.

HYDROELECTRIC DEVELOPMENT ON THE TUOLUMNE

By 1983, existing hydroelectric developments on the Tuolumne captured 90 percent of its water and more than 70 percent of its power generating capacity—enough to supply drinking water to nearly two million Californians, irrigate 230,000 acres of farmland in California's Central Valley, and generate electricity to power some 400,000 homes. The city and county of San Francisco drew 300 million gallons of a water a day from the Hetch Hetchy Reservoir, located inside Yosemite, and from two additional reservoirs on tributaries of the Tuolumne. The Hetch Hetchy System's three powerhouses provided nearly 300 megawatts of electrical capacity, which the San Francisco Public Utilities Commission sold to municipal departments of the city and to nearby utility districts and industrial customers. Thirty miles downstream, the New Don Pedro Dam and Reservoir provided electricity and irrigation water to the Modesto and Turlock Irrigation Districts (MID and TID).

The two irrigation districts distributed irrigation water and power to the city of Modesto, several smaller towns, and 230,000 acres of farmland in Stanislaus and Merced counties.[1] Located less than 100 miles west of San Francisco, in California's Central Valley, the two districts contained some of the richest farmland in the world, as well as a burgeoning population of professionals, industrial workers and retirees. Electricity consumption in the MID-TID service area had increased more rapidly than in California as a whole from 1965-75, thanks to a dramatic increase in irrigated acreage and an influx of agricultural processors and other industries who had moved their plants from the metropolitan areas to Central Valley towns. A 1975 study by the consulting firm Arthur D. Little predicted that rapid economic growth would continue in the MID-TID service area through the year 2000. In 1979, a study of electricity

demand in the MID service area by consultants Hittman and Associates found that the area's industrial growth had slowed somewhat, but predicted that electricity demand would still grow at an annual rate of 4.1 percent.

By 1983, the 150-megawatt (MW) power station at New Don Pedro Dam met only half the electricity demand in the two irrigation districts, forcing them to purchase additional power from the statewide utility, Pacific Gas and Electric Company (PG&E), and from San Francisco's Hetch Hetchy system. Using Hittman's 4.1 percent annual growth predictions, district planners projected that the gap between demand and generating capacity would continue to grow, to about 500 MW in 1995 and 600 MW in 2000 (Exhibit 1). Historically, MID and TID customers had enjoyed some of the lowest electricity rates in the nation, but rates began to rise in the early eighties as the districts invested in new sources and bought more PG&E power to keep up with rising demand. District planners expected electricity prices to rise further after 1985, when they would have to renegotiate the price for power purchased from Hetch Hetchy.

Faced with rising demand for electricity and rising prices for outside sources, managers of both irrigation districts turned to the last undeveloped stretch of the Tuolumne, and to a 1968 engineering study originally done for San Francisco which recommended construction of two new hydroelectric facilities on the river—one at the mouth of the Clavey River and another at Wards Ferry, just above the New Don Pedro Dam. In 1976, San Francisco and the two irrigation districts had applied to the Federal

EXHIBIT 1

Combined MID and TID Projected Demand Requirements vs Resources

Source: R. W. Beck and Associates, Clavey-Wards Ferry Project. Phase II Feasibility Evaluation, for Modesto and Turlock Irrigation Districts.

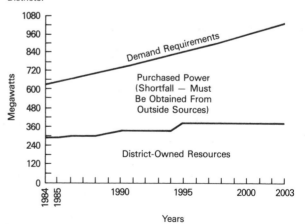

---

[1] Irrigation districts are governed by five-member boards elected to staggered four-year terms by the area residents.

Energy Regulatory Commission (FERC) for a preliminary permit to conduct a feasibility study of the so-called Clavey-Wards Ferry (CWF) proposal. But the year before, Congress had asked the U.S. Departments of Agriculture and Interior to study the Tuolumne's eligibility for preservation as a "wild and scenic" river, and FERC was forbidden to act on the permit application until the end of the three-year federal study period. The river study concluded that the entire 83 miles of river that flows through Yosemite National Park and the Stanislaus National Forest possessed "outstandingly remarkable scenic qualities" and should be included in the nation's wild and scenic rivers system. Although Congress never acted on President Carter's 1979 request to preserve the river, his request delayed FERC action on the permit application until 1982. San Francisco and the irrigation districts remained interested in the project, commissioning three updated economic reports on the project during this period. Finally, in April 1983, FERC granted the preliminary permit. MID, TID, and the city and county of San Francisco promptly hired the engineering consulting firm of R.W. Beck and Associates to perform a detailed three-year feasibility study of the Clavey-Wards Ferry proposal.

THE CLAVEY-WARDS FERRY PROJECT

As described in the FERC preliminary permit application, the CWF development would generate 980 gigawatt-hours (GWh) annually from two separate generating installations, the Clavey unit and the Wards Ferry unit (Exhibit 2). The Clavey unit would include two new dams and reservoirs and a 5.1 mile diversion tunnel. Jawbone Diversion Dam, 175 feet high and 255 feet long, would be located on the Tuolumne River just downstream from its confluence with Cherry Creek. The nearby Jawbone Creek Diversion Dam and Pipeline would divert Jawbone Creek flows into the new Jawbone Reservoir behind the Jawbone Diversion Dam. From Jawbone Reservoir, the Jawbone Ridge Tunnel would carry water to Clavey Reservoir. The Hunter Point Dam and Clavey Reservoir would be located on the Clavey River almost six miles upstream from its confluence with the Tuolumne. A 2.4 mile pressure tunnel would link the Clavey Reservoir to two 150-MW generating units in the Clavey Powerhouse, to be located underground near the headwaters of the planned Wards Ferry Reservoir.

The Wards Ferry Unit would include a 450-

EXHIBIT 2
The Clavey-Wards Ferry Proposal

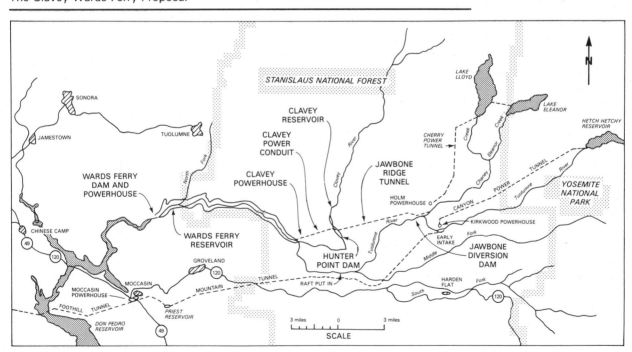

Source: R. W. Beck and Associates, *Clavey-Wards Ferry Project. Phase II Feasibility Evaluation,* for Modesto and Turlock Irrigation Districts.

foot-high, 1,060-foot-long rockfill Wards Ferry Dam, which would create the Wards Ferry Reservoir. The reservoir would have a usable storage of about 92,300 acre-feet[2]—providing an annual water supply of 12,000 acre-feet—and would store and regulate Tuolumne River flows for power generation and water supply. The Wards Ferry Powerhouse, which would be located underground in the dam's south abutment, would house two 50-MW generating units.

Beck estimated that construction of the CWF project could be completed in 1995, allowing for preparatory studies, FERC licensing and a $4\frac{1}{2}$ year construction period. Total capital costs were estimated at $860 million in 1995 dollars. The consultants estimated that by constructing CWF, the two irrigation districts would enjoy a net savings of $29 million in the first year of operation over the projected costs of purchasing power from PG&E; the CWF option would cost $18 million less in the first year than constructing or joining other utilities in new fossil-fuel plants.

Both proponents and opponents of the Clavey-Wards Ferry proposal agreed that its construction would substantially change existing conditions on the Tuolumne. The planned Wards Ferry Reservoir would inundate approximately 1,200 acres of the Tuolumne River Canyon, including traditional mule deer winter habitats and approximately 12 miles of trout spawning beds and stream habitat on the Tuolumne. Upriver, the Clavey unit was expected to reduce riverflows in some fifteen miles of the Tuolumne and six miles of the Clavey. Dam management would also cause abrupt changes in waterflows in these sections of the two rivers.

THE CASE FOR CLAVEY-WARDS FERRY

Proponents of the Clavey-Wards Ferry project argued that the dams would provide a cheap, clean, renewable source of energy to help the districts keep pace with their steadily rising demands. "We needed a source of power," explained Turlock Irrigation District manager Ernest Geddes. "We needed a reliable and economical source. . . . If you look at what are the options, I could build a nuclear plant, or an oil-fired plant or a coal plant, or a hydro plant. . . . [Clavey-Wards Ferry] was the most economical alternative."

For Tuolumne County, which had endorsed the project, Clavey-Wards Ferry would help answer its

desperate need for water. Distant communities like San Francisco had long ago appropriated most of the water which flowed through this sparsely populated county in the Sierra foothills, which is dominated by Yosemite National Park and Stanislaus National Forest. In the early eighties, Tuolumne County was one of the fastest growing in the state—its population was expected to grow from 40,000 to 60,000 between 1985 and 2000—and its small water supply was already strained. Under an agreement with MID and TID, the county would get 12,000 acre feet of water annually from Clavey-Wards Ferry, and a third of the revenue from the project's sales of excess power. (The county planned to dedicate those revenues to developing other water supplies.) The estimated 250 construction jobs and dozens of permanent jobs the project would require were also appealing in the county, where seasonal unemployment had reached 21 percent in the winter of 1983.

The project proponents argued that the changes Clavey-Wards Ferry would bring to Tuolumne Canyon would increase recreational opportunities in the area (Exhibit 3). The development would bring new roads, opening the wilderness to tourists and permitting the development of more campsites. The new Wards Ferry Reservoir would offer opportunities for flatwater fishing, boating and swimming. Proponents promised to maintain trout fishing opportunities by setting minimum flow levels at Jawbone Dam and Clavey Dam in consultation with state and federal fisheries agencies. And, they argued, the reduced flows between Jawbone Dam and Lumsden campground might improve fishing conditions, particularly for fly fishing.

Proponents conceded that the dams would reduce the Tuolumne's main whitewater run from 18 miles to 6.6 miles. But Geddes maintained that the dam at Jawbone Creek would increase raftable days by 20-25 percent by holding back the heavy spring runoff that sometimes made the river too wild to navigate in June and early July. (Dam proponents also pointed out that the Lumsden-Wards Ferry run would probably be too wild for rafting without the existing dams at Cherry Creek and Hetch Hetchy.) A more moderate, controlled flow, he said, would allow rafters to make the trip in their own small boats, rather than paying for professional river guides. Besides, they said, flatwater recreation was more popular and allowed a greater density of use than wilderness pursuits like rafting and hiking. "Rafting's a special interest thing," said Jerry Bellah, a member of the Tuolumne County Board of Supervisors. "I've lived here 23 years and I've never rafted the river. Not that many people do it."

---

[2]An acre-foot equals 325,851 gallons—the amount of water required to flood one acre of land to a depth of one foot.

EXHIBIT 3

Effects of Clavey-Wards Ferry and Ponderosa Alternatives on Existing Environment

Item	Existing Baseline Conditions	Conditions with Clavey-Wards Ferry Alternative
Lake recreation	• None on affected reach of the Tuolumne between Don Pedro & Hetch-Hetchy Reservoir	• Creates opportunities at Wards Ferry Reservoir
Whitewater rafting	• 18-mile long, Class IV run below Lumsden Campground used by two commercial companies & individuals. • Experts-only Cherry Creek run (kyaking and rafting)	• Reduce main run to 6.6 miles and reduce number of raftable days. Run will not support commercial operations. • Eliminate Cherry Creek Run because of flow diversions
Fly fishing	• Concentrated at and above Lumsden Campground	• Minimum flow releases would preserve fly-fishing above Lumsden Campground
Lake fishing	• None between Don Pedro & Hetch-Hetchy Reservoirs	• Creates opportunities at Wards Ferry Reservoir
Camping	• Limited to three developed campgrounds with 23 campsites. 14 undeveloped sites on Tuolumne used by river boaters	• Lakeside campsites would be developed at Wards Ferry Reservoir. Some undeveloped sites would be inundated.
Hiking, hunting and other dispersed activities	• Hiking and hunting concentrated in hills above Tuolumne Canyon	• Same as existing conditions but improved access to canyon areas.
River access	• Very limited	• Improved
Visual character	• Flowing rivers in rugged canyons Tuolumne flows controlled by releases from Holm with limited evidence of recent human occupation.	• Considerable portions of canyon bottoms converted to lakes. Two dams on Tuolumne, access roads and transmission line.
Water supply	• None for Tuolumne County	• Provide supply from Wards Ferry Reservoir
Flood control	• At Don Pedro Reservoir	• Improve capability
Cultural resources	• Area contains known cultural sites	• Potential for inundation or activity at sites
Terrestrial habitat	• Canyons include winter range of mule deer. Habitat of peregrine falcon and bald eagle and possibly rare snail.	• Inundation causes loss of mule deer winter range and possible interruption of migration routes. Increased human access may make falcon and eagle habitat less favorable.
Aquatic habitat	• Fish habitat limited by flow variability especially upstream of South Fork. No man-made barriers to fish migration between Don Pedro Reservoir and Early Intake	• Habitat improvement upstream of South Fork due to more constant flow conditions. Below South Fork, Hunter Point and Wards Ferry dams would convert habitat from riverine to reservoir.

Source: R. W. Beck and Associates, *Clavey-Wards Ferry Project. Phase II Feasibility Evaluation,* for Modesto and Turlock Irrigation Districts.

THE OPPOSITION

In a sense, the modern environmental protection movement began with an earlier fight over the Tuolumne's future. In the early 1900s, naturalist John Muir led an impassioned campaign to prevent San Francisco from damming the Tuolumne and flooding the Hetch Hetchy Valley, which Muir and his followers felt was as beautiful as the neighboring Yosemite Valley. "Dam Hetch Hetchy!" he wrote, during the first nationwide letter-writing campaign to Congress on an environmental issue. "As well dam for water tanks the people's cathedrals and churches, for no holier temple has ever been consecrated by the heart of man."

Muir lost the battle when Congress passed the Raker Act of 1913, which permitted the city and county of San Francisco to build six dams and reservoirs in the Tuolumne watershed. He died before the dam was completed—of a broken heart, according to conservationist folklore—but from the Hetch Hetchy fight, the Sierra Club emerged as a strong voice for environmental protection.

By the early eighties, the fight to save the remaining 30 wild miles of the Tuolumne took on symbolic importance for environmentalists, who were frustrated by their agonizingly slow progress in protecting the nation's most spectacular rivers from development. When the Wild and Scenic Rivers Act was passed in 1968, conservationists hoped its protective system would include a hundred rivers by 1978 and 200 by 1990. But by 1978, only 16 rivers had been added to the original eight, and by 1980, only a few more—most of them in Alaska—had won federal protection from Congress. The battle to save Tuolumne Canyon thus seemed to conservationists a test of the nation's commitment to the preservation of wild and scenic rivers. "If we can't win this one," John Amodio of the Tuolumne River Preservation Trust told *California* magazine, "you have to wonder, where can we win?"

THE CASE AGAINST CLAVEY-WARDS FERRY

Opponents of the CWF project believed it would decimate the Tuolumne and Clavey fisheries, eliminate all whitewater boating potential, adversely affect the canyon's wildlife population, and destroy forever the isolated, wilderness character that drew hikers and campers to the area. The Wards Ferry Reservoir would inundate two-thirds of the 18-mile whitewater run between Lumsden and Wards Ferry and virtually dry up the remaining section (minimum project flow releases there were scheduled at 35-75 cubic feet per second [cfs], just a fraction of the 1,000 cfs that professional river guides said were necessary for whitewater rafting). They argued that the Wards Ferry Reservoir would inundate 12 miles of prime trout spawning beds and stream habitat, while the Wards Ferry Dam would block spawning runs necessary to perpetuate the trout population downstream in the New Don Pedro Reservoir. The Clavey Reservoir would inundate more than a mile of stream habitat on the Clavey River and block the passage of fish. Average flows in the lower reach of the Clavey, and in the Tuolumne below Jawbone Diversion, would not meet US Fish and Wildlife Service recommendations for maintaining the fish population. In addition, the fragile non-trout fish population in the lower Clavey would be threatened by flow changes and the encroachment of other species from the Wards Ferry Reservoir. The river fisheries also would be harmed by changes in seasonal flows, changes in water temperature and dissolved oxygen content from water releases from different levels of the reservoirs, and construction-related changes in turbidity and sediment transport. Construction activities, increased human presence in the area and the erection of electrical transmission lines would destroy the canyon's scenic beauty and threaten several rare species of birds, particularly the endangered Southern Bald Eagle. And a 1982 California Department of Water Resources report warned that the project would block several traditional migration routes used by the Yosemite deer.

Opponents also argued that the new recreational opportunities created by Wards Ferry Reservoir would be extremely limited. The project consultants had acknowledged the reservoir would be a long, narrow and deep lake which would be sunless most of the time. Furthermore, surface water levels would fluctuate by almost 100 feet, and access to the lake would be difficult given the canyon's steep, narrow sides. The fishing opportunities of the reservoir were equally uncertain, opponents argued, citing a former state Department of Fish and Game biologist's estimate that the reservoir would contain less than 10 pounds of fish per acre, compared to the free-flowing Tuolumne's 1,000 pounds of fish per acre. Even the project consultants had acknowledged area fishermen's preference for river fishing, and the federal wild and scenic rivers study had pointed out that "reservoir fisheries are in abundance in the Sierra foothills, whereas river trout fisheries of the quality of the Tuolumne are a rarity in the state."

The opponents complained that neither Beck nor the irrigation districts had adequately considered alternative sources of energy. They pointed out that the irrigation districts would be able to buy surplus off-peak energy from coal-fired power plants in the Southwest and Northwest, and from hydroelectric plants in the Pacific Northwest. They also argued that the districts had not adequately considered ways that conservation and load management could be used to meet the system's capacity needs.

ORGANIZING THE FIGHT

The Tuolumne River Preservation Trust was formed in 1981 to coordinate efforts of conservationists, rafting and fishing enthusiasts, and California residents who opposed further development on the Tuolumne. Led by two Bay Area Sierra Club members, the Trust helped to make the Tuolumne battle a cause celebre in California, garnering widespread media coverage, celebrity attention and political support. By the summer of 1983, the campaign to save the Tuolumne had also picked up important support in San Francisco and the state capitol. Both the state Department of Fish and Game and Department of Water Resources opposed further development on the Tuolumne, as did San Francisco Mayor Dianne Feinstein, and the city's Board of Supervisors. (The city's Public Utilities Commission was still a nominal participant in the feasibility study, however.) At the same time, the Trust was lobbying hard to persuade California's junior senator, Republican Pete Wilson, to include the Tuolumne River Canyon in his wilderness bill, S. 1515. The Trust also hoped to win Wilson's endorsement for S. 142, a bill proposed by California's senior senator, Democrat Alan Cranston, to declare the Tuolumne a wild and scenic river.

In June of 1983, the Trust asked economists at the Environmental Defense Fund (EDF) to prepare an economic evaluation of the Clavey-Wards Ferry project, including its environmental costs. The group intended to use the study in its lobbying efforts. But if its run at congressional protection for the Tuolumne failed, a comprehensive quantitative accounting of the project's private and environmental costs could help them fight the project before the Federal Energy Regulatory Commission and the California State Water Resources Control Board. The project proponents would have to obtain a construction license from FERC, and a water rights permit from the state board; both agencies operated under legal mandates which allowed them to approve a project only if its benefits to the public exceeded its costs.

EDF had its own, wider interest in the Trust's proposal for an economic evaluation of Clavey-Wards Ferry. With 7,000 members in California and nearly 50,000 nationwide, the group focused its research, lobbying and organizing efforts on promoting long-run improvements in natural resource management. EDF had won a reputation for making economic arguments for environmental causes in the early 1970s, when the group had worked to convince utilities that marginal cost pricing would encourage energy conservation and save money. Early in 1983, EDF was searching for a way to deal with an unintended consequence of an earlier environmentalist triumph—the 1978 amendments to the Public Utilities Regulatory Policies Act (PURPA), which required utility companies to buy excess power produced by independent facilities. The new rules had been supported by environmentalists as an incentive for the development of cogeneration energy; in practice they also spawned a new boom in small hydroelectric development. Since 1978, hydro project applications to FERC had increased by 2,000 percent, and in the early 1980s, FERC was evaluating hundreds of applications to dam up rivers throughout the Sierras.

EDF felt that FERC's approval of hydro projects in the past had consistently undervalued their environmental costs, because of the agency's practice of weighing a qualitative judgment of environmental losses against the more easily quantified net economic benefits to the project developers. The Trust's offer of funding for an economic assessment of the Clavey-Wards Ferry project's environmental costs gave EDF the chance to present FERC—and other environmental advocacy groups—with a method for quantifying the environmental effects of hydroelectric development. As Robert Stavins, the principal author of EDF's Tuolumne study recalled: "Rather than looking at it from a narrow, financial perspective, [we believed] we could look at it from a broader, social perspective by trying to internalize some of the environmental externalities."

While the techniques EDF would use were not new to economists, environmental advocacy groups had traditionally resisted the use of cost-benefit analysis in making decisions about environmental policy—the chairman of the Natural Resources Defense Council, for instance, has called the use of cost-benefit analysis in setting toxics standards "immoral." But most conservation advocates also recognized the power of economic arguments in the political world. "Environmentalists in general will support cost-benefit analysis when it confirms their preconceived position," explained EDF senior economist Zach Willey. "But when it doesn't, it's more controversial. I think, by and large, environmentalists are skeptical of cost-benefit analysis; they've seen how it's been used and will come up with all kinds of arguments about how it's not possible to quantify many environmental values. . . . [But EDF's Tuolumne study] was not inconsistent with the emotional view of many environmentalists that the environment is priceless. In fact, it was consistent in that it added some of the value of the environment to a particular decision.''

COUNTING THE COSTS AND BENEFITS

Although Stavins drew much of his raw data from the Beck studies of the Clavey-Wards Ferry project, his analysis differed from theirs in two crucial ways. For one, his cost-benefit model was designed to add the project's environmental, or "external," costs and benefits onto the "internal," or financial, cost-benefit analysis that Beck had prepared. Stavins' estimate of environmental costs and benefits was admittedly incomplete. Although he recognized the project's environmental impacts could range from destruction of historic sites to threatening endangered bird species, he had to rest his calculations on the river's principal (and most easily quantified) existing recreational uses—trout fishing and whitewater rafting. As the CWF's "external" benefits, Stavins counted the value of the CWF's projected water supply, and the flatwater fishing and boating opportunities that would be available at the planned Wards Ferry Reservoir.

Secondly, Stavins took issue with Beck's decision to estimate the project's benefits and costs for only its first year of operation, since such an approach did not account for the uneven streams of benefits and costs which would be spread out over 50 to 100 years in such a project. Stavins elected instead to estimate the project's benefit/cost streams over the entire likely life of the project. His analysis produced estimates of the project's levelized annual costs and benefits by finding their present value of 50 years, inflated at six percent, discounted at 10.72 percent, and then levelized at 10.72 percent over 50 years. He chose the 50-year planning period in keeping with FERC guidelines, and assumed the project would come on line in 1994, adding three years to Beck's assumed four-year construction period. (Stavins believed that Beck's assumption was overly optimistic, given the US Army Corps of Engineers estimate that hydroelectric projects even smaller than the Wards Ferry Dam required a six-year construction period.) The 10.72 discount rate was Stavins' estimation of the likely rate at which the districts would be able to float 40-year bonds, based on the Modesto

Irrigation District's actual sales in 1983 of tax-exempt energy project revenue bonds. This choice was in keeping with FERC recommendations that for non-federal projects the overall cost of money to the project developers should be used as the discount rate.

Stavins estimated the project's total levelized annual project benefits at slightly less than $188 million (Exhibit 4). The biggest share of that was the project's $184 million in electricity benefits, which he measured by using the standard industry practice of calculating the avoided cost of the least expensive alternative means of meeting an identical load. Beck, too, had used this method, but had based its analysis of benefits on a mix of coal and combustion turbine capacity and its associated energy. Stavins' least cost mix of alternative energy sources included purchase of coal energy off-peak from southwest and northwest utilities, purchase of off-peak hydro energy from the northwest, with peak energy and capacity provided by the district's own combustion turbines, and conservation and load management measures. He also counted the project's expected impact on fishing into the benefit side of the analysis, by estimating the project's energy generation at some 295 GWh less than Beck's projections, assuming the project operators preserved enough of the Tuolumne's original flows to protect the river's fish stock.[3]

Other benefits included water yield, which Stavins valued at $1.6 million, based on Beck's estimates that the water would be worth about $105/acre-foot in 1990. And he valued the project's "external" benefits—the 1,600 user-days of flatwater boating and 4,000 user-days of fishing that the Department of Interior had predicted for the Ward's Ferry Reservoir—at $327,000 a year. To place a dollar value on this benefit, Stavins chose the "unit-day" method, which relies on expert opinion to approximate the average willingness-to-pay of users for recreational resources.[4]

Valuing the project's costs was more complicated. Using Beck's 1980 estimates of the project's construction costs, Stavins produced an annual level-

---

[3]Stavins structured a monthly schedule of flows available for energy generation, based on Beck's estimates of Tuolumne river flows minus flow releases recommended by the U.S. Fish and Wildlife Service as necessary to maintain river fisheries.

[4]Stavins said he chose this method based on Water Resources Council guidelines, which suggest using the unit-day value method if the project meets the following three conditions: the site does not involve specialized, highly skilled recreational activities for which opportunities are limited; the number of visits per year likely to be affected by the proposed project does not exceed 750,000; and the expected recreation costs do not exceed 25 percent of total project costs.

EXHIBIT 4

Social Benefits, Clavey-Wards Ferry Project

(1) Levelized annual energy benefit[1] (Table 4: [(2) + (3) + (5) − (4)]])	$146,720,000
(2) Levelized annual capacity benefit[2] (Table 4: [(1) + (6)]])	$ 37,500,000
(3) Annual benefit of increased firm yield of water for MID/TID (11,900 AF × $105/AF in 1990, 4 years at 6% to 1994)	$ 1,577,000
(4) Levelized annual benefit of increased firm yield [(3) × 2.148]	$ 3,388,000
(5) Total internal levelized annual benefits [(1) + (2) + (4)]	$187,608,000
(6) Annual flatwater boating benefit on Wards Ferry Reservoir (1,600 user-days × $20/day, 1994)	$ 32,000
(7) Annual reservoir fishing benefit (4,000 user-days × $30/day, 1994)	$ 120,000
(8) Total external levelized annual benefits [(6) + (7) × 2.148]	$ 327,000
(9) Total levelized annual project benefits [(5) + (8)]	$187,935,000

[1]Annual energy benefit refers to the avoided cost of running the least expensive alternative to the project.

[2]Annual capacity benefit refers to the avoided cost of constructing the capacity to provide the least expensive alternative.

Source: Reprinted with permission from *The Tuolumne River: Preservation or Development? An Economic Assessment* (Berkeley: Environmental Defense Fund, Inc., 1984).

ized "internal" cost estimate of $134 million. To estimate the project's "external costs," which he defined as the value of Tuolumne River whitewater rafting opportunities to both users and non-users, Stavins constructed a regional travel cost model. He began by estimating the willingness to pay, or consumer surplus, of users, using data on the river's current use to determine per capita visitation rates and costs from various geographic regions (Exhibits 5 and 6).

Then he econometrically estimated a so-called "participation function," which would be used to derive the net per capita economic value of the river's recreational opportunities for each area. The per capita figures were then converted to regional total values, and added together to produce an aggregate economic value. Stavins originally estimated the participation function using three alternative forms: linear, which produced a consumer surplus estimate of $16.6 million; double logarithmic, which estimated the consumer surplus at $2.1 million; and semilogarithmic, which produced an estimate of $3.1 million (Exhibit 7). In the final analysis, Stavins chose the semilog results, which produced a levelized annual consumer surplus estimate of $3 million. To that he added an estimate of user fees and producer surplus (Exhibit 8).

Stavins then turned to estimating rafting's "option value"—the amount interested non-users would be willing to pay to insure access to rafting on the river at some future time. Stavins surveyed the economic literature, and found nine studies that had quantified intrinsic recreational values as a positive fraction of user values (Exhibit 9). The nine studies used survey questions to elicit people's willingness to pay to preserve a recreational opportunity; they exhibited ratios of non-use value to use value ranging from 0.47 to 1.39, with a weighted average of 0.60. Thus, on average, non-user recreational value per household interested in the project was found to be approximately 60 percent of user recreational value per household. Stavins believed that he could multiply this number by his consumer surplus estimates to estimate the per capita option value for various geographic regions. But than he had to identify the relevant population of interested non-users. Stavins chose to use Sierra Club membership as a proxy for the population of interested non-users. To be somewhat conservative, he estimated the total California option value as 60 percent of the total California per capita consumer surplus, multiplied by the full California Sierra Club membership; for other regions of the U.S., he took 45 percent of the total consumer

EXHIBIT 5

Data Used in Travel Cost Model (TCM) of Tuolumne River Whitewater Recreation

Region	Average Travel Cost[1] from Region to Site ($)	Per Capita Use from Region ($\times 10^{-6}$)
Humboldt	643.31	70.080
Butte	566.76	11.316
Santa Rosa	441.13	491.137
Yolo	456.09	2059.277
Tahoe-Reno	538.84	752.949
Sacramento	430.22	868.768
El Dorado	401.27	991.147
West Bay	485.56	1510.583
East Bay	470.34	1360.516
South Bay	468.03	716.121
Stockton	384.20	1200.421
Tuolumne	347.48	5315.727
Fresno	474.19	176.380
Los Angeles	629.28	271.385
San Diego	730.78	191.908
Pacific Northwest	1207.16	15.361
Nevada (less Washoe County)	660.27	65.049
West	894.24	33.340
Mountain	1443.66	38.310
Plains	1728.90	1.764
Great Lakes	1991.95	4.690
Atlantic	2065.78	4.492
New England	2102.11	2.752
Southeast	1920.41	0.992

[1]Average travel cost for a representative user from a given region, i, consists of three principal components: actual transportation cost, opportunity cost of time spent traveling to and from the site, and opportunity cost of time spent on the site:

$$TC_i = TPC_i + OCT_i + OCS_i$$

Source: Reprinted with permission from *The Tuolumne River: Preservation or Development? An Economic Assessment* (Berkeley: Environmental Defense Fund, Inc., 1984).

EXHIBIT 6

Commercial Whitewater Recreation Tuolumne River, 1982

Outfitter	Passenger Use Days
A. A. Wet and Wild	440
American River Touring Association	1162
Echo: The Wilderness Company	1077
OARS	576
Outdoor Adventures	783
Outdoors Unlimited	804
Sierra Mac River Trips	377
Wilderness Waterways	585
All Outdoors	83
Sobek Expeditions	327
Zephyr River Expeditions	122
Total	6336

Source: Steve Cutwright, American River Touring Association, as printed in *The Tuolumne River: Preservation or Development? An Economic Assessment* (Berkeley: Environmental Defense Fund, 1984).

EXHIBIT 7

Ordinary Least Squares (OLS) Estimation[1] of Whitewater Recreation Participation Functions, Tuolumne River Canyon, California, 1994

(a)
$$Q_i = 1.43876 \times 10^{-3} - (8.55382 \times 10^{-7}) TC_i$$
$$ (3.77)** (-2.42)*$$
$$R^2 = .211 \quad F_{1,22} = 5.87 \quad n = 24$$

(b)
$$\ln Q_i = \ln 15.72846 - 3.767194 \ln TC_i$$
$$ (6.62)** (-10.51)**$$
$$R^2 = .834 \quad F_{1,22} = 110.49 \quad n = 24$$

(c)
$$\ln Q_i = -5.90043 - 0.00362 TC_i$$
$$ (-13.19)** (-8.73)**$$
$$R^2 = .776 \quad F_{1,22} = 76.152 \quad n = 24$$

[1]t-values are given in parentheses.

Asterisks indicate: *significant at the a = 0.05 level; and **significant at the a = 0.01 level, two tailed tests, degrees of freedom = 22.

Source: Reprinted with permission from *The Tuolumne River: Preservation or Development? An Economic Assessment* (Berkeley: Environmental Defense Fund, Inc., 1984).

EXHIBIT 8

Social Costs, Clavey-Wards Ferry Project

(1) Levelized annual internal costs	$134,224,000
(2) 1994 consumers' surplus of users	$ 3,099,000
(3) 1994 user fees (1983 fee, $3, at 6%/year for 11 years)	$ 128,000
(4) 1994 producers' surplus (.125 profit × $350 at 6% for 11 years × 6,400)	$ 532,000
(5) 1994 Option Value (consumer surplus/user × option value × proxy population)	$ 33,503,000

      CA: $184.14 × 0.60 × 130,836
           = $14,455,000
    Other: $392.91 × 0.45 × 215,459/2
           = $19,048,000

(6) 1994 total recreational value [(2) + (3) + (4) + (5)]	$ 37,261,000
(7) Levelized annual cost of recreational value (present value of 50 years, inflated at 6%, discounted at 10.72%, then levelized at 10.71% over 50 years)	$ 80,039,000
(8) Total of private and recreational annual cost [(1) + (7)]	$214,263,000

Source: Reprinted with permission from *The Tuolumne River: Preservation or Development? An Economic Assessment* (Berkeley: Environmental Defense Fund, Inc., 1984).

EXHIBIT 9

Use and Intrinsic Values of Environmental Resources from Previous Empirical Studies, 1974–1983

Study	Site	Estimates ($1994/Household/yr)[1]		Ratio of Nonuse to Use
		Use	Nonuse	
Meyer 1974	Fraser River, British Columbia	1943	1051	0.54
Horvath 1974	Southeastern U.S.	5914	3296	0.56
Dornbusch and Falcke 1974	Communities along seven U.S. bodies of water	—	—	1.39
Meyer 1973	Fraser River, British Columbia	601	754	1.25
Walsh, Greenley, Young, McKean and Prato 1978	South Platte River, Colorado	264	138	0.52
Mitchell and Carson 1981	U.S. national	540	253	0.47
Cronin 1982	Potomac River	88	63	0.72
Desvousges, Smith and McGivney 1983	Monongahela River	109	71	0.65
Cronin (forthcoming)	Potomac River	92	73	0.79
	Average values	1194	712	0.60[2]

[1] Inflated at CPI to 1982 and at 6%/year to 1994.
[2] Does nto include results from Dornbusch and Falcke 1974.
Source: Reprinted with permission from *The Tuolumne River: Preservation or Development? An Economic Assessment* (Berkeley: Environmental Defense Fund, Inc., 1984). Citing Ann Fisher and Robert Raucher, ''Intrinsic Benefits of Improved Water Quality: Conceptual and Empirical Pespectives.'' *Advances in Applied Microeconomics,* ed. V. Kerry Smith (Greenwich CT: JAI Press, Inc., 1984).

EXHIBIT 10

Estimating the Option Value Associated with Whitewater Boating
on the Tuolumne River

California	
Consumer surplus per user from TCM model, based upon actual Tuolumne River rafting data	$184.14
Nonuser/user value ratio, based upon previous empirical research summarized by Fisher and Raucher (1983)	× 0.60
Estimated per-capital California option value	$110.48
California membership of Sierra Club	× 130,836
Estimated 1994 total California option value	$14,455,000

Other Regions of the U.S.	
Consumer surplus per user from TCM model, based upon actual Tuolumne River rafting data	$392.91
Nonuser/user value ratio, based upon previous empirical research summarized by Fisher and Raucher (1983) and reduced to account for effect of remoteness from site	× 0.45
Estimated per-capital non-California option value	$176.81
Non-California membership of Sierra Club, reduced by one-half to account for effect of remoteness from site	× 107,730
Estimated 1994 total non-California option value	$19,048,000
Estimated total U.S. option value (1994)	$33,503,000

Source: Reprinted with permission from *The Tuolumne River: Preservation or Development? An Economic Assessment* (Berkeley: Environmental Defense Fund, Inc., 1984).

surplus, multiplied by half the non-California Sierra Club membership (Exhibit 10). All told, he produced an option value estimate of $33.5 million.

In the final analysis, Stavins estimated the annual social costs of the Clavey-Wards Ferry development at $214 million, outweighing its benefits by some $26 million. The calculations assigned the Clavey-Wards Ferry proposal a cost-benefit ratio of 0.877, indicating that the project would return about $.88 of benefits to society for each $1.00 invested in the project.

ASSIGNMENT FOR CLASS

Consider the decision of the Tuolumne River Preservation Trust to have the Environmental Defense Fund engage in a quantitative cost-benefit analysis of the proposed hydroelectric development of the Tuolumne River:

1. What are the sources of the Tuolumne River's value in its undeveloped state? Which of these values do you think can be quantified and which cannot?

2. Are there any values raised by the case that you think should not be quantified as a matter of public policy? If so, what are they and what alternatives would you turn to in answering the question of whether the Tuolumne ought to be dammed?

3. For those values of an undeveloped Tuolumne that can be quantified, is the quantification in the case convincing? Why or why not?

The Sawhill Commission:
Weighing a State Takeover of LILCO

The truth of the matter is that [Cuomo] said, "I'm not letting the plant open, I'm not letting the plant open, I'm not letting the plant open," and then people said to him, "Are you crazy? This is a four billion dollar investment—who the hell is going to pick it up?"

> —Karen Burstein, Sawhill Commission member

PUBLIC POWER FOR LONG ISLAND?

On January 30, 1986, New York Governor Mario Cuomo announced the creation of a blue-ribbon panel to study "the feasibility and economic viability of replacing the Long Island Lighting Company (LILCO) with a publicly owned utility." The panel was the governor's latest effort to resolve the long-running battle between electric ratepayers on Long Island, and LILCO, whose rates were among the highest in the country. At the center of the battle was the Shoreham nuclear power plant, located in Suffolk County, on the northeast shore of Long Island. Twenty years in the planning and building, the 809 megawatt Shoreham plant threatened to double the price of electricity on Long Island, already almost twice the national average for investor-owned utilities (see Exhibit 1). Officially titled the Long Island Public Power Panel, the group became known as the Sawhill Commission, after its chairman, Dr. John Sawhill, a director of the international consulting firm McKinsey & Company, Inc. The commission was charged with deciding if a takeover of LILCO would actually save money, and suggesting how the state might accomplish a takeover if it were advantageous to do so.

HISTORY

Like most of the private utilities that built nuclear plants in the early seventies, LILCO experienced numerous problems with the Shoreham plant—including high labor costs, work stoppages, low productivity, theft, design delays on the part of Stone & Webster (the architect/engi-neer for the project), defective parts and equipment, and management problems—all of which led to tremendous cost overruns and countless delays in construction. The actual construction of the plant took twelve years, and was finally completed early in 1985, at an estimated total cost of $4.5 billion.[1] Even then, LILCO's difficulties with the plant were far from over: the company immediately ran into licensing problems when both state and county officials refused to participate in evacuation plans. By the time of the Sawhill Commission, one Nuclear Regulatory Commission (NRC) board had already denied LILCO a license for the facility, and many considered the plant a nuclear white elephant. NRC efforts to license the plant were still underway, however, and the plant was running under a low-power license.

Shoreham brought financial burdens as well as safety concerns to Long Island residents, some of whom had opposed the plant since the planning stages. Critics of LILCO management felt vindicated when a six-year study by the New York Public Service Commission (PSC) concluded that $1.4 billion of Shoreham's total cost had been spent imprudently. Under New York law, costs judged imprudent could not be passed on to consumers; they had to be absorbed by the stockholders. Of the remaining $3.1 billion in Shoreham costs, 60 percent, or $1.8 billion, had been included in the rate base as of LILCO's January 26, 1986 rate increase. By 1986, Shoreham accounted for 26 percent of the company's rate of 11.5 cents per kilowatt hour (kwh); even without Shoreham in the rate base, LILCO's price for electricity would have been 8.51 cents per kwh, or 37 percent higher than the national average for investor-owned utilities, because of its reliance on oil-burning plants (see Exhibit 1). The high rates and the evacuation uncertainties increased the opposition to the plant; Maurice Barbash, who headed Citizens to Replace LILCO, said that by late 1985, "seventy percent of the people [on Long Island] wanted to get rid

---

[1] For a more complete picture of Shoreham, see Harvard Business School cases #1-385-249, 1-385-251, and 3-683-052.

This case was written by Nancy Kates under the direction of Professors Josæe A. Gomez-Ibañez and Joseph Kalt for use at the John F. Kennedy School of Government, Harvard University. (1087)

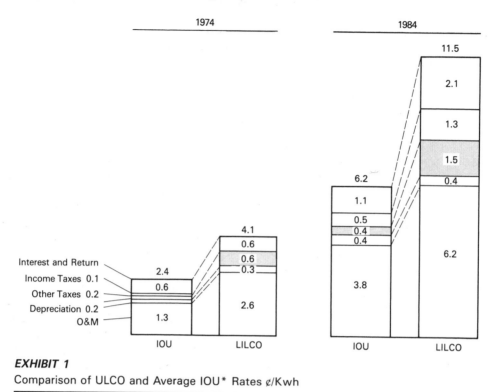

EXHIBIT 1

Comparison of ULCO and Average IOU* Rates ¢/Kwh

*Average investor owned utility in the United States.

Source: ULCO annual report; DOE/EIA, staff analysis, as printed in the *Report of the Long Island Public Power Panel,* June 24, 1986.

of LILCO and replace it with a public power authority."

With the public dead set against the plant, the governor decided to form a special commission to consider a state takeover of the company. Several Cuomo panels had already studied Shoreham, but their studies had been inconclusive,[2] and the state still had no clear-cut strategy for dealing with the imbroglio. When Cuomo approached the New York state legislature, it approved a budget of $500,000 for the commission and set a deadline of April 30 for the panel's report. This time, the legislators wanted a quick and definitive analysis of the merits of a public takeover. "They were asking themselves," said Frank Murray, Cuomo's deputy secretary for energy

[2]These panels were the Marburger Commission, headed by John Marburger III of the State University of New York at Stony Brook, which concluded in 1983 that Suffolk County had not acted unreasonably in rejecting the company's evacuation plan, but whose findings were disputed since the group was marked by extreme divisiveness; and an internal group—created in 1983 to study a public takeover and headed by Cuomo's secretary, Michael Del Guidice—which by 1985 had evolved into the Governor's Special Task Force on Public Power on Long Island, headed by Vincent Tese of New York City's Urban Development Corporation.

and environment, "'was the governor going to study this issue to death?', death being the point at which the legislature goes home for the summer."

By the time the Sawhill Commission got underway, two key measures were pending in the legislature. The first, known as the "used and useful" bill, proposed that "utility customers should not be required to bear the cost of a plant which failed to operate," and required utilities to go into full operation forty-two months after they received low-power testing licenses. The proposed legislation effectively granted LILCO a deadline of January 1989 to resolve its licensing problems, or else lose the right to pass through Shoreham costs. A second bill authorized the state to create a Long Island Power Authority (LIPA) for purposes of a public takeover of LILCO, by purchase or condemnation of assets or stock. Known as the LIPA bill, the measure stipulated that the state could take over the company only if the public power authority would have lower electric rates than LILCO, and that the new entity would be exempt from PSC ratemaking authority. The bill set a deadline of January 15, 1987 for appointing the LIPA board, which made the task of the Sawhill Commission all the more urgent.

THE SAWHILL COMMISSION

The seven members of the panel included a number of experts in the fields of finance and energy; panelists were picked partly for their credibility with the media. At least four—three of them well-known energy experts—were perceived by Long Islanders as overly sympathetic to the private utility industry: Sawhill, the former deputy secretary of the Department of Energy; Alfred Kahn, an economist at Cornell and the former chairman of the New York PSC; William Hogan, a professor at the Kennedy School of Government at Harvard; and Kevin Collins, head of the Municipal Securities Division of The First Boston Corporation. In actuality, several of the business-oriented panel members were quite sympathetic to the idea of public power: John Bierwirth was the chairman of Grumman Corporation, the biggest employer on Long Island and LILCO's major industrial customer, and Leonard Rosen, a partner at the law firm of Wachtell, Lipton, Rosen & Katz in New York City, lived on Long Island and was concerned about Shoreham safety.[3]

Public power advocates in particular worried that the panel was weighted in LILCO's favor. Observed Marjorie Harrison of the Long Island Public Power Project, one of the main "stop Shoreham" groups:

> The Sawhill Commission, which was made up of people very much in the mainstream of the financial establishment, with a few exceptions, like Karen Burstein, clearly was not going to be party to putting forth a proposal which was . . . predicated upon the stockholders and bondholders taking a real haircut on the Shoreham debt.

The panel began its study in February 1986, with a formidable task ahead. With the aid of outside consultants, the State Energy Office staff, and John Sawhill's own staff at McKinsey, the commission had to come up with a cost comparison of LILCO and a public power authority, which for study purposes was called LIPA, as in the pending legislation. But the Sawhill Commission version of LIPA differed in a number of ways from the public power authority described in the pending legislation, departing, for example, from the "used and useful" bill in its interpretation of that concept.

LIPA

In order to answer the larger question of whether public power would save money over LILCO, the panel had to ask itself what kind of institution LIPA would be, and how it would operate. Panel members envisioned LIPA as a non-profit state power authority serving Long Island. LIPA would employ a traditional, somewhat conservative municipal power authority structure, especially in its financing. Since public entities were allowed to issue tax-exempt bonds paying below-market interest, the Sawhill Commission projected that LIPA would be able to borrow money at nine percent, instead of the 11 percent market rate paid by LILCO. Under the panel's structure, LIPA might be eligible for an A bond rating (LILCO debt was rated BB- by Standard & Poor's), because of two factors: conservative coverage ratios and a managerially responsible board of directors.[4] In the case of LIPA, the Sawhill Commission calculated coverage based on the idea that the authority would reduce its total debt every year through repayment of principal. (LILCO's coverage ratios were based on repayment of interest only.) LIPA, like LILCO, would probably have to capitalize its debt service in the first few years, but the panel believed that LIPA would be a stronger entity than LILCO, since they expected LIPA to set its own rates. Therefore, the new authority would not be subject to increasing PSC reluctance to allow Shoreham's capitalized costs into the rate base. The panel report noted, however, that the power authority would need a strong, independent governing board, but it did not specifically address the viability of the elected 15-member board proposed in the LIPA legislation. An elected board was perceived as essential by the drafters of the legislation, who were responding to the demands of anti-Shoreham activists and frustrated ratepayers. After years of struggling with high electric rates, the public wanted someone they could hold accountable.

---

[3]The other panel member was Karen Burstein, president of the New York State Civil Service Commission and a former member of the PSC; Burstein had been a strong consumer advocate for many years.

[4]A coverage ratio is the amount of money brought in, in revenues, minus the operating expenses, divided by the amount needed to service the debt. For example, a company with a 2.0 coverage ratio has enough money to pay its yearly debts twice over. Higher coverage ratios allow companies to build up debt reserve funds, providing a cushion for periods in which reserves are low.

LIPA'S IMPACT ON COSTS

1. Fuel Prices and Alternative Electricity Supply

Two weeks after the first meeting, Sawhill recommended that the panel divide itself into subcommittees, one to study the economic viability of public power, headed by Bill Hogan, and the other to look at the feasibility question, chaired by Leonard Rosen. The first task for Hogan's group was to make assumptions about a range of factors that would have a significant impact on the cost of producing electricity, including fuel prices, electric load growth on Long Island, and the availability and cost of alternative methods for meeting the load growth. If the as-yet-unlicensed Shoreham did operate, alternative energy prices and availability would become less important, since the plant could provide additional capacity. And although the commission report wavered on this issue, the panel generally assumed that LILCO would operate the plant if a license could be obtained, and that a public power authority would probably not, for political reasons. However, the panel modeled rate projections for four separate scenarios: Shoreham operation versus non-operation by both LIPA and LILCO. Under the Shoreham abandonment case, the commission assumed both LILCO and LIPA would be able to recover $3.1 billion, or the prudent cost of the plant. Since both LILCO and LIPA would have to replace some of the lost capacity if Shoreham were abandoned, supply requirements would increase operations and maintenance costs. Conversely, post-operation capital additions on the plant would add expense if Shoreham did operate. Surprisingly, the panel found that operating the facility would save only about $200 million (net present value) over the life of the plant, unless the cost of supplying alternative power rose significantly above projected rates.

Moreover, it was not clear to the commission that the plant was actually needed, especially after 1991, when a planned 345 megawatt transmission line would come on line. The State Energy Office (SEO) predicted that even without Shoreham, Long Island could get by in the short term by conserving, importing power, and implementing small power technologies. LILCO itself had testified before the 1983 Marburger Commission that the plant would not be needed before 1994.

The panel, however, was more cautious. Its report stated that "the Long Island power system may have some difficulty in importing sufficient power to meet its reliability needs through 1991," and concurred with an earlier PSC suggestion that the com-

pany build combustion turbines to ensure reliability whether or not Shoreham operated. This was consistent with the SEO estimate that an in-service Shoreham would operate at 58 percent of its capacity, and the Long Island would therefore need additional capacity when the plant was shut down. Both LILCO and the PSC forecast capacity factors above 58 percent, but the panel chose to go with the more conservative estimate.[5]

Bill Hogan, who lobbied for the cautious approach to alternative supply plans, explained why the gas turbines made sense even with Shoreham:

> If you were thinking of all the things that you would do, in order to solve the reliability in power problem, the last thing on the list would be to turn on a big nuclear power plant. . . . If some fluke occurs and they have to shut the thing down, they're going to have to have those turbines out there anyhow, just to turn on in case.

On the other hand, a drastic increase in oil prices—from the then-current price of $15/barrel—would dramatically increase the cost of alternative energy if Shoreham did not operate, since most of the replacement power would be generated by oil-burning plants. For example, the commission calculated that $27/barrel oil would increase projected public power rates by 30 percent. In its final report, the panel assumed a $19/barrel oil price with no real increase over the next 15 years.

2. Operations and Maintenance

In making their rate projections for the panel, the SEO analysts assumed that operations and maintenance (O&M) costs would be the same for LIPA and LILCO.[6] If Shoreham did not operate, the analysts estimated O&M costs would be nine percent higher,

---

[5]All nuclear power plants shut down periodically for refueling, repairs, NRC inspections, tests, and other reasons. Capacity factor estimates were calculated by studying other plants in New York and the nation. According to SEO Deputy Commissioner Bill Davis, boiling-water, salt-water-cooled plants like Shoreham, run without a twin reactor by utilities without prior experience operating nuclear plants, have very low capacity factors.

[6]SEO rate projections for LILCO were checked by several outside consultants to the panel, including Energy Management Associates, Inc., Arthur Andersen & Co., as well as PSC analysts and several Sawhill Commission staff members. The SEO's LIPA estimates were reviewed by Salomon Brothers, Inc., and the panel staff. Various parties to the commission's proceedings questioned the thoroughness of the PSC review, due to ongoing tensions between the PSC and the SEO.

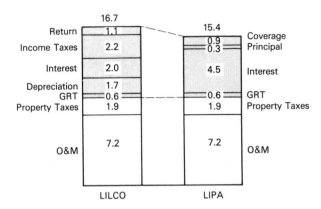

EXHIBIT 2

Rate Component Comparison—Shoreham Abandoned[1]
LILCO vs. LIPA Levelized ¢/kwh

---

[1]Oil at $19/barrel.

Source: Report of the Long Island Public Power Panel, June 24, 1986.

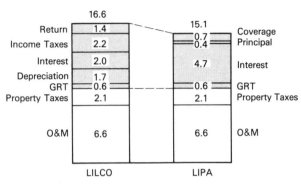

EXHIBIT 3

Rate Component Comparison — Shoreham Operation[1]
LILCO vs. LIPA Levelized ¢/kwh

---

[1]Oil at $19/barrel.

Source: Report of the Long Island Public Power Panel, June 24, 1986.

but their calculations assumed the same increase for both concerns (see Exhibits 2 and 3). "We wanted to keep the comparison as fair as possible," remembered Rick Peters of McKinsey & Co., one of the principal staff members for the commission. "We looked at a couple of studies of public and private entities in the United States, and found no compelling evidence that one is better than the other," in terms of efficiency. Some panel members may have privately disagreed with that assumption. Leonard Rosen, for example, said he "personally wouldn't have long-term confidence that the public sector would run the utility more cheaply than the private. I would expect it would be the other way [around]. . . ." A report prepared by the National Economic Research Associates, Inc. (NERA) for LILCO, which listed several indicators of the company's operating efficiency, was consistent with Rosen's doubts: LILCO's figure for gross plant in service per megawatt of demand was 30 percent below average for New York State, its 1985 total wages paid per kwh of sales were the lowest in the state, and the thermal efficiency of its generating plants was better than average for New York utilities.[7]

3. Taxes

LIPA's perceived tax advantages were significant in comparison to LILCO's. In contrast to several other studies,[8] the Sawhill Commission analysis assumed a

$200 million federal tax liability for LIPA, versus a $1.6 billion (net present value) tax burden for LILCO over the 15-year study period. LIPA's $200 million would be owed for Investment Tax Credit (ITC) recapture, a repayment of the tax break LILCO received for making capital investments in its plants. Although the panel noted the possibility of a $550 to $600 million tax liability for LIPA due to such recapture if it were to purchase LILCO with Shoreham, its rate projections assumed no depreciation recapture. A public entity buying LILCO with Shoreham would be liable for this tax if the IRS ruled the takeover an asset purchase, rather than a stock purchase. While the panel examined the tax assumptions made by Smith Barney, Harris Upham & Co., Inc., in its study for Suffolk County, as well as one conducted by EBASCO Business Consulting Company for LILCO, the panel took issue with points in both studies, and relied on its own tax consultants, Arthur Andersen & Co., who felt additional taxes could be avoided, depending on the mechanics of the actual takeover.

LILCO CEO William Catacosinos hotly disputed the panel's estimates of the company's federal tax liability, and said that "LILCO will actually pay less than $1.0 billion and that is under the current tax law." He expected tax liability to drop beginning in 1987 under the revised federal tax law (panel computer runs used the old tax guidelines). Furthermore, in a study conducted for LILCO, EBASCO assumed LIPA would inherit $613 million in federal taxes, including both ITC and depreciation recapture.

---

[7]NERA report, p. e-2.

[8]One of the difficulties faced by the panel was the number of conflicting reports that had previously been issued by various parties to the dispute. In addition to the six outside consultants employed

by the Sawhill Commission, members received information from three consultants hired by LILCO and six consultants hired by Suffolk County, which was conducting its own investigation of a possible takeover.

Another tax advantage for LIPA which the panel found significant was its ability to issue unlimited tax-exempt bonds: because the bonds would incur no federal tax liability, they could be sold at rates below the market rate for taxable bonds. In response, LILCO argued that it was eligible to issue low coupon, tax-exempt industrial development bonds (IDBs), and that it planned to refinance $2.5 billion of its long-term debt with IDBs over the next five years. Bill Hogan took issue with that, noting,

> LILCO can come back and say—the IDBs are best example—"well, we can get tax-exempt financing, too, all you have to do is let us." The answer is yes, that's right, all we have to do is let you.

There was some question as to whether or not such a refinancing would be feasible, because of the rules governing the use of IDBs, especially the federally imposed cap of $2.5 billion per year for New York state. Under federal law, the governor of every state controls IDB allocation. It was the consensus of the panel that even if the state had enough surplus volume to allocate $500 million, or one fifth of the state total, to LILCO each year for five years, the governor would be unlikely to do so.

In addition to its federal tax burden, the panel assumed that LIPA would not be liable for state and local taxes but it would make payments in lieu of them. State taxes were principally the four percent gross receipts tax (GRT) on revenues, while local tax liabilities were for property taxes. LILCO currently paid both state and local taxes, although the company expected its property tax assessment for Shoreham to drop 50 percent if a lawsuit against Suffolk County proved successful. Smith Barney, by contrast, assumed in its analysis that LIPA would not make payments in lieu of GRT; the panel disagreed, but estimated savings in the range of $500–750 million over the next 15 years if Smith Barney were right.

LIPA'S BENEFITS TO RATEPAYERS

Based on its assumptions and calculations covering taxes, interest rates, alternative supply, etc., the panel concluded that electricity furnished by LIPA would be seven to nine percent cheaper than LILCO electricity, depending on what happened with Shoreham. Under "worst-case" assumptions—i.e., that LILCO would operate Shoreham but LIPA would not—the panel projected LIPA rates would still be seven percent below LILCO rates.[9] However, all projected savings from LIPA were extremely sensitive to four factors: the purchase price for LIPA; the interest rate on LIPA debt; the coverage ratio for LIPA; and the future price of oil (see Exhibits 4–9). For example, LIPA's nine percent advantage over LILCO (which assumed both would operate Shoreham) would fall to four percent if LIPA paid a market interest rate of 11 percent instead of a municipal bond rate of nine percent. Because of the size of the stock purchase and the amount of debt needed to buy the company, ratepayer savings were very sensitive to purchase price and coverage ratios: a lower purchase price would increase savings from LIPA, and a higher coverage ratio would significantly reduce them. Jeff Cohen, a principal staff member for the commission, remembered the process of drafting the report, which specifically avoided characterizing projected ratepayer savings:

> There was care taken with the words, so that adverbs and adjectives [used in the report] became important. Seven percent savings from one perspective could be cast as "merely seven

EXHIBIT 4
Ratepayer Savings from LIPA
Percent

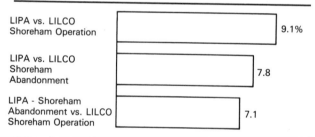

LIPA vs. LILCO Shoreham Operation	9.1%
LIPA vs. LILCO Shoreham Abandonment	7.8
LIPA - Shoreham Abandonment vs. LILCO Shoreham Operation	7.1

Source: Report of the Long Island Public Power Panel, June 24, 1986.

[9]These rates were calculated with a base case $18 purchase price, used only for the purpose of comparison. The panel calculated $18/share as the approximate adjusted book value of the company. LILCO stock was selling for $11/share at the time. Book value is calculated as the value of the assets, minus depreciation, using one of two methods: original cost less depreciation (OCLD), or replacement cost new less depreciation (RCNLD). The commission calculated $18/share using the OCLD method, and then adjusted that book value by subtracting the $1.4 billion disallowance for Shoreham, as well as $256 million for LILCO's share of the expected imprudence in the Nine Mile Point II plant (in which it had an 18 percent interest). Further adjustment was made by adding in the tax benefit of the imprudencies, which would accrue to the stockholders. The panel figure for the adjusted book value per share was slightly higher than LILCO's own figure for the same calculation, $16.92.

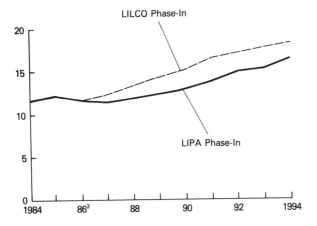

EXHIBIT 5

Comparison of Rate Patterns LILCO[1] vs. LIPA[2]
Nominal ¢/kwh

[1]Shoreham Operation.
[2]Shoreham abandonment.
[3]Projected.

Source: Report of the Long Island Public Power Panel, June 24, 1986.

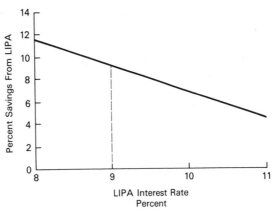

EXHIBIT 7

Sensitivity of Ratepayer Savings to LIPA Interest
Rate[1] Shoreham Operation Percent Savings from LIPA

LIPA interest rate
Percent
[1]$19 per barrel oil prices, $18 per share purchase price.

Source: Report of the Long Island Public Power Panel, June 24, 1986.

percent," or "an astoundingly great seven percent savings." Some panelists may well think that seven percent or eight percent . . . savings is a lot, others may think it's not worth a candle. The panel chose to cast its report in a way that all could subscribe to it without getting into that judgment.

Having determined that LIPA would save money, the panel turned to its feasibility subcommittee, which was studying various takeover strategies.

TAKEOVER STRATEGIES

Leonard Rosen's feasibility group had measured alternative takeover strategies for LIPA, against a set of criteria developed early in the process: control over the acquisition price; certainty of completing the takeover once it began; ability to complete the takeover quickly, without costly delays in the middle of the process; and absence of substantial litigation. Two basic takeover methods were available: the state could buy LILCO, or take it under the law of eminent domain. A purchase could be accomplished

EXHIBIT 6

Sensitivity of Ratepayer Savings to Purchase Price[1]
Shoreham Operation Percent Savings from LIPA

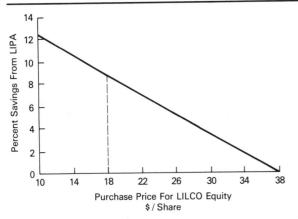

Purchase price for LILCO equity $/share
[1]$19 per barrel oil prices.

Source: Report of the Long Island Public Power Panel, June 24, 1986.

EXHIBIT 8

Sensitivity of Ratepayer Savings to LIPA Coverage[1]
Shoreham Operation

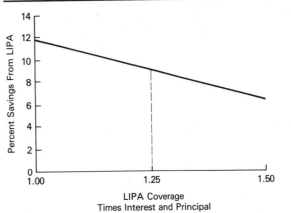

LIPA Coverage
Times Interest and Principal
[1]$19 per barrel oil prices, $18 per share purchase price.

Source: Report of the Long Island Public Power Panel, June 24, 1986.

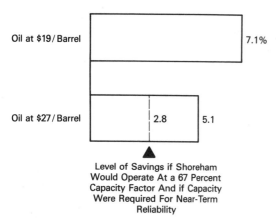

Oil at $19/Barrel — 7.1%

Oil at $27/Barrel — 2.8 | 5.1

Level of Savings if Shoreham
Would Operate At a 67 Percent
Capacity Factor And if Capacity
Were Required For Near-Term
Reliability

EXHIBIT 9

Sensitivity of Ratepayer Savings to Oil Prices[1] LILCO
Shoreham Operation vs. LIPA Shoreham
Abandonment

[1] $18/share purchase price.

Source: Report of the Long Island Public Power Panel, June 24, 1986.

through either a hostile tender offer or a negotiated deal approved by the stockholders and the board of directors. Of these options, only a negotiated deal appeared to satisfy all four criteria.

Condemnation, for example, the traditional method of takeover under eminent domain, would not let LIPA control the acquisition price, because New York eminent domain laws had been changed so as to require the purchaser to take title of the property—an irreversible step—before a court determination of a fair purchase price. Condemnation involved years of litigation, and even if the process were sped up, it could be a prohibitively expensive method for gaining control of LILCO, depending on the theory of valuation adopted by the court. Historically, courts have used a number of factors, such as market value, net asset value, book value, and earnings to determine just compensation in stock condemnation cases. In a report prepared for LILCO, the law firm of Shea & Gould argued that a fair price for the company under asset condemnation would be in excess of $16 billion, using the valuation method of "replacement cost new less depreciation" (RCNLD), which involved paying the condemnee enough to build an identical company from scratch. By contrast, if LIPA were to pay a price at or near market value, a stock condemnation could cost as little as $1.2 billion.

A hostile takeover presented similar risks and uncertainties. As the panel report noted, "Any tender offer of this magnitude by a state public power agency for the stock of a major investor-owned utility would certainly be unprecedented."

While a hostile tender offer would be legally feasible, it would leave LIPA vulnerable to protracted litigation, and would require the approval of two-thirds of the shareholders, a majority of the common equity holders, and a majority of the preferred stock holders. Even an unsuccessful tender would be quite expensive for the state, since the investment bankers would charge commitment fees of approximately one percent on the short-term debt needed to commence a takeover, payable whether or not the debt were issued. In the case of LILCO, the short-term debt would cost $1-3 billion, and there would still be no guarantee that stockholders would go along with the deal. As Leonard Rosen said, "They could [spend] in the range of $10, 20, 30 million and not make it." According to Rosen, Salomon Brothers Inc., which served as the investment banking consultant to the panel, thought Wall Street would react very negatively to a hostile tender.

New York State law also presented a considerable obstacle to a hostile tender. The state's tough new anti-takeover statute virtually prohibited hostile acquisitions, although it had never been applied. As Rick Peters put it, "The state's not going to be the first one to violate its takeover law." Many panel members felt that changing the law or amending it to allow for extraordinary exceptions was possible, but unwise. "There was quite a debate about the advisability of a hostile takeover strategy," remembered Peters. "There were those that felt it was just bad public policy. . . . If you're a businessman, do you want to move to a state where the state government is going to take a run at your business?" Rosen, however, a bankruptcy lawyer and founding partner of one of the most prestigious mergers and acquisitions law firms in the country, thought a hostile tender was at least feasible as a strategy. The panel report concluded that a negotiated deal approved by the stockholders and management would avoid litigation, delay, and the uncertainties presented by the other takeover strategies; it was clearly the most realistic method for acquiring LILCO. Nevertheless, the commission included all three options in its report, despite the obvious difficulties with two of the three.

POTENTIAL PROBLEMS WITH LIPA

In its study of the merits of public power for Long Island, the Sawhill Commission glossed over some serious operational problems presented by LIPA. Two potential difficulties with LIPA concerned the response of the bond markets to the venture. First, LIPA's board of directors posed a catch-22 for the new power authority; the elected board demanded by irate ratepayers might well prove unsatisfactory to Wall Street analysts. "I think our investment banker's opinion was that that wouldn't fly," recalled staff member Rick Peters.

> There's no way you'd get an "A" [bond] rating if they had elected officials, because that [structure] provided incentives for granting insufficient [electric] rates that would jeopardize the bond ratings. I think the panel really felt that we needed a very strong governing board that wouldn't be subject to politics.

No specific mention of how to resolve the governance impasse was made in the report, although members of the panel and outside observers assumed there would be additional legislation if the state were to commence a takeover.

A second, more global consideration was the size of the initial bond offering needed to purchase LILCO. Other entities requiring a market for their tax-exempt municipal bonds were concerned that a large LIPA offering might adversely affect their ability to issue debt. A letter sent to Governor Cuomo from the Erie County Industrial Development Agency (ECIDA) in Buffalo warned:

> The sheer magnitude of the tax exempt bond financing required to acquire LILCO could have a disruptive effect on the market for tax exempt bonds, with issuers facing possible interest rate increases or an inability to access a saturated market.

ECIDA also cautioned that the pending 1986 federal tax bill could subject public power authority debt to a cap on non-essential function bonds, "thus excluding a variety of other public benefit issuers from access to tax-exempt financing." The panel took the questions raised by ECIDA into account, but did not extensively study the hypothetical effects of a LIPA debt issue on the municipal bond markets.

FINANCING LIPA

The Sawhill Commission considered several models for the financial structure of the proposed power authority. Each model involved a transition from a debt-and-equity-structured investor-owned utility to a debt-only public utility, which would issue its own bonds as needed. All of the plans called for LIPA to function as the sole guarantor, using its revenues for

debt service. One key variable in the financial structure of the public entity was the coverage ratio. A higher ratio would be more expensive—since more capital would be tied up in a debt reserve fund—but safer, because a lower coverage ratio would have less cushion against a sudden drop in revenue. After looking into coverage ratios at a number of North American public utilities, the panel found that actual cash coverage ranged from 3.6 for the Los Angeles Department of Water and Power to 0.9 for Ontario (Canada) Hydro, which had credit guarantees from the provincial government; the existing New York public power authority, NYPA,[10] had a coverage ratio of 1.15. Various proposed plans gave LIPA ratios ranging from 1.1 to 1.25.

The other major financial decision facing the panel was the question of LILCO's existing $3 billion debt, which could be assumed or refunded (paid off in a lump sum during the takeover by issuing new debt) when the public power authority came into existence. Refunding would save money over time, because new debt could be issued at lower rates than the old LILCO debt, but this solution would front-load the takeover costs. Despite the potential savings, staff member Jeff Cohen said the panel's consultants opposed refunding because of the amount of new debt required:

> It was big enough as is that Salomon [Brothers, the panel's investment banking advisor] was concerned about its unprecedented size, and anything to make it bigger made its real world marketability that much more doubtful.

Proponents of refunding countered that assuming LILCO's debt would still involve sizeable up-front costs: significant amounts of old debt would soon be maturing, and LIPA would need an additional $1.4 billion over the next five years to pay for it (see Exhibits 10 and 11). Refunding advocates also argued that assuming the LILCO debt would give LIPA a slightly lower credit rating than refunding, since new LIPA debt would be subordinated to old LILCO debt. Others argued, on the other hand, that assuming the debt would be less expensive, because LIPA would have to pay coverage on its new debt but *not* on assumed LILCO debt.

---

[10]NYPA was established to sell low-cost electricity from two upstate hydroelectric projects, Niagara and St. Lawrence. Although the Niagara plan was required by law to sell half of its output to public power entities, the Sawhill Commission did not assume that LIPA would be eligible for NYPA hydro, because a transfer to Long Island ratepayers "would be at the direct expense of ratepayers elsewhere in the state," as its report noted.

EXHIBIT 10
Long Term Debt and Trust Obligations at December 31
(In thousands of dollars)

Rate of Interest	Series	Due	1985	1984	1983
First Mortgage Bonds (excludes Pledged Bonds)					
3¼ %	G	1984	$ —	$ —	$ 15,000
3⅜	H	1985	—	15,000	15,000
4¾	I	1986	20,000	20,000	20,000
4⅛	J	1988	20,000	20,000	20,000
5	L	1991	25,000	25,000	25,000
4.40	M	1993	40,000	40,000	40,000
4⅝	N	1994	25,000	25,000	25,000
4.55	O	1995	25,000	25,000	25,000
5¼	P	1996	40,000	40,000	40,000
5½	Q	1997	35,000	35,000	35,000
8.20	R	1999	35,000	35,000	35,000
9⅛	S	2000	25,000	25,000	25,000
7¼	U	2001	40,000	40,000	40,000
7½	V	2001	50,000	50,000	50,000
7⅝	W	2002	50,000	50,000	50,000
8⅛	X	2003	60,000	60,000	60,000
Total First Mortgage Bonds			490,000	505,000	520,000
Less — Current Maturities			20,000	15,000	15,000
Total—Less Current Maturities			470,000	490,000	505,000
General and Refunding Bonds					
9⅞% Series Due 1984			—	—	90,000
9⅝% Series Due 2006			70,000	70,000	70,000
8⅝% Series Due 2006			50,000	50,000	50,000
8⅝% Series Due 2007			85,000	85,000	85,000
9.20% Series Due 2008			75,000	75,000	75,000
9.75% Series Due 1999			91,000	94,000	96,000
14¼% Series Due 2010			50,000	50,000	50,000
15.75% Series Due 1991			100,000	100,000	100,000
17⅜% Series Due 2011			50,000	50,000	50,000
16¾% Series Due 1991			50,000	50,000	50,000
18% Series Due 2011			50,000	50,000	50,000
17% Serie sDue 1991			50,000	50,000	50,000
17⅛% Series Due 2012			100,000	100,000	100,000
15¼% Series Due 2012			100,000	100,000	100,000
12⅝% Series Due 1992			75,000	75,000	75,000
13½% Series Due 2013			105,000	105,000	105,000
17½% Series Due 1989			100,000	100,000	—
½% Series Due 1993			225,000	250,000	—
13¼% Series Due 1995			225,000	—	—
Total General and Refunding Bonds			1,651,000	1,454,000	1,196,000
Less—Bonds held by pledgee			—	121,500	—
Less—Current Maturities			3,000	3,000	92,000
Total—Less Current Maturities			1,648,000	1,329,500	1,104,000
Third Mortgage[1]					
1982 RCA			231,759	250,000	250,000
Eurodollar RCA			75,000	150,000	150,000
Intermediate Term Notes			97,339	105,000	105,000
Resources Trust			163,003	176,437	203,362
Construction Trust			471,089	509,184	510,122
Total Third Mortgage			1,038,190	1,190,621	1,218,484
Less—Current Maturities			661,903	75,000	—

EXHIBIT 10 (cont.)

Total—Less Current Maturities	376,287	1,115,621	1,218,484
Other Long Term Debt			
1984 RCA	30,000	36,000	—
Authority Financing Notes			
6½% to 8¼% Due 2006-2016	216,675	66,675	66,675
Grid Note	7,230	—	—
Promissory Note 8½% Due 1985	—	46	102
Total Other Long Term Debt	253,905	102,721	66,777
Less—Current Maturities	30,000	36,046	56
Total—Less Current Maturities	223,905	66,675	66,721
Total Long Term Debt and Trust Obligations—Less Current Maturities	$2,718,192	$3,001,796	$2,894,205

The aggregate of the Company's long-term debt due in the next five years is $714,903,000 (1986), $31,000,000 (1987), $420,000,000 (1988), $140,000,000 (1989), and $83,000,000 (1990).

[1]Amounts shown for 1983 were outstanding under each respective lending agreement but were not secured under the Third Mortgage.

Source: Long Island Lighting Company, *Annual Report,* 1985.

EXHIBIT 11

Comparison of Financial Requirements—LIPA[1] 1987-94

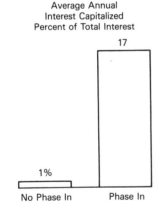

Average Annual
Interest Capitalized
Percent of Total Interest

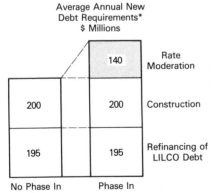

Average Annual New
Debt Requirements*
$ Millions

[1]Shoreham abandonment.
[2]Before internally available funds.
Source: Report of the Long Island Public Power Panel, June 24, 1986.

WHAT PRICE FOR LIPA?

One thorny issue raised by all of the various proposed financing plans was the purchase price, which the state would have to determine before commencing a takeover. LILCO and its consultants claimed that a fair price would be between $20 and $30 per share, since the company would argue in court "that the State has taken actions in the past that depressed the price of the stock well below book value, and is now trying to buy the property . . . at an artificially depressed price." The Sawhill Commission noted in its report that LILCO common stock had ranged from $6 to $15 per share during the 52 weeks before the report was released, and that Smith Barney had used a price of $14 per share. However, the panel decided to use $18 per share, its calculation of the adjusted book value, rather than an approximation of the market value of the stock, although it found that ratepayer savings were quite sensitive to purchase price (see footnote 9).

Some observers criticized the panel for using an $18 figure in the report, claiming that a price so far above the market price would "poison the pot" and limit the governor's flexibility in his upcoming negotiations with LILCO, even though the report presented it as a fair or reasonable price for the purpose of economic analysis, but not necessarily a recommended figure. Sawhill "made a mistake in basing his figures on an $18 buyout," said Maurice Barbash of Citizens to Replace LILCO. "I couldn't see why a stock that was selling for $11 or $12 had to go for $18." Many of the journalists who wrote about the commission referred to the figure as the price the state would be willing to pay, and one municipal bond newsletter published by an investment banking house actually referred to the figure as "LIPA's $18 per share offer."[11] "We certainly did not get into the business of telling the state how much it could pay for LILCO," countered staff member Rick Peters. "But what we did want to do was come up with a number that we thought was fair. . . . What's fair in a regulated environment would have been adjusted book value. . . . In a perfect world, if our regulators gave LILCO its cost of capital, the market value of

LILCO's stock should be equal to book value. I mean, that's what the future flow of earnings is worth." Bill Hogan put it another way:

This is often discussed in the mindset that this is T. Boone Cuomo[12] coming in to buy this company. This is not. This is Governor Cuomo coming in to buy this company, and he has a different responsibility. And because it is a regulated entity, where the state determines its future economic health, it has a dual responsibility.

---

[11]Corporate Bond Research, Electric Utilities, L.F. Rothschild, Unterberg, Towbin, July 7, 1986.

[12]A reference to the famed corporate raider, T. Boone Pickens, Jr.

ASSIGNMENT FOR CLASS DISCUSSION

Come to class prepared to explain whether and why, or why not, you are in favor of a state takeover of LILCO. In considering your recommendations, please consider:

1. Would such a takeover lower electric rates for Long Island residents, and why?

2. What assumptions about the proposed Long Island Power Authority are necessary to answer the first question the way that you did?

3. What effects would such a takeover have on other parties, such as federal taxpayers, New York state taxpayers, and bondholders?

The Department of Transportation and Airport Landing Slots

I fail to see how it can be argued that because we have given the right to the airlines to possible windfall profits from operating slots, we should give them further windfall profits from selling the slots. To do so would be the equivalent of saying that because I have given my children the right to live in my house while they are growing up, it should be of no significance to also give them the right to sell the house.

—Rep. Norman Y. Mineta (D-CA)

An airport landing "slot" is the name the Federal Aviation Administration (FAA) gives to an intangible but

valuable commodity: the right of an airplane to use a specific airport at a specified time. Slots constitute key assets of a commercial airline. The right to fly means little without the right to take off and land at major cities during periods of peak travel demand.

During the early 1980s, a series of events—ranging from airline deregulation to the air traffic controllers' strike—gradually forced the Department of Transportation (DOT)—umbrella agency for the FAA—to consider how best the government should allocate the finite number of airport landing slots. Among the options Secretary of Transportation Elizabeth Dole would consider were: continuing a longstanding system allowing airport-based

---

This case was written by Vlad Jenkins under the direction of Professors José Gomez-Ibañez and John Meyer for use at the Kennedy School of Government, Harvard University. (1087)

committees of airlines to distribute the slots, with federal intervention a possibility in case of deadlock; conferring upon "incumbent" airlines the right to keep the slots they had and sell them without interference; auctioning all existing slots to the highest bidder and permitting an open market in slots once the auction was over.

THE FAA AND SCHEDULING COMMITTEES

The FAA introduced slot regulations in April 1969, in an attempt to deal with chronic congestion and delay at four high-density airports: New York's Kennedy and LaGuardia, Washington's National and Chicago's O'Hare. As the organization responsible for operating the Air Traffic Control system, the FAA determined the number of slots for each airport and divided the slots among three categories of users: air carriers, commuter airlines, and general aviation. The semi-annual allocation to specific airlines was accomplished at each airport by separate air carrier and commuter airline scheduling committees operating under a limited grant of antitrust immunity. Representatives of incumbent airlines as well as Civil Aeronautics Board (CAB)-certified potential entrants participated in the committees and had to reach unanimous agreements. The FAA reserved the right to intervene in case of deadlock and make administrative allocations.

This structure provided a sufficient incentive for incumbents to accommodate the few entrants who appeared in the 1970s. However, the competitive environment created by the Airline Deregulation Act of 1978 placed strains on the scheduling committee system. Demand for slots increased as more new airlines appeared, established airlines restructured their routes, and more passengers than ever before took advantage of the lower fares. A scheduling committee became deadlocked for the first time in the fall of 1980; the FAA reluctantly intervened and awarded slots at Washington National to the newly established New York Air.

The FAA became even more involved in the allocation of slots after the 1981 Professional Air Traffic Controllers Organization (PATCO) strike. The sharp reduction in the capacity of the system led the FAA to lower the number of slots at the four high-density airports, impose similar slot constraints at an additional 18 airports, and allocate slots among individual airlines by administrative action. As new air traffic controllers restored the system's capacity, the FAA continued to allocate each group of restored slots to individual airlines, deciding between the claims of new entrants and incumbents who had suffered cutbacks. In its new capacity to control entry, the FAA incurred the wrath of Alfred E. Kahn, former chairman of the CAB, and other proponents of airline deregulation. Kahn wrote in a March 21, 1982 letter to *The Washington Post:*

> The market does not solve all our problems; but it takes a special kind of idiocy to refuse to let it do jobs that it obviously can do. The FAA has consistently demonstrated its manifest preference for thoroughly regulatory remedies.

By the summer of 1982, the FAA was feeling not only the pressures of pro-market officials in the Reagan administration but also the sheer administrative burden of allocating over 9000 slots at the 22 "pacer" airports. As an experiment, the agency established a one-time temporary market—whereby airlines could freely buy and sell slots—as a way to facilitate the distribution of slots for the fall schedule. During an initial period of four weeks, and an additional two-week extension granted at the request of the industry, the FAA received 322 requests for slot transactions. Prices in recorded transactions ranged from $12,000 to $500,000 per slot, depending on the airport and time of day. Airlines were allowed to hold on to acquired slots under the same legal terms that had prevailed before the experiment. The FAA reserved the ultimate right to withdraw and reallocate slots.

The FAA remained skeptical about the results of the "buy-sell experiment" and attempted to resurrect the scheduling committees for the next round of allocations in the spring of 1983. By then the FAA had removed slot constraints from the 18 airports that had been restricted following the PATCO strike. At the four high-density airports, the FAA restored the slot quotas to their pre-strike levels, thereby enabling the scheduling committees to reach agreement. But, in the fall of 1983, the FAA offered no more additional slots and incumbents were asked to accommodate new entrants through reductions in their own holdings of slots. The Washington National committee, after dozens of meetings, reached a deadlock. Shelton Jackson, an official in the DOT Policy Analysis Division who had been working with the FAA and the scheduling committees, explained the collapse of the process:

> The FAA would threaten an allocation, and the threat of an allocation was sometimes sufficient to make someone give up his slot or do something for new entry. But it was becoming increasingly time consuming to rattle around as if we were going to do something. We didn't know what we were going to do. And usually nothing was what we would do.

In August 1983, the FAA simply issued a ruling that preserved the existing allocation of slots at Washington National for the following six months. By the spring of 1984, it had become clear that the threat of an allocation by the FAA amounted to nothing more than the preservation of the status quo. All four committees became deadlocked.

TWO PROPOSED RULES

By 1984 officials in the DOT Office of the Secretary had become increasingly sympathetic to the market solution advocated by the Office of Management and Budget (OMB), the Federal Trade Commission (FTC), and the Council of Economic Advisers (CEA). These pro-market officials challenged the committee scheme as "a remnant of the closed-club regulatory era of the airline industry" and reasoned that only in a market situation would airlines fill scarce slots with flights that were of highest value to consumers. Undaunted, the FAA continued to argue that a market for slots would allow large airlines to deprive small airlines and small communities of access to congested airports, and that airlines with marketable slots would oppose the needed expansion of airport capacity.

The FAA forestalled any action to change the committee system until prompted by the major airlines. Until the 1982 experiment, most incumbents had been wary of a slot market, having been impressed by estimates in a 1979 study contracted by the FAA that an initial auction of slots at Washington National could raise over $500 million. However, the experience of the 1982 temporary market, which had not involved an auction, made many regard the market system as a feasible and preferable alternative. In the spring of 1984, faced with intractable deadlock, a majority of the carriers on the Washington National committee petitioned the DOT and FAA to issue a Notice of Proposed Rulemaking (NPRM), and to institute a free-market mechanism as the "least of all evils."

On June 1, 1984, the FAA issued a notice proposing that air carrier slots be bought and sold freely, and implying that incumbent airlines would be able to hold on to their slots; the proposed rule received the enthusiastic support of OMB, FTC, CEA, and most major airlines. The FAA also invited comment on an alternative notice, which proposed to preserve the scheduling committee system and to provide a regulatory allocation mechanism if a committee reached an impasse; this approach was endorsed by

new entrants, small air carriers, general aviation, state and local governments, and airport operators.

Following a review of comments received in response to the NPRMs the DOT Office of Policy and the FAA summarized the cases for the buy-sell rule and the scheduling committee rule, respectively. In the process, the two organizations disagreed in three major areas: effects on competition and service to small communities, effects on airport capacity and access, and the possibility of windfall profits should the buy-sell rule be adopted without an initial auction.

EFFECTS ON COMPETITION AND SMALL COMMUNITIES

Ever since the 1982 buy-sell experiment, the FAA had warned that a market for slots would benefit large carriers with "deep pockets" at the expense of small airlines and small communities. In December 1982, Secretary of Transportation Drew Lewis conveyed the FAA's concerns in a letter to David Stockman, director of OMB and a strong advocate of a market for slots:

> The buying and selling of slots tends to benefit the high bidders, not necessarily the traveling public. The largest carriers, serving the high-density markets, have the cash resources to outbid the smaller carriers serving the lesser markets. The travel options available to the public would therefore be limited, if not curtailed, and almost certainly the airlines would pass the higher costs along to the public.

Secretary Lewis' letter was followed by an FAA study of the 1982 experiment that revealed a pattern of sales from small commuter airlines to large carriers. (See Exhibits 1–4.) As a group, the major air carriers increased their slots at "pacer" airports by 91, at the expense of regional and commuter airlines, with United Airlines gaining the greatest number. The transactions also resulted in more flights from large hub airports and fewer from smaller airports, with Princeton, New Jersey losing as many as 88 percent of its departures. The FAA drew attention in particular to the example of Pioneer Airlines, which, by selling its Denver slots to United, had deprived a number of small airports in Nebraska of direct service to Denver.

Some of the major carriers (e.g., Delta and USAir), smaller airlines, and general aviation organi-

EXHIBIT 1

Net Change in Slots Held by Air Carriers as a Result of Slot Sales and Uneven Trades

Carriers That Increased Slots Held at the 22 Pacer Airports			
United Airlines	+43 slots	Pilgrim	+3 slots
People Express	+26 slots	American Int'l	+2 slots
Continental	+17 slots	Southwest	+2 slots
USAir	+14 slots	Texas Int'l	+2 slots
Northwest	+10 slots	Westair	+2 slots
Pan American	+6 slots	Frontier	+1 slot
Eastern	+4 slots	Ozark	+1 slot
Princeton-Boston	+4 slots	Piedmont	+1 slot
Arrow	+3 slots	Simmons	+1 slot
		Total	+142 slots

Carriers That Reduced Slots Held at the 22 Pacer Airports			
Princeton	−22 slots	Air Midwest	−2 slots
Pioneer	−12 slots	Air Nevada	−2 slots
North American	−11 slots	American Central	−2 slots
Christman	−10 slots	Aspen	−2 slots
Air Florida	−8 slots	Centennial	−2 slots
New York Air	−8 slots	Empire	−2 slots
Rocky Mountain	−7 slots	Fleming Int'l	−2 slots
Lakeland	−6 slots	Green Hills	−2 slots
Metro	−6 slots	Liberty	−2 slots
Chapparal	−4 slots	TWA	−2 slots
Freedom	−4 slots	Western	−2 slots
Wings	−4 slots	Air US	−1 slot
Altair	−3 slots	American	−1 slot
Commuter	−3 slots	Cumberland	−1 slot
Silver State	−3 slots	Skyline Motors	−1 slot
Trans Missouri	−3 slots	Trans Colorado	−1 slot
		Will's	−1 slot
		Total	−142 slots

Note: The above data show the *net* results for transactions involving all 192 slots that were either sold or traded on an uneven basis.

Source: U.S. Department of Transportation.

zations issued similar warnings in the responses to the NPRMs. According to USAir:

> The proponents of buy-sell underestimate the ability of the largest carriers to use their financial power to dominate particular airports and markets. The large carriers' well-developed hubs maximize the value of flights connecting to those hubs, thereby enabling those carriers to outbid small carriers for the same slots. In addition, there is a substantial risk that large carriers may be willing to devote resources to acquire slots and utilize them for unprofitable flights if necessary to keep their competitors out of the market.

USAir presented estimates of revenue generated by aircraft of different sizes serving different route lengths and argued that buy-sell would result in a shift in service to longer-haul, higher-density markets served by larger aircraft. (See Exhibit 5.)

A number of small communities also expressed their concern that they might lose, or never obtain, direct service to the congested airports. For example, an editorial in the *San Jose Mercury News* forecast that under a market system:

> San Jose air travelers would be left to the mercy of the major carriers. The FAA could no longer reallocate slots or force an airline to sell a number of JFK slots to another carrier that wished to inaugurate San Jose-JFK service. That strikes us as unfair to the 500,000 Silicon Valley residents who fly to New York City each year, and it explains why 480,000 of them drove to San Francisco to get on a plane.

EXHIBIT 2

Net Change in Slots Held at the 22 Pacer Airports by Class of Carrier

Major	American, Continental, Delta, Eastern, Northwest, Pan Am, Republic, TWA, United, USAir, Western	+91
Nationals	AirCal, Air Florida, Alaska, Aloha, Capitol, Frontier, Hawaiian, Ozark, Piedmont, PSA, Southwest, Texas International, Transamerica, Wien, World	−3
Large regionals	Air Midwest, Air New England, Air Wisconsin, Altair, Aspen, Bar Harbor, Britt, Cascade, Empire, Golden Gate, Golden West, Henson, Metro, Metro International, Midway, Mississippi Valley, Muse, New York Air, Pennsylvania Airlines, People Express, Pilgrim, Prinair, Provincetown/Boston, Ransome, Rocky Mountain, Suburban	+3
Small regional/charters	All others, including: Air Nevada, Air US, American Central, American International, Arrow, Centennial, Chapparal, Christman, Commuter, Cumberland, Fleming International, Freedom, Green Hills, Lakeland, Liberty, North American, Pioneer, Princeton, Silver State, Simmons, Skyline, Trans Colorado, Trans Missouri, Westair, Will's, Wings	−91

Note: The above data show the *net* results for transactions involving all 192 slots that were either sold or traded on an uneven basis.

Source: U.S. Department of Transportation.

EXHIBIT 3

Net Change in Service at Airports
Airports with Net Loss in Departures Associated with Slot Sales

Airport	Departures Lost[1]	Total Arrivals in OAG May '82[2]	% Departures Lost	Total Arrivals in OAG May '83[3]	Change in Arrivals '82–'83
Princeton, NJ	−22	25	88	0	−25
Charleston, WV	−5	31	16	29	−2
Abilene, TX	−4	31	12	18	−13
Blue Bell, PA	−4	31	12	35	4
Gillette, WY	−4	16	25	12	−4
Laramie, WY	−4	12	33	6	−6
Madison, WI	−4	46	8	39	−7
Phil/Wilmington, DE	−7	395	1	374	−21
Pueblo, CO	−4	13	30	15	+2
Clear Lake City, TX	−3	22	13	24	+2
Jefferson City, MO	−3	10	30	9	−1
Marathon, FL	−3	12	25	8	−4
Beaumont, TX	−2	20	10	18	−2
Binghamton, NY	−2	41	4	41	0
Cheyenne, WY	−2	15	13	17	2
Chicago, IL (Midway)	−2	51	3	49	−2
Cortez, CO	−2	8	25	8	0
Dayton, OH	−2	74	2	106	32
Detroit, MI	−2	280	.7	324	44
Eau Claire, WI	−2	18	11	17	−1
Fort Lauderdale, FL	−2	126	1	150	24
Grand Canyon, AZ	−2	40	5	32	−8
Hyannis, MA	−2	51	3	71	20
Lansing, MI	−2	32	6	29	−3
New York, NY (JFK)	−2	265	.7	268	3
Providence, RI	−2	39	5	62	23

EXHIBIT 3
(continued)

Airport	Departures Lost[1]	Total Arrivals in OAG May '82[2]	% Departures Lost	Total Arrivals in OAG May '83[3]	Change in Arrivals '82–'83
St. Louis, MO	−2	325	.6	425	100
Toledo, OH	−2	35	5	59	14
Washington, DC (Dulles)	−.2	59	3	78	19
Akron/Canton, OH	−1	25	4	27	2
Alamosa, CO	−1	3	33	3	0
Allentown, PA	−1	51	1	45	−6
Aspen, CO	−1	10	10	9	−1
Beloit, WI	−1	10	10	7	−3
Charleston, SC	−1	36	2	38	2
Colorado Springs, CO	−1	26	3	36	10
Columbia, MO	−1	10	10	13	3
Durango, CO	−1	13	7	23	10
Erie, PA	−1	13	7	14	1
Farmington, MI	−1	29	3	30	1
Flint, MI	−1	19	5	18	−1
Greensboro, NC	−1	68	1	73	5
Gunnison, CO	−1	10	10	5	−5
Jacksonville, FL	−2	74	2	117	43
Kansas City, MO	−1	203	.4	208	5
Lake Charles, LA	−1	25	4	23	−2
Latrobe, PA	−1	15	6	13	−2
Miami, FL	−1	282	.3	281	−1
Montrose, CO	−1	6	16	7	1
Rifle, CO	−1	3	33	3	0
Sioux Falls, SD	−1	23	4	31	8
Tampa, FL	−1	252	.3	283	31
Utica, NY	−1	13	7	14	1
Waterloo, IA	−1	19	5	32	13
West Palm Beach, FL	−2	85	2	110	25
White Plains, NY	−1	20	5	29	9
Williston, ND	−1	9	11	8	−1
Youngstown, OH	−1	16	6	18	2
	−132	3491	3.8%	3831	390

[1]These numbers are based only on the effects of transactions involving slot sales or uneven trades.

[2]Prior to policy. Domestic arrivals only.

[3]One year after policy. Domestic arrivals only.

Source: U.S. Department of Transportation.

The advocates of a market solution, on the other hand, contended that neither small airlines not small communities had reason to fear. The FTC, in its submission in support of the buy-sell NPRM, had addressed the concern that large airlines would use their advantage in bidding for slots to gain control over the market:

It would not be profitable for an airline to buy a slot to operate a low-valued flight simply because it has the cash to do so. Moreover, a carrier that expects to offer a high-valued flight, but is short of cash, should be able to borrow to finance the needed slot. The ability of a car-

rier to finance slot and equipment purchases depends in large part on the expected profitability of the use to which the slots or equipment will be put.

Noting that one indicator of the future profitability of an airline was its previous profit performance, the FTC paper presented evidence that large airlines were less profitable than their smaller rivals. (See Exhibit 6.)

Both OMB and the CEA asserted that a market for slots would not create a barrier to entry. "First," argued the CEA, "landing slots would constitute only a small fraction of an airline's operating costs,"

EXHIBIT 4

Net Change in Service at Airports
Airports with Net Gain in Departures Associated with Slot Sales

Airport	Departures Gained[1]	Total Arrivals in OAG May '82[2]	% Departures Gained	Total Arrivals in OAG May '83[3]	Change in Arrivals '82–'83
Baltimore, MD	+10	190	5	223	33
Norfolk, VA	+9	80	11	85	5
Boston, MA	+6	358	1	417	59
Denver, CO	+6	522	1	562	40
Newark, NJ	+11	240	4	311	71
Dallas, TX	+5	651	.7	569	−82
Boise, ID	+3	54	5	49	−5
Chicago, IL (O'Hare)	+5	776	.6	859	83
Cleveland, OH	+3	184	1	213	29
Grand Rapids, MI	+3	40	7	43	3
Harrisburg, PA	+3	35	8	43	8
Minneapolis, MN	+3	260	1	320	60
Pittsburgh, PA	+3	371	.8	396	25
San Antonio, TX	+3	106	2	98	−8
Wichita, KS	+3	60	5	64	4
Lincoln, NE	+2	20	10	28	8
Memphis, TN	+2	260	.7	273	13
Milwaukee, WI	+2	130	1	127	−3
Nashville, TN	+2	110	1	112	2
New Orleans, LA	+2	202	.9	186	−16
New York, NY (LaGuardia)	+2	366	.5	408	42
Oakland, CA	+2	70	2	79	9
Omaha, NE	+2	73	2	90	17
Phoenix, AZ	+2	250	.8	272	22
Raleigh, NC	+2	99	2	95	−4
Reno, NV	+2	75	2	72	−3
Sacramento, CA	+2	93	2	98	5
Syracuse, NY	+2	101	1	124	23
Tampa, FL	+2	252	.7	283	31
Unspecified Airport	+2	—			
Alburquerque, NM	+1	106	.9	113	7
Bridgeport, CT	+2	18	5	23	5
Buffalo, NY	+1	110	.9	110	0
Charlotte, NC	+1	222	4	274	52
Des Moines, IA	+1	49	2	61	12
Elmira, NY	+1	14	7	18	4
Eugene, OR	+1	25	4	22	−3
Fresno, CA	+1	38	2	47	9
Honolulu, HI	+1	10	10	n/a	n/a
Houston, TX	+1	321	.3	324	3
Long Island, NY	+1	23	4	46	23
Martha's Vineyard, MA	+1	21	4	49	28
New London, CT	+2	22	4	37	15
Oklahoma City, OK	+1	100	1	95	−5
Orlando, FL	+1	190	.5	196	6
Richmond, VA	+1	71	1	101	30
Saginaw, MI	+1	23	4	26	3
Salt Lake City, UT	+1	171	.5	179	8
Santa Barbara, CA	+1	33	3	46	13
San Francisco, CA	+1	341	.2	393	52
San Jose, CA	+1	87	1	105	18
Washington, DC (National)	+1	338	.2	361	23
Wilkes-Barre, PA	+1	26	3	35	9
Total	+131	8,387	1.6%	9,160	783

[1]These numbers are based only on the effects of transactions involving slot sales or uneven trades.
[2]Prior to policy. Domestic arrivals only.
[3]One year after policy. Domestic arrivals only.
Source: U.S. Department of Transportation.

EXHIBIT 5
Revenue Generated by Different Flight Length

Equipment	Seats	300 Miles	750 Miles	1,250 Miles
DC-9-30	110	$9,223	$15,587	$19,734
B-757	185	$15,512	$26,214	$33,189
L-1011	293	$24,568	$41,518	$52,564

Source: Civil Aeronautics Board, *Air Carrier Financial Statistics,* June 1982.

hundreds of thousands of dollars at most, compared with the tens of millions of dollars it costs to buy a jet aircraft. Second, the CEA continued:

> Most barriers to entry occur because a new firm is putting its money at risk by entering into an industry. If the firm subsequently decides to leave the market, it cannot recoup its sunk costs, such as the depreciation of its assets. The price of slots is not a sunk cost. Since slots do not depreciate, any firm that wishes to sell its slots should be able to get its money back.

In fact, OMB argued, under the market system there would be "*less* of an entry barrier than [in] the committee system, which gave the illusion of easy entry by allowing a few slots to anyone—but not necessarily enough for economic viability, and certainly not as many as some carriers would purchase in a market." According to OMB, the 1982 experiment had demonstrated the benefits of a market system to new entrants. Whereas the FAA noted the loss of direct service from Nebraska airports to Denver, supporters of a market for slots highlighted a different example. After a series of frustrated appeals to the Washington National committee, People Express was finally able to enter the market in 1982 by purchasing six slots for about $1.75 million.

As for the argument that some small communities might lose direct service to congested airports,

the paper prepared by the DOT Office of Policy asserted that "[small] communities would not lose access. Travelers from small communities might have to fly first to an uncongested smaller hub airport to connect with a flight to a congested airport."

AIRPORT EXPANSION AND ACCESS

The FAA's second concern was that a buy-sell rule would diminish the willingness of airlines to participate in the expansion of airport capacity. Edward P. Faberman, deputy chief counsel of the FAA, made this argument in discussions with DOT officials:

> The administrator [of FAA] and the agency felt very strongly that what we need in this country is more airports. We were concerned that by creating this price tag on carriers' slots, the carriers would then be very reluctant to do anything which would lessen its value. Therefore, while we were talking about expansion at O'Hare or building a new airport, the carriers out there all of a sudden would oppose that.

It was also on the question of airport capacity that economists in the FAA issued their strongest challenge to the pro-market economists in the Reagan administration. John Rodgers, director of the FAA's Economic Analysis Branch, explained that al-

EXHIBIT 6
Operating Revenues and Operating Profit/Equity by Carrier Group

Carrier Group	Operating Revenues (Millions of Dollars per Year)	Operating Profit/Equity	
		1981	1982
Majors	over 1,000	0.3%	−16.5%
Nationals	75–1,000	15.8%	2.4%
Large regionals	10–75	−3.7%	−1.6%
Medium regionals	under 10	—	8.1%

Source: Civil Aeronautics Board, *Air Carrier Financial Statistics,* June 1982.

though "everybody that ever took an economics degree, or even any course, was in favor of [buy-sell]," one of the fundamental reasons for justifying the market system from a welfare perspective was missing:

> The first [reason] is that the market system is an efficient allocator in that it provides better services to those who are most willing to pay for them. But in the same breath the argument is made that the free market stimulates increased supply; it provides incentives for profits, and it brings additional producers into the market. And unfortunately, that one half of the equation is in fact missing in that no one has yet figured how to create additional airport capacity where needed. So in those situations welfare economics may say that the market may not in fact be an appropriate mechanism, and that what you have in fact is a regional monopoly. Whenever you have a monopoly, generally speaking, you have public regulation.

Finally, FAA officials feared that the implementation of a buy-sell rule would be used by local airport operators as a precedent to limit access to airports. The comments of the Airport Operators Council International (AOCI) appeared to confirm the FAA's concerns. The AOCI argued that the FAA's slot restrictions were based on considerations other than air traffic safety and that, therefore, the FAA was infringing on the airport proprietors' authority "to allocate airport capacity (runways, gates, terminals, and noise capacity) through traditional airport/tenant relations." The AOCI suggested the use of scheduling committees with an enhanced deadlock-breaking mechanism that would withdraw by lottery 25 percent of incumbents' slots. The proceeds from auctioning the withdrawn slots would be "kept within the air transportation system and used for the creation of additional capacity."

AOCI's eagerness to use auctions to collect revenues caused the FAA to warn that a buy-sell policy would "establish a precedent in the use of the market which may spread to non-high-density airports." Faberman explained:

> The Port Authority of New York has for years been making noises about implementing its own auction to determine who comes into the airport. That was a concern to us because we saw this national system going into place where people would have to bid on slots and on access, and there would be problems with new entrants.

Economists at OMB, CEA, and the FTC countered these arguments with another lesson in economics. The FAA's concerns about potential opposition to expansion of airport capacity were based, they contended, on the mistaken impression that slots would derive their value from the establishment of a market. An FTC study of airfares during the 1982 buy-sell experiment stated:

> Economic theory implies that it is slot scarcity that causes airline fares to be higher, not slot marketability. Whether or not slots are marketable, they have value because limited air traffic control capacity and FAA restrictions make them scarce. If a slot market existed, the price of each slot would merely reflect the prevailing level of slot scarcity at a particular airport during a particular hour of the day.

The study estimated that the average fare (operating revenue per passenger mile) was already from two to five percent higher in slot-constrained markets than in other markets. These findings seemed to be supported by casual observations that flights into slot-constrained airports were consistently more expensive than flights into nearby unconstrained airports (e.g., LaGuardia instead of Newark, National instead of Dulles). (See Exhibit 7.)

Finally, pro-market economists concluded, airlines that had use of scarce slots already faced strong incentives to oppose any airport expansion schemes that would diminish the value of their slots. The marketability of slots would hardly alter their value to incumbent airlines and, therefore, would not heighten the airlines' interest in preserving the value of this scarce resource.

INITIAL ALLOCATION: EFFICIENCY AND WINDFALL PROFITS

The transition to a market system also raised the difficult choice between holding an initial auction and preserving the existing allocation. The major airlines insisted on a "grandfather" provision that would allow incumbents to keep slots they were already using. In joint comments to the NPRMs, eleven major air carriers defended this approach as both fair and efficient:

> Grandfather rights recognize the investments and commitments in personnel, equipment, terminal development, and planning by existing carriers. Moreover, any other method of allocating large numbers of slots at one time,

EXHIBIT 7
Comparative Fares (Lowest Available)

	To/From LaGuardia	*To/From Newark*
To/from Buffalo	$50 (USAir)	$42 (USAir) 39 (People Express)
To/from Chicago	$200 (United)	$119 (United) 79 (People Express)
To/from St. Louis	$99 (TWA)	$69 (TWA) 49 (People Express)
To/from Houston	$109 (Continental)	$79 (Continental) 79 (People Express)

	To/From National	*To/From Dulles*
To/from Houston	$140 (Continental) 109 (People Express)	$119 (Continental) 79 (People Express)
To/from Orlando	$115 (New York Air) 108 (People Express)	$89 (New York Air) 69 (People Express)
To/from Tampa	$115 (New York Air)	$69 (New York Air)
To/from Boston	$115 (New York Air) 59 (People Express)	$99 (New York Air) 35 (People Express)

Source: U.S. House of Representatives, Committee on Public Works and Transportation, Hearing 99-33, September 10, 1985.

whether by lottery, auction, or other procedure, has the potential of considerably disrupting operations and service patterns at high-density airports, which is not in the public interest.

A major obstacle to "grandfathering" was the perception of many that incumbents might derive enormous windfall profits. According to the AOCI, for example, "slots would be given away 'free' to a user who, in return, is allowed to sell his interest for a 100 percent profit."

On this issue, OMB and the CEA held somewhat differing views. CEA member William A. Niskanen, Jr. argued outright that "an auction of existing slots would be the most efficient," and found "regrettable" any policy that would "give rather than sell this resource to the airlines."

First, an auction should not cause service disruptions that will render [airlines'] investments worthless. If Delta has upgraded its O'Hare terminal, then clearly O'Hare flights are worth a good deal of money to Delta. Thus, Delta would be the high bidder on a number of O'Hare slots sold in an auction.

Second, even if for some reason such an airline does not receive slots, its investments would not be wasted. It is important to recognize that Delta would be able to liquidate its

holdings; their investment in airport facilities is a fixed cost, not a sunk cost.

Recognizing that it might be infeasible to sell all slots at once, Niskanen proposed that auctions proceed over a period of five years, with 20 percent of slots, selected by lottery, auctioned every year.

OMB claimed that the reasoning behind the windfall profits argument was based on "economic error: the real 'windfall' occurred when the carriers received the slots for nothing in the first place. Permitting slot sales would not create the economic value of the slots, but only reveal that value in monetary terms." In the CEA comments, Niskanen countered the view that "the present slot windfall has become institutionalized": "This argument certainly does not apply to the allocation of any new slots. There is no reason for the government to continue the granting of windfalls in the future."

OMB acknowledged that "it might appear unfair if the incumbent airlines were suddenly permitted to cash in on their slots, the value of which 'rightfully' belongs to the government." But, the agency pointed out, the FAA would have to receive additional congressional authority in order to undertake auctions anywhere other than at National Airport (where it could act under its legal authority as the airport's proprietor).

Sam Fairchild, who represented the OMB Office for Information and Regulatory Affairs in the discussions with DOT, was convinced that any proposal to start a market for slots with an initial auction would meet the strong opposition of major airlines and would fail in Congress. Therefore, Fairchild regarded those who made the argument about windfalls with skepticism:

> All the opponents said "Well, let's have an auction." Here is their argument: "We know that no one is going to approve an auction, so let's insist on having an auction and that way kill the whole policy." The CEA and the DOJ [Department of Justice] wanted auctions, and their arguments were excellent economic arguments—and those guys I have a lot of respect for. But we knew that Congress would have to act to approve auctions, and they would never act to do so.

A LAST ALTERNATIVE

For the FAA, the combination of concerns about the implications of a buy-sell rule was sufficient to warrant another effort to resurrect the committee system. The FAA contended that "scheduling committees had functioned adequately in the past," and reminded critics that since 1978 the number of operating carriers had increased from 10 to 19 at National, from 14 to 24 at LaGuardia, and from 33 to 48 at O'Hare. The scheduling committee system, the FAA concluded, "simply needs some adjustment."

In December 1984, following a review of comments to the NPRMs, the FAA made its final recommendations to Secretary Dole. In order to increase the incentive for scheduling committees to reach agreement, the FAA proposed a deadlock-breaking mechanism that would withdraw by lottery five percent of the slots held by the incumbents. These slots, along with any unused or newly available slots, would then be allocated by another lottery. That procedure would set aside 15 percent of the slots for new entrants, and would give incumbents preference in accordance with the number of slots they already held. The FAA reasoned that "such 'free slots' might allow more carriers, which are not as well financed, to gain access than would market approaches." Also, multiple trades and inter-airport trades would be allowed so as to increase the flexibility of carriers in adjusting to changing market conditions.

DOT's Office of Policy, on the other hand, endorsed the initial buy-sell rule with grandfathering rights, but also mentioned the possibility of periodic auctions by the federal government. Such an approach, the Office of Policy explained, "would be more equitable than grandfathering for the initial allocation," and would "largely avoid the potential for collusion among the dominant carriers to restrict competition, which would occur from an improperly structured buy-sell proposal." Nevertheless, the Office of Policy recommended against the use of a periodic or any other type of auction, citing the possibility of massive disruptions in service, the carriers' objection that this would impose a tremendous hardship on the industry, and the difficulties of passing legislation allowing the federal government to auction slots.

According to DOT economist Cindy Burbank, the Office Policy also anticipated an unwelcome amount of controversy because "it wasn't clear what you would do with the proceeds of such an auction." Some representatives of OMB would have argued that the money should go to the Treasury, whereas airport operators had already suggested that the money should be used for improvements in the air traffic system.

THE 1985 CONGRESSIONAL HEARINGS

Secretary Dole refrained from making an early decision among the options presented by the FAA and the DOT Office of Policy. Instead, Dole assigned the Office of the General Counsel to work with the FAA and the Office of Policy, address a number of unresolved sub-issues that had been raised in the public comments, and develop the final language for the options. Over the next few months, Sam Podberesky, on behalf of the Office of the General Counsel, attended over twenty meetings with representatives of the FAA, OMB, and the DOT Office of Policy.

> The marching orders we had from the secretary—the approach we took was to stay openminded, too. We would try to convince OMB that the FAA's position was the right position, that it had fewer problems and was easier to implement.

However, Podberesky contended, representatives from OMB held to their staunch belief in the market alternative:

> Because of OMB's desires to further market approaches to solving these kinds of problems, they viewed slot allocation as a trial horse that

they wanted to use, and they pushed very, very hard.

OMB made it clear from the beginning that they felt the market approach was the way to go, and they took the position: "Convince us that something else should be used instead. If you think that's the case, come in and tell us why."

Approval by officials from the OMB Office for Information and Regulatory Affairs was critical to the policymaking process. That office wielded the authority to rule on all proposed regulations and information collection requirements of federal agencies. Cindy Burbank believed that if DOT were to choose an option radically different from the market solution advocated by the OMB, "it probably wouldn't go much further. And there wouldn't be much we could do other than perhaps the secretary appealing directly to the president."

Even though the meetings failed to resolve the fundamental dispute between OMB and the FAA, they continued along, with a growing agenda of sub-issues identified by the Office of the Secretary. By the fall of 1985, over a year after the NPRMs had been issued, observers from the airline industry and Congress had become annoyed with DOT's indecision. Finally, Rep. Norman Y. Mineta (D-CA), chairman of the Subcommittee on Aviation of the House Committee on Public Works and Transportation, organized hearings to examine the government's policies regarding airport slots.

The three days of hearings revealed neither commenters nor comments different from those that first appeared in response to the 1984 NPRMs. However, most of the participants seized the opportunity to express their frustration with DOT's procrastination. Anticipating a DOT ruling, the scheduling committees had even less of an incentive to reach agreement, and, in the case of National Airport, had remained deadlocked for over two years. (See Exhibit 8.) Most airline and airport representatives supported Mineta when he lectured DOT representatives that "it's essential that DOT deal with this situation promptly by completing its rulemaking. Almost any outcome in the rulemaking would be preferable to the stalemate which has developed." Mineta went on to extract from Matthew V. Scocozza, assistant secretary for policy, and Edward Faberman, deputy chief counsel of the FAA, a pledge that DOT would issue a final rule by December 1, 1985.

In an October 31, 1985 letter to Secretary Dole, Mineta and Rep. John Paul Hammerschmidt (R-

EXHIBIT 8

DCA Slot Allocation

Carrier	Summer 1983	Spring 1985
Eastern	107	107
USAir	86	86
New York Air	56	56
Piedmont	52	52
Northwest	40	40
United	34	34
TWA	34	34
American	30	30
Delta	30	30
Pan Am	22	22
Air Florida	12	0
Midway	10	22
People Express	12	12
Ozark	6	6
Republic	6	6
Empire	6	6
Air One	4	4
Continental	4	4
Western	4	4
Braniff	0	4

Source: U.S. House of Representatives, Committee on Public Works and Transportation, Hearing 99-33, October 22, 1985.

AR), the subcommittee's ranking minority member, urged her to take action by the December 1 deadline, but refrained from endorsing any specific option. However, Mineta and Hammerschmidt did express a strong opposition to any solution that would "grant incumbents grandfather rights to all of their slots and then allow them to sell these slots. The combination of grandfathering and buy-sell," they explained, "would maximize the windfall profits for incumbents who would be selling slots which they obtained at no cost from the government."

In November 1985, Secretary Dole was nearing a final decision. Officials in the Office of the Secretary were convinced that a combination of "grandfathering and buy-sell" would trigger legislation in both houses that would likely overturn such a rule. Sam Podberesky recognized that FAA administrator Donald D. Engen had reason to be particularly concerned about the windfall profits argument. "He's the one that's going to have to go up on the Hill and defend this. And it is very hard to argue against those who claim that this is just throwing money to the big established airlines." On the other hand, OMB continued to believe that the congressional legislation necessary for auctions would fail in the face of vehement opposition from incumbent airlines.

ASSIGNMENT FOR CLASS DISCUSSION

Come to class prepared to recommend whether Secretary Dole should accept the FAA's recommendation to strengthen scheduling committees or instead establish a market for slots. If you are recommending the establishment of a market, the secretary would like to know what form this market should take (i.e., slots grandfathered to incumbents with subsequent resale allowed, a one-time auction with resale, periodic auctions with no resale, etc.)

In formulating your recommendation, please consider:

1. How do you evaluate the arguments that a market in slots will reduce competition and service to small communities?
2. What are the purposes of establishing a market in slots and what do they imply for the form or design of that market?